ALTERNATIVE HISTORIOGRAPHIES OF THE DIGITAL HUMANITIES

Before you start to read this book, take this moment to think about making a donation to punctum books, an independent non-profit press,

@ https://punctumbooks.com/support/

If you're reading the e-book, you can click on the image below to go directly to our donations site. Any amount, no matter the size, is appreciated and will help us to keep our ship of fools afloat. Contributions from dedicated readers will also help us to keep our commons open and to cultivate new work that can't find a welcoming port elsewhere. Our adventure is not possible without your support.

Vive la Open Access.

Fig. 1. Hieronymus Bosch, *Ship of Fools* (1490–1500)

First published in 2021 by punctum books, Earth, Milky Way.
https://punctumbooks.com

ISBN-13: 978-1-953035-57-8 (print)
ISBN-13: 978-1-953035-58-5 (ePDF)

DOI: 10.53288/0274.1.00

LCCN: 2021937406
Library of Congress Cataloging Data is available from the Library of Congress

Book design: Vincent W.J. van Gerven Oei
Cover image: Inca. Quipu, 1400–1532. Cotton, 20½ × 34⅝ in. (52 × 88 cm). Brooklyn Museum, Gift of Mrs. Eugene Schaefer, 36.413. CC-BY.

HIC SVNT MONSTRA

Alternative Historiographies of the Digital Humanities

Edited by Dorothy Kim & Adeline Koh

Contents

Praxis

Methods

Indigenous Futures

Break (Up, Down, Out, In) DH and Black Futurities

Acknowledgments

This volume was originally organized and planned by Adeline Koh. I inherited this volume after she decided to move permanently out of academia. We miss her and her generous community-building work. I would like to acknowledge the writers who have continued through this editorial transition and also had to deal with this last year of COVID-19 where people lost partners, mothers, fathers, children, siblings, and other family and close friends. Many of those in this collection have also dealt with unbearable grief during the writing, editing, and revision of this volume. I am incredibly humbled by your work and generosity for this volume even in the wake of years of racial violence and now a pandemic. My thanks to Edmond Y. Chang for helping me curate and organize the Black Futures section of this collection. My thanks to the anonymous peer reviewers of the different articles who gave such generous feedback. I am also grateful to the anonymous peer reviewer of the whole volume who helped clarify what we were doing in getting a volume on historical reckonings together and who gave us trenchant feedback about how to clarify and refine our aims. My thanks to punctum books and Vincent W.J. van Gerven Oei for publishing this volume and his editorial care. My thanks to Cara DuBois and Nicholas Hoffman who did amazing jobs with copyediting this in various stages.

INTRODUCTION

Media Histories, Media Archaeologies, and the Politics and Genealogies of the Digital Humanities

Dorothy Kim

To begin to discuss alternative genealogies and histories of the digital humanities, we have to first discuss the genealogy of the digital as the site of settler colonialism and transatlantic chattel slavery. I am indebted to Jessie Daniel's discussion in "The Algorithmic Rise of the Alt-Right" that succinctly points to this undergirded issue.[1] Historically, the early architects of cyberspace always imagined the internet as an extension of US manifest destiny, a "frontier" for "freedom." As Jessie Daniels explains, you can see this in the Electronic Frontier Foundation and the manifesto of its founder, John Perry Barlow.[2] He writes:

> Governments of the Industrial World, you weary giants of flesh and steel, I come from Cyberspace, the new home of Mind. On behalf of the future, I ask you of the past to leave

1 Jessie Daniels, "The Algorithmic Rise of the 'Alt-Right,'" *Contexts* 17, no. 1 (February 2018): 60–65.

2 Ibid.

us alone. You are not welcome among us. You have no sovereignty where we gather.

We have no elected government, nor are we likely to have one, so I address you with no greater authority than that with which liberty itself always speaks. I declare the global social space we are building to be naturally independent of the tyrannies you seek to impose on us. You have no moral right to rule us nor do you possess any methods of enforcement we have true reason to fear. [...]

We are creating a world that all may enter without privilege or prejudice accorded by race, economic power, military force, or station of birth. [...]

Our identities have no bodies, so, unlike you, we cannot obtain order by physical coercion. We believe that from ethics, enlightened self-interest, and the commonweal, our governance will emerge. [...]

These increasingly hostile and colonial measures place us in the same position as those previous lovers of freedom and self-determination who had to reject the authorities of distant, uninformed powers. We must declare our virtual selves immune to your sovereignty, even as we continue to consent to your rule over our bodies. We will spread ourselves across the Planet so that no one can arrest our thoughts.

We will create a civilization of the Mind in Cyberspace. May it be more humane and fair than the world your governments have made before.

Davos, Switzerland
February 8, 1996[3]

This idea of a colorblind, bodiless digital frontier of freedom is the frame-out of the digital worlds we deal with now. Daniels, Lisa Nakamura, and other scholars have debunked this myth

3 John Perry Barlow, "A Declaration of the Independence of Cyberspace," *Electronic Frontier Foundation*, https://www.eff.org/cyberspace-independence.

that the internet is free of racism, colorblind, and/or free of actually gendered, raced bodies.[4] Daniels explains that Silicon Valley CEOs and engineers have mined this ethos while developing the third-party platforms on which we move through our daily social, commercial, and academic transactions.[5] They are invested in this "raceless" and disembodied internet that is imagined as a frontier utopia. As the internet is based on the centrality of coding in a monolingual English and American framework, it thus participates in the narrative of American exceptionalism, the digital jeremiad on the hill.[6] The digital then is based on settler colonialism viewed as a version of the American West. Yet from these terms, we know it only spells out further settler colonial genocide, stolen land turned into white property, and unending epistemic and devastating erasure of Indigenous people and culture.

What further compounds this is the fact that digital structures are deeply raced: embedded in these digital structures lies the architecture of US chattel slavery. Daniels points to Anna Everett's work.[7] In her 2001 monograph, *The Revolution Will Be Digitized: Afrocentricity and the Digital Public Sphere,* and in her reprinted 2002 article, "The Revolution Will Be Digitized: Afrocentricity and the Digital Public Sphere,"[8] she describes the

4 See Jesse Daniels, *Cyber Racism: White Supremacy Online and the New Attack on Civil Rights, Perspectives on a Multiracial America* (Lanham: Rowman & Littlefield, 2009) and Lisa Nakamura, "Cyberrace," *PMLA* 123, no. 5 (2008): 1673–82.

5 Daniels, "The Algorithmic Rise of the 'Alt-Right,'"

6 See Michelle Moravec, "Exceptionalism in Digital Humanities: Community, Collaboration, and Consensus," in *Disrupting the Digital Humanities,* eds. Dorothy Kim and Jesse Stommel (Earth: punctum books, 2018), 169–96 and Gretchen McCullock, "Coding Is for Everyone — As Long as You Speak English," *Wired,* April 8, 2019, https://www.wired.com/story/coding-is-for-everyoneas-long-as-you-speak-english/.

7 Daniels, "Rise of the 'Alt-Right.'"

8 Anna Everett, "The Revolution Will Be Digitized: Afrocentricity and the Digital Public Sphere," *Social Text* 20, no. 2 (Summer 2002): 125. See also Anna Everett, *The Revolution Will Be Digitized: Afrocentricity and the Digital Public Sphere* (Utrecht: Uitgave Faculteit der Letteren, 2001).

embedded North American chattel slavery manifest in turning on her personal computer. She writes:

> In powering up my PC, I am confronted with DOS-based text that gives me pause. Before access to the MMX technology powering my system is granted, I am alerted to this opening textual encoding: "Pri. Master Disk, Pri. Slave Disk, Sec. Master, Sec. Slave." Programmed here is a virtual hierarchy organizing my computer's software operations. Given the nature of my subject matter, it might not be surprising that I am perpetually taken aback by the programmed boot-up language informing me that my access to the cyber frontier indeed is predicated upon a digitally configured "master/slave" relationship. As the on-screen text runs through its remaining string of required boot-up language and codes, I often wonder why programmers chose such signifiers that hark back to our nation's ignominious past.[9]

This structural, violent, anti-Black naming continued into the controversies surrounding the language of standard computer programs, including Python.[10] It was only in the last two years that Python finally removed the Master/Slave language from its computing language.[11] Github only began discussing this removal in the aftermath of the #GeorgeFloyd protests in Minnesota.[12] The digital world, the internet, is an extension of US settler colonialism, the digital arm of US manifest destiny that already structures through its system the frames of US chattel slavery. Thus, we cannot begin a discussion of the alternative ge-

9 Everett, "The Revolution Will Be Digitized," 125.

10 "Master Slave Communication," *Python Testing Infrastructure*, https://pyti.readthedocs.io/en/latest/master-slave.html.

11 Daniel Oberhaus, "'Master/Slave' Terminology Was Removed from Python Programming Language," *Motherboard: Tech by Vice*, September 13, 2018, https://motherboard.vice.com/en_us/article/8x7akv/masterslave-terminology-was-removed-from-python-programming-language.

12 Elizabeth Landau, "Tech Confronts Its Use of the Labels 'Master' and 'Slave,'" *Wired*, July 6, 2020, https://www.wired.com/story/tech-confronts-use-labels-master-slave/.

nealogies and historiographies of the digital humanities without discussing this genealogy of the digital.

At DHSI 2019, Arun Jacob, one of the writers included in this volume, presented a talk that examined digital platforms and tools through the lens of a critical media archaeology that is politicized, raced, gendered, and considers the issues currently related to surveillance, security, and the complex interconnection between digital media development and the military-industrial complex. Jacob defines media archaeology vis-à-vis Jussi Parikka's *What Is Media Archaeology* (2012)[13] as "a field that attempts to understand new and emerging media through close examination of the past, and especially through critical scrutiny of dominant progressivist narratives of popular commercial media."[14] Jacob's presentation included an analysis of several different digital tools and their histories.

One of these tools is the ubiquitous ArcGIS. By examining its history, its genealogy, along with a media archaeology methodology that also references Parrikka's *A Geology of Media,*[15] we can rethink the digital humanities through an examination of the history of the media tool or platform or practice as well as an examination of its structures. In this way, Jacob follows the origin genealogy of ArcGIS and ESRI to Laura and Jack Dangermound, who established the ESRI in 1969 for "digital mapping and analysis services."[16] Jacob excavates the history of ESRI in relation to its military-industrial complex history and even its current capabilities to transform into "Military Tools for ArcGIS" as a straightforward "extension" of the ArcGIS

13 Jussi Parikka, *What Is Media Archaeology?* (Cambridge: Polity, 2012).

14 Arun Jacob's Digital Humanities Summer Institute 2019 presentation is available here: https://docs.google.com/presentation/d/1OhTECuxOJDVEo9jyydjTA2FBrPCD72pa8iam7blK1ns/edit#slide=id.g5b4675e386_0_53. See also Wikipedia: https://en.wikipedia.org/wiki/Media_archaeology.

15 Jussi Parikka, *A Geology of Media* (Minneapolis: University of Minnesota Press, 2015).

16 Jacob cites Miguel Helft, "The Godfather of Digital Maps," *Forbes*, February 10, 2016, https://www.forbes.com/sites/miguelhelft/2016/02/10/the-godfather-of-digital-maps/#4b55009e4da9.

desktop.[17] This is juxtaposed with the favorable press that the Dangermounds have gotten for their environmental conservation work — in particular, the Conservation land, the Coastal Ranch at Point Conception, as well as the Dangermound Endowed Chair in Conservation Studies at UCSB.[18] Gender is an interesting point of analysis with this genealogy of the digital humanities because, as a husband and wife team, this includes the participation of a white woman in the formation, building, and work to create a digital geospatial system primarily used to find war targets. Jacob charts a historical genealogy of ESRI, which has a huge share of the GIS business, that also intersects with a philanthropic, "conservation," and environmental profile that ESRI and its founders project. Thus, one of the main areas of digital humanities — digital mapping — often built on the ESRI platform, has and continues to have a history that is intertwined with the military-industrial complex, war, and ongoing violent settler colonialism. It is through media archaeology, microhistory, and a wider net in addressing community praxis — the ways in which the internet's most toxic elements can enter into the research and pedagogical experience — that many of the essays in this collection resituate the genealogies and historiographies of the digital humanities. Thus, these essays address whiteness, fascism, race, decoloniality, feminist materiality, toxic masculine gamer cultures, queer digital histories, multilingualism, the military-industrial complex and the history of area studies and environmental studies, Indigenous futures, Black futurities, Black diasporic protest, Black digital social media, Black

17 Jacob's discussion of the ArcGIS desktop: https://docs.google.com/presentation/d/1OhTECuxOJDVEo9jyydjTA2FBrPCD72pa8iam7blK1ns/edit#slide=id.g5b4675e386_0_118.

18 Ibid. Jacob points to the following press releases: "The Nature Conservancy Preserves 24,000-acre Coastal Ranch at Point Conception with $165 Million Gift from Esri Founders," *The Nature Conservancy*, December 21, 2017, https://www.nature.org/en-us/explore/newsroom/the-nature-conservancy-preserves-24000-acre-coastal-ranch-at-point-conceptio/ and "Preserving Nature: UC Santa Barbara announces Dangermond Endowed Chair in Conservation Studies," *The Current*, 2017, https://www.news.ucsb.edu/2017/018606/preserving-nature.

feminist archival praxis, cultural studies, digital archives of the global South, and the spectre of IBM as the origin myth of DH.

Within these essays, a main focus is on the question of power in thinking about genealogies, history, praxis, pedagogy, and futures of the digital humanities. However, this book engages with three main historical methodologies — media archaeology, the discussion of historiography in relation to "big data" and big humanities/digital humanities; and the discussion of silence and history making. Media archaeology as a methodology is characterized as "a sobering conceptual friction in the way that certain theorists identified with the field, such as Geert Lovink, use it to undertake 'a hermeneutic reading of the 'new' against the grain of the past, rather than telling of the histories of technologies from past to present.'"[19] This volume is an instantiation of media archaeology and particularly its tendencies to go "against the grain" and push back against "progress model" narratives. Erkki Huhtamo and Jussi Parikka explain that: "Media archaeologists have challenged the rejection of history by modern media culture and theory alike by pointing out hitherto unnoticed continuities and ruptures... On the basis of their discoveries, media archaeologists have begun to construct alternate histories of suppressed, neglected, and forgotten media that do not point teleologically to the present media-cultural condition as their "perfection.""[20] This volume rethinks media archaeology in relation to "alternate histories" as well as potential "futures" particularly in regards to how power, different marginal groups, have been embedded in these "suppressed, neglected, and forgotten media" histories.

---

19 Lori Emerson, *Reading Writing Interfaces* (Minneapolis: University of Minnesota Press, 2014), xii. See also Geert Lovink, *My First Recession: Critical Internet Cultures in Transition* (Rotterdam: Nai Publishers, 2004), 11.

20 Erkki Huhtamo and Jussi Parikka, "Introduction: An Archaeology of Media Archaeology," in *Media Archaeology: Approaches, Applications, and Implications*, eds. Erkki Huhtamo and Jussi Parikka (Berkeley: University of California Press, 2011), 3.

The second historical methodological discussion is in relation to longer considerations of history and big data. In particular, the debates in historiography about different models of historical inquiry predicated on a genealogy based on 19th-century German models of *Wissenschaft*. This discussion reconsiders the conflict between the methodologies championed by Theodor Mommsen vision of a Big Humanities in his systematic collection and collaborative "industrial" model vs. Friedrich Nietzsche's critique of *Wissenschaft* in which he supported a vision that "philology was a way of life and the philologist was an ethical persona."[21] This discourse about the longer histories of "big data" projects and their methodological priorities in contrast to the individual scholar and his/her interpretive interaction with the past leaves out precisely the history of the workers, what Mommsen termed *Arbeiter* in what was ostensibly his large-scale Big Humanities "database" project of classical epigraphs.[22] However, this examination rarely addresses the issue of how "the history of the workers" or even the "individual scholar and his/her(/their) interpretive interaction with the past" can in fact also be a history of fascism and white supremacist actors. What do you do when we know that Nietzsche was a primary source for Germany's 20th-century fascism and the current far right?[23] How do these questions about different kinds of knowledge production also then intersect with the work of Black queer feminists in the Combahee River Collective and how intersectionality, identity politics, and autoethnography especially of BIWOC create friction with Nietzsche's idea of the "ethical philologist" and whose imagined lived experiences gets to interpret the past.[24] In fact, in

21 Chad Wellmon, "Loyal Workers and Distinguished Scholars: Big Humanities and the Ethics of Knowledge," *Modern Intellectual History* 16, no. 1 (2019): 116.

22 Ibid., 97, 108.

23 Ibid., 108–13. Sean Illing, "The Alt-Right Is Drunk on Bad Readings of Nietzsche. The Nazis Were Too," *Vox*, December 30, 2018, https://www.vox.com/2017/8/17/16140846/alt-right-nietzsche-richard-spencer-nazism.

24 Keeanga Yamahtta Taylor, ed., *How We Get Free: Black Feminism and the Combahee River Collective* (Chicago: Haymarket Boooks, 2017).

reassessing the work philology, scholars have discussed the raciolinguistic bent of the "Romance of Philology" and especially the romance of Germanic philology (English national and German national)[25] in relation to racialized white nationalism. The ethical Germanic philologist can be a white supremacist, if not potentially a fascist. The field of philology is ripe with a raciolinguistic focus on genealogical origins as a form of raciolinguistic white supremacy. Big Humanities, in either *Wissenschaft* vision, cannot escape its entanglement with white supremacy and with nineteenth and twentieth-century fascism.

Finally, in Michel-Rolph Trouillot's *Silencing the Past: Power and the Production of History*, he writes that by examining the process of history we can "discover the differential exercise of power that makes some narratives possible and silences others."[26] This volume on *Alternative Historiographies of the Digital Humanities* examines the process of history in the narrative of the digital humanities. This volume's raison-d'être in considering DH's historical narrative is to dissect power. In essence, as Trouillot explains: "Power is constitutive of the story. Tracking power through various 'moments' simply helps emphasize the fundamentally processual character of historical production"[27] Trouillot's discussion of the four-stage system of silences — from "the making of sources," "the making of archives," "the making of narratives," "the making of history" — highlights the locations where silences enter the process of history.[28] He explains that "any historical narrative is a particular bundle of silences, the result of a unique process, and the operation required to deconstruct these silences will vary accordingly."[29] It is the silences

25 See Shyama Rajendran, "Undoing 'the Vernacular': Dismantling Structures of Raciolinguistic Supremacy," *Literature Compass* 16 (2019): e12544 and Yasemin Yildiz, *Beyond the Mother Tongue: The Postmonolingual Condition* (New York: Fordham University Press, 2012).

26 Michel-Rolph Trouillot, *Silencing the Past: Power and the Production of History* (Boston: Beacon Press, 1995), 25.

27 Ibid., 28.

28 Ibid., 26.

29 Ibid., 27.

in these alternative media histories that many of these essays highlight and these are not just silences of the past and present, but also silences about the digital future.

Alternative Historiographies of the Digital Humanities resists a linear history of the digital humanities — a straight line from the beginnings of humanities computing. By discussing alternatives histories of the digital humanities that address queer gaming; feminist game studies praxis; Cold War military-industrial complex computation; the creation of the environmental humanities; monolingual discontent in DH; the hidden history of DH in English studies; radical media praxis; cultural studies and DH; indigenous futurities; Pacific Rim postcolonial DH; the issue of scale and DH; Black feminist praxis; Global African feminist protest; Black feminist archives; and the racialized silences in topic modeling; the radical, indigenous, feminist histories of the digital database; and the possibilities for an antifascist DH, this collection hopes to re-set discussions of the DH and its attending straight, white origin myths. Thus, this collection hopes to reexamine the silences in such a straight and white masculinist history and show how power comes into play to shape this straight, white DH narrative.

The collection includes work from Edmond Y. Chang, David Golumbia, Alenda Y. Chang, Domenico Fiormonte, Alexandra Juhasz, Carly A. Kocurek, Viola Lasmana, Siobhan Senier, Anastasia Salter, Bridget Blodgett, Cathy J. Schuland-Vials, Arun Jacob, Jordan Clapper, Ravynn K. Stringfield, Nalubega Ross, Jamal Russell, Christy Hyman. The volume is organized into six sections: Presents; Histories; Praxis; Method; Indigenous Futures; and Black Futurities. In Presents, I interview David Golumbia about Digital Humanities and/with White Supremacy to think about the histories of fascism and white supremacy in relation to the digital and what it means to reckon with digital humanities' fascist politics and historiographies. Carly Kocurek's "Towards a Digital Cultural Studies: The Legacy of Cultural Studies and the Future of Digital Humanities," thinks about the potential for remixing methods in which "the framework proposed here is a call to action for digital humanities, like cultural studies, is aware of the degree to which it is always already engaged in the work of cultural politics."[30] A number of the pieces, including Arun Jacob's "Punching Holes in the International Busa Machine Narrative," Cathy J. Schlund-Vials "Cold War Computations and Imitation Games: Recalibrating the Origins of Asian American Studies," and Dorothy Kim's "Embodying the Database: Race, Gender, and Social Justice," reexamine the origin myth of the digital humanities to reassess Father Busa's hagiography and work in relation to media archaeology, politics, Cold War maneuvers, mechanized genocide, the Third Reich, and the military-industrial complex as it has organized fields including Asian studies. This is a reassessment of comparative genealogies — vis-à-vis Foucault — as well as ways to tell an alternative history of the Jesuit hagiography we have so far been unwilling to reexamine for its narrative use in embellishing an origin hagiography/historiography for digital humanities.

Cathy Schlund-Vials and Edmond Y. Chang also rethink the military-industrial complex and the legacies of the queer father of 20th-century computer science, Alan Turing. Chang's essay is also a form of new alternative praxis in which a critical essay is also a text game. His chapter is a transition into the section on Praxis. A number of pieces considers alternative praxis in rethinking these histories — whether it is an essay that is a game or a reevaluation of feminist media praxis. Alexandra Juhasz's "The Self-Reflexive Praxis at the Heart of DH," becomes a form of autoethnography about teaching YouTube in prison pedagogy while simultaneously rethinking the digital humanities genealogy back to BIWOC feminist critical theory. Bridget Blodgett and Anastasia Salter's, "Training Design 2: Ideological Conflicts in Feminist Games+Digital Humanities," considers the problems of audience and designer as those toxic cultural worlds come into the world of digital games pedagogy. They advocate for a "counter-canon" in order to push back against toxic masculinity, white supremacy, and racism in video games.

30 Carly A. Kocurek, "Towards a Digital Cultural Studies: The Legacy of Cultural Studies and the Future of Digital Humanities" (this volume).

In "An Indigenist Internet for Indigenous Futures: DH Beyond the Academy and 'Preservation,'" Siobhan Senier gives a larger view of Indigenous digital humanities that addresses Indigenous futurities and moves away from the touchstone of Indigenous "preservation." Senier thinks of the Indigeneity+digital as a method that requires co-creators, are reciprocal, respectful, and thinks through how digital media can create communities and futurity. Jordan Clapper's "The Ancestors in the Machine: Indigenous Futurity and Games," examines how different kinds of games can be "indigenized" and what the future may hold for Indigenous games and gaming.

Other pieces intertwine the digital humanities with other fields and a reevaluation of methods — distance reading, archives, area studies, Asian studies, cultural studies, literary studies, and environmental studies — in order to reexamine how the intersections and juxtapositions reveal silences in these histories. In Methods, Viola Lasmana's "Towards a Diligent Humanites: Digital Cultures and Archives of Post-1965 Indonesia," rethinks digital humanities as a methodology that allows alternative trajectories, and in this case, beyond academic digital humanities, for a "diligent humanities, practiced and theorized with care, with a hermeneutics that is attentive to the frictions between multiple scales of analyses, scales of production, as well as scales of tensions between the global and the local."[31] Domenico Fiormonte's "Taxation Against Overrepresentation: The Consequences of Monolingualism for Digital Humanities" begins with a self-reflexive discussion of the author's situatedness, begins to unpack the work of Walter Mignolo and Linda Tuhiwai Smith to discuss decoloniality, translation, language, and how "the technical is always political."[32] And finally, in Alenda Y. Chang's article, "Pitching the 'Big Tent' Outside: An Argument for the Digital Environmental Humanities," she discusses

31 Viola Lasmana, "Toward a Diligent Humanities: Digital Cultural Productions in Post-1965 Indonesia" (this volume).

32 Domenico Fiormonte, "Taxation against Overrepresentation? The Consequences of Monolingualism for Digital Humanities" (this volume).

the emergence of two different fields — digital humanities and environmental humanities, and also their intersections.

The volume finishes with a meditation on Break (Up, Down, Out, In) DH and Black Futurities. It opens with Ravynn K. Stringfield's essay "Breaking and (Re)Making" in which she states in the first sentence: "The interesting thing about the digital humanities is that it is exceptionally fragile."[33] Christy Hyman's piece, "Black Scholars and Disciplinary Gatekeeping," invokes Afrofuturism to discuss the archive of Black life and the constant disciplinary gates that will not allow Black scholars to use Black methodology to recover and bear witnesses to these archival narratives and their silences. Nalubega Ross's chapter, "Dr. Nyanzi's Protests: Silences, Futures, and the Present," considers the African feminist Dr. Stella Nyanzi's poem, "Feminist in High Heels" as a counter-poem and a form of feminist digital protest that broke out of its prison environment onto viral digital networks. And finally, Jamal Russell asks about Black futurities in topic modeling if there is no given to context of how the model is created and no context on the data itself. What he wonders is the future of Black DH in topic modeling?

DH must reckon with its past to reevaluate its methods, praxis, vision, politics now in order to create a different antiracist, decolonial, and just future. However, we cannot create this without reckoning with the digital humanities complex, often violent, fascist, and difficult genealogies and histories. We are not the only field in the midst of a reckoning. I take inspiration from Zoe Todd's discussion of anthropology's reckoning in her piece, "The Decolonial Turn 2.0: The Reckoning."[34] Todd channels the work of Rinaldo Walcott's *Queer Returns: Essays on Multiculturalism, Diaspora, and Black Studies*.[35] She writes:

33 Ravynn K. Stringfield, "Breaking and (Re)Making" (this volume).

34 Zoe Todd, "The Decolonial Turn 2.0: The Reckoning," *anthrodendum*, June 15, 2018, https://anthrodendum.org/2018/06/15/the-decolonial-turn-2-0-the-reckoning/.

35 Rinaldo Walcott, *Queer Returns: Essays on Multiculturalism, Diaspora, and Black Studies* (London, Ontario, Canada: Insomniac Press, 2016).

> Anthropology continues to be a colonial and exclusionary discipline, and that in order to reckon with its structural violences we need — in a nod to the work of Dr. Rinaldo Walcott (2016) in his text "Queer Returns" — a decolonial (re)turn in anthropology. I am inspired here by Walcott (2016:1), who notes, in engaging with his previous thinking and writing, the value in a "return to scenes of previous engagements in ways that demonstrate growth, change, and doubt." In imagining a Decolonial Turn 2.0 or Decolonial (re)turn for Anthropology, I envision an engagement that forces us to return to the 'scenes of apprehension' (Simpson 2014) through which Anthropology imagines, reproduces, and promulgates itself as largely, still, a white, male, and colonial discipline.[36]

My hope is that this volume begins that work of digital humanities reckoning with its past, its historiographies, as a way to confront its historical and current structural violences. I believe this is the only way to imagine a just digital humanities future.

In addition, I hope this book is a way to subvert the very forms of power it critiques by being published by an open-access press supported by university libraries. So much of the digital humanities and its genealogical histories have involved large amounts of funding tied to the military-industrial complex and the academic-industrial complex that have often been about devastating violence and harm. In addition, the six areas that this book has organized its essays — Presents; Histories; Praxis; Methods; Indigenous Futures; and Black Futurities — should make clear another way to discuss the digital humanities. So moving beyond definitions or debates, what I lay out here is an alternative path to examine the present, the future, and the past through a situated politics as well as a way forward in thinking about how to address digital humanities' long genealogy in its complicity to military power, fascism, settler colonialism, chattel slavery, violence against LGBTQIA+ people, toxic masculine digital cultures, the Anthropocene and environmental disaster,

36 Todd, "The Decolonial Turn 2.0."

archives of violence, the price of American monolingualism, Indigenous games and archives, Black digital methods and futurities, etc. The way to move forward is to precisely examine our praxis and our methods in order to think about the digital humanities as a process of scholarly, critical, discursive ways to always examine power.

Bibliography

Barlow, John Perry. "A Declaration of the Independence of Cyberspace." *Electronic Frontier Foundation*. https://www.eff.org/cyberspace-independence.

Daniels, Jessie. "The Algorithmic Rise of the 'Alt-Right.'" *Contexts* 17, no. 1 (February 2018): 60–65. DOI: 10.1177/1536504218766547.

Daniels, Jessie. *Cyber Racism: White Supremacy Online and the New Attack on Civil Rights*. Lanham: Rowman & Littlefield, 2009.

Emerson, Lori. *Reading Writing Interfaces*. Minneapolis: University of Minnesota Press, 2014.

Everett, Anna. "The Revolution Will Be Digitized: Afrocentricity and the Digital Public Sphere." *Social Text* 20, no. 2 (Summer 2002): 125–46. https://muse.jhu.edu/article/31928.

Everett, Anna. *The Revolution Will Be Digitized: Afrocentricity and the Digital Public Sphere*. Utrecht: Uitgave Faculteit der Letteren, 2001.

Helft, Miguel. "The Godfather of Digital Maps." *Forbes*, February 10, 2016. https://www.forbes.com/sites/miguelhelft/2016/02/10/the-godfather-of-digital-maps/.

Huhtamo, Erkki, and Jussi Parikka. "Introduction: An Archaeology of Media Archaeology." In *Media Archaeology: Approaches, Applications, and Implications*, edited by Erkki Huhtamo and Jussi Parikka, 1–24. Berkeley: University of California Press, 2011.

Illing, Sean. "The Alt-Right Is Drunk on Bad Readings of Nietzsche. The Nazis Were Too." *Vox*, December 30, 2018. https://www.vox.com/2017/8/17/16140846/alt-right-nietzsche-richard-spencer-nazism.

Jacob, Arun. "#DHSI19_Unconference_Media Anarchaeology: Critical Theory & Digital Humanities," presentation at the Digital Humanities Summer Institute, 2019.

Landau, Elizabeth. "Tech Confronts Its Use of the Labels 'Master' and 'Slave.'" *Wired,* July 6, 2020. https://www.wired.com/story/tech-confronts-use-labels-master-slave/.

Lovink, Geert. *My First Recession: Critical Internet Cultures in Transition.* Rotterdam: Nai Publishers, 2004.

Moravec, Michelle. "Exceptionalism in Digital Humanities: Community, Collaboration, and Consensus." In *Disrupting the Digital Humanities,* edited by Dorothy Kim and Jesse Stommel, 169–96. Earth: punctum books, 2018.

"Master Slave Communication." *Python Testing Infrastructure.* https://pyti.readthedocs.io/en/latest/master-slave.html.

McCullock, Gretchen. "Coding Is for Everyone — As Long as You Speak English." *Wired,* April 8, 2019. https://www.wired.com/story/coding-is-for-everyoneas-long-as-you-speak-english/.

Nakamura, Lisa. "Cyberrace." *PMLA* 123, no. 5 (2008): 1673–82. DOI: 10.1632/pmla.2008.123.5.1673.

Oberhaus, Daniel. "'Master/Slave' Terminology Was Removed from Python Programming Language." *Motherboard: Tech by Vice,* September 13, 2018. https://motherboard.vice.com/en_us/article/8x7akv/masterslave-terminology-was-removed-from-python-programming-language.

Parikka, Jussi. *A Geology of Media.* Minneapolis: University of Minnesota Press, 2015.

———. *What Is Media Archaeology?* Cambridge: Polity, 2012.

"The Nature Conservancy Preserves 24,000-acre Coastal Ranch at Point Conception with $165 Million Gift from Esri Founders." *The Nature Conservancy,* December 21, 2017. https://www.nature.org/en-us/explore/newsroom/the-nature-conservancy-preserves-24000-acre-coastal-ranch-at-point-conceptio/.

"Preserving Nature: UC Santa Barbara Announces Dangermond Endowed Chair in Conservation Studies." *The Current,* 2017. https://www.news.ucsb.edu/2017/018606/preserving-nature.

Rajendran, Shyama. "Undoing 'the Vernacular': Dismantling Structures of Raciolinguistic Supremacy." *Literature Compass* 16 (2019): e12544. DOI: 10.1111/lic3.12544.

Taylor, Keeanga-Yamahtta, ed. *How We Get Free: Black Feminism and the Combahee River Collective.* Chicago: Haymarket Books, 2017.

Todd, Zoe. "The Decolonial Turn 2.0: The Reckoning." *anthrodendum,* June 15, 2018, https://anthrodendum.org/2018/06/15/the-decolonial-turn-2-0-the-reckoning/.

Trouillot, Michel-Rolph. *Silencing the Past: Power and the Production of History.* Boston: Beacon Press, 1995.

Walcott, Rinaldo. *Queer Returns: Essays on Multiculturalism, Diaspora, and Black Studies.* London: Insomniac Press, 2016.

Wellmon, Chad. "Loyal Workers and Distinguished Scholars: Big Humanities and the Ethics of Knowledge." *Modern Intellectual History* 16, no. 1 (April 2019): 87–126. DOI: 10.1017/S1479244317000129.

Yildiz, Yasemin. *Beyond the Mother Tongue: The Postmonolingual Condition.* New York: Fordham University Press, 2012.

Presents

2

Digital Humanities and/as White Supremacy: A Conversation about Reckonings

David Golumbia & Dorothy Kim

DOROTHY KIM: One of the ways in which I have tried to think about this volume in regards to Alternative Historiographies is to organize with a mind towards different areas and histories that do not get discussed — Asian American, Indigenous, Global, etc. — but I think a big white elephant in the room is to discuss, especially now, as we have seen since the 2016 US election into this COVID-19 moment, into the 2020 elections and its aftermath is the history of white supremacy and DH (digital studies, media studies, etc.). What do you think are the most salient parts of this historiography that must be known and consistently highlighted?

DAVID GOLUMBIA: I appreciate the opportunity to talk about this with you, especially now. We are talking during the protests in favor of racial justice prompted by the murder of George Floyd and other violence against Black communities. Those are the reasons I have decided to talk about this again and at this moment, even though I have previously pledged not to write or speak about DH again, as I explain at the end of this discussion, in response to what I see as a remarkable but symptomatic pattern of proto-fascist social media use on the part of DH practitioners that targets not just me but everyone who speaks critically about it.

That seems to me to open up a space for discourse about race and DH. We are finally starting to see in the various bastions of technical power in our world (especially major tech companies like Google, Facebook, Twitter, Reddit, and so on, but also at least some of the tech advocacy groups like the ones around Wikipedia) the beginnings of an acknowledgment that they strongly support white supremacy, and that when critics point this out, it is a mark of that white supremacy to immediately attack the critic and to deny and dissemble about the accusations. Yet this pattern of denial and dissembling is exactly what I've encountered since I began speaking out about DH, and frankly, since I know most of the prominent critics of DH, whether understood as "inside" or "outside" of DH proper — another construction I'd like to talk more about later — they too have encountered exactly the same pattern.

So, I hope that we might be at a moment when, if we look at the long history of critiques of DH that point out its uncomfortable relationship with white supremacy, we might finally be a place where DH might take these concerns seriously rather than attacking critics. Unfortunately, I think that there are structural reasons why DH, like many other institutions and practices that strongly identify with technological development as social progress, will be unable to push back very hard on the white supremacy with which it is deeply entwined, and these are closely aligned with the reasons that it cannot afford to take seriously critiques directed at the para-discipline.

Since the title of this volume is *Alternative Historiographies,* I wonder if we can talk about the historiography of DH a bit in this regard. One of the truly infuriating (to me at least) aspects of talking about this topic is that we are often nowadays met with the claim that DH has somehow always been about the work of minority and marginalized populations, or even primarily about those populations — despite the fact that the field itself is remarkably white, even now, especially when compared with the other humanities fields within and around which it operates, and that this is a truism that many of those with feet in both the non-DH and DH aspects of literary studies (including Martha Nell Smith, Tara McPherson, and even Alan Liu) have acknowledged from the earliest days. What do you think of these claims about the origins of DH?

DOROTHY: I think the history of DH and white supremacy is deeply entrenched and has been for a while. I mean in relation to my own piece, there is still a Busa award, so you have to wonder how people really thought about why this was fine even when he made it clear in DH pieces he wrote how entangled he was with IBM (not to mention the fact, he admits that he was an Italian fascist) and how entrenched all that was. I think what you are describing is how these alternative historiographies to the mainstream history of white DH is picked up and used as a diversity shield. It's a form of what Sara Ahmed discusses in *On Being Included* in regards to the academic and institutional diversity industrial complex.[1] I do think that the history of the digital humanities does have a long history that involves the work of BIPOC and other marginalized groups, but I also believe that work is not exactly what is getting the grants, getting the support, nor even getting the kind of recognition for that work. If white DH is picking these projects and histories as a way to say "we are diverse" it is also entangled in a form of what Cheryl L. Harris discusses in "Whiteness as Property."[2]

DAVID: I want to focus in a bit on the "diversity shield" and the scholarship you mention in the latter part of your response. There is a prominent thread of thinking about this going back to the very early days, perhaps best exemplified in Martha Nell

1 Sara Ahmed, *On Being Included: Racism and Diversity in Institutional Life* (Durham: Duke University Press, 2012).

2 Cheryl I. Harris, "Whiteness as Property," *Harvard Law Review* 106, no. 8 (1993): 1709–91.

Smith's essay "The Human Touch" and Tara McPherson's essay "Why Are the Digital Humanities So White?"[3] All of this work, like yours and mine, talks about the directly material question of ways that DH hires, foundation support, conferences, role in university administrations, and publications look retrograde when compared to English in particular, but also other humanities fields: the representation of minorities is much lower in DH than in the fields it claims to partner with. But even more pointedly, the critiques are about structural racism. They don't just note the material reality I've just mentioned: they ask why it is that a new field of English (and of course you and I are both English professors by training, and I have many times pointed out that it was English in particular that the DH formation targets: DH projects in disciplines like History are much less controversial and much less problematic than in English) has developed in which all the work that literature departments have been doing to increase minority representation has been turned upside-down: why *this* subfield in particular? To answer that question requires reading fairly widely in Black studies, in critical race studies, in "theory" per se, and in the kinds of critical work about digital technology that is almost always published as "digital studies" or "media studies" and almost never as DH.

Yet the reception of this critical work in DH, and this is what is so incredibly frustrating, is to ignore all of this and to focus on the "diversity shield." Rather than comparing the hiring of white people vs non-white people in English departments, which is one of the main topics many critics have talked about, this response just says, "well, we've hired a few minority scholars." Rather than engaging with the long work of studying race and racism, this response says, "we have started digitization projects in Black history" or, even worse, "it's not our fault because the

3 See Martha Nell Smith, "The Human Touch Software of the Highest Order: Revisiting Editing as Interpretation," *Textual Cultures* 2, no. 1 (2007): 1–15 and Tara McPherson, "Why Are the Digital Humanities So White? or Thinking the Histories of Race and Computation," in *Debates in the Digital Humanities*, ed. Matthew K. Gold (Minneapolis: University of Minnesota Press, 2012).

only texts in the public domain are by white people." Even to the final point about criticism of the digital per se, the answers tend to be very cribbed, and to point to the fact that the history of computerization is not all white and even less all male.

What is remarkable to me in these responses is that they are often word-for-word the same responses we see from the leaders of all digital technology organizations, whether corporations or even non-corporate institutions, when it turns out that structural support for white supremacy is pervasive. Rather than saying something like, "of course all institutions in the US have roots in white supremacy, and we need to do some real self-examination about what ours is" — which is in very broad strokes what the response of the humanities academy has been, over many decades — the answer always is, "we're not racist." Which is the kind of answer only someone who was committed to not understanding racism would give.

DOROTHY: Much of the work that has undergirded the white supremacy and fascist problems in digital right now has come from media studies, communication studies, digital studies, and not "digital humanities." The discussion of tech and structural racism, tech, and the white supremacy problem have really dug deep in these areas or with pieces like Safiya Noble's *Algorithms of Oppression*, Ruha Benjamin's *Race after Technology*, and even Lisa Nakamura's call in *Film Quarterly*, "Watching White Supremacy on Digital Video Platforms: 'Screw Your Optics, I'm Going In,'" that have demanded that the white supremacy and fascist problems on these digital spaces be addressed and combated.[4] In the Fall of 2020, the White House and Trump administration penned an executive order precisely about banning

4 See Safiya Umoja Noble, *Algorithms of Oppression: How Search Engines Reinforce Racism* (New York: NYU Press, 2018); Ruha Benjamin, *Race after Technology: Abolitionist Tools for the New Jim Code* (Cambridge: Polity Press, 2019); and Lisa Nakamura, "Watching White Supremacy on Digital Video Platforms: 'Screw Your Optics, I'm Going In,'" *Film Quarterly* 72, no. 3 (2019): 19–22.

critical race theory and terms like "structural racism."[5] What would you say about both the groundwork that has been done in relation to tech, digital, and white supremacy and fascism in specific other fields (media studies, communications, LIS, etc.) and what is the clear overt government policing of critical race theory in our politics? What has been going on now in digital humanities? I don't think structures of white supremacy can be dismantled without naming, describing, understanding its machinery, so this is me asking, what do you think is going on and how do we deal with this? In addition, beyond just academic areas, there is also the critique that has been happening both in Library and Information Science (and a long-standing critique about white librarianship) and also academic technology.[6] Many areas where people are doing DH work in relation to the university are and having ongoing racial reckonings in relation to white supremacy.

DAVID: This is one of the reasons I have tried in my work to focus on DH as an institutional formation and ideology, a set of rhetorical moves and associations and forces rather than a method or set of methods. I have long said and long observed that DH was developed as a reactionary formation against the kinds of critical apparatuses that emerged from the 1970s through the 1990s

5 "Executive Order 13950 of September 22, 2020, Combating Race and Sex Stereotyping," *Federal Register* 85, no. 188 (September 28, 2020): 60683. EO 13950 was revoked by "Executive Order 13985 of January 20, 2021, Advancing Racial Equity and Support for Underserved Communities Through the Federal Government," *Federal Register* 86, no. 14 (January 25, 2021): 7009.

6 See Lindsay McKenzie, "Racism and the American Library Association," *Inside Higher Ed,* February 1, 2019, https://www.insidehighered.com/news/2019/02/01/american-library-association-criticized-response-racism-complaint and Angela Galvan, "Soliciting Performance, Hiding Bias: Whiteness and Librarianship," *In the Library with the Lead Pipe,* June 3, 2015, http://www.inthelibrarywiththeleadpipe.org/2015/soliciting-performance-hiding-bias-whiteness-and-librarianship/. See also Audrey Watters' work and her forthcoming book *Teaching Machines: The History of Personalized Learning* (Cambridge: MIT Press, forthcoming August 2021).

in literary studies in particular. I am falsely accused of "conspiracy theory" for saying this, but it bears repeating: the change from "humanities computing" to "digital humanities" was a deliberate rebranding that happened in a series of workshops at the University of Virginia around the year 2000, directed in particular by Jerome McGann and Johanna Drucker along with a handful of graduate students, and with funding from Mellon and the NEH. I was the first person hired in the world as a "digital humanist" with the grant money they received to realize this rebranding. It took me several years to fully grasp this, but they were furious with me for teaching and writing about race in particular, as well as cultural topics in general. I taught a class called "Race and the Digital" in my third or fourth year at UVa, imagining it was par for the course; only later I learned that senior DHers at UVa had actually *complained* about my teaching the class as if it violated some unspoken precept of DH in particular. I cannot stress this enough: their animus toward these topics was well-known at the time, and as time went on, they expressed it more and more overtly to me repeatedly. DH was designed as a replacement for "theory" and "cultural studies." It was to be the "new thing" that took over English departments and rid us of those mistaken old topics. The senior DH people at UVa were notorious for coming to faculty meetings and lectures and classes and saying things like "it's all digital now" when people insisted on what you and I might agree are the substantive questions of literary and cultural studies, always with the explicit purpose of shutting down discussion of these questions. It is no accident, by the way, that long-time UVa English professor Rita Felski's full-throated embrace of right-wing political thinking about culture developed in that place and at that time.[7] It was all of a piece: anything to get rid of critical thinking in general, but racial politics in particular.

7 See Sheila Liming, "Fighting Words," review of *Hooked: Art and Attachment,* by Rita Felski, *Los Angeles Review of Books,* December 14, 2020, https://lareviewofbooks.org/article/fighting-words/.

Now, I should say that I think it is very dangerous to engage in thinking that dips into genetic fallacies. The fact that DH was conceived in this way does not mean that somehow everyone who practices it has bought into these grounding assumptions, and in fact the work of critics like you and me and many others has pushed DH to say that it is not in fact a bastion of white supremacy. But as we've been talking about, too often these responses themselves smack of white supremacist denialism, including the "diversity shield." And again and again and again, the most obvious thing is that the DH practitioners who defend the field overtly reject what the rest of us in literary and cultural studies embrace as foundational: reading the texts that critique white supremacy, from slave narratives to W.E.B. Du Bois to James Baldwin to Toni Morrison to vast amounts of contemporary writing. This is where you see the real gap, and one of the structural ways in which DH strongly resembles other rightist hotbeds of digital agitation: they reject the description of themselves as racist, but also reject the descriptions of racism from those who have done the most to define and understand it. They turn racism into what Eduardo Bonilla-Silva, among many others, calls "color-blindness," and that is a right-wing, anti-theoretical understanding of racism.[8] It is really remarkable when we start talking with academics about racism and their first move is to dismiss the vast bulk of academic work about racism, if they are even familiar with it.

One recent and dispiriting example of these dynamics is found in Nan Z. Da's *Critical Inquiry* article about what she calls "computational literary studies" and the "discussion" that happened around it, especially on social media.[9] Whether you agree with its conclusions or not (of course I largely do agree with them), Da's article is extremely careful and strongly evidence-driven. She looks specifically at the kinds of claims DH

8 See Eduardo Bonilla-Silva, *Racism without Racists: Color-Blind Racism and the Persistence of Racial Inequality in America*, 5th edn. (Lanham: Rowman & Littlefield, 2018).

9 Nan Z. Da, "The Computational Case against Computational Literary Studies," *Critical Inquiry* 45, no. 3 (2019): 601–39.

itself makes for some of its methods, and shows that on these terms, DH repeatedly fails to deliver what it promises. This is a harsh critique to be sure. That's not unusual in any academic discipline, which may be a bad thing about academia altogether, or maybe it's just the nature of impassioned human beings exchanging ideas about things they disagree about. DH is in no way unique in this. But having read a lot of academic debates in a lot of fields in my decades as a professor, this one stands out for the fact that a large number of responses to Da radically mis-state her argument at best, and at worst take what should be bizarre and irrelevant secondary pot shots at her.

Like every other person who has tried to critique DH for its institutional politics and for the claims it makes about its own work, Da was trashed personally and professionally, including her pretty large body of non-DH work. As always, one of the main responses was the characteristic "No True Scotsman" argument,[10] where no matter how central the examples are that one chooses, one is always told that actually, today, now, much better examples exist that resolve all the problems the critic identifies, even though we can't actually even point at those other examples. Worst of all, though, Da was accused of "erasing" the work of people of color, even though not a single thing about her argument in any way hinged on the race of the researchers who wrote the studies she examined. And these critiques came just as much from white people within DH who seemed to have overlooked the fact that Da herself is a woman of color.

The disingenuousness of this response reminds me very much of the way fascists respond to the work of Black intellectuals. Keyword potshots are used to distract from substance; facts are denied right in the face of near-irrefutable evidence; "facts" that favor fascists are asserted despite them being highly unlikely at best; and people asserting critiques of fascism are accused of being "the real fascists." And this takes a particular form in digital technology, as once technology promoters learned that

10 "No True Scotsman," *Internet Encyclopedia of Philosophy*, https://iep.utm.edu/fallacy/#NoTrueScotsman.

activists were holding their feet to the fire about the negative racial consequences of their technologies, the promoters turned around and accused these activists of actually being the ones who were harming people of color. Just as in the Da case, white men tell women of color that actually they are the ones who are harming people of color, and doing so by refusing to accept the beneficence of digital tools that are in too many ways just tools for the powerful to gain even more power.

The most famous example of this I know of is the shockingly dishonest technology promoter and "professor" Jeff Jarvis, who has learned what a productive line of argument this is, despite it being shockingly contrary to both common sense and scholarly observation.[11] In a fairly recent (2019) conversation with the technologist and technology critic Andrew Keen, Jarvis claims that what he calls (very inexactly) "populism" is a result of "old white men who are threatened by technological change."[12] In Keen's words, to Jarvis, because "the Internet...enables the new voices of movements like Black Lives Matter and Me Too, it is — by definition — progressive." Believing this requires one to overlook entirely the fact that, as Keen puts it, "reactionary old white men like Steve Bannon and Donald Trump are actually very skilled at using the internet to build their movements and distribute their messages" — and Keen's politics are not even ones I share for the most part, but here he comes out far to the left of Jarvis who likely is a liberal with regard to ordinary electoral politics, but repeatedly takes the side of the far right when it comes to technology.

Remember that Jarvis says this in 2019, when the empirical grounding for Keen's response was beyond obvious (and beyond clear to the majority of digital media scholars in all the non-DH fields). Digital technology may have salutary effects for progressive social movements — if it did not have some such ef-

11 See, e.g., Jeff Jarvis, *What Would Google Do? Reverse-Engineering the Fastest-Growing Company in the History of the World* (New York: HarperCollins, 2009).

12 Andrew Keen, interview with Jeff Jarvis, *Keen On,* May 21, 2019, http://www.ajkeen.com/podcast/episode19.

fects, would these topics even be open for discussion? — but by far the dominant effects, at least so far, are to give enormous and unprecedented power to right-wing populist and fascist movements all over the world, including in what had historically been relatively stable democracies like the US and UK, as non-DH scholars have pointed out again and again,[13] to the almost-total silence of the supposed digital technology "experts" in DH (who, nevertheless, when people like me say that DH is partly about the elimination of critique of the digital from the humanities academy, repeatedly have almost nothing to say, or even engage in outright denialism, about the obvious and poisonous uses of digital technology). To look at this situation and say that actually these technologies are pushing society in a progressive direction requires a willful distortion of underlying facts that is already tinged with the reality distortions we expect of fascist movements themselves: that it is being said by someone with a history of protecting and advancing the interests of technology against all criticisms, no matter the facts on hand, makes it shocking.

This is almost exactly the pattern we see in the cycle of critiques of DH and "responses" to it. Those who respond are, like Jarvis, thoroughly and institutionally embedded in a formation that goes well beyond a "method," but entails a willful commitment to the progressive nature of technological change that is deeply resistant to self-examination. (This is part of why DH is so hard to define, although to be fair, one senior DHer, Ted Underwood, has occasionally acknowledged that this commitment to technology-as-progress is what's at the heart of DH.) Whatever DH means, it means institutional and personal power to those who champion it, power associated with the view that digital technology is on balance good for society, and for the most part, those people are white. They are certainly white to a much higher percentage when compared with the other humanities fields

13 See in addition to works by authors like Benjamin and Noble cited above, Jen Schradie, *The Revolution that Wasn't: How Digital Activism Favors Conservatives* (Cambridge: Harvard University Press, 2019) and Virginia Eubanks, *Digital Dead End: Fighting for Social Justice in the Information Age* (Cambridge: MIT Press, 2011).

DH can't help but work to supplant. So while DH jobs and dollars displace people of color in English and other departments, DH promoters have to tell us that DH is actually there to promote exactly what is being displaced by it.

One of the things that is so galling about this is that nearly everyone not part of DH sees it. I am always shocked by the number and wide range of professors and graduate students who tell me that they see the white supremacy, the proto-fascist anti-intellectualism, the shifting target of study, and all the other things I have been speaking about for decades when they look at DH. Almost to a one, the people who dismiss these observations are directly invested in DH — that is, they have positions, institutional roles and awards that depend not just on them being literary scholars or historians or whatever, but specifically on doing work that feeds the idea that there is such a thing as DH, that it stands apart from the rest of the disciplines they say they are a part of, and at times, that it is politically salutary or exists for purposes of social justice. So on the one hand you have people who really do embrace both the politics and methods of literary study and see DH as more or less destructive to that; on the other hand you have DHers, who freely express animus toward non-DH work, but then claim that they are the victims and the non-DHers are insane conspiracy theorists for pointing out DH's destructiveness.

One wants to say: really? Are you *really* arguing that first, so many senior English professors (and junior professors, and graduate students) are completely not-credible about the substance and institutional politics of our own discipline? Let alone that, second, you are saying this in the *very same breath* that you say it's crazy to think that DH has animus toward that discipline? How could those two thoughts be even remotely compatible? It is a typical mark of ideological and proto-fascist formations that they sit on remarkable instances of cognitive dissonance and become angry, not reflective, when these are pointed out. Identifying these areas of contradiction is often taken as a hallmark of literary and cultural studies, but suddenly, we have the very odd spectacle of DHers who generally reject the work of cultural interpretation telling those of us who do continue to specialize in it, that DHers are "actually" the specialists in cultural interpretation when it comes to our own field.

DOROTHY: So maybe this is the question that I see happening not just in DH, though the historiography and genealogies there are long and deeply entrenched with white supremacy and fascism, but also in other fields. I see this in medieval studies and I see similar tactics and rhetoric used in other traditional "white" canon fields. I mean medieval studies just happens to be an extreme version since the field is so white and so deeply embedded with current political fascism. I think Black and ethnic studies has had a long history of dealing with these rhetorical moves and tactics as well as naming these operations, identifying these tactics, breaking down the components of these white supremacist moves: the "white liberal," the "I have #BlackLivesMatter signs on my lawn," but will continue to work through the practices of white fragility and white innocence and eventually what Carol Anderson calls "white rage."[14] I have been particularly flummoxed and frustrated in medieval studies by this seeming inability to reckon with what I think of as critical whiteness studies in the field. And I see a similar pattern in DH. As someone who is told by white scholars all the time, like Da, that I am the one harming BIPOC scholars in medieval studies, yhere is no racial reckoning. Instead, it is often a continued disinformation pattern there (also from purported white scholars who say they are liberal but seem fine to hang out digitally and socially with medieval studies' fascist pundits) in which I am called the fascist, and I am the violent one. This is a really standard pattern discussed by Koritha Mitchell as "Know Your Place Aggression."[15]

And there is definitely some very interesting revisionist digital historiography going on there in relation to Jarvis. What is

14 Carol Anderson, *White Rage: The Unspoken Truth of Our Racial Divide* (New York: Bloomsbury, 2016).

15 Koritha Mitchell, "Identifying White Mediocrity and Know-Your-Place Aggression: A Form of Self-Care," *African American Review* 51, no. 4 (2018): 253–62.

fascinating is that even as people like Jessie Daniels and other scholars have pointed to how media savvy the far right has been for a long time (from film, to newsletters, to usenet, to forums, to email, to the internet, to now social media, etc.)[16] there is this strange way that these two histories are not discussed as parallel and in fact affecting each other. The rise of the digital far right and their influence, denizens, political organizing is matched by the rise of hashtag activism, #BlackLivesMatter, and other social justice organizing online and they have been directly in a digital fight in relation to information, disinformation, etc., for a long time. It's amazing to imagine these blinkered recent historical lenses that do not understand that the far right used the Black feminist hashtag activists[17] as target practice to refine their digital tactics — swarming, doxxing, swatting, bots, Black face digital ventriloquism a la Cointelpro — before they went and used that on #GamerGate and then more widely in the political arena,[18] which we now see in the culmination #StealTheVote and QAnon violent political factions.

It horrifies me that we cannot even grapple with the most recent digital past, let alone a longer digital historiography to understand what we are dealing with and what is going on. How will this help DH and basically the work it fuels in these large political arenas as we grapple with its whiteness, white supremacy, and fascist reckoning? I feel that all of our fields are in a long-term moment of reckoning. Here I am thinking of Zoe Todd's description in anthropology of reckoning in her piece "The Decolonial Turn 2.0: The Reckoning" from a few years ago. She writes this:

---

16 See Jessie Daniels, "The Algorithmic Rise of the 'Alt-Right,'" *Contexts* 17, no. 1 (2018): 60–5.

17 I'Nasah Crockett, "'Raving Amazons': Antiblackness and Misogynoir in Social Media," *Model View Culture*, June 30, 2014, https://modelviewculture.com/pieces/raving-amazons-antiblackness-and-misogynoir-in-social-media.

18 Rachelle Hampton, "The Black Feminists Who Saw the Alt-Right Threat Coming," *Slate*, April 23, 2019, https://slate.com/technology/2019/04/black-feminists-alt-right-twitter-gamergate.html.

> I submit that situations like the *HAU* Journal scandal reinforce the fact that Anthropology continues to be a colonial and exclusionary discipline, and that in order to reckon with its structural violences we need—in a nod to the work of Dr. Rinaldo Walcott (2016) in his text 'Queer Returns'—a decolonial (re)turn in anthropology. I am inspired here by Walcott (2016: 1), who notes, in engaging with his previous thinking and writing, the value in a "return to scenes of previous engagements in ways that demonstrate growth, change, and doubt."
>
> In imagining a Decolonial Turn 2.0 or Decolonial (re)turn for Anthropology, I envision an engagement that that forces us to return to the 'scenes of apprehension' (Simpson 2014) through which Anthropology imagines, reproduces, and promulgates itself as largely, still, a white, male, and colonial discipline. Working through Walcott and Simpson's significant contributions to the fields of decolonization, I imagine, here, what it means to visit these moments and entanglements of anthropological knowledge production, and illustrate what has been at stake for me in my own experiences in the discipline. I delve into moments and case studies here that have, largely, inspired many of my writings about decolonizing anthropology, but which I have, until now, shied away from exploring more explicitly for fear of backlash and retribution.[19]

This has been turning in my mind for so many of my different fields for several years and very much embedded in the introduction of this collection. I would also point out that Todd has been very public in her description of finally actually leaving anthropology because it was unsustainable and the toxicity and white supremacist settler colonialism literally killing her. Even

19 Zoe Todd, "The Decolonial Turn 2.0: The Reckoning," *anthro{dendum}*, June 15, 2018, https://anthrodendum.org/2018/06/15/the-decolonial-turn-2-0-the-reckoning/. Todd cites Rinaldo Walcott, *Queer Returns: Essays on Multiculturalism, Diaspora, and Black Studies* (London: Insomniac Press, 2016).

as she has framed out the most searing, clear, critical, but necessary explanation of what needs to be done to reckon in a deeply entangled white supremacist field, she had to leave to live.[20] What does that say when she and others have pointed out the actual handful of Indigenous scholars in anthropology?

I agree with what you are discussing as some sort of techno-utopia when we have been in a cycle of at least 4-5 years (since 2016's US Elections) of a mainstream understanding that digital is about techno-dystopia at the very least if not a fascist, white supremacy surveillance machine. I wonder about this since waves and moves to certain literary theories or methods also have come with the support of various kinds of white supremacist structures. I am thinking about the history of New Criticism which was entirely about trying to disentangle politics for literary criticism and the humanities and was supported by the CIA. In the 1990s, literary theory was grappling with ethnic studies and critical race theory while new historicism was on the rise as a way to step around having, in fact, to deal with race at all. Now, I see a similar move made in ecocriticism who have only recently been critiqued for ignoring race, see for example Jennifer James's work or the critiques to a particularly terrible piece that includes Donna Haraway amongst others talking about the Anthropocene.[21] In the critique of the latter from Katherine

20 Douglas Quan, "Inside the 'Indigenization' of Canada's Universities: Progress — But Also Accusations of Tokenism, Broken Promises and 'Ethnic Fraud,'" *Toronto Star*, February 27, 2021, https://www.thestar.com/news/canada/2021/02/27/inside-the-indigenization-of-canadas-universities-progress-but-also-accusations-of-tokenism-broken-promises-and-ethnic-fraud.html.

21 See Jennifer James, "'Buried in Guano': Race, Labor and Sustainability," *American Literary History* 24, no. 1 (2012): 115–42; Jennifer James, "Ecomelancholia: Slavery, War, and Black Ecological Imaginings," in *Environmental Criticism for the Twenty-First Century*, eds. Stephanie LeMenager, Teresa Shewry, and Ken Hiltner (New York: Routledge, 2011), 163–78; Fikile Nxumalo, "Situating Indigenous and Black Childhoods in the Anthropocene," in *Research Handbook on Childhoodnature: Assemblages of Childhood and Nature Research*, eds. Amy Cutter-Mackenzie-Knowles, Karen Malone, and Elisabeth Barratt Hacking (New York: Springer, 2018), 1–22; and Heather Davis and Zoe Todd, "On the

McKitterick (recently online) and also from the work of Black geography, the critique has pointed out the complete lack of addressing racial capitalism and the critiques of the "plantation" as a system.[22] Or the turn to aesthetics which often is a weird turn to form as literary appreciation and somehow does not address any identity politics, especially race. Kyla Wazana Tompkins writes about this problem in this "new aesthetics" turn.[23] There seems to always be these kinds of retranchist, whitelash recyclings. However, I think what makes DH particularly difficult is the issue of acceleration, speed, and funding. Daniels discusses this in relation to white supremacy and digital media. I think there is a similar problem here. These other areas are literary theoretical turns that often take a decade or two to hash out. They usually are not massively funded by government and foundations (in the case of the US) and they usually are not the conversation of mainstream politics in a late fascist and capitalist moment. What I see as an urgency in discussions and reckoning with DH historiographies is that we need to immediately take stock of what's going on because the acceleration of digital in relation to fascism and white supremacy and then how digital is then weaponized to harm and kill BIPOC groups and also other marginalized communities is incredibly urgent. We do not have time to hash this out for a decade or two.

DAVID: This is fascinating and so important and I'm not sure I can begin to adequately talk about it. One of the things that immediately stands out to me is that, of all longstanding academic

---

Importance of a Date, or, Decolonizing the Anthropocene," *ACME: An International Journal for Critical Geographies* 16, no. 4 (2017): 761–80. See the aforementioned controversial piece: Donna Haraway et al., "Anthropologists Are Talking—About the Anthropocene," *Ethnos* 81, no. 3 (2016): 535–564.

22 Janae Davis et al., "Anthropocene, Capitalocene, … Plantationocene? A Manifesto for Ecological Justice in an Age of Global Crises," *Geography Compass* 13, no. 5 (2019): e12438.

23 See Kyla Wazana Tompkins, "Response to Michelle N. Huang and Chad Shomura," *Lateral* 6, no. 1 (2017) and "On the Limits and Promise of New Materialist Philosophy," *Lateral* 5, no. 1 (2016).

disciplines, anthropology is the one that has been most open to discussions of inherent colonialism and discrimination.

I have worked near and directly with anthropologists, especially linguistic anthropologists, at various points during my career, and out of all the fields that existed in the pre-civil rights university, it is one of the few that has been most open to decolonial work, for relatively obvious reasons. It is one of those that is most open to thinking about its own discriminatory heritage. At the same time, and I want to tread carefully here, it is also one that at times seems to think that it already knows what decolonial thought requires, as Todd writes repeatedly in that piece: it already knows the answer, already knows it is doing good work, and so doesn't want to hear from anyone who is critical of it.

I am going to digress here for a moment because it may be instructive. In an earlier part of my career I did a lot of work on languages spoken by Indigenous people worldwide, in particular with linguists who worked on some Cree[24] groups in Canada and Arapesh[25] speakers in Papua New Guinea. The linguists who I worked with were incredibly sensitive and thoughtful to issues not just of exploitation but of exchange and reciprocity — they worked hard to build real relationships with the people whose language they were studying, to provide materials for language instruction and revitalization in return for the information they were "collecting," to give them credit in any published work, and so on. This is in part related to the worldwide interest in what linguists call "Endangered Languages."

I talk about this in my piece "Postcolonial Studies, Digital Humanities, and the Politics of Language" from 2013 which was also featured in the Postcolonial Digital Humanities project you were involved with, so I won't go into great detail here.[26] I just want to note here that there are at least two major kinds of project that get lumped under Endangered Languages: lan-

24 *Algonquian Linguistic Atlas*, https://www.atlas-ling.ca/.

25 *Arapesh Grammar and Digital Language Archive*, http://www.arapesh.org/.

26 David Golumbia, "Postcolonial Studies, Digital Humanities, and the Politics of Language," *uncomputing*, May 31, 2013, http://www.uncomputing.org/?p=241.

guage *documentation*, and language *revitalization*. Both of these are very important and in many ways complement each other. But there was a fascinating bifurcation among the linguists, anthropologists, and Indigenous community members working on these projects. On the one hand, some of them, in a group that was mostly made up of academics, were those who focused on language documentation: getting an accurate record of languages that have only a few speakers left. The value of this documentation to both communities and researchers is inarguable. Yet I found it remarkable how some in this group considered the languages "already dead," the project of revitalization hopeless, and any attempt to prevent the active destruction of the language to be "quaint." They often had very little evidence to support this contention.

The other group, which to be fair includes both academics and community members, tended to focus on revitalization as a critical goal that cannot be separated from documentation. Even from an academic perspective, languages are much better studied when people still speak them, as opposed to being exclusively available in documentation. The resistance to this approach was remarkable. Community activists would say that they did not think the languages were necessarily going to die; some academics and policy makers would dismiss these statements out of hand.

I should say that I did some of this work at the University of Virginia. The attitude of the digital humanists there toward this work was shocking: dismissive, racist, and neocolonialist, and yet at the same time, openly acknowledging that the people making these judgments had virtually no exposure to the languages or the people who speak them. In fact, it is fair to say that the fact that I did this work, even when it involved sophisticated digital technology, counted against my reputation as a digital humanist. This despite the fact that some of these same faculty members claimed to work closely with the anthropologists at the same university who worked closely with Indigenous community members, in my opinion very respectfully.

DOROTHY: What you are describing is so much of what Linda Tuhiwai Smith discusses in *Decolonized Methodologies*[27] especially her comments about how "research is violence" and the idea of how Indigenous communities are only the research objects. That series of comments you relate about the academic researchers is textbook settler colonial studies, as Patrick Wolfe formulates as basically already genocide studies in "Settler Colonialism and the Elimination of the Native."[28] The insistence of "language death" is an insistence on eliminating the native, on imagining research study on the foundation of genocide. Also, languages that were imagined as "dead" in relation to oral speakers have been brought back with more living speakers, so I am not sure what the insistence on "death" is about other than settler colonial white supremacy.

One of the things that I often wonder if literary DH folks forget is that in other fields, particularly social science, there are entire discussions of methodologies, power relations, working with communities, etc. that have a longer genealogy in thinking about data, data ethics, communities, and what that means in research justice. I think one of the other genealogies you are pointing out here is to linguistics and the work of linguistics. One of the backgrounds I don't discuss as much in my main digital humanities work in the medieval scholarly textual archive is that I was trained as a historical linguist and so when I am thinking about DH work I am also thinking about my training in historical linguistics, their understanding of data, and then the conversations happening in computational linguistics.

Since this has been a long conversation throughout 2020 and we were trying to finish this conversation in January 2021, at this point, I cannot stop thinking about the recent spate of violent fascist events (and how they are all organized online — Parler, Twitter, Facebook, etc.). I am thinking about what happened in

27 Linda Tuhiwai Smith, *Decolonized Methodologies: Research and Indigenous Peoples*, 2nd edn. (London: Zed Books, 2012).

28 Patrick Wolfe, "Settler Colonialism and the Elimination of the Native," *Journal of Genocide Research* 8, no. 4 (2006): 387–409.

the violent white supremacist coup attack on the Capitol on January 6. I think this is rolling in my mind (for a number of reasons) because the responses by the particularly "white liberal" media and also the politicians fell into the rhetoric of "this is not us," "this is not what America is," and then would denounce the violence, but then refuse to name, identify, describe, understand what this was: white supremacy, fascism, a coup, stochastic terrorism, white terrorism. That pattern is what I see often in a version of whiteness in DH. Critical whiteness studies, a subset and often integral in work in critical race theory, is entirely about naming, identifying, explaining, describing the machinery and structures of whiteness. In the case of our current US politics, many people online — journalists, academics, activists, etc. — asked, how are you going to fight fascism and white supremacy if you cannot even name it, let alone understand its moves, let alone understand its agendas, goals, processes, in order to counteract it.

I feel that the similar backlash that you and others, including Da have received in naming the whiteness and particularly the fascist violence in some of these digital structures, methods, and histories. How can you dismantle white supremacy if you do not identify, name, describe, understand how it works, its agenda, in order to counteract and fight against it? I feel like this is also the line in which people forget the long history of critique about "diversity" initiatives (Sara Ahmed, etc.) and the problems with token representation that doesn't actually really get their hands into the white supremacist structure and reckon with it.

I think one of the best discussions of a critical DH is the introduction and special issue of the *American Studies Quarterly* on critical digital humanities. But there, they address and identify the white supremacist structures even as they work through various CRT, antiracist, LGBTQIA+, and other methodologies and discussions. What does it mean that such an issue is spearheaded within American Studies and the American Studies Association rather than DH spaces? What does it mean that some of the people doing this work are denouncing that they are doing DH? And why?

DAVID: Here's the thing. I hadn't known about that issue because I don't follow DH very closely anymore, and reading your description, I had hoped that what you said is correct. Then I went and read the introduction, and I just don't see the kind of self-reflection you mention in much of a substantive way. Yes, there are nods to two non-DH articles that talk about race and technology, but as a digital studies scholar it is remarkable to me how little engagement we find there with the vast array of scholarship that draws direct connections between the development and deployment of digital technology and white supremacy and other forms of fascism. (Although I don't want to discount the fact that in that special issue at least there is some nod toward understanding the problem of digital politics, which is not par for the course in DH, and I think this is what you mean about these ideas coming up in American Studies as opposed to the main part of DH.)

This may help to put a point to the longstanding conflict I have had with DH. DH sometimes claims to be "critical": at times people within DH have very dismissively said to me and others that DH scholars are "the most critical" scholars they themselves know when it comes to digital technology and its affordances. I see myself working in a tradition of scholarship that reaches back to figures like Jacques Ellul, Theodore Roszak, Langdon Winner, and especially Lewis Mumford. To all these thinkers, the very idea of digitizing the world — at least in any "real" form that we could understand that process, meaning real computers as we see them in the world, the way power is structured in our world, and so on — was inevitably linked indirectly and/or directly to fascism. Mumford, perhaps the most important of all these thinkers, saw computerization as part of a "megatechnic bribe,"[29] a fundamentally authoritarian technological phenomenon whose most significant effects are in a sense epistemologi-

29 "Zachary Loeb — From Megatechnic Bribe to Megatechnic Blackmail: Mumford's 'Megamachine' after the Digital Turn," *b20*, July 30, 2018, https://www.boundary2.org/2018/07/loeb/.

cal.[30] Within that frame, we cannot think about how the whole enterprise might be politically charged, down to its foundations.

We expect, even if we do not like it, academic fields to rise up that are unable to have that thought at all: engineering, computer science, business, and so on. Digital humanities is remarkable because it is the embodiment of that thought within the one place we look to offer resistance: it inserts into the humanities a fundamental inability to think about the political impact of technology. It is continually finding ways to justify and expand on the "utility" of technology while rejecting any real attempts to think about it critically.

This is not to say that individual DH scholars do not sometimes incorporate this thinking, or teach it. But it's as if the thinking is wrapped inside a cocoon: at the end of the day, we must come back to justifying technology and its positive benefits for thinking, while downplaying its negative political effects. Once a scholar goes over to focusing on those negative or fascistic effects, they no longer "count" as DH, and the fact of no longer "counting" licenses the most brutal and dishonest attacks imaginable. Right there you have the us-them dynamic that many scholars put at the heart of fascism,[31] and the constant handwringing about the definition of DH, including very famous statements about DH having something to do with the totally floating idea of "who's in and who's out"[32] — who is with us and who is against us — fits right into the distinctly fascistic politics of digital technology into which DH buys without reflection.

It's odd to reflect on this, because what I've just said might be a little controversial to some in digital studies, but in general, the digital studies scholars with whom I work will take that kind

---

30 "Authoritarian and Democratic Technics, Revisited," *LibrarianShipwreck*, January 13, 2021, https://wp.me/p38S12-124.

31 Jason Stanley, *How Fascism Works: The Politics of Us and Them* (New York: Random House, 2018).

32 Stephen Ramsay, "Who's In and Who's Out," in *Defining Digital Humanities: A Reader*, eds. Melissa Terras, Julianne Nyhan, and Edward Vanhoutte (New York: Routledge, 2016), 239–42.

of sentiment as obviously true and supported by huge amounts of scholarship on fascism, on white supremacy, and on digital technology. Look at Safiya Noble, Ruha Benjamin, Charlton McIlwain, Virginia Eubanks, Fred Turner, and so many others. I only know of two groups near digital studies who do not just disagree with but vociferously attack scholars who make this kind of claim: first, the highly industry-aligned parts of the media studies world that are directly involved in the production of digital technology, especially in games production departments (which only count as media studies in some specific institutional environments) and places like the MIT Media Lab, and along with them industry-consultant academics like Jeff Jarvis and Clay Shirky. And the other of course is DH. It cannot allow itself to think that fascism is not at the heart of DH but of digital technology itself. In my opinion, that might be understandable, if still appalling, in games production parts of the university and other parts explicitly dedicated to the development of technology skills. In humanities departments it is beyond the pale to see that one of the most pressing issues of our time cannot be thought. And of course, as thinkers from Arendt to Jason Stanley to Timothy Snyder to so many others have shown, being unable or unwilling to acknowledge the fascism at the heart of our politics is itself a core feature of fascism.

I have said it before and will say it again, though I have too much experience to imagine it can be heard: I could not care less whether people do good scholarly work with digital tools. I think it's beyond obvious that we all do that, using all kinds of digital tools. Good work is good work. As an institutional formation, DH is not about "doing good work with digital tools." It is about making unthinkable the fascism at the heart of digital technology. That is its most fundamental commitment. To me, that is incompatible with the mission of the humanities. That's what has to go.

DOROTHY: So what may be more central, and possibly what you are seeing is not as substantially addressed in the American Studies special issue—though it was a special issue that happened because the *American Quarterly* did an entire DH review segment that involved white men who seemed completely unaware of the work in DH and deeply grounded in white epistemologies and completely ignored the American Studies DH caucus so was organized as a form of repair — is a systematic reckoning with fascism and white supremacy. I think this was not probably their main agenda but rather to think about critical digital methods that can do work with different, especially BIPOC, communities that resist, subvert, steal, break, bend, etc., the system and the work rather in the vein of Harney and Moten's discussion of the "undercommons."[33] It may be that communication, digital studies, and several other fields are really more overt about the reckoning with political fascism and also the dismantling of political democracy. So in this vein, I think about the very long genealogy of digital studies and communication in and around this in relation to race, white supremacy, fascism:[34] Jessie Daniels, Anna Everett, Lisa Nakamura, Andre Brock, Meredith Clark, Ruha Benjamin, Safiya Noble, Moya Bailey, Sarah J. Jackson, Marisa Parham, Kim Gallon, Wendy Chun, etc. I actually think we probably need both. People working to address and dismantle the genealogy, the histories, the structures of white supremacy and fascism and those who show different ways to work, resist in the "maroon" spaces that Harney and Moten discuss. I actually think what is being missed and I think back to you, Daniel Allington, and Sarah Brouillette's article in *LARB* and its various critiques which I felt often didn't get the point, is that the piece and all of your work were pointing to the white supremacist, neoliberal, capitalist structure of this digital machine in the university.[35] It is, in fact, a form of digital critical whiteness studies, but people did not actually get what

33 Fred Moten and Stefano Harney, *The Undercommons: Fugitive Planning and Black Study* (New York: Minor Compositions, 2013).

34 See Amber M. Hamilton, "A Genealogy of Critical Race and Digital Studies: Past, Present, and Future," *Sociology of Race and Ethnicity* 6, no. 3 (2020): 292–301.

35 Daniel Allington, Sarah Brouillette, and David Golumbia, "Neoliberal Tools (and Archives): A Political History of Digital Humanities," *Los*

was going on. A lot more of the digital critical whiteness studies has happened in digital studies, communication, media studies, etc. Less so in digital humanities and this is what I have really tried to grapple with in this volume.

We actually need both things and as you know, and you and I have discussed, it is toxic as hell for BIPOC, LGBTQIA+, and other groups targeted by the fascists and far right to work on white supremacy and fascism. The amount of toxic horribleness, the inundation of that level of gaslighting misinformation white supremacy, and then the danger itself in working in these spaces to get that kind of research and material, it is not safe usually for BIPOC, LGBTQIA+, and other groups that are targets and it takes a massive toll on researchers and journalists who work in these spaces. It requires a completely different level of safety protocols, security issues, not to mention managing one's potential violent threat levels, and then the fact that certain fascist and white supremacist people you may wish to have access to, interview, etc., would probably go ahead and try to violently harm BIPOC, LGBTQIA+, and other people in groups targeted. And maybe this is because of my complicated situatedness in relation to medieval studies and the fascist far right, but I do not know if people understand that to do this kind of critical whiteness studies work — to become a researcher of the KKK, far right, white supremacist ecosystem — is an entirely different set of safety, harm, research issues that in fact, I would be happy that white people, and especially white men did, and brought us back the information. This is incredibly horrific, trauma-inducing, dangerous to the researcher both physically and in terms of mental health, work. It is a form of labor that I actually want white people to do because it is an entire other minefield for BIPOC, LGBTQIA+, and other people in groups targeted because we would constantly have to think of both physical violent threats and the mental health toxic toll all the time. For example, I actually am so grateful to the alt-right research group you were run-

---

Angeles Review of Books, May 1, 2016, https://lareviewofbooks.org/article/neoliberal-tools-archives-political-history-digital-humanities/.

ning when I was under attack and those journalists, researchers, who were white men who went and checked all the dark spaces of the web for me to check on the chatter because I would not have been able to do that without an incredible amount of trauma and anyone else who is a target would have also had to be dealt with traumatic toxicity just to do that. This is form of white labor and trauma work that is a way to work on critical digital whiteness studies.

I think the work that I see in the American Studies special issue and introduction and also the work of the digital labs run in so many spaces has been thinking about digital, critical race especially in relation to Black feminist, Latinx, Asian American, Indigenous feminist genealogies — work that has created spaces to create, remix, break, grow, live in the cracks, apertures, and intersections of the larger white supremacist academic and digital machine: Jessica Marie Johnson's Sex and Slavery Lab at Johns Hopkins University;[36] the work of Johnson and Yomaira C. Figueroa Vásquez on electricmarronage;[37] Kim Gallon's COVID Black organization;[38] Tao leigh Goffe's Dark Laboratory;[39] Ruha Benjamin's Ida B. Wells Just Data Lab;[40] the work of Deep Lab;[41] Wendy Chun's Digital Democracies Institute;[42] Marisa Parham's work at MITH, AADHum, and the Immersive Realities Lab for the Humanities at the University of Maryland;[43] Kim

36 Jessica Marie Johnson, "This Week: @jmjafrx Launches the Sex & Slavery Lab #unboundJHU," *Diaspora Hypertext, the Blog,* March 7, 2018, https://dh.jmjafrx.com/2018/03/07/this-week-jmjafrx-launches-the-sex-slavery-lab-unboundjhu/.

37 *Taller Electric Marronage,* https://www.electricmarronage.com/.

38 *CovidBlack,* https://www.covidblack.org/.

39 *Dark Laboratory,* https://www.darklaboratory.com/.

40 *Ida B. Wells Just Data Lab,* https://www.thejustdatalab.com/.

41 *Deep Lab,* http://www.deeplab.net/.

42 *Digital Democracies Institute,* https://digitaldemocracies.org/.

43 See "Marisa Parham Named Director of UMD's African American History, Culture and Digital Humanities Initiative," *University of Maryland College of Arts and Humanities,* March 6, 2020, https://arhu.umd.edu/news/marisa-parham-named-director-umds-african-american-history-culture-and-digital-humanities; "About AADHum," *African American History,*

TallBear's Relab;[44] and numerous other specific labs or groups. In addition, the long-standing and important project *Chicana por mi Raza* that has spent over a decade doing community-based, feminist, intersectional history and memory work but have never received the funding, support, and accolades it deserves.[45] Likewise, I think of the long-term work of things likes #TransformDH and HASTAC as early and ongoing versions of creating alternative spaces.

Johnson discussed this in her *LARB* piece as seeing her work as part of doing the work of the undercommons for BIPOC creators, researchers, students, communities.[46] This is then the work of a digital CRT that has been happening and been done in various spaces, moments, intersections for a while. I also think of Simone Browne's discussion of "dark sousveillance" in *Dark Matters* in which you can take the technologies of white supremacist surveillance and turns those tools back onto the white supremacist structures.[47]

I think what has happened in DH is that the other part of critical race theory work, the critical whiteness studies work, has not actually been done to address the racial reckoning the field needs in relation to white epistemologies, white historiographies, and the white structures, white entanglements with the neoliberal military academic industrial complexes. You need this too and for me, as a WOC researcher, it is more productive and fruitful for me to do the kind of organizing, community building, creating, remixing, work of the digital undercommons that a lot of the work I highlighted in these labs and groups are

---

Culture and Digital Humanities, https://aadhum.umd.edu/asante/about/; and *Immersive Realities Lab for the Humanities*, https://irlhumanities.org/.

44 *Relab*, https://re-lab.ca/.

45 María Cotera and Linda Garcia Merchant, *Chicana por mi Raza Digital Memory Project and Archive*, https://chicanapormiraza.org/.

46 Melissa Dinsman, "The Digital in the Humanities: An Interview with Jessica Marie Johnson," *Los Angeles Review of Books*, July 23, 2016, https://lareviewofbooks.org/article/digital-humanities-interview-jessica-marie-johnson/.

47 Simone Browne, *Dark Matters: On the Surveillance of Blackness* (Durham: Duke University Press, 2015), 21–24.

doing. However, I know we also need the white supremacist and fascist reckoning work. DH has not really done that in the ways other fields have — including work in gender and queer studies (one only needs to look at the discussions of Black, Indigenous, and postcolonial feminism and queer of color critique to figure that one out). It's also a problem in other more traditional fields, I can tell you medieval studies has not done this work, I know because I keep having to write articles doing this white supremacist epistemology, methodology, historiography work. It is frustrating but who else is there to do it to be able to really explain these histories and how they have influenced ontologies, methodologies, praxis?

Maybe the question then is wider and also narrower. First, as we are wrapping up this interview in the month of a US insurrection (and yes, I know I am being deeply Anglo- and US- centric, but as I point out in the introduction to this volume, the entirety of digital infrastructure is an extension of American Empire, everyone's got to deal with that lens of translation and it affects us all), and I have seen a looped series of posts, memes, tweets about "how to save the US from fascism" means the humanities. I have also seen some specific critiques of how there are some massive issues with this. In my other field, medieval and even amongst premodernists, there have been a loop of these kinds of "the humanities will save you from fascism." I find this a huge problem because it imagines a mythical history of antifascist humanities work when that is demonstrably not the case. Something I point out in a number of pieces in this volume. But also something pointed out from the history of STEM and physics. Chanda Prescod-Weinstein, I remember, discussed this in a Twitter thread long ago as she was reading Alan D. Beyerchen's *Scientists under Hitler: Politics and the Physics Community in the Third Reich*. She discussed how Beyerchen's book points out that the physicists in 1930s Germany were antifascist and rejected Hitler, but the issue in the German higher education circles were the humanities faculty members, several who supported fascism.[48] The humanities and academics in the humanities have a long history with fascism and the far right. For example, we can now point to Richard Spencer and his multiple degrees from UVa and the University of Chicago in the Humanities. This is also the case with Stephen Miller. What is with the historical field amnesia to imagine that humanities "will save you from fascism"? Even Trump's multiple executive orders was about bolstering the "humanities" but in opposition to critical race theory — whether it was about the US history curriculum, medieval saints' days, or even neoclassical decoration. Really, I think the point is that critical race theory will save you from fascism.

DAVID: It is clear that fascists hate the humanities, and have targeted them for destruction since the late 1960s. Their assault on the humanities has taken many forms, including direct attack via right-wing extremists like David Horowitz and his Trump-administration acolyte Stephen Miller, the financialization of universities (which is, by the way, incredibly dishonest: despite what the "run the university as a business" people say, it turns out that humanities are incredibly profitable for universities whereas the supposedly profit-friendly units like business and engineering are very expensive), and the constant currying of humanities approaches that twist and undermine progressive approaches. Teaching feminist theory in humanities departments might well help to resist fascism, but teaching "feminism" in the mode of Christina Hoff-Sommers will only do the opposite.

So no, the humanities does not automatically save anyone from fascism. Indeed, it's remarkable how many far-right figures have experience in the humanities — and at a personal-political level, how nasty and unethical many humanities professors are

48 Alan D. Beyerchen, *Scientists under Hitler: Politics and the Physics Community in the Third Reich* (New Haven: Yale University Press, 1977). See also Chanda Prescod-Weinstein, Sarah Tuttle, and Joseph Osmundson, "We Are the Scientists against a Fascist Government," *The Establishment*, February 2, 2017, https://medium.com/the-establishment/we-are-the-scientists-against-a-fascist-government-d44043da274e.

and have been. At the same time, a society that does not teach the humanities, or that requires the humanities to be taught in a nationalistic and reality-denying fashion (I'm thinking here of the ludicrous "1776 Report" the Trump administration released in its final days),[49] seems especially bound to devolve into fascism.

I have to admit, as dark and critical as my work has always been, I have been shocked to see how far we were able to fall, both inside and outside the academy. From where I sit, English and other core humanities departments are so marginalized within universities as to have become almost entirely ineffective. Were it not for their highly profitable nature and the fact that they often employ many of a given university's minority scholars, they might already have been eliminated. DH has played a critical role in helping administrators to think that English professors are not researchers, do not produce important thought, and do not deserve the same kinds of respect that "profitable" research in STEM fields produce, or the institutional clout that the frankly absurd business and leadership faculty have.

DH is not alone responsible for this calamity, but its continual and entirely unjustified refrain, that it represents the "future" of fields that would have been perfectly well able to determine our own futures without it, has hurt literary studies tremendously. As I've said for decades now, the apparently unintentional side effect (although in the minds of senior DH people, it was very much intentional) of making the rest of the humanities look backwards has taken hold very strongly. Having been near several faculty searches driven by administrators where DH or its truly disingenuous offshoot rebranding "public humanities" (which is neither public nor humanities, and actual humanities work that is public does not count) have been at issue, it's been remarkable how little input faculty have in these situations

---

49 Gillian Brockell, "'A hack job,' 'outright lies': Trump Commission's '1776 Report' Outrages Historians," *Washington Post*, January 19, 2021, https://www.washingtonpost.com/history/2021/01/19/1776-report-historians-trump/.

compared to ordinary searches. Given that I am the most senior person in my department who can be seen as DH from some directions, and that most of my departmental faculty colleagues do not go off recommending or demanding DH on their own, it's been remarkable to see repeated requests from the administration come down that reject everything about my own role in the university in the name of some vaguely-stated promises that don't even make sense on the surface (for example, there is absolutely no undergraduate demand for "digital humanities" courses per se, and if there were, I and several other colleagues could easily offer them: the main reason we don't is that students won't sign up for them — which makes administrative demands to hire *more* DH specialists truly hard to comprehend, unless the point is to diminish student demand for humanities classes even more).

But stepping back, from where I sit, I could never have imagined English departments changing as much as they have from the early 1990s when I was in graduate school until today. DH has certainly played a part, but in a way it's also a symptom of many other pressures and changes across the university, in liberal arts units, and in English departments in particular. It is also the case that in my experience English professors may be very good at understanding political vectors very close to their own interests and experiences (within a particular movie or book, for example), but have a much less-clearer grasp of a variety of institutional politics that directly affect us. This can frequently result in playing into the hands of some of the worst administrative impulses, both inside and outside the institution. The variety of strategies for accommodating the political right, for example — the constant pressure to "depoliticize" interpretation, from very smart people who pretend ignorance about the right-wing usefulness of their work like Felski, to any number of efforts to revive "formalism"[50] while claiming against all evi-

50 David J. Alworth, "Form's Function," review of *Forms: Whole, Rhythm, Hierarchy, Network,* by Caroline Levine, *Los Angeles Review of Books,* March 20, 2015, https://lareviewofbooks.org/article/forms-function/.

dence that political interpretations have not cared about form, to efforts to rewrite the history of recent criticism as somehow apolitical[51] while systematically ignoring the work of Black critics and other BIPOC scholars — all strike me as incredibly depressing, as something like Obama preemptively giving ground to the Congressional GOP as if these offerings would result in compromise. They fail to understand that the political right has declared war on history first and foremost, on accuracy, on keeping to the actual words of texts, on being clear about our ideas, and other values that *can* be at the heart of humanities education (and I utter all these apparently Enlightenment value terms fully aware of the necessity of subjecting them to rigorous critique, but also — as I think Derrida in his best modes makes clear — not jettisoning them or dismissing their importance in achieving the things we consider most important, like justice).

This is one of the reasons that DH's continual prevarication over its goals and methods worries me so much, and always has. It refuses to talk honestly about itself, and on the rare occasions when it does, some of which we've mentioned here, that awareness gets swallowed by an "eternal September" of ignorance. That's partly because it is constituted in such a way that memory and critical knowledge are impossible. But the fact is that ideological formations that cannot admit their own contradictions are central characteristics of fascism. And no matter how many times we have these conversations, no matter how many half-baked efforts are made to "add some data about race" into DH work,[52] DH keeps coming back to these same circular and pointless debates and attacks on critics from what are supposed to be its own disciplines. *Institutionally,* not personally — that is to say, *structurally,* in much the same way that we talk about struc-

51 Dermot Ryan, review of *Literary Criticism: A Concise Political History,* by Joseph North, *b2o,* January 29, 2018, https://www.boundary2.org/2018/01/dermot-ryan-review-of-joseph-norths-literary-criticism-a-concise-political-history/.

52 Mark Algee-Hewitt, J.D. Porter, and Hannah Walser, "Representing Race and Ethnicity in American Fiction, 1789–1920," *Journal of Cultural Analytics* 12 (2020): 28–60.

tural racism as well as personal racist attitudes — DH is about discrediting and disempowering the humanities, especially English. And along with some of the other efforts I've mentioned, it's been shockingly successful in this regard. And this in turn has helped to make the humanities much less successful than they had started to be in pushing back against the many forms of white supremacy and fascism that structure both the academy and society.

I want to say one thing that I know you may disagree with. As admirable as many of the projects you mention are, I find the whole genre troubling, for the reasons we discussed above with regard to the "diversity shield." DH as a field now *needs* projects like this to respond to critiques mounted by many of us, including you and me, about the racial politics of digital technology itself, and so of DH. As far as I know, at least half of the projects you mention do not brand themselves as DH, and although I understand that some of these scholars may benefit from this branding, it benefits the reactionary forces within digital technology much more.

The last time I spoke publicly about DH, I gave an invited keynote talk at a non-DH conference, specifically about DH's racial politics, along some of the lines we have discussed here. It is due to these events that like other critics I have been bullied by DH practitioners into not speaking about it again. In very typical proto-fascist fashion, everything I said in that talk was misrepresented. As I learned later, one of the conference staff members was live-tweeting my talk, very literally misstating nearly every sentence I was reported to have said (and since I spoke from a prepared text this was especially clear — I was truly shocked by comparing the tweets with what I'd actually said. It's also worth mentioning that, due to a long history with this kind of thing, I specifically asked the audience not to tweet my talk, a request which even the conference organizers saw no reason to respect). There were quite a few Black professors and students in the audience, some of whom came up to me afterwards to thank me for the talk. Yet there were also many DH practitioners in the audience, some of whom claimed that my talk was antifeminist because they are women, they practice DH, and therefore all critiques of DH are antifeminist. This was the takeaway from the talk that circulated widely and immediately on social media, in which I was portrayed, as I have been many times before, as a victimizer, in ways that clearly and obviously misrepresented the entire content of my talk, which was overtly in support of Black students and scholars in our profession. Since then I and others have heard reports of this talk from people who liked it and people who hated it, and it is really something to hear each of them describe it, because an ordinary person could never reconcile them into a single event: they are that starkly different.

I think even a few years later and in the wake of Trump-era racial justice activism, this kind of obscene misprision of comments about racial justice would be intolerable, but it is notable that in that case "feminism" was used as a shield against a race critique. (It should be needless to say that my talk included virtually no comments about gender per se, certainly nothing diminishing or attacking the contributions of women, but *only* about how DH has helped to reverse the advances Black scholars and students have made in literary studies over the past few decades, critiques that have largely been developed by women like Smith and McPherson, both of whose work I discussed favorably in my talk.) Both digital technology promoters and reactionary forces in the academy are incredibly practiced at using social justice claims dishonestly, to insist that technology is actually there to help the disadvantaged, despite the manifest harms it does. I have long argued in my work, and I developed this line of argument before DH as a brand had even been mooted, that computerization carries with it a profoundly reactionary cultural politics. The cynical use of minorities to rebut this more fundamental claim about cultural politics has become one of its most effective techniques to shut down critics. I want to be clear: those projects absolutely should continue and expand; what I am asking is who is served by associating these projects with the DH brand, especially when these are projects, unlike some of those Da talks about, that deserve to be and would be successful if they were evaluated and funded as any other scholarship is.

DOROTHY: What you are describing is the topic of Jessie Daniels book coming out in the Fall, *Nice White Ladies*.[53] The white feminism and the toxic fascist feminism are something I discuss in an essay in this volume in asking have we asked about who has done the early computational database work and the fascist feminism involved in it. And I agree with you, so many of these projects need the funding, support, resources, and they will not get it or not enough of it, and yet, the projects themselves may be used to continue a sort of "diversity shield" narrative in DH that refuses to reckon with its white supremacist and fascist issues. And yes, it's very interesting that a number of areas, particularly in around American Studies, do not want to call their work DH work. This is the digital racial reckoning that DH has not had and that other fields in the university, the university, etc. are also having, though to varying effects. I don't think we can really address the white supremacy and fascist dismantling without a thorough accounting and reckoning. I am going to end it here but with this quote from Lee Bebout's *Whiteness on the Border* that I hope connects what I see as a long history of white supremacy and fascism writ large in DH's historiography but with what we have talked about here as a form of "everyday whiteness" or quotidian white supremacy:

> While critical whiteness studies has developed as a formalized field of inquiry in recent years, its roots can be traced back to key African American intellectuals such as W.E.B. Du Bois and James Baldwin. These influential thinkers believed that addressing the problem of race required going to the source, understanding the experiences and racial logics that fashion and are reinforced by whiteness. Here, one must think of white supremacy not as people in pointy white hoods or small-town country bigots as is popularly conceptualized, but rather as a system of racial logics and social

53 Jessie Daniels, *Nice White Ladies: The Truth about White Supremacy, Our Role in It, and How We Can Help Dismantle It* (New York: Seal Press, forthcoming October 2021).

> relations of which we are all inheritors, and that often goes unrecognized as water to fish. Critical whiteness studies has persuasively argued that white supremacy — as structural racial inequality — thrives today not because of the actions and beliefs of fringe, aberrant whites but because of the ideology, actions, and inactions of what Karyn McKinney has termed "everyday whiteness." That is, racial inequality is secured through "commonsense" logics that deny and undergird the status quo. Indeed, John Hope Franklin and others have incisively demonstrated how contemporary articulations of color blindness are both seductive to well-intentioned people and a tremendous obstacle to the freedom movements of African Americans and other peoples of color. Here, I would contend that the investments of "everyday whiteness," color blindness, and aberrant, explicitly supremacist forms of whiteness, are mutually dependent and influencing. Through depictions of aberrant whites (e.g., skinheads and the KKK), everyday whites are able to deny their positioning within a racial system. Likewise, the "possessive investment" of everyday whiteness gives legitimacy and cover to the fears and desires of the more explicit hate groups.[54]

I wonder in this moment, as we have seen years of real mobs of overt white supremacists and fascists in our mainstream newsfeeds, whether this will finally push us to a reckoning especially with the quotidian "everyday whiteness" that has gotten us here. I think you and I are possibly on the same page here that cynically, we don't think so. The white supremacist machine will continue to avoid or shield from a real, substantive reckoning. Though for me, I am cynical about this in a number of humanities fields. So, DH is not exceptional in that case though its formation and shape are specific.

54 Lee Bebout, *Whiteness on the Border: Mapping the US Racial Imagination in Brown and White* (New York: NYU Press, 2016), 5.

Bibliography

"About AADHum." *African American History, Culture and Digital Humanities.* https://aadhum.umd.edu/asante/about/.

Ahmed, Sarah. *On Being Included: Racism and Diversity in Institutional Life.* Durham: Duke University Press, 2012.

Algee-Hewitt, Mark, J.D. Porter, and Hannah Walser. "Representing Race and Ethnicity in American Fiction, 1789–1920." *Journal of Cultural Analytics* 12 (2020): 28–60. DOI: 10.22148/001c.18509.

Algonquian Linguistic Atlas. https://www.atlas-ling.ca/.

Alworth, David J. "Form's Function." Review of *Forms: Whole, Rhythm, Hierarchy, Network,* by Caroline Levine, *Los Angeles Review of Books,* March 20, 2015. https://lareviewofbooks.org/article/forms-function/.

Allington, Daniel, Sarah Brouillette, and David Golumbia. "Neoliberal Tools (and Archives): A Political History of Digital Humanities." *Los Angeles Review of Books,* May 1, 2016. https://lareviewofbooks.org/article/neoliberal-tools-archives-political-history-digital-humanities/.

Anderson, Carol. *White Rage: The Unspoken Truth of Our Racial Divide.* New York: Bloomsbury, 2016.

Arapesh Grammar and Digital Language Archive. http://www.arapesh.org/.

"Authoritarian and Democratic Technics, Revisited." *LibrarianShipwreck,* January 13, 2021. https://wp.me/p38S12-124.

Bebout, Lee. *Whiteness on the Border: Mapping the US Racial Imagination in Brown and White.* New York: NYU Press, 2016.

Benjamin, Ruha. *Race after Technology: Abolitionist Tools for the New Jim Code.* Cambridge: Polity Press, 2019.

Beyerchen, Alan D. *Scientists Under Hitler: Politics and the Physics Community in the Third Reich.* New Haven: Yale University Press, 1977.

Bonilla-Silva, Eduardo. *Racism without Racists: Color-Blind Racism and the Persistence of Racial Inequality in America.* 5th edition. Lanham: Rowman & Littlefield, 2018.

Brockell, Gillian. "'A hack job,' 'outright lies': Trump Commission's '1776 Report' Outrages Historians." *Washington Post,* January 19, 2021. https://www.washingtonpost.com/history/2021/01/19/1776-report-historians-trump/.

Browne, Simone. *Dark Matters: On the Surveillance of Blackness.* Durham: Duke University Press, 2015.

Cotera, María, and Linda Garcia Merchant. *Chicana por mi Raza Digital Memory Project and Archive.* https://chicanapormiraza.org/.

CovidBlack. https://www.covidblack.org/.

Crockett, I'Nasah. "'Raving Amazons': Antiblackness and Misogynoir in Social Media." *Model View Culture,* June 30, 2014. https://modelviewculture.com/pieces/raving-amazons-antiblackness-and-misogynoir-in-social-media.

Da, Nan Z. "The Computational Case against Computational Literary Studies." *Critical Inquiry* 45, no. 3 (2019): 601–39. DOI: 10.1086/702594.

Daniels, Jessie. "The Algorithmic Rise of the 'Alt-Right.'" *Contexts* 17, no. 1 (2018): 60–65. https://contexts.org/articles/the-algorithmic-rise-of-the-alt-right/.

Daniels, Jessie. *Nice White Ladies: The Truth about White Supremacy, Our Role in It, and How We Can Help Dismantle It.* New York: Seal Press, forthcoming October 2021.

Dark Laboratory. https://www.darklaboratory.com/.

Davis, Heather, and Zoe Todd. "On the Importance of a Date, or, Decolonizing the Anthropocene." *ACME: An International Journal for Critical Geographies* 16, no. 4 (2017): 761–80. https://acme-journal.org/index.php/acme/article/view/1539.

Davis, Janae, Alex A. Moulton, Levi Van Sant, and Brian Williams. "Anthropocene, Capitalocene, … Plantationocene? A Manifesto for Ecological Justice in an Age of Global Crises." *Geography Compass* 13, no. 5 (2019): e12438. DOI: 10.1111/gec3.12438.

Deep Lab. http://www.deeplab.net/.

Digital Democracies Institute. https://digitaldemocracies.org/.

Dinsman, Melissa. "The Digital in the Humanities: An Interview with Jessica Marie Johnson." *Los Angeles Review of Books,* July 23, 2016. https://lareviewofbooks.org/article/digital-humanities-interview-jessica-marie-johnson/.

Eubanks, Virginia. *Digital Dead End: Fighting for Social Justice in the Information Age.* Cambridge: MIT Press, 2011.

"Executive Order 13950 of September 22, 2020, Combating Race and Sex Stereotyping." *Federal Register* 85, no. 188 (September 28, 2020): 60683. https://en.wikisource.org/wiki/Page%3AExecutive_Order_13950.pdf/1.

"Executive Order 13985 of January 20, 2021, Advancing Racial Equity and Support for Underserved Communities Through the Federal Government." *Federal Register* 86, no. 14 (January 25, 2021): 7009. https://en.wikisource.org/wiki/Page%3AExecutive_Order_13985.pdf/1.

Galvan, Angela. "Soliciting Performance, Hiding Bias: Whiteness and Librarianship." *In the Library with the Lead Pipe,* June 3, 2015. http://www.inthelibrarywiththeleadpipe.org/2015/soliciting-performance-hiding-bias-whiteness-and-librarianship/.

Golumbia, David. "Postcolonial Studies, Digital Humanities, and the Politics of Language." *uncomputing,* May 31, 2013. http://www.uncomputing.org/?p=241.

Hamilton, Amber M. "A Genealogy of Critical Race and Digital Studies: Past, Present, and Future." *Sociology of Race and Ethnicity* 6, no. 3 (2020): 292–301. DOI: 10.1177/2332649220922577.

Hampton, Rachelle. "The Black Feminists Who Saw the Alt-Right Threat Coming." *Slate,* April 23, 2019. https://slate.com/technology/2019/04/black-feminists-alt-right-twitter-gamergate.html.

Haraway, Donna, Noboru Ishikawa, Scott F. Gilbert, Kenneth Olwig, Anna L. Tsing, and Nils Bubandt. "Anthropologists Are Talking — About the Anthropocene." *Ethnos* 81, no. 3 (2016): 535–64. DOI: 10.1080/00141844.2015.1105838.

Harris, Cheryl I. "Whiteness As Property." *Harvard Law Review* 106, no. 8 (1993): 1709–91. DOI: 10.2307/1341787.

Ida B. Wells Just Data Lab. https://www.thejustdatalab.com/.

Immersive Realities Lab for the Humanities. https://irlhumanities.org/.

James, Jennifer. "'Buried in Guano': Race, Labor and Sustainability." *American Literary History* 24, no. 1 (2012): 115–42.

James, Jennifer. "Ecomelancholia: Slavery, War, and Black Ecological Imaginings." In *Environmental Criticism for the Twenty-First Century,* edited by Stephanie LeMenager, Teresa Shewry, and Ken Hiltner, 163–78. New York: Routledge, 2011. https://www.jstor.org/stable/41329630.

Jarvis, Jeff. *What Would Google Do? Reverse-Engineering the Fastest-Growing Company in the History of the World.* New York: HarperCollins, 2009.

Johnson, Jessica Marie. "This Week: @jmjafrx Launches the Sex & Slavery Lab #unboundJHU." *Diaspora Hypertext, the Blog,* March 7. 2018, https://dh.jmjafrx.com/2018/03/07/this-week-jmjafrx-launches-the-sex-slavery-lab-unboundjhu/.

Keen, Andrew. Interview with Jeff Jarvis. *Keen On,* May 21, 2019. http://www.ajkeen.com/podcast/episode19.

Liming, Sheila. "Fighting Words." Review of *Hooked: Art and Attachment,* by Rita Felski. *Los Angeles Review of Books,* December 14, 2020. https://lareviewofbooks.org/article/fighting-words/.

"Marisa Parham Named Director of UMD's African American History, Culture and Digital Humanities Initiative." *University of Maryland College of Arts and Humanities,* March 6, 2020, https://arhu.umd.edu/news/marisa-parham-named-director-umds-african-american-history-culture-and-digital-humanities.

McKenzie, Lindsay. "Racism and the American Library Association." *Inside Higher Ed,* February 1, 2019, https://www.insidehighered.com/news/2019/02/01/american-library-association-criticized-response-racism-complaint.

McPherson, Tara. "Why Are the Digital Humanities So White? or Thinking the Histories of Race and Computation." In *Debates in the Digital Humanities,* edited by Matthew K. Gold. Minneapolis: University of Minnesota Press, 2012. https://dhdebates.gc.cuny.edu/read/untitled-88c11800-9446-469b-a3be-3fdb36bfbd1e/section/20df8acd-9ab9-4f35-8a5d-e91aa5f4a0ea#ch09.

Mitchell, Koritha. "Identifying White Mediocrity and Know-Your-Place Aggression: A Form of Self-Care." *African American Review* 51, no. 4 (2018): 253–62. DOI: 10.1353/afa.2018.0045.

Moten, Fred, and Stefano Harney. *The Undercommons: Fugitive Planning and Black Study.* New York: Minor Compositions, 2013.

Nakamura, Lisa. "Watching White Supremacy on Digital Video Platforms: 'Screw Your Optics, I'm Going In.'" *Film Quarterly* 72, no. 3 (2019): 19–22. DOI: 10.1525/fq.2019.72.3.19.

"No True Scotsman." *Internet Encyclopedia of Philosophy.* https://iep.utm.edu/fallacy/#NoTrueScotsman.

Noble, Safiya Umoja. *Algorithms of Oppression: How Search Engines Reinforce Racism.* New York: NYU Press, 2018.

Nxumalo, Fikile. "Situating Indigenous and Black Childhoods in the Anthropocene." In *Research Handbook on Childhoodnature: Assemblages of Childhood and Nature Research,* edited by Amy Cutter-Mackenzie-Knowles, Karen Malone, and Elisabeth Barratt Hacking, 1–22. New York: Springer, 2018.

Prescod-Weinstein, Chanda, Sarah Tuttle, and Joseph Osmundson. "We Are the Scientists against a Fascist Government." *The Establishment,* February 2, 2017, https://medium.com/the-establishment/we-are-the-scientists-against-a-fascist-government-d44043da274e.

Quan, Douglas. "Inside the 'Indigenization' of Canada's Universities: Progress — But Also Accusations of Tokenism, Broken Promises and 'Ethnic Fraud.'" *Toronto Star,* February 27, 2021. https://www.thestar.com/news/canada/2021/02/27/inside-the-indigenization-of-canadas-universities-progress-but-also-accusations-of-tokenism-broken-promises-and-ethnic-fraud.html.

Ramsay, Stephen. "Who's In and Who's Out." In *Defining Digital Humanities: A Reader,* edited by Melissa Terras, Julianne Nyhan, and Edward Vanhoutte, 239–42. New York: Routledge, 2016.

Relab. https://re-lab.ca/.

Ryan, Dermot. Review of *Literary Criticism: A Concise Political History,* by Joseph North. *b2o,* January 29, 2018, https://www.boundary2.org/2018/01/dermot-ryan-review-of-joseph-norths-literary-criticism-a-concise-political-history/.

Schradie, Jen. T*he Revolution that Wasn't: How Digital Activism Favors Conservatives.* Cambridge: Harvard University Press, 2019.

Smith, Linda Tuhiwai. *Decolonized Methodologies: Research and Indigenous Peoples.* 2nd edition. London: Zed Books, 2012.

Smith, Martha Nell. "The Human Touch Software of the Highest Order: Revisiting Editing as Interpretation." *Textual Cultures* 2, no. 1 (2007): 1–15. https://muse.jhu.edu/article/251864.

Stanley, Jason. *How Fascism Works: The Politics of Us and Them.* New York: Random House, 2018.

Taller Electric Marronage. https://www.electricmarronage.com/.

Todd, Zoe. "The Decolonial Turn 2.0: The Reckoning." *anthro{dendum},* June 15, 2018, https://anthrodendum.org/2018/06/15/the-decolonial-turn-2-0-the-reckoning/.

Tompkins, Kyla Wazana. "On the Limits and Promise of New Materialist Philosophy." *Lateral* 5, no. 1 (2016). http://csalateral.org/issue/5-1/forum-alt-humanities-new-materialist-philosophy-tompkins/.

———. "Response to Michelle N. Huang and Chad Shomura." *Lateral* 6, no. 1 (2017). https://csalateral.org/issue/6-1/forum-alt-humanities-new-materalist-philosophy-response-tompkins/.

Walcott, Rinaldo. *Queer Returns: Essays on Multiculturalism, Diaspora, and Black Studies.* London: Insomniac Press, 2016.
Watters, Audrey. *Teaching Machines: The History of Personalized Learning.* Cambridge: MIT Press, forthcoming August 2021.
Wolfe, Patrick. "Settler Colonialism and the Elimination of the Native." *Journal of Genocide Research* 8, no. 4 (2006): 387–409. DOI: 10.1080/14623520601056240.
"Zachary Loeb — From Megatechnic Bribe to Megatechnic Blackmail: Mumford's 'Megamachine' after the Digital Turn." *b2o,* July 30, 2018.https://www.boundary2.org/2018/07/loeb/.

3

Towards a Digital Cultural Studies: The Legacy of Cultural Studies and the Future of Digital Humanities

Carly A. Kocurek

> *"However far modern science and technics have fallen short of their inherent possibilities, they have taught mankind at least one lesson: Nothing is impossible."*
> —Lewis Mumford, *Technics and Civilization*

In his groundbreaking 1957 work, *The Uses of Literacy: Aspects of Working Class Life*, the sociologist and literary scholar Richard Hoggart weaves together sociological analysis, autobiography, and close reading to examine the rise of an American-inflected mass culture in midcentury England. Part lament at the loss of British working class culture, Hoggart's book also served as a call to action for academics to take seriously the lived experience of working class people. Raymond Williams published a similarly radical book in 1958; in *Culture and Society*, Williams takes on the notion of culture itself, arguing that British conceptions of culture from the eighteenth through twentieth centuries have developed in part as a response to the Industrial Revolution. Writing in the 1980s about the evolution and history of cultural studies, Stuart Hall pointed to the deceptive upheaval at play in both these works and in the works they inspired.[1] Both in the 1950s and now, cultural studies is a radical project. Interdisciplinary or even antidisciplinary, the field demands scholarship that is not only engaged theoretically and empirically, but politically as well. To do the work of cultural studies is to always be engaged with the political ramifications of that work and to push for more sophisticated understanding of how systems of power and control are established, exercised, and disrupted through culture. In a moment marked by a rise in white supremacist activities both in the US and around the world, this project is increasingly urgent.

In this chapter, I argue that one way of increasing the diversity of participants is by increasing the diversity of perspectives, positions, and fields valued. The humanities is more and more widespread — I would argue delightfully so — in the types of questions researchers ask and the types of projects they produce; it is simultaneously growing, slowly at least, in diversity among the researchers themselves. The overwhelming homogeneity of Digital Humanities stands in sharp contrast to the growing visibility of fields like gender and ethnic studies. The contrast is thrown into sharper relief when we consider the degree to which these vibrant fields are absent from digital humanities' theoretically big tent. I am interested in the possibilities of cross-pollinating digital humanities with cultural studies in part because I see the radicalism of cultural studies as a potential path towards a digital humanities that is diverse in meaningful ways, that not only engages in cultural criticism that is rightfully framed within broader political discourses, but that creates an environment in which the righteous legacies of intellectual vanguard are carried forward like flaming torches, where a recentering of the work of people of color, of women, of queer people, of those outside of or at the margins of the academy is seen not only as possible, but foundational. We come not to burn, but to light a path for ourselves.

1 Stuart Hall, "Cultural Studies: Two Paradigms," *Media, Culture & Society* 2, no. 1 (1980): 57–72.

I propose an alternate history of the digital humanities that traces the field not to humanities computing, but instead to the provocations of cultural studies. In doing so, I ask key questions about the purpose and utility of digital humanities scholarship for addressing social, cultural, and historical problems. What might a digital humanities directly shaped by Marxist and feminist traditions look like? How might the legacy of radicalism inherent to cultural studies help energize, redirect, and empower digital humanities as publicly engaged scholarship? How can and should digital humanists draw on the works of scholars not only like Hoggart, Hall, and their Birmingham colleagues, but the broader field including scholars like Gloria Anzaldúa, Andrew Ross, and Janice Radway?

While considering these questions, I highlight the successes and limitations of current digital humanities models and propose a loose framework for a digital humanities that takes seriously its debt to cultural studies. I begin by surveying key texts in cultural studies and highlighting how digital humanities projects have or could extend the types of work carried out in these historic texts. Then, I identify key characteristics of digital cultural studies, and finally detail a tentative framework for the cultivation of future projects. Alternate histories are a means of re-centering and re-grounding, but they are also an opportunity to imagine alternative futures; fundamentally, this chapter is a work of speculative nonfiction, an imagining of a digital humanities that is deeply engaged in questions of public concern and cultural immediacy, and one that not only draws from but is led by the deep well of diversity that is increasingly evident elsewhere in the humanities. Ultimately, the framework proposed here is a call to action for a digital humanities that, like cultural studies, is aware of the degree to which it is always already engaged in the work of cultural politics.

A Call to Arms

Digital humanities can and should engage with the diversity of human experiences and concerns. However, the field has struggled with diversity at a number of levels, which is evident not only in who fits in to mainstream digital humanities discourse, but also in the types of work that are most visible in the field. In analyzing submissions for Digital Humanities 2015, for example, Scott Weingart found some striking trends; 21 percent of submissions were tagged as involving Text Analysis, and Literary Studies accounted for 20 percent of submissions not only in 2015, but in the preceding two years.[2] There is nothing wrong with these approaches or fields, but what is striking is the absence of a number of fields that have become prominent in the broader discourse of the humanities, and in particular in what I would call the cultural studies-inflected humanities, while remaining marginal to digital humanities. As both Weingart and Jacqueline Wernimont point out, gender studies is nearly absent from the same pool of submissions, with only 1.2 percent of submissions marked as "gender studies."[3] Weingart concludes his analysis noting that while most of the trends are unsurprising, they can be seen as disappointing: "The fact that the status is pretty quo is worthy of note, because many were hoping that a global DH would seem more diverse, or appreciably different, in some way."

The status quo of ideas and fields that Weingart highlights is intertwined with a status quo of people and participants. Miriam Posner has written, for example, about how the insistence that everyone in digital humanities learn to code is embedded in a broader context in which women face significant challenges to gaining coding skill.[4] As a result, the elevation of coding as the essential foundation of digital humanities work can mar-

2 Scott Weingart, "Submissions to Digital Humanities 2015 (pt. 2)," *The Scottbot Irregular,* November 6, 2014, http://www.scottbot.net/HIAL/index.html@p=41053.html.

3 @profwernimont (Jacqueline Wernimont), *Twitter,* November 6, 2014, 15:40 UTC, https://twitter.com/profwernimont/status/530384290392342528.

4 Miriam Posner, "Some Things to Think about Before You Exhort Everyone to Code," *Miriam Posner's Blog,* February 29, 2012, http://miriamposner.com/blog/some-things-to-think-about-before-you-exhort-everyone-to-code/.

ginalize women in the field. Similarly, Bethany Nowviskie has suggested that data mining has become a kind of "gentleman's sport" in part because both funders and scholars have engaged in a particular rhetorical framing of the associated practices.[5] In her address to the DH 2015 conference held in Sydney Australia, Deb Verhoeven begins by asking a series of questions regarding Australian flora and fauna. How many in the audience have seen a funnel-web spider? A koala? These seemingly humorous questions circle towards a damning one: "Now for the worst and most elusive of creatures. How many of you yesterday saw a woman on this stage? [pause] Or anyone who isn't just a standard issue bloke?" With these questions, Verhoeven launches a fiery speech titled "Has Anyone Seen a Woman?," in which she condemns the conference's "parade of patriarchs" and the universalizing of one (white, male, cisgender, heterosexual, western) perspective. "Do this because you embrace diversity in all its complexity, not because you have checklists or policies, but because you recognize that the real story of DH is more heterogeneous and more complex and more vibrant than you have allowed it to be to date."[6] In her speech, Verhoeven directly addresses "standard issue blokes," calling for increased diversity at one of digital humanities most visible and best attended annual conferences. The marginalization of both gender studies as a topic and women as scholars is intertwined, and it is also not an isolated problem, but one entangled within a complex nexus of marginalization of both scholars and scholarly thought. The invisibility of women, of people of color, of people who are lesbian, gay, bisexual, transgender, genderqueer — of people who aren't "standard issue blokes" — across digital humanities remains profound. If we want to make things better, we must actively practice the commitment to diversity so many of us claim. If the submissions to conferences and publications are not di-

5 Bethany Nowviskie, "What Do Girls Dig?" *Bethany Nowviskie*, April 7, 2011, http://nowviskie.org/2011/what-do-girls-dig/.

6 Bestqualitycrab (Deb Verhoeven), "Has Anyone Seen a Woman?" *Vimeo*, November 6, 2015, https://vimeo.com/144863312.

verse, we should actively solicit work to diversify the pool in consideration and also ensure that our programming committees and editorial boards are not homogenous. In constructing panels and events, we should make sure that nobody can come up and ask, like Verhoeven, to "show me a woman." These types of simple steps are not a complete solution, but they are concrete steps to be taken in improving the current state of affairs. If we are claiming digital humanities is a big tent, a broad, representative field, we must do the work to make it so. If we value, at all, the complexity of human experience, something that should be the very heart of the humanities, it is a moral imperative that we do so.

In the quote at the beginning of this chapter, Mumford suggests that technology teaches us that "anything is possible," and I would suggest this is true, but horribly so: anything is possible, including the reinscription of existing inequalities. The historians among us, in particular, have watched countless alleged revolutions in technology turn into these types of reinscriptions. If we are not careful about the ways in which we enact our own biases, if digital humanities is not pushed to become transformative, then it is nothing more than a new verse in an old, disappointing song, another opportunity for technology to efface the specificities of culture and history, to reinforce old hierarchies of power, and to continue to neglect the real crises of human experience in favor of propping up obsolete canons.

Cultural Studies: A Historical Primer

Cultural studies as a field is often traced back to the book by Richard Hoggart I mentioned earlier, but I do not wish, particularly in a volume that celebrates the complexities of fields' historical origins, to posit a neat timeline from Hoggart to the present. For one thing, there are many scholars who helped contribute to the formation of the field; Américo Paredes, for whom the University of Texas's Center for Cultural Studies is named, immediately springs to mind. But, further, what I wish to propose here is a reconfiguration that opens up possibilities and that draws on many threads rather than substituting one neatly packaged timeline for another. If there is one thing that my training as a historian has taught me, it is that timelines can too easily be tools for reinforcing power and that they cannot come close to revealing the intricacies of history itself. So, here as elsewhere, I think of history as a tangle of threads. Each thread can be a timeline of its own, but the threads intersect, they divert each other and twine together, and not one could be removed from the tangle without altering the entire mess. As Stuart Hall has said:

> In serious, critical intellectual work, there are no "absolute beginnings" and few unbroken continuities. Neither the endless unwinding of "tradition", so beloved on the History of Ideas, nor the absolutism of the "epistemological rupture", punctuating Thought into its "false" and "correct" parts [...] will do. What we find, instead, is an untidy but characteristic unevenness of development. What is important are the significant breaks — where old lines of thought disrupted, older constellations displaced, and elements, old and new, are regrouped around a different set of premises and themes.[7]

Hoggart certainly shaped the field, but Hoggart's contemporaries and colleagues, who cofounded the Birmingham School of Cultural Studies alongside him, cannot be left out, nor can the researchers who worked simultaneously and after them to expand the field.

Stuart Hall's work has become foundational to thinking across an array of humanities disciplines; contemporary media studies is difficult to imagine without the work of Raymond Williams, and, as Hall points out, Hoggart and Williams, working simultaneously, are each radical in their own way. Angela McRobbie has effectively challenged the centering of popular culture around male pursuits by taking seriously the cultural practices and fascinations of teenage girls, and Janice Radway's

7 Hall, "Cultural Studies," 57.

work similarly takes up the women who read and find community and satisfaction in romance novels and the broader middlebrow reading culture.[8] Angela Davis has forged a career that is itself a model of how scholarly work and political activism can form a palimpsest, focusing on issues such as racial justice and prison abolition.[9] Gloria Anzaldúa worked across written forms to address the complexities of the borderlands through cultural, feminist, and queer theory. Andrew Ross's scholarship on contemporary labor practices dovetails with activist work in the anti-sweatshop movement, in supporting student workers' unions, in Occupy Wall Street and in related debtors' movements, and in efforts to improve migrant labor standards in the United Arab Emirates. This is a somewhat scattershot list of scholars. There are hundreds who could be included, but what the scholars on this list have in common is a commitment to taking seriously the conditions of people's daily lives and to valuing the possibilities of work that spills over the conventionally understood edges of the academy. Anzaldúa, for example, wrote children's books, Paredes worked in both creative writing and folklore throughout his academic career, Ross has helped with Strike Debt, a "nationwide movement of debt resisters fighting for economic justice and democratic freedom."[10] In short, I would argue what binds these scholars together, what makes it sensible to include them on a single list is not necessarily influence, although they

---

8 See Angela McRobbie, *Feminism and Youth Culture: From "Jackie" to "Just Seventeen"* (Boston: Unwin Hyman, 1991) and Angela McRobbie and Jenny Garber, "Girls and Subcultures," in *Resistance through Rituals: Youth Subcultures in Post-War Britain,* eds. Stuart Hall and Tony Jefferson (London: Routledge, 1975), 177–88 for more on gendered cultural practices. See Janice A. Radway, *A Feeling for Books: The Book-of-the-Month Club, Literary Taste, and Middle-Class Desire* (Chapel Hill: University of North Carolina Press, 1997) and *Reading the Romance: Women, Patriarchy, and Popular Literature* (Chapel Hill: University of North Carolina Press, 1984) for more on women's pleasure in reading.

9 For further reading, see Angela Davis, *Women, Culture & Politics* (New York: Random House, 1989) and *Women, Race & Class* (New York: Vintage, 1983).

10 *Strike Debt,* http://strikedebt.org/.

are influential, but rather an interest in and commitment to the often experimental possibilities of critically engaged academic work.

If we must imagine a lineage for digital humanities, why wouldn't we imagine one that includes predecessors who have, themselves, fought for and forged a humanities that is enamored of possibility, of scholarship not just as monograph or journal article, but as poetry, as children's literature, as art, as political action? Of a body of scholars that includes not only those of us ensconced in the academy, but all committed to understanding and improving the human condition? Cultural studies is a radical critique, one that has had a profound effect on disciplines including history, literature, and anthropology, among others; if digital humanities were to become such a radical critique, think of the transformations, of the vital interventions, we could have. Such a lineage both makes possible and demands a digital humanities that is diverse both in the composition of its practitioners and in its intellectual concerns and output. At this point, I want to consider a handful of works by the scholars I have mentioned, considering the specifics of form, audience, and production. Then, building on the outlined works, I move to a proposal for what a cultural studies-inflected digital humanities might look like.

Some Existing and Theoretical Works

Cultural studies has produced a myriad of notable works. Here, I would like to briefly discuss a few, including Américo Paredes's *"With His Pistol in His Hand": A Border Ballad and Its Hero,* Raymond Williams's *Television: Technology and Cultural Form,* and Janice Radway's *Reading the Romance: Women, Patriarchy, and Popular Literature.* These three books are in some ways significantly different from each other. The scholars who produced them are working in different home disciplines and in various types of cultural and institutional contexts, and have turned their attention to a somewhat disparate objects of study: a border song sung both north and south of the Rio Grande, the television as medium, and the popular genre of the romance novel as read by American women. However, the three scholars and their books share a concern with the cultural practices and concerns of the daily lives of average people. All three scholars have also proven profoundly influential. Paredes's work has shaped not only the study of folklore, but of borderlands, popular music, and regional culture; Williams remains so widely read and well regarded that the entirety of the 2014 Flow Conference was organized in response to and conversation with *Television*; Radway's studies of women's reading practices are a cornerstone for now decades of scholarship in literary, media, and American studies that take seriously feminized culture that is still so easily dismissed.

The strengths of these projects — their radical mixing of methods and willingness to work between and even outside of disciplines, their rigorous use of theory, and their commitment to taking seriously lived culture — can be found in many works of cultural studies, and are dependent upon an approach that is willing to push at the existing boundaries of scholarly work and question the often limiting conventional wisdom about which people and subjects are worth critical study. For example, Williams's *Television* is important for its effort to understand how television worked at multiple levels and is a landmark text in part because he chose to look at a maligned and often dismissed medium. Similarly, Radway investigated the importance of romance novels, considering them as a form that facilitated pleasure, escape, and community in ways that are deeply meaningful for many readers; in doing so, she raised profound questions about what, exactly, makes literature valuable or worthy of study. And, Paredes was a tireless champion for Mexican American Studies. While *"With a Pistol in His Hand"* is Paredes's first book, it is only one entry into a rich bibliography of works exploring the complexities of border culture.

All three of these works are concerned with cultural expressions often dismissed as "bad objects," as things unworthy of serious attention, but in giving serious attention to television, romance, and the music of the border, they do not rehabilitate these artifacts but rather demonstrate their existing importance and build a foundation for our understanding of broad areas of cultural production and practice. These three key books shifted critical understanding of culture and remain influential because of their radicalism even as, through the distance of years, they often appear decreasingly radical. This longstanding influence is a testament to the longstanding impact they have had, but also a call to action to seek out new boundaries to test.

Digital humanities has the promise of radicalism, and the field is often celebrated as disruptive, innovative, and expansive. But, much of digital humanities is deeply enmeshed with more traditional conceptualizations of what the humanities can and should be. We see many projects, for example, on the works of William Shakespeare and on the US Civil War.[11] I do not wish to suggest these are bad projects; many of them are reflective of innovative approaches to topics of well established significance, and some, like Global Shakespeares, are making interesting interventions in the framing of particular topics and providing excellent resources to boot.

However, projects on these types of subjects are often among the best funded, and often have high levels of visibility along with that funding. For example, a listing of digital humanities projects that fall under the National Endowment for the Humanities's "Standing Together: The Humanities and the Experience of War" speaks to the prominence of war history in US

---

11 See, for example, the "The Folger Shakespeare," *Folger Shakespeare Library*, https://shakespeare.folger.edu/; "Video and Performance Archive," *MIT Global Shakespeares*, https://globalshakespeares.mit.edu/; and Hugh Macrae Richmond, "Shakespeare's Staging: Media Resources for Students and Teachers," *University of California Berkeley*, 2016, https://shakespeare.berkeley.edu/ for more on Shakespeare. See "House Divided: The Civil War Research Engine at Dickinson College," *Dickinson College*, 2007, http://housedivided.dickinson.edu/; "Civil War Digital Tour," *The Caroline Marshall Draughon Center for the Arts and Humanities, Auburn University*, 2015, https://cla.auburn.edu/cah/programs/civil-war-digital-tour/; and "Hidden Patterns of the Civil War," *Digital Scholarship Lab, University of Richmond*, 2010, https://dsl.richmond.edu/civilwar/ for more on the Civil War.

history and includes two projects (out of a total of seven) focused on the Civil War.[12] Edward Castranova's ill-fated effort to render Shakespearean society into a massively multiplayer environment, "Arden," received $250,000 in funding and extensive media coverage.[13] There are reasons to study Shakespeare and the Civil War, and certainly new tools make possible new and fruitful approaches to these topics. However, we should be careful that the digital humanities does not only reinforce the old canon of humanistic knowledge with its old biases, inequalities, exclusivities, and inaccessabilities.

Digital Cultural Studies

Cultural studies works like those I have discussed to this point are, by and large, far from digital, but they are both deeply radical and deeply engaged with the core questions of the humanities. It is in their radicalism, and in their interest in the daily concerns of people's lived cultural experiences and encounters, that I see a useful model for reconceiving the digital humanities. Fundamental to this chapter is a consideration of what the digital humanities might look like as the child not of humanities computing, but of cultural studies. In this section, I turn to outlining what that might look like.

First, such a digital humanities would necessarily be engaged in radical experimentation: experimentation in research approaches, in publishing models, and in approaches to subjects. Second, a cultural studies-inflected digital humanities would be strongly engaged with the study of media and popular culture and invested in our understanding of the complexities of race, gender, sexuality, socioeconomic class, and other facets of cultural identity. Additionally, a digital humanities framed in this

12 "Funded Projects in Digital Humanities," *National Endowment for the Humanities*, https://www.neh.gov/veterans/funded-projects-in-digital-humanities.

13 Akela Talemasca, "Edward Castronova Reveals Lessons Learned from Arden," *Engadget*, March 23, 2008, https://www.engadget.com/2008/03/23/edward-castronova-reveals-lessons-learned-from-arden/.

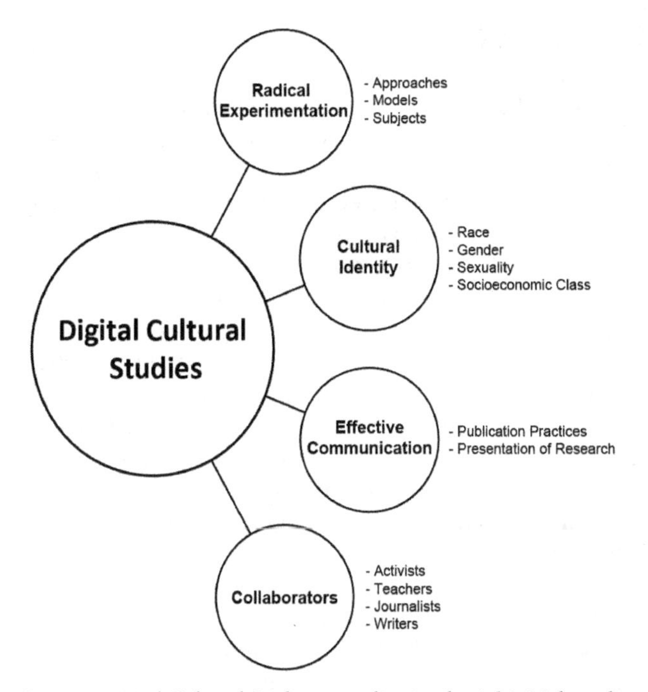

Figure 1. Digital Cultural Studies, visualization by Athir Mahmud.

way would necessarily be concerned with effective communication and publication practices and ensure that the presentation of research is at least as sophisticated as the means in which that research is conducted. There are absolutely projects happening now that do work in this way — including some of the Civil War and Shakespeare projects already mentioned, and projects like Scalar have proven the value in experimenting with the presentation of even more conventional scholarship while also making room for radical efforts at constructing knowledge.[14] Recent anthologies like Elizabeth Losh and Jacqueline Wernimont's *Bodies of Information: Intersectional Feminism and Digital Humani-*

14 Tara McPherson, *Feminist in a Software Lab: Difference and Design* (Cambridge: Harvard University Press, 2018).

ties and Jentery Sayers's *Making Things and Drawing Boundaries: Experiments in the Digital Humanities* both showcase vibrant examples of what feminist and queer scholarship in DH can offer. This is not a situation in which we should throw the baby out with the bathwater, but rather one in which we should think carefully about whose practices and concerns we are drawing inspiration from and who our work serves and why.

A cultural studies-inflected digital humanities, a digital cultural studies, would always be concerned with its own political and cultural positioning and impact (see fig. 1). It would focus on lived culture, on daily life. It would be necessarily concerned with race, with gender, with sexuality, with cultural, political, and economic inequalities. And it should present as a field that includes the work not only of those of us safely ensconced in the academy, but of those working in the increasingly diffuse array of alt-ac positions and those so often, so vaguely, called "independent scholars": researchers working outside the academy because they work in the growing pool of adjunct academic laborers or because they have no clear formal claim to academic legitimacy at all. There should be room for us to work alongside and learn from activists, teachers, journalists, writers, community leaders, and those who engage with significant cultural work not out of professional obligation, but out of personal devotion. Digital cultural studies should be responsive and inclusive, radical not because it can be, but because it must be. There are many approaches to diversifying fields, but changing our approaches, questioning the types of knowledge we produce and legitimate, is an absolutely vital one. Digital cultural studies should be a field that can not only, as Verhoeven demands, "show me a woman," but also show me forms of knowledge production in which women are welcome and in which women's concerns are valued. This is true not only, of course, of women, but of people of color, of queer people, of everyone who isn't a "standard issue bloke."

Conclusion

I began with a quote from Lewis Mumford because Mumford, so famously invested in the march of progress, so skilled in turning a sharp at the expense of those who he believed to be charlatans or crooks or dinosaurs, is an unsurprising convert to the power and potential of technological advancement. Those of us wading into the waters of digital humanities, even those of us who are cynics at heart, are often similarly enthralled. The Mumford proclaiming that "nothing is impossible," is a marginally optimistic Mumford, but the degree to which he, and many of us, can be dazzled by technology, even technologies that "have fallen short of their inherent possibilities," should give us pause. Perhaps "nothing is impossible," but from the perspective of the twenty-first century, we can look back to technology after technology that, we were told gleefully, would change the world: radio, cable television, the VCR. I'm sure by now some readers are clearing their throats, waiting for me to warn against technological determinism, and this is my warning: technology, even technology that is leaps and bounds beyond what we might have imagined, is not inherently radical, and neither is its use.

Nothing is impossible, says Mumford, but I would argue that nothing is also possible — it is depressingly easy for new technologies to reinscribe our current inequalities. We can use new technologies to continue business as usual. For example, the VCR, at one point allegedly primed to revolutionize education, simply displaced the classroom film strip with the classroom VHS, another generation of often ill-conceived educational media, used long past the point where it was badly dated.[15] Technologies on their own are not prone to radical transformation. It is in our use and deployment of technologies that we see that if not anything, at least something, is possible. Digital humanities can

15 The VCR, of course, has been hugely important for distribution and production, enabling entire new areas of production, such as the "straight to video model." My point is not that VCRs are not important, but rather that they did not achieve what many breathlessly promised they would.

and should be a field in which something is possible — where we can conceive of scholarship that is, for example, broadly accessible to the public, or that relies on large-scale collaboration to a degree that remains rare in the humanities, or that is responsive to the pressing cultural, political, and educational concerns of the broader population, scholarship that is agile, accessible, innovative. Digital humanists have the potential to produce work, in short, that evokes some of the most successful innovations of cultural studies while continuing to push beyond the limitations of existing research and publication standards and tools. The digital tools we are using are not inherently radical, but they have radical potential, if we can bring ourselves to wield them properly.

Bibliography

Bestqualitycrab (Deb Verhoeven). "Has Anyone Seen a Woman?" *Vimeo*. November 6, 2015. https://vimeo.com/144863312.

"Civil War Digital Tour." *The Caroline Marshall Draughon Center for the Arts and Humanities, Auburn University*, 2015. https://cla.auburn.edu/cah/programs/civil-war-digital-tour/.

"Civil War Letters." *Hamilton*, 2015. https://www.hamilton.edu/academics/centers/digital-humanities-initiative/projects/civil-war-letters.

Davis, Angela Y. *Angela Davis: An Autobiography*. New York: Random House, 1974.

———. *Blues Legacies and Black Feminism: Gertrude "Ma" Rainey, Bessie Smith, and Billie Holiday*. New York: Pantheon, 1998.

———. *Women, Culture & Politics*. New York: Random House, 1989.

———. *Women, Race & Class*. New York: Vintage, 1983.

"Funded Projects in Digital Humanities." *National Endowment for the Humanities*. https://www.neh.gov/veterans/funded-projects-in-digital-humanities.

Hall, Stuart. "Cultural Studies: Two Paradigms." *Media, Culture & Society* 2, no. 1 (1980): 57–72. DOI: 10.1177/016344378000200106.

"Hidden Patterns of the Civil War." *Digital Scholarship Lab, University of Richmond*, 2010. https://dsl.richmond.edu/civilwar/.

Hoggart, Richard. *The Uses of Literacy: Aspects of Working-class Life with Special References to Publications and Entertainments*. London: Chatto and Windus, 1957.

"House Divided: The Civil War Research Engine at Dickinson College." *Dickinson College*, 2007. http://housedivided.dickinson.edu/.

Losh, Elizabeth, and Jacqueline Wernimont, eds. *Bodies of Information: Intersectional Feminism and Digital*

Humanities. Minneapolis: University of Minnesota Press, 2018.

McPherson, Tara. *Feminist in a Software Lab: Difference and Design.* Cambridge: Harvard University Press, 2018.

McRobbie, Angela. *Feminism and Youth Culture: From "Jackie" to "Just Seventeen."* Boston: Unwin Hyman, 1991.

——— and Jenny Garber. "Girls and Subcultures." In *Resistance through Rituals Youth Subcultures in Post-War Britain,* edited by Stuart Hall and Tony Jefferson, 177–88. London: Routledge, 1975.

Nowviskie, Bethany. "What Do Girls Dig?" *Bethany Nowviskie.* April 7, 2011. http://nowviskie.org/2011/what-do-girls-dig/.

Posner, Miriam. "Some Things to Think about Before You Exhort Everyone to Code." *Miriam Posner's Blog.* February 29, 2012. http://miriamposner.com/blog/some-things-to-think-about-before-you-exhort-everyone-to-code/.

@profwernimont (Jacqueline Wernimont). *Twitter.* November 6, 2014, 15:40 UTC. https://twitter.com/profwernimont/status/530384290392342528.

Radway, Janice A. *A Feeling for Books: The Book-of-the-Month Club, Literary Taste, and Middle-Class Desire.* Chapel Hill: University of North Carolina Press, 1997.

———. *Reading the Romance: Women, Patriarchy, and Popular Literature.* Chapel Hill: University of North Carolina Press, 1984.

Richmond, Hugh Macrae. "Shakespeare's Staging: Media Resources for Students and Teachers." *University of California Berkeley,* 2016. https://shakespeare.berkeley.edu/.

Sayers, Jentery, ed. *Making Things and Drawing Boundaries: Experiments in the Digital Humanities.* Minneapolis, University of Minnesota Press, 2017.

Strike Debt. http://strikedebt.org/.

Talemasca, Akela. "Edward Castronova Reveals Lessons Learned from Arden." *Engadget.* March 23, 2008. https://www.engadget.com/2008/03/23/edward-castronova-reveals-lessons-learned-from-arden/.

"The Folger Shakespeare." *Folger Shakespeare Library.* https://shakespeare.folger.edu/.
"Video and Performance Archive." MIT *Global Shakespeares.* https://globalshakespeares.mit.edu/.
Weingart, Scott. "Submissions to Digital Humanities 2015 (pt. 2)." *The Scottbot Irregular.* November 6, 2014. http://www.scottbot.net/HIAL/index.html@p=41053.html.
Williams, Raymond. *Culture and Society: 1780–1950.* Aylesbury: Penguin, 1963.

Histories

4

Cold War Computations and Imitation Games: Recalibrating the Origins of Asian American Studies

Cathy J. Schlund-Vials

Genealogy [. . .] requires patience and a knowledge of details and it depends on a vast accumulation of source material [. . .]. In short, genealogy demands relentless erudition. Genealogy does not oppose itself to history as the lofty and profound gaze of the philosopher might compare to the molelike perspective of the scholar; on the contrary, it rejects the metahistorical deployment of ideal significations and indefinite teleologies. It opposes itself to the search for "origins."
—Michel Foucault, "Nietzsche, Genealogy, History"

Interdisciplinarity becomes much more than a matter contained within the academy. It becomes the episteme that organizes the regimes of representation for academy, state, and capital.
—Roderick Ferguson, *The Reorder of Things*

In her contribution to the edited anthology *A Companion to Digital Humanities,* Susan Hockey presents readers with a now recognizable genealogy for digital humanities vis-à-vis a brief history of humanities computing.[1] Noting that "unlike many other interdisciplinary experiments, humanities computing has a very well-known beginning," Hockey congruently recounts an origin story which features as primary protagonist Father Roberto Busa.[2] Intent on what Hockey characterizes as the "monumental task" of "mak[ing] an *index verborum* of all the words in the works of St. Thomas Aquinas and related authors, which totaled some 11 million words of medieval Latin," the Italian Jesuit priest approached International Business Machines (IBM) in 1949.[3] It was through this tactical computational relationship — wherein scholarly endeavor was inexorably linked to corporate venture — that digital humanities as identifiable multidiscipline was "born." These auspicious beginnings, as Hockey succinctly depicts, render visible the ways in which humanities computing was, from the outset, a *bicultural* enterprise that deployed "the rigor and systematic unambiguous procedural methodologies characteristic of the sciences" to "address problems within the humanities that had hitherto been most often treated in *serendipitous* fashion" (emphasis added).[4] Inadvertently yet tellingly, Hockey's foundational account — which privileges a distinct narrative of scholastically-driven venture capital — corresponds to an oft-accessed dominant script about the digital humanities. To clarify, such a narrative casts the field as a neoliberal-friendly interdiscipline which embraces "corporate world" technological innovation while eschewing "real world" politics. These business-oriented registers and apolitical affects are reiterated in Hockey's subsequent digital humanities (hereafter "DH") overview, which moves from Busa's mid-

1 See Susan Hockey, "The History of Humanities Computing," in *A Companion to Digital Humanities*, eds. Susan Schreibman, Ray Siemens, and John Unsworth (New York: Blackwell Publishing, 2004), http://www.digitalhumanities.org/companion/. Hockey's chapter begins in the 1940s (particularly 1949) and maps the development of humanities computing from the mid-twentieth century to the turn of the twenty-first century.

2 Ibid.

3 Ibid.

4 Ibid.

century indexical endeavor to the late-century rise of both the personal computer in the 1980s and the internet in the 1990s.

Notwithstanding the deliberative persuasiveness of Hockey's postwar computational recapitulation, and despite its connections to a long-standing positivist humanism and more recent neoliberal triumphalism, this chapter offers a deviating view of humanities computing and DH by way of a largely underutilized, politically inflected *comparative* genealogy. Guided in part by Michel Foucault's genealogical insistence in the introductory epigraph that such a method militates against searches for "origin" and destabilizes the "metahistorical deployment of ideal significations and indefinite teleologies," this chapter on the one hand examines to varying degrees and divergent ends how the rise of humanities computing necessarily occurred in synchronous tandem with the ongoing racialization of Asian Americans and the post–1949 institutionalization of area studies (specifically Asian studies) as Cold War interdiscipline.[5] In so doing, I access as a foundational premise Rey Chow's provocative reading that Asian studies as *internationalized episteme* engaged from its programmatic inception a "strategic logic" that was "fully inscribed into the politics and ideology of war."[6]

5 This "foreign policy" assessment of mid-century Asian studies is evident in Dean Acheson's "Speech on the Far East," which was delivered soon after the so-characterized "fall of China" in 1949. On January 12, 1950, Acheson averred, "I am frequently asked: Has the State Department got an Asian policy? And it seems to me that that discloses such a depth of ignorance that it is very hard to begin to deal with it. The peoples of Asia are so incredibly diverse and their problems are so incredibly diverse that how could anyone, even the most utter charlatan, believe that he had a uniform policy which would deal with all of them. On the other hand, there are very important similarities in ideas and in problems among the peoples of Asia and so what we come to, after we understand these diversities and these common attitudes of mind, is the fact that there must be certain similarities of approach, and there must be great dissimilarities in action." Dean Acheson, "Speech on the Far East," *CIA Library*, https://www.cia.gov/library/readingroom/docs/1950-01-12.pdf.

6 See Rey Chow, *The Age of the World Target: Self-Referentiality in War, Theory, and Comparative Work* (Durham: Duke University Press, 2006), 40–41.

These bellicose judgements and war-driven dogmas, evident in the frenetic, mass production of imperial and militarily-relevant knowledge about people, cultures, and regimes "over there," make perceptible — as Chow avers — the extent to which Asian studies served as a way of not just re-seeing the world but tactically rendering it a viable target.[7] Influenced by Chow's field assessment vis-à-vis calculated investments and embattled stakes, I consider in this chapter the ways in which Asian Americans were transnationally and analogously "inscribed into the politics and ideology" of nativist conflict and global war. In particular, as the paradoxical objects of pre-Cold War exclusion and postwar inclusion, Asian immigrants and Asian Americans were, as this chapter maintains, *differentially targeted* in mid-century domestic initiatives and US foreign policy. Indeed, situated in the aftermath of Japanese American internment (1942–1946), set adjacent to the "fall of China" (1949), and investigated in conjunction with an ever-expanding "military industrial complex" which supported scientists, engineers, and Orientalist scholars (1950s–1960s), I unreservedly push for a complementary genealogy which marries fields of seemingly conflicting yet nevertheless interconnected inquiry: humanities computing and Asian American studies.[8]

On the other hand, such critical juxtaposing — which ineludibly involves a syncretic assessment of mid-century debates over machine intelligence, post–1949 international relations, and early Cold War *realpolitik* — presages this chapter's overriding recalibration of and negotiation with Asian American studies

7 According to Chow, in the postwar period, to "conceive the world as a target is to conceive it as an object to be destroyed." See Chow, *The Age of the World Target,* 31.

8 With regard to this observation of "conflict," I am accessing what has become a "mainstream academic" characterization of digital humanities as innovative, cutting-edge, and technologically transformative; whereas digital humanities is cast as constantly changing, Asian studies has been classified as "traditional" and critiqued (rather unfairly) as a static interdiscipline. This misreading of Asian studies is evocatively disabused in Kuan-Hsing Chen's *Asia as Method: Toward Deimperialization* (Durham: Duke University Press, 2010).

through the appropriately efficacious logics of Cold War DH.[9] Whereas the master narrative of Asian American studies as race-based interdisciplinary links field formation to the civil rights and Third World liberation movements of the 1950s and 1960s, and while many fix the legibility of "Asian America" as identifiable body politic to shifts in immigration legislation/refugee initiative (e.g., the 1965 Hart-Celler Act and the 1975 Indochinese Refugee Assistance and Migration Act) and transpacific turns within contemporaneous foreign policy (for instance, US involvement in the second Indochina War), this chapter considers an alternative genealogy vis-à-vis its meditation upon the early Cold War era (1945–1955).[10] Integral to my mid-century emphasis is a consideration of disparate discursive histories that make urgently visible an uneasy, oft-ignored interconnectedness, particularly with regard to humanities computing and

---

9 This idea of "critical juxtapositioning" emerges from Yên Lê Espiritu's compelling insistence to bring into dialogue ostensibly divergent fields and narratives. See *Body Counts: Militarized Refuge(es)* (Berkeley: University of California Press, 2014).

10 The 1965 Immigration and Nationality Act is credited for enabling the first en masse migration of Asian immigrants in US history. What follows is a confessedly quick overview of anti-Asian immigration policy. Asian immigrants were disproportionately targeted in a series of exclusionary immigration prohibitions which commence with the 1875 Page Act (which prohibited in most instances the migration of Asian women to the United States) and the 1882 Chinese Exclusion Act; indeed, the Chinese remain the only group specifically named in immigration legislation and the prohibitions reflect both the racist concerns of nineteenth-century/early twentieth-century white labor and nativist anxieties. These provisions were extended to other Asian immigrant groups, including South Asians, Japanese, Filipinos, and Koreans. While the 1952 McCarran-Walter Act enabled Asian immigrant naturalization, what remained were country-based quotas that disproportionately privileged "Western," predominately white nation-states. The 1965 Immigration and Nationality Act eschewed country-based quotas in favor of a hemispheric division which allowed for the legal migration of 120,000 immigrants (per year) from the so-classified Western Hemisphere and 170,000 immigrants from the so-known Eastern Hemisphere. Not only did the act "open the door" to Asian migrants; it also enabled immigration from Latin America.

Ethnic Studies subfield.[11] Such interlocked modalities — which bring into view the larger racial project of US empire via the real and imagined Asian/American subject — concomitantly reflect, refract, and resist state-sanctioned surveillance at home (specifically immigration/incarceration/naturalization policies) and militarized violence abroad (particularly in terms of US warmaking in Asia).

By dialogically positioning these domestic racial formations alongside Chow's aforementioned characterization of Asian studies and emergence of humanities computing (or DH), this chapter builds on what Tara McPherson observes is an identifiable yet underexplored relationship between "[c]ertain modes of racial visibility and knowing [which] coincide or dovetail with specific ways of organizing data."[12] As McPherson further avers:

> [I]f digital computing underwrites today's information economy and is the central technology of post-World War II America, these technologized ways of seeing and knowing took shape in a world also struggling with shifting knowledges about and representations of race. If [...] racial formations serve as fundamental organizing principles of social relations in the United States [...] how might we understand the in-

11 This connection is very much at the forefront of Anne Cong-Huyen's recently published "Asian/American and the Digital|Technological Thus Far," *Verge: Studies in Global Asias* 1, no. 1 (Spring 2015): 100–108. According to Cong-Huyen, "To some, it may seem as if Asian studies and Asian American studies have had limited engagement with big tent digital humanities and have instead been siloed within area studies and American ethnic studies, and even from each other. However, scholarship in these areas has long been engaged with the digital, the technological, and the unseen politics therein" (101).

12 See Tara McPherson, "Why Are the Digital Humanities So White? Or Thinking the Histories of Race and Computation," in *Debates in the Digital Humanities*, ed. Matthew K. Gold (Minneapolis: University of Minnesota Press, 2012), https://dhdebates.gc.cuny.edu/read/untitled-88c11800-9446-469b-a3be-3fdb36bfbd1e/section/20df8acd-9ab9-4f35-8a5d-e91aa5f4a0ea#ch09.

> fusion of racial organizing principles into the technological organization of knowledge after World War II?[13]

Influenced by McPherson's argument about "technologized ways of seeing," and guided by the question, "how might we understand the infusion of racial organizing principles into the technological organization of knowledge" in the post-war period, I concentrate on two outwardly unrelated albeit contemporaneous "events": the publication of Alan M. Turing's "Computing Machinery and Intelligence" (1950) and the passage of the McCarran-Walter Act (1952).

Expressly, I commence in this chapter with a brief evaluation of Turing's meditation on computational ability and consider how the mathematician's contemplation of artificial intelligence — which pivots on establishing a machine's *imitative capacity* proves a valuable frame to evaluate what Lisa Lowe has fruitfully categorized as the "violent inclusion" of Asian Americans at home (in the United States) via immigration law, surveillance/incarceration, and model minoritization.[14] This assessment of "violent inclusion" and its intimate association with Asian America presages a more in-depth consideration of Japanese/Japanese American internment and a concurrent deliberation on the McCarran-Walter Act, which removed — for the first time in US history — racial requirements for naturalized citizenship.[15] Notwithstanding such seemingly "progressive" citizenship politics, the act maintained conservative anti-communist protocols which targeted purported "enemies within" via euphemistically characterized "emergency detention" and

---

13 Ibid.

14 See Lisa Lowe, *Immigrant Acts: On Asian American Cultural Politics* (Durham: Duke University Press, 1996).

15 The Naturalization Act of 1790 required would-be citizens to be "free white persons"; this was later amended in 1870 to include "those of African descent." Asian immigrants fell between these two race-based poles and were deemed — in a series of court cases in 1878 (*In re Ah Yup*), 1922 (*Ozawa v. United States*), and 1923 (*United States v. Thind*) — "aliens ineligible for citizenship." In 1943, as per wartime logics and political alliances, Chinese and South Asian immigrants were allowed to naturalize.

politically-based deportation.[16] These naturalized anti-communist politics and denaturalized anti-immigrant projects foreground a concluding focus on the ways in which a recalibration of Asian American studies as re-envisioned computational discipline and progressive data mining endeavor renders obvious the field's ongoing relevance, particularly with regard to critical evaluations of the contemporary "War on Terror."

All in all, as "revisionist" contemplation, this chapter's emphases on *other* temporalities and *divergent* origin points unquestionably coheres with the overall genealogical focus of this collection and is indebted to Adeline Koh's right-minded insistence that we rethink, deconstruct, and dismantle the monolithic "social contract governing the digital humanities." In reevaluating the aforementioned computational "origins" of DH (vis-à-vis Busa, IBM, and humanities computing), Koh issues the following directive: she compels us to move away "from the argument that the digital humanities has its roots within the field of humanities computing and within that field alone" on the grounds that this thinking has engendered a problematic "social contract" predicated on "civility/niceness and technical knowledge."[17] On one level, such civility (as Koh brings to light) makes troublingly difficult a complete appraisal of a field which — notwithstanding self-characterizations of objectivity and self-declarations "otherwise" — was necessarily a product of Cold War politics, was uniquely suited to the polemical task of mid-century racialization, and is presently fixed to the exclusionary logics of the neoliberal university. On another level, Koh's contractual critique corresponds to Roderick Ferguson's equally evocative, epigraphical characterization of institutional-

16 For a compelling analysis about mid-century deportation politics and their connection to race and racialization, please see Joseph Keith's *Unbecoming Americans: Writing Race and Nation from the Shadow of Citizenship, 1945–1960* (New Brunswick: Rutgers University Press, 2012).

17 See Adeline Koh, "Niceness, Building, and Opening the Genealogy of the Digital Humanities: Beyond the Social Contract of Humanities Computing," *differences: A Journal of Feminist Cultural Studies* 25, no. 1 (2014): 95.

ized interdisciplinarity as an organizing episteme that necessarily moves beyond the academy and involves both regimes of racialized representation and the polemics of imperial statecraft.[18]

Imitation Games, Japanese American Internment, and the McCarren-Walter Act

Considered by many to be *the* formative paper on artificial intelligence, Alan Turing's "Computing Machinery and Intelligence" (published in *Mind*) commences with this seemingly simple, now-familiar question: "Can machines think?"[19] Within the space of the essay's first paragraph, Turing quickly dismisses this provocative query on denotative grounds: noting that the terms "machine" and "think" carry different and often incompatible meanings, Turing concludes — at the level of nomenclature and due to inexact definition — that such an interrogative path is *subjectively* flawed. This overt engagement with the idiosyncratic, wherein one's reaction to a phenomenon is reflective of personal tastes and refractive of individual proclivities, correspondingly forms the basis of what the mathematician-turned-pioneering computer scientist successively designates as a formulaic "imitation game."

As Turing describes, such a simulation is comprised of three entities (a man, "Player A"; a woman, Player B"; and an interrogator, "Player C," who "may be [of] either sex"). The interrogator

> stays in a room apart from the other two. The object of the game for the interrogator is to determine which of the other two is the man and which is the woman [...]. In order that tones of voice may not help the interrogator the answers should be written, or better still, typewritten. The ideal ar-

18 Koh, "Niceness, Building, and Opening the Genealogy of the Digital Humanities."

19 See Alan M. Turing, "Computing Machinery and Intelligence," *Mind* 59, no. 236 (1959): 433.

> rangement is to have a teleprinter communicating between the two rooms.[20]

Accordingly, the interrogator (Player C) asks a series of questions to determine the respective genders of Player A and Player B. Player A is charged with the task of answering in a manner that leads the interrogator to the incorrect conclusion. By contrast, Player B is expected to direct the interrogator to the correct answer. While his initial game description utilizes three human actors, Turing further revises the simulation to accommodate a key machine presence; in this amended scenario, the machine assumes the programmed position of Player A. Artificial intelligence is subsequently indexed according to whether or not the machine can act indiscriminately from its human counterpart.[21]

To be sure, this concise summation of the so-known "imitation game" does not completely attend to the complexity of Turing's hypothesis with regard to the possibility (or probability) of artificial intelligence, nor does this foray into mid-century computational science answer the question which both presages and drives the simulation (e.g., the aforementioned, "Can machines think?"). Nevertheless, the prevailing performative logic of Turing's mid-century contest, principally with regard to the bifurcated characterization of identifiable interrogators as contradistinguished from imposters, offers — even if inadvertently — a distinct analytic that is *a propos* a past/present US imaginary of racialized state-authorized surveillance, xenophobic World War II-era incarceration, and, as the conclusion to this chapter as-

20 Ibid.

21 Ibid., 449–55. Upon establishing the "imitative" registers of his revised game, Turing enumerates what he characterizes as nine common objections against artificial intelligence which include the following: 1) religious objection (predicated on the idea of a human "soul"); 2) "Heads in the Sand" objection (based on sublime avoidance); 3) mathematical objections (which highlight the computational limitations of computer logic); 4) consciousness (as humanistic); 5) "disabilities" which involve (dis)attributing human qualities onto machines; 6) lack of originality (termed "Lady Lovelace's Objection"); 7) nervous system continuity; 8) informality of behavior; and 9) extra-sensory perception.

serts, "War on Terror" reconnaissance.[22] As further (inter)disciplinary context, this peculiar line of inquiry, which takes as a first premise the primacy of race in the making of the US state (as regulatory body) and American nation (as imagined collective), is very much fixed to a comparative ethnic studies/Asian American studies framework. Following suit, Turing's "imitation game" strikes a distinctly emblematic chord when situated adjacent to US immigration history, policy, and practice. Since the concerted codification of immigration law in the mid-nineteenth century, government officials and border patrol officers have indefatigably policed, detained, and questioned newly arrived European, Asian, and Latin American migrants to ascertain their viability vis-à-vis bureaucratic legality at waystations on the East and West Coasts and at various checkpoints in the Pacific Northwest and American Southwest.[23]

These simulative engagements — wherein the state is charged with the task of delineating through interrogation and examination ideal citizens from perilous subjects — are analogously pertinent to the racist rationalizations that undergirded the forced detention and relocation of an estimated 120,000 Japanese and

---

22 To be sure, this line of imaginative inquiry diverges from Turing's original argument, which is very much focused on machine intelligence. Even so, as theoretical optic, the "imitation game" allows for a critical juxtapositioning of multiple fields which have arbitrarily been characterized as discrete disciplines notwithstanding the fact that politics do not occur in a vacuum.

23 The most famous of these waystations was New York's Ellis Island, a principle port of European immigrant entry on the East Coast; its West Coast counterpart, San Francisco's Angel Island, was the primary entry point for Asian immigrants. As key reference, see Mae M. Ngai's *Impossible Subjects: Illegal Aliens and the Making of Modern America* (Princeton: Princeton University Press, 2004). Even less intentional yet likewise analogous is the extent to which Turing's "imitation game" serves as an apt frame to recollect the long-standing racialization of Asians in the United States via a series of immigration prohibitions which precipitated the rise of so-termed Chinese "paper sons," who attempted to enter the United States using fraudulent immigration papers. These individuals would usually pay a third party that established an identity as the progeny of a native-born Chinese American. Upon arrival, these individuals were forced to answer a series of questions to prove this "familial bond."

Japanese Americans during World War II. Within the dominant political imaginary, such subjects were, in the days, weeks, and months that followed the December 7, 1941, bombing of Pearl Harbor, regarded as "enemies of the state" due to their nonwhite status (as "perpetual foreigners"), religious practices (principally Buddhism), and assumed affiliations with imperial Japan (as transnational subjects).[24] Accordingly, as Eiichiro Azuma and Kandice Chuh contend, first- and second-generation Japanese Americans occupied a vexed space "between two empires" (e.g., the United States and Japan) and inhabited a paradoxical place as denaturalized US subjects. To surmise and summarize, as "violently included" subjects, Japanese Americans were respectively placed in the untenable position of proving political allegiance via military service and loyalty oath.[25]

Notwithstanding these resonances, Turing's "imitation game" is by virtue of publication date synchronous with and a product of the early Cold War period. Correspondingly, the rules which govern it — unintentionally and uncannily — echo the ways in which US state actors stressed, vis-à-vis contemporaneous con-

---

24 This essay deliberately uses the term "incarceration" as a means of accentuating the racist, carceral actualities of Japanese American internment. Such usage coheres with what Lane Hirabayashi and other Asian American historians assert is a more accurate nomenclature. However, earlier mentions to "internment" are intended to use a more recognizable formulation as a means of introducing the event.

25 See Eiichiro Azuma's *Between Two Empires: Race, History, and Transnationalism in Japanese America* (New York: Oxford University Press, 2004) and Kandice Chuh's *Imagine Otherwise: On Asian Americanist Critique* (Durham: Duke University Press, 2003). The en masse incarceration of Japanese Americans (inclusive of first-generation *Issei*, second-generation *Nisei* and *Kibei*, and third-generation *Sansei*) is an undeniable field touchstone for Asian American studies. As many have noted, while the dominant reading of what has come to be known as "the internment" pivots on an assessment of "necessary" wartime logics and states of exception, the treatment of Japanese Americans is consistent with a multi-decade nativism and anti-Asian racism. This longue durée reading — particularly when juxtaposed with the forced migrations of Native peoples and Africans/African Americans in the 18th and 19th centuries — makes clear how such a policy was not the exception but rather the rule of the US racial state.

gressional committee and legislative act, the ongoing need to identify allies and categorize antagonists at home and abroad. Domestically then, Turing's "imitation game" makes "Cold War sense" when considered alongside the vehemently anti-communist dictates of the Red Scare and the McCarthy era. To wit, the game's superseding concern with strategic performance and overriding obsession with tactical detection coheres with the "discovery-oriented" ambitions of the House Un-American Activities Committee, an investigative assemblage in the US House of Representatives that was originally founded in 1938 to uncover fascist connections "in-country" but is better remembered as an anti-Communist governmental apparatus which attempted to root out, by any means necessary, so-classified "enemies within." While the committee's anti-Communist activities are by and large well-known, less acknowledged is its connection to the above-discussed mass incarceration of Japanese/Japanese Americans. Indeed, it was the House Un-American Activities Committee (under the conservative leadership of Senator Martin Dies, Democrat from Texas) that issued the "Yellow Report," which in its biased aggregation of ethnographic data supported en masse relocation and incarceration, promulgating a "fifth column" assessment of Japanese Americans which prefigured a collective status as a national security threat.[26]

While the history of Japanese/Japanese American incarceration and the actuality of the Red Scare make blatantly discernible the exclusionary logics of the United States as regulated state *and* affective nation, and whereas the logics of inimical

26 In particular, the "Yellow Report" argued that Japanese Americans represented potential espionage threats due to alleged devotion to the Japanese emperor, observance of Buddhist practice, and the number of Japanese fishermen on the West Coast. This characterization militated against the findings of a previously written report by Army contractor C.B. Munson, who stressed that Japanese and Japanese Americans on the West Coast posed no serious threat to national security. This report very much worked in tandem with Executive Order 9066, issued February 19, 1942 by President Franklin D. Roosevelt. For more information about the Yellow Report, see Dillon S. Myer, *Uprooted Americans* (Tucson: University of Arizona Press, 1971), 19.

identification pivot on a racialized evaluation of imitative selfhood, less obvious is the extent to which seemingly inclusionary shifts in immigration/naturalization law problematically adhered to past/present *derivative* assessments of the Asian immigrant body as assimilated, co-opted, and contained subject. To recapitulate and clarify, while the passage of the 1952 McCarran-Walter Act ostensibly ushered in a new era of accessible citizenship for Asian immigrants via non-racial requirement, it necessarily did so through the imitative logics of US naturalization, which required a simultaneous repudiation of country-of-origin affiliations and wholesale acceptance of settlement-nation politics.[27] Significantly, as Robert G. Lee maintains, the rehabilitation of Asian immigrant bodies from "aliens ineligible for citizenship" to assimilated model minorities was consistent with a state-sponsored global agenda which included increased transpacific militarization (for instance, in Guam, the Philippines, and Japan) and involved US wars in Asia (e.g., the Korean War and the second Indochina War).[28]

Perhaps most germane to this chapter's hybrid Asian Americanist/DH focus, the McCarran-Walter Act was resolutely fixed to a binaried Cold War computation that pitted potential amicable subject against impending inimical threat. Congruently, a chief provision involved the ability to deport immigrants and naturalized citizens engaged in "subversive acts"; other requirements included an unwavering adherence to country-based quotas, a critical, meta-assessment of the nation's labor needs, and the stringent prohibition of Communist Party "fellow travelers."[29] As Senator Pat McCarran (D-NV) averred soon after the act's June 1952 passage:

---

27 See Cathy J. Schlund-Vials, *Modeling Citizenship: Jewish and Asian American Writing* (Philadelphia: Temple University Press, 2011).

28 See Robert G. Lee, *Orientals: Asian Americans in Popular Culture* (Philadelphia: Temple University Press, 1999).

29 In so doing, the 1952 McCarran-Walter Act was consistent with the previously passed "Subversive Activities Control Act of 1950," which carried an "Emergency Detention" provision. President Harry S. Truman

> I believe that this nation is the last hope of Western civilization and if this oasis of the world shall be overrun, perverted, contaminated or destroyed, then the last flickering light of humanity will be extinguished. I take no issue with those who would praise the contributions which have been made to our society by people of many races, of varied creeds, and colors [...]. However, we have in the United States today hard-core, indigestible blocs which have not become integrated into the American way of life, but which, on the contrary are its deadly enemies. Today, as never before, untold millions are storming our gates for admission and those gates are cracking under the strain. The solution of the problems of Europe and Asia will not come through a transplanting of those problems *en masse* to the United States.[30]

In emphasizing the prospective "contamination" to "Western civilization" by "hard-core, indigestible blocks which have not become integrated into the American way of life," McCarran makes clear the extent to which the act was—from its inception and by design—intended to identify "untold millions" of immigrant targets. Whereas the act has largely been heralded as a "watershed moment" within Asian American studies on the basis of unheralded naturalization access, what remains undermined is the degree to which it was not so much progressive but rather consistent in its Cold War demarcation of friends and enemies.

By way of conclusion, this critical recalibration of the McCarran-Walter Act is necessarily informed by Turing's "imitation game," which makes possible an interrogative interpretation of its less-than-progressive aims; as further complement, such an analysis takes seriously the ways in which the act's prejudicial objectives, which attempt to stem the tide of contamination

vetoed both acts on the grounds that they were discriminatory and "un-American."

30 Senator Pat McCarran, Congressional Record, March 2, 1953. See U.S. *Congressional Record,* 99 Cong. Rec., pt. 2 (1953), 1518.

through categorization, are consistent with the logics of humanities computing. To read Asian American history through the schema of humanities computing makes possible a politically-relevant recalibration of Asian America as a formation which remains intimately fixed to the past/present legacies of US statecraft and war-making. Put alternatively, this mode of evaluation accentuates a consistency with regard to US immigration agenda and US foreign policy, particularly in a post-September 11th imaginary comprised of compulsory detentions at Guantanamo Bay, deportations of criminalized permanent residents (particularly Southeast Asians and Central Americans), covert renditions of "enemy combatants" to locations unverified, clandestine collections of telephone metadata by the NSA (National Security Administration), along with the increased surveillance of South Asian and Arab Americans as per the U.S.A. PATRIOT Act.[31] As parallel schema, DH provides a useful analytic upon which to remap alternative trajectories — or genealogies — for Asian American studies, an interdiscipline which simultaneously reflects Cold War apologetics, Civil Rights-era politics, and contemporary "War on Terror" logics.

31 See Arshad Ahmed's "The US PATRIOT Act: Impact on the Arab and Muslim American Community" Report. This report was generated under the auspices of the Institute for Social Policy and Understanding (ISPU). According to the Institute's site, the ISPU is an independent, nonpartisan think tank and research organization committed to conducting objective, empirical research and offering expert policy analysis on some of the most pressing issues facing the United States. These issues include U.S. foreign policy, national security, the economy, and public health." The ISPU is specifically focused on issues facing "American Muslims and Muslim communities around the world." Available online at https://www.ispu.org/the-usa-patriot-act-impact-on-the-arab-and-muslim-american-community/.

Bibliography

Acheson, Dean. "Speech on the Far East." CIA *Library*. https://www.cia.gov/library/readingroom/docs/1950-01-12.pdf.

Ahmed, Arshad. "The US PATRIOT Act: Impact on the Arab and Muslim American Community." *Institute for Social Policy and Understanding*, January 1, 2004. https://www.ispu.org/the-usa-patriot-act-impact-on-the-arab-and-muslim-american-community/.

Azuma, Eiichiro. *Between Two Empires: Race, History, and Transnationalism in Japanese America.* New York: Oxford University Press, 2004.

Chen, Kuan-Hsing. *Asia as Method: Toward Deimperialization.* Durham: Duke University Press, 2010.

Chinese Exclusion Act. H.R. 5804, 47th Cong. 1882.

Chow, Rey. *The Age of the World Target: Self-Referentiality in War, Theory, and Comparative Work.* Durham: Duke University Press, 2006.

Chuh, Kandice. *Imagine Otherwise: On Asian Americanist Critique.* Durham: Duke University Press, 2003.

Cong-Huyen, Anne. "Asian/American and the Digital|Technological Thus Far." *Verge: Global Asias* 1, no. 1 (2015): 100–108. DOI: 10.5749/vergstudglobasia.1.1.0100.

E.O. 9066. General Records of the Unites States Government, Record Group 11, issued February 19, 1942.

Espiritu, Yên Lê. *Body Counts: Militarized Refug(es).* Berkeley: University of California Press, 2014.

Ferguson, Roderick. *The Reorder of Things: The University and Its Pedagogies of Minority Difference.* Minneapolis: University of Minnesota Press, 2012.

Foucault, Michel. "Nietzsche, Genealogy, History." In *Language, Counter-Memory, Practice: Selected Essays and Interviews,* edited by Donald F. Bouchard, translated by Donald F. Bouchard and Sherry Simon, 139–64. Ithaca: Cornell University Press, 1980.

Hockey, Susan. "The History of Humanities Computing." In *A Companion to Digital Humanities,* edited by Susan

Schreibman, Ray Siemens, and John Unsworth. New York: Blackwell Publishing, 2004. http://www.digitalhumanities.org/companion/.
Immigration and Nationality Act. H.R. 2580, 89th Cong. 1965.
In re Ah Yup. I F. Cas, 223 (D. Cal. 1878).
Keith, Joseph. *Unbecoming Americans: Writing Race and Nation from the Shadow of Citizenship, 1945–1960*. New Brunswick: Rutgers University Press, 2012.
Koh, Adeline. "Niceness, Building, and Opening the Genealogy of the Digital Humanities: Beyond the Social Contract of Humanities Computing." *differences: A Journal of Feminist Cultural Studies* 25, no. 1 (2014): 93–106. DOI: 10.1215/10407391-2420015.
Lee, Robert G. *Orientals: Asian Americans in Popular Culture.* Philadelphia: Temple University Press, 1999.
Lowe, Lisa. *Immigrant Acts: On Asian American Cultural Politics*. Durham: Duke University Press, 1996.
McCarran-Walter Act. H.R. 5678, 82nd Cong. 1952.
McPherson, Tara. "Why are the Digital Humanities So White? Or Thinking the Histories of Race and Computation." In *Debates in the Digital Humanities,* edited by Matthew K. Gold. Minneapolis: University of Minnesota Press, 2012, https://dhdebates.gc.cuny.edu/read/untitled-88c11800-9446-469b-a3be-3fdb36bfbd1e/section/20df8acd-9ab9-4f35-8a5d-e91aa5f4a0ea#ch09.
Myer, Dillon S. *Uprooted Americans.* Tucson: University of Arizona Press, 1971.
Naturalization Act. 1 Stat. 103, 1st Cong. 1790, amended 1870.
Ngai, Mae M. *Impossible Subjects: Illegal Aliens and the Making of Modern America*. Princeton: Princeton University Press, 2004.
Page Act. H.R. 4747, 43rd Cong. 1875.
Schlund-Vials, Cathy J. *Modeling Citizenship: Jewish and Asian American Writing*. Philadelphia: Temple University Press, 2011.

Schreibman, Susan, Ray Siemens, and John Unsworth, eds. *A Companion to Digital Humanities*. New York: Blackwell Publishing, 2004.

Subversive Activities Control Act. S. 4037, 81st Cong. 1950.

Takao Ozawa v. United States. 260 U.S. 178 (1922).

Turing, Alan M. "Computing Machinery and Intelligence." *Mind* 59, no. 236 (1950): 433–460. DOI: 10.1093/mind/LIX.236.433.

United States v. Bhagat Singh Thind. 261 U.S. 204 (1923).

U.S. Congress. *Congressional Record*. 99 Cong. Rec., pt. 2, 1953.

5

Punching Holes in the International Busa Machine Narrative

Arun Jacob

The fabled origin story of humanities computing takes place in 1946 when Jesuit Priest Father Roberto Busa and Thomas J. Watson Sr., the CEO of International Business Machines (IBM), meet, exchange pleasantries, and lay the groundwork for producing an index of the complete writings of Saint Thomas Aquinas.[1] Busa and Watson's meeting marks the genesis of the field since the theologian was able to acquire the material, technical, and financial support from the technocrat in order to engage in his scholarly endeavor, developing a linguistic corpus using computing technologies. This illustrious digitization project of sorting and indexing eleven million medieval Latin words in the works of St. Thomas Aquinas produced a touchstone for humanities computing the *Index Thomisticus*.[2] Busa along with IBM technicians developed machine-readable concordances

1 See Thomas Nelson Winter, "Roberto Busa, S.J., and the Invention of the Machine-Generated Concordance," *The Classical Bulletin* 75, no. 1 (1999): 3–20.

2 Susan Hockey, "The History of Humanities Computing." In A *Companion to Digital Humanities*, eds. Susan Schrelbman, Ray Siemens, and John Unsworth (Oxford: Blackwell, 2004), 4.

and in the process produced a bibliography that was searchable through a telephonic coupler. Busa's pioneering work, which "explored the concept of presence according to Thomas Aquinas" by repurposing business machines developed primarily for record keeping to generate automated concordances, has been widely celebrated as the genesis of humanities computing later christened digital humanities.[3]

In this paper I will be studying how the cultural memory of Fr. Roberto Busa's humanities computing project has been shaped, formed, and contoured in contemporary digital humanities scholarly discourse. By broaching the topic of the provenance of computational approaches to humanities and by revisiting the origins of the traditions and practices of computer assisted text analysis, it becomes evident how, as Torgovnick claims, "As part of a social bargain, individuals and groups agree to look away from unsettling histories, which then form the latent contents of cultural memory — not erased from memory (Halbwachs's concept) so much as a consequential, even active absence: the hole, to put it colloquially, that completes the donut, necessary for the donut's very shape."[4] By studying the narrative arcs that lead up to and/or are left out from the genealogical history of the field of digital humanities I hope to offer a counter-hegemonic cultural memory. My narrative critique strives to locate the genesis of the field of humanities computing at Busa's feet and venerating him as the great man of digital humanities. I take my cue from Ramon Reichert's assertion that neither Busa's research question nor his methodological procedure was novel.[5] I trace the lineage of the field of study by teasing out the longer history of the computing infrastructure that was at Busa's disposal and critically perusing the media archeology of punch-card tech-

3 R. Busa, "The Annals of Humanities Computing: The Index Thomisticus," *Computers and the Humanities* 14, no. 2 (October 1980): 83.

4 Marianna Torgovnick, *The War Complex: World War II in Our Time* (Chicago: University of Chicago Press, 2008), 3.

5 Ramon Reichert, "Big Humanities Project," in *Encyclopedia of Big Data*, eds. Laurie A. Schintler and Connie L. McNeely (Basel: Springer International Publishing, 2017), 2.

nologies through curated corporate histories and their relation to cultural memories.

The conventional historiography that pivots around Busa's founding father storyline and his *savoir faire* silences the socio-econo-political lived realities of the space-time where and when work on humanities computing took place. Haunting the timeline when Busa was working on the *Index Thomisticus* include details[6] like how during World War II Busa served as a military chaplain in the auxiliary corps of the Italian Army from 1940–1943.[7] As a graduate student in the Pontifical Gregorian University in Rome working on his dissertation on Thomistic theology, Busa was seemingly unaffected being "surrounded by bombings, Germans, partisans, poor food and disasters of all sorts."[8] I found it quite disconcerting that a man of the cloth was so socially disaffected by the catastrophes happening around him. Zygmunt Bauman theorizes that in a bureaucracy moral concerns are not discussed; rather, the object of bureaucratic labor is to produce flawless work.[9] The excellence with which the task is performed is the only metric of concern for the bureaucrat; there is no room for ethical concerns in this operational paradigm. I would opine that Busa's research project is symptomatic of the schemata that Bauman describes in his apparent lack of social concern. As much as the field of digital humanities owes to its founding father, it is worth explicating that Busa's pioneering research in humanities computing resides at the intersection of the workings of three gargantuan bureaucracies: academia, the Catholic Church, and the IBM corporation. As a Jesuit priest,

6 Roberto Busa went to high school with Albino Luciani, the future Pope John Paul I. See Marco Passarotti, "One Hundred Years Ago: In Memory of Father Roberto Busa SJ," paper presentation, The Third Workshop on Annotation of Corpora for Research in the Humanities (ACRH-3), Sofia, Bulgarian Academy of Sciences, December 12, 2013.

7 Ibid.

8 Steven E. Jones, *Roberto Busa, S.J., and the Emergence of Humanities Computing: The Priest and the Punched Cards* (London: Routledge, 2016), 35.

9 Zygmunt Bauman, *Modernity and the Holocaust* (Ithaca: Cornell University Press, 1989), 98.

Busa reported to the ecclesiastical office of Pope Pius XII, and in his industry-university collaborative endeavor, he liaised with Thomas J. Watson Sr., the CEO of IBM. Both Pope Pius XII and Thomas Watson leave behind very troubling legacies and unsettling histories vis-à-vis their respective relationships with the Third Reich.[10]

The sanitized digital humanities origin story fails to acknowledge the provenance of the punch-card technology and the purpose for which the technologies were originally constructed. Before there was humanities computing, there was computational social science. The IBM punch-card technology Busa used has a history of being used by the Nazi regime, which has been wiped clean from digital humanities historiographies. I am of the opinion that if we are to acknowledge punch-card technology as an essential part of the genesis of digital humanities, we must be cognizant of the logic of hierarchy and inequality that is baked into the history of punch cards. IBM punch cards were the data processing technology used by the Third Reich to instrumentalize race science, operationalize surveillance, and in the process automatize human extermination.[11] Thomas J. Watson, recipient of the Order of the German Eagle and president of the International Chamber of Commerce in 1937, was personally involved in IBM's project management of Hitler's extermination campaign.[12] The New Deal policies that curtailed American corporate operations in Europe did not affect IBM because of the personal relationships that Watson had cultivated with US

10 See John Cornwell, *Hitler's Pope: The Secret History of Pius XII* (New York: Penguin Books, 2008); Robert A. Ventresca, *Soldier of Christ: The Life of Pope Pius XII* (Cambridge: Harvard University Press, 2013); Paul O'Shea, *A Cross Too Heavy: Pope Pius XII and the Jews of Europe* (New York: Palgrave Macmillan, 2011); and Edwin Black, *IBM and the Holocaust: The Strategic Alliance Between Nazi Germany and America's Most Powerful Corporation* (Washington, DC: Dialog Press, 2012.)

11 Black, *IBM and the Holocaust*, 10.

12 Ibid., 147; Kevin Maney, *The Maverick and His Machine: Thomas Watson, Sr., and the Making of IBM* (Hoboken: J. Wiley & Sons, 2003), 208.

Presidents Roosevelt, Truman, and Eisenhower.[13] IBM subsidiaries were fully functional during World War II and operating business ventures through units in Germany and Switzerland.[14] IBM's German subsidiary Dehomag (Deutsche Hollerith-Maschinen Gesellschaft mbH or German Hollerith Machines LLC) redesigned the Hollerith punch cards originally used in the Hollerith Machine to electronically tabulate census returns to track people and perform the information and tabulation tasks required to operationalize the Third Reich's Holocaust.[15] Using Dehomag's punch-card technology, the Third Reich was able to produce the final solution precisely and accurately on account of the superior information processing and database management systems that IBM's cybernetic infrastructure provided. The rationality of the bureaucrats who were looking for the most efficient and effective system to exterminate the Jews during World War II explicate how technology and ideology were sutured together under Nazism. Dehomag's technical expertise yokes the Nazi system of totalitarian control and coordination to the vulgar extreme of IBM's capitalist enterprise.

My own research endeavor is in locating the Torgovnickian absent-presence in the origin story of digital humanities. Engaging in a hauntological reading of the great-man narrative, I hope to unveil the spectral revenants that lurk underneath the surface by carefully teasing out the provenance of the punch-card technology, the particularities of the political economy within which the technology emerged, and historically contextualizing the social and cultural affordances that enabled the technology to be adopted. By mobilizing Paul Ricœur's "hermeneutics of suspicion," I will be peering into the nooks and crannies of the cultural record to find what has been unsaid in and/or left out from the cannons of digital humanities in order to argue

13 Ibid.; David L. Stebenne, "Thomas J. Watson and the Business-Government Relationship, 1933–1956," *Enterprise & Society* 6, no. 1 (2005): 49.

14 Stebenne, "Thomas J. Watson and the Business-Government Relationship," 49.

15 Black, *IBM and the Holocaust*, 265.

that identifying some of the socio-cultural contexts that shaped Busa's work and further probing these contexts reveal how this domain of research emerged.[16] By recalling, recollecting, and remembering the cultural legacies of the genesis of humanities computing, I wish to suture the problematic histories of Busa's project to the contemporary technoscape and unsettle the original disciplinary narrative. I am of the opinion that it is worth investing some scholarly energies into cultivating an "ethics of memory" to critically peruse the culture, climate, and values of the space-time from where the *Index Thomisticus* originated, and into inculcating in digital humanists a "duty to remember" a more nuanced origin story with blemishes, flaws, and follies and all.[17]

I found that the most fertile ground from where to begin analyzing the relation of history and memory in Busa's narrative was by critically reviewing a gap in the literature that stemmed from his own admission of ignorance when he wrote:

> Although some say that I am the pioneer of the computers in the humanities, such a title needs a good deal of nuancing… [O]n the stacks of the IBM library in New York City I had spotted a book (whose title I have forgotten), which was printed some time between 1920 and 1940: in it someone mentioned that it was possible to make lists of names by means of punched cards.[18]

The founding father of the digital humanities openly confessing that he was aware that someone else at IBM had created machine-generated concordances several years prior to his own attempts was at once both intriguing and infuriating to me. What was the object of including such a vague and inchoate statement in this piece? While reading this passage, I began asking myself,

16 Paul Ricœur, *Memory, History, Forgetting* (Chicago: University of Chicago Press, 2004), 30.

17 Ibid., 89.

18 Busa, "The Annals of Humanities Computing," 84.

is it possible this man was feigning ignorance of the origins of machine-generated concordances? Was there malicious intent on Busa's part in excluding the details of the progenitor of the IBM punch-card technology? Busa has been described on several occasions as a meticulous and methodical researcher; to have written such a sloppy entry signaled to me that something was terribly awry.[19] For a scholar revered as an academic giant in the fields of philological, linguistic, and literary computing to leave out crucial details such as the title of the book he read, the author of the aforementioned book, the publication year, and so on did seem very peculiar and made it seem that something was amiss. This intuition prompted me to pursue the spectral voices haunting Busa's academic legacy and destabilizing the narrative built around the *Index Thomisticus*. I was transfixed by the question of what could possibly have been Busa's rationale for obfuscating the aforementioned text and/or obliterating the cultural record in the process?

I gathered it was essential to acquaint myself with the punch-card technology that Busa was working with, namely the IBM 858 Cardatype accounting machines, a series of storage-and-retrieval devices. Busa mentions the 858 Cardatype by name in the text as the technology that he had access to in order to work on his project. But upon cross checking with the IBM Archives, I found that the IBM 858 Cardatype was developed in 1955.[20] Nico Sprokel writes that Busa was working on his doctorate in 1942, writing index cards by hand to produce a lexicographic and linguistic corpus of the *Index Thomisticus*.[21] Since Busa's project began several years before this particular make and model of the IBM punch card machine was in service, I suspect Busa and his research team used earlier models of IBM machines over the

19 Passarotti, "One Hundred Years Ago," 17; Winter, "Roberto Busa, S.J." 16; Geoffrey Rockwell, "The Index Thomisticus as Project," *Theoreti.ca*, March 14, 2016, http://theoreti.ca/?p = 6096; Julianne Nyhan and Marco Passarotti, *One Origin of Digital Humanities: Fr. Roberto Busa in His Own Words* (Cham: Springer International Publishing, 2019).

20 Busa, "The Annals of Humanities Computing," 84.

21 Nico Sprokel, "The 'Index Thomisticus,'" *Gregorianum* 59, no. 4 (1978): 739.

years. In 1949, when Busa was commencing the project, Thomas Winter writes that Busa seemed acutely aware of the nitty-gritty details of the specific workings of the technical venture. Busa was very knowledgeable of the appurtenances that he would need to accomplish the empirical undertaking.[22] I find it fascinating that a Jesuit priest had the project management skills and technological know-how to generate an engineering bill of materials that precisely met his project's technical needs.[23] In *Varia Specimina,* Busa's first published report of the project, he describes his research methodology and the technical glitches that he encountered while repurposing the punched-card tabulators to work on his humanities computing project, with a glint of techno-optimism shining through in his writing.[24] Busa's technical prowess and intuitive knowledge of the glitches that the IBM punch cards would produce suggests to me that he may have had an intimate working knowledge of these tabulating machines. I am interested in how, when, and where Busa may have come in contact with punch cards to gain this prior knowledge about their technicalities and engineering paraphernalia.

The IBM 858 Cardatype accounting machine that Busa mentions in his writing is an example of a turnkey solution IBM offered to its business customers.[25] IBM would offer to its business clients a turnkey computer system comprised of computer

22 Winter, "Roberto Busa, S.J.," 6.

23 It is only once an antitrust suit (U.S. *v.* IBM) is filed against IBM in January 1969 that the specifications of the IBM punch-card machines are made available to the public. Dr. Cuthbert Hurd explicates all the components required to build an IBM punch-card machine in his sworn testimony to the Justice Department (ibid.). Hurd was a mathematician who worked for the Atomic Energy Commission's laboratory before joining IBM in 1949 to work on implementing punch-card machine technology into IBM's engineering laboratories and workshops (Thomas J. Watson and Peter Petre, *Father, Son & Co.: My Life at IBM and Beyond* [New York: Bantam Books, 2000], 224). Hurd's testimony presents in the written word the technology that Busa would have worked with and/or the punch- card machines that he would have seen at the site visit with IBM CEO Thomas J. Watson Sr. in 1949.

24 Winter, "Roberto Busa, S.J.," 6.

25 Ibid., 10.

hardware, software, and applications developed and sold specifically for the customer to meet the individual client's requirements. Perusing the 858 Cardatype Accounting Machine catalogue from August 20, 1957,[26] I noticed that the machine was comprised of a control unit, a transmitting typewriter and non-transmitting typewriter, an auxiliary keyboard, a cardatype card punch, a tape punch, and an arithmetic unit. IBM marketed the 858 Cardatype Accounting Machine as a complete business solution and billed their customers for each of the aforementioned components separately. IBM did not sell their equipment to their customers; rather they leased the hardware to customers and offered a service and maintenance contract for the upkeep of the equipment. The tapes, ribbons, cards, and the like used in the "Accounting Machine" were exclusive and proprietary to IBM.

I find Busa's discursive slippage problematic because by using IBM's sales and marketing term "Accounting Machine" in his writing, Busa glosses over the nuances of working with punch card technologies; not a single machine is being deployed here but rather a whole slew of machines, which are in turn then serviced by an army of IBM service personnel, organizational staff, administrative employees, and keypunch operators. I'd argue that Busa's choice of words indicates how little he valued the working people who laboured on the operation of the machine. This becomes obvious in Busa's private disclosure to Edward Vanhoutte where it is described that, "[f]or his complete *Index Thomisticus,* Busa calculated that the stack of punch cards would have weighed 500 tonnes, occupying 108 m^3 with a length of 90 m, a depth of 1 m, and a height of 1.20 m. By 1975, when the *Index Thomisticus* was completed and started to appear on 65,000 pages in 56 volumes (Busa, 1974–1980) some 10,631,973 tokens were processed."[27] While there is no acknowledgement of

26 IBM *Equiment Summary,* August 20, 1957, http://www.bitsavers.org/pdf/ibm/punchedCard/Training/Card_Equipment_Summary_Aug57.pdf.

27 Edward Vanhoutte, "The Gates of Hell: History and Definition of Digital | Humanities | Computing," in *Defining the Digital Humanities: A Reader,* eds. Melissa Terras, Julianne Nyhan, and Edward Vanhoutte (Surrey: Ashgate, 2013), 119–56.

the labor that went into creating these punch cards, the quantitative data that Busa produces about the punch cards are duly noted in the cultural record and presented as historical fact. Each one of the punch cards that made up the five hundred tons were each individually entered by female punch-card operators. Punch-card operators completed an apprenticeship at Busa's training institute in Milan, where they learned how to input, verify, and interpret the keypunch operations. Melissa Terras writes that Busa chose females over males, preferably those who did not know Latin, to make sure they were conscientious and would not insert their own interpretations into the text.[28] There are photographs taken in Gallarate, Italy, of female punch-card operators working on Busa's project. But these photographs have not been catalogued properly,[29] therefore, it is not possible to discern when they were taken and/or the identities of the subjects in the photographic texts. These female punch-card operators are the midwives of knowledge creation, and they are left out of the origin story of digital humanities. I argue this is because Busa didn't see himself as one of the working people who labored on the research initiative and that he preferred the corporate marketing discourse.

Busa's use of IBM's marketing jargon suggests to me where his loyalties were, who he swore allegiances to, and who he associated himself with in the public-private partnership. IBM offered this research project material and financial support for several decades. I thought it would be abundantly clear to Busa, as a religious scholar at the Pontifical Gregorian University, that publicly funded research ought be for public good not private

28 David J. Birnbaum, Sheila Bonde, and Mike Kestemont, "The Digital Middle Ages: An Introduction," *Speculum* 92, no. 1 (October 2017): S2.

29 Marco Passarotti at CIRCSE Research Centre, Università Cattolica del Sacro Cuore, Milan, Italy can grant permission to have the images made available under a Creative Commons CC-BY-NC license. Melissa Terras has a few of these images available on her blog from October 15, 2013, "For Ada Lovelace Day—Father Busa's Female Punch Card Operatives," *Melissa Terras' Blog*, October 15, 2013, https://melissaterras.blogspot.ca/2013/10/for-ada-lovelace-day-father-busas.html.

benefit. Moreover, as a priest I expected Busa to value the link between Christianity, secular government, and society. To quote from the scriptures, in the Gospel according to Matthew, Christ says, "Render unto Caesar the things that are Caesar's, and unto God the things that are God's."[30] Busa does not disclose in his writings the nature of the financial arrangement between IBM and the academic institution where his research project was housed. Writing about the *Index Thomisticus*, Geoffrey Rockwell mentions how our memory infrastructures are designed to preserve knowledge generated by projects without adequate knowledge of the workings of the project. He also notes that the Busa archives demonstrate that one of the side effects of obtaining corporate sponsorship to conduct the project was that IBM was looking for influence and publicity in return for bankrolling the project.[31] I would maintain that Busa's project was a corporate social responsibility project and public relations campaign for IBM.

Lars Heide points out that, "As early as 1926, IBM had decided not to base punched-card multiplications on an improved tabulator but to build a separate non-printing machine that could read figures from a punched card, perform the required arithmetic operations, and punch the outcome on the same or a successive card."[32] This exemplifies IBM's market orientation for developing technological solutions. IBM did not pursue the more technically efficient and/or cost-effective engineering solution, rather they invested their corporate energies into developing technologies that systemically prioritized the generation of profit over technical prowess. To this effect, James W. Bryce's design of a separate punched-card multiplier was patented in 1928 and implemented in the IBM Type 600 Machine in 1931 (and upgraded later that year to the Type 601 to calculate mul-

30 Matthew 22:21, KJV.

31 Rockwell, "The Index Thomisticus as Project," *Theoreti.ca*, March 14, 2016, http://theoreti.ca/?p=6096.

32 Lars Heide, *Punched-Card Systems and the Early Information Explosion, 1880–1945* (Baltimore: Johns Hopkins University Press, 2009), 124.

tiplication and addition).[33] IBM punch-card machines were not streamlined for technical efficiency because the mission of the business venture was to maximize the number of number of punch cards sold, therefore any process that would undermine the sale and commerce of punch cards was antithetical to the corporate mission.

In 1928, Dehomag, IBM's German subsidiary company, had brought Austrian engineer Gustav Tauschek's patent for a punched-card multiplier to the company's attention. Tauschek had filed for the patent in Germany in 1926, and he was awarded the patent in 1928. IBM saw the potential in Tauschek's patent and hired him on a contract from 1931 to 1935, buying his numerous patents. IBM's strategy in hiring Tauschek was to make sure that no rival would capitalize on his intellectual property. IBM had made such a move in the past when the company bought out John Thomas Schaaff's electric typewriter and census tabulating machine patents and John Royden Peirce's bookkeeping machine patents.[34] In 1935, the United States Patent Office denied Gustav Tauschek's patent application, therefore denying his control of the rights to punched-card multiplication in the United States. Tauschek was let go from his contract at IBM around the same time. Meanwhile, IBM implemented several of Tauschek's patents in their product lines in the years to come.[35]

Gustav Tauschek was a technical wizard whose other inventions include the first electromagnetic drum storage device and patenting the technology for optical character recognition in 1929.[36] From 1926–1930, Tauschek worked for the military technology group Rheinmetall (Rheinische Metallwaaren-und Maschinenfabrik AG or Rhine Metalware and Machine Factory Joint-Stock Company), where he developed the electro-me-

33 Ibid.

34 Ibid., 104; Brian Randall, ed., *The Origins of Digital Computers: Selected Papers*, Vol. 1 (Berlin: Springer-Verlag, 1975), ch. 3, "Tabulating Machines," 127.

35 Heide, *Punched-Card Systems*, 124–25.

36 Walter D. Jones, "Watson and Me: A Life at IBM," IEEE *Annals of the History of Computing* 25, no. 3 (July 2003): 12–13.

chanical punched-card accounting machine. Tauschek's punch-card machine prototype from 1928 was never mass produced, and Rheinmetall sold off the company's punch-card technologies to Dehomag, IBM's German subsidiary[37] Even though Tauschek's inventions never made it to market, I would imagine IBM acquired all the technical drawings, papers, monographs, and other writings that documented in detail how the punch-card technology could be operationalized. This leads me to believe that the mysterious book that Busa mentioned having come across in the book stacks of IBM's corporate library could very well have been one of the the works of Gustav Tauschek. Since Tauschek's writings about the punch-card machine prototype were now in the possession of IBM, I am of the opinion that it is not beyond a reasonable doubt that Busa may have been referring to one of Tauschek's texts that detailed a scenario for using punch cards that could work for the machine-generated concordance project. Giving Tauschek credit for developing the tools and techniques that Busa would go on to use two to three decades later also requires taking into account the social, cultural, political, and economic context from within which these technologies were researched and developed.

Rheinmetall, the company that Tauschek worked for, was an arms and ammunitions manufacturing firm. By acknowledging Tauschek as a pioneer in the field is to draw a direct link between humanities computing and the Nazi military-industrial complex. Dehomag, IBM's German subsidiary, was responsible for developing punch-card technologies for the Third Reich.[38] Although punch-card technology was used in census operations since the 1890s for processing and tabulating data,[39] it was innovated upon, instrumentalized, and weaponized to execute the race science and surveillance agenda of the Third Reich. IBM's Dehomag was instrumental in the Nazi administrative efforts

37 Ibid., 12.

38 Black, *IBM and the Holocaust*, 370.

39 Emerson W. Pugh, *Building IBM: Shaping an Industry and Its Technology* (Cambridge: MIT Press, 1995), 13.

to record the vital statistics of every resident and coordinate and conduct a comprehensive surveillance program that was intent on arriving at the Final Solution.[40] Therefore, Busa was not merely repurposing business machines developed primarily for record keeping, he was repurposing innovations in computing technologies, developed by the military-industrial complex, that were funded and used to operationalize the ideological agenda of the Nazi government.

I would argue that the allure of punch-card technology and its innovations to both Busa and the Nazis as administrators and bureaucrats was its capacity to resolve the vexing problem of organizing a large, ill-defined data set. The punched-card technology served the utilitarian purpose of helping Busa find his way through a massive corpus of Latin words, sorting, sifting, and organizing his database just as it helped the Nazis locate and persecute groups of people: Jews, Roma peoples, LGBT peoples, BIPOC, people with disabilities, labor unionists, anarchists, communists, and artists. Both the priest and the Nazi empire were seduced by the same temptress, namely IBM and its modern market ideology and "the practicality that confers the maximum priority to results, and forgets about the means used to reach those results."[41] In other words, IBM offered their clients an innovative business solution for their respective big data problems.

IBM's prowess, as I have noted before, is not in providing their clients with the most technically elegant solutions but rather offering their client a market-ready solution from their existing stable of technology solutions and communicating to the client that IBM's technology is the one best suited for them and will be the one to ameliorate all the clients' predicaments. By this logic, it was not Busa who used the IBM punch-card technology on his

40 D.M. Luebke and S. Milton, "Locating the Victim: An Overview of Census-Taking, Tabulation Technology and Persecution in Nazi Germany," IEEE *Annals of the History of Computing* 16, no. 3 (Autumn/Fall 1994): 27.

41 Eloy Portillo and Pedro Costa, "The Role of Technological Acceleration in the Crisis of Modernity: A View by Paul Virilio," paper presentation, 2010 IEEE International Symposium on Technology and Society, Wollongong, NSW, Australia, June, 2010.

lexical text analysis project but rather it was IBM that was looking to enter the textual analytics market. IBM found in Busa a client who would be an evangelist for their punch-card technology solutions to others in his field of work. IBM was trading on Busa's ecclesiastic credentials to purge the punch-card technology of its' Nazi legacies. The punch-card system that IBM had sold to Busa was a tried, tested, and true technology solution that had already gone through its product development stages. Popper and Buskirk breakdown the evolution of a technology through a marketplace, or technology lifecycle (TLC) into six basic phases: "cutting edge, state of the art, advanced, mainstream, mature, decline."[42] At the time when Busa's project was being initiated the punch card was a mainstream product. I would speculate that IBM was trying to generate positive press coverage for its punch-card technology through Busa and his humanities computing project. The media exposure that IBM would receive for Busa's project[43] would connect punch-cards with the priest in the collective cultural memory.

42 Edward T. Popper and Bruce D. Buskirk, "Technology Life Cycles in Industrial Markets," *Industrial Marketing Management* 21, no. 1 (1992): 24.

43 IBM has had its products engage in media spectacles to gain media attention. I remember the press coverage that IBM received in 1996 when the IBM supercomputer Deep Blue defeated the reigning world chess champion Gary Kasparov. In 2011, IBM's artificial intelligence technology Watson appeared on the popular television show *Jeopardy*. In 2016, IBM Watson garnered a lot of media attention for creating the first AI-made film trailer for *Morgan* (dir. Luke Scott) (20th Century Studios, "Morgan | IBM Creates First Movie Trailer by AI [HD] | 20th Century FOX," *YouTube*, August 31, 2016, https://www.youtube.com/watch?v=gJEzuYynaiw). These examples suggest to me that IBM's corporate communication strategy aims to generate media content that will evoke positive feelings in people's collective cultural memories. In 2017, IBM Watson, also served as the army's equipment advisor solution using Internet of Things (IoT) to provide predictive battlefield analytics for military vehicles. But there is minimal press coverage given to IBM's cutting-edge military-industrial ventures, suggesting that IBM only advertises technologies that are in the advanced or mainstream stage of their technological life cycle while IBM's cutting edge or state-of-the-art military technologies receive very little media exposure. IBM Watson is being currently used by the US Department of Defense for Artificial

The *Index Thomisticus* was at once both Busa's research project and an IBM public relations project. IBM provided Busa with an off-the-shelf technology for which they did not have to incur any additional new research and development costs. The various computing technologies that went into the punch-card machine had been previously developed and well established in the marketplace. IBM's predecessor Herman Hollerith's Tabulating Machine Company had developed a system for compiling census statistics in the 1880s. The general statistics technology was developed in 1894 and was stabilized by 1907 leading to the creation of adding machines. Bookkeeping technologies were developed in 1906. These calculating machines could add, subtract, multiply and divide and had market lifespan of thirty years or so. The punch-card technology was developed in 1933 and stabilized by 1936 when the eighty column IBM cards were in production. Punch cards had a market lifespan of thirty years or so. The history of information systems based on punched cards is made possible firstly by the transnational memory network of patent laws and regulations that allows one generation of product innovations to build upon the other[44] and secondly by the material supplies necessary for the production of punch cards. IBM had a stranglehold on the bill of materials needed to produce the standardised product, including high quality paper which was not easily available during the World Wars. To comprehend the political economy of punch cards is to understand the reification of power. This data processing technology that was capturing, circulating, and storing data that was in turn becoming the raw material to feed the racial surveillance apparatus of the Third Reich. Aly and Heim explicate how the connections between "the politics of modernization and the politics of annihilation" can best be understood by focusing on how young, career-minded technocrats and academics were able to execute

Intelligence-based predictive maintenance solutions for their military assets.

44 Pierre-E. Mounier-Kuhn, "Reviewed Work: Punched-Card Systems and the Early Information Explosion, 1880–1945 by Lars Heide," *Business History Review* 85, no. 1 (2011): 235; Heide, *Punched-Card Systems*, 124.

their plans because they were able to have their ideas sanctioned by those in the upper echelons of the National Socialist state hierarchy. The open and permeable information flows between the Nazi state and the technocratic apparatus enabled Gustav Tauschek's (and by extension Roberto Busa's) research.

Reading Busa's account of how he used the IBM Punch Card machines to sequence, collate, and correlate data from the *Index Thomisticus,* it was evident that Busa was truly a technocrat at heart and a religious specialist only by vocational training. Edward Vanhoutte writes, "The story goes that Busa met Ellison around 1954, congratulated him on his computing work, and went back to IBM to transfer the punch cards onto magnetic tape and use computer technology and programming for the publication of his Dead Sea Scrolls project in 1957."[45] I would opine that Busa's conduct is quite unbecoming of a Jesuit priest, as he seems to have broken the tenth commandment, which instructs that, "Thou shalt not covet thy neighbour's house, thou shalt not covet thy neighbour's wife, nor his manservant, nor his maidservant, nor his ox, nor his ass, nor any thing that is thy neighbour's."[46] When Busa learned about how Rev. John W. Ellison used Remington magnetic tapes to prepare a concordance of the Bible, he was jealous of the headway Ellison was making and demanded that IBM give him access to more advanced technological resources so that he too could make more progress on his project.[47] Gluttony, greed, lust, pride, sloth, envy, and wrath are the cardinal sins in Christian teaching. The revelation that Busa was envious of Ellison's progress shows how lackluster his commitment to the cardinal and theological values was. This behavior is antithetical to the Jesuit tradition, customs, and practices. Jesuit priests are members of a religious community who have taken vows of poverty, chastity, and obedience, living in the community, sharing everything. The Jesuit order is known

45 Vanhoutte, "The Gates of Hell: History and Definition of Digital | Humanities | Computing," 127–28.

46 Exodus 20:17, KJV.

47 Busa, "The Annals of Humanities Computing," 85.

for their liberation theology, a social justice-oriented Christian theology that emphasizes a concern for the liberation of the oppressed and marginalized. Busa was working with technology that was drenched in the blood of the oppressed. Yet he does not insert his Jesuit social justice commitment to his work. Busa's pedestrian concerns over the velocity with which the project could be completed suggests how he had been subsumed by the political economy of speed. Busa had been exnominated by the essences of capitalism, the never-ending *blitzkrieg* of the circulation of capital, technology, and speed. In this account Busa's technological rationality becomes evident; he was seduced by the efficiencies afforded by the technological innovations, which established how he had been thoroughly interpellated into IBM's logic of militarized techno-science.

Probing the cultural memories that haunt the origin story of digital humanities, it becomes evident that the scholarly discourse exhibits an indifference to the humanistic and social concerns of the twenty-first century, namely big data, biometrics, techno-politics, surveillance systems, and so on. Carroll Pursell writes, "As many of the founding generation [of American invention] feared, a technology not subordinated to our highest political aspirations has become a bulwark of our worst."[48] As a humanistic discipline, digital humanities scholarship must begin to excavate the problematic histories of the field and engage with the lineage of these data collection and data processing methodologies. The abject memories and grotesque legacies of IBM's punch cards can be traced back to Fr. Roberto Busa's humanities computing project. The traditions and practices of computer assisted text analysis project is strife with direct links to how the technology was used to what Simone Browne describes as "reduce flesh to pure information."[49] To summarize I believe that when acknowledging the punch-card technology

48 Carroll Pursell, *The Machine in America: A Social History of Technology* (Baltimore: Johns Hopkins University Press, 2007), xiii.

49 Simone Browne, *Dark Matters: On the Surveillance of Blackness* (Durham: Duke University Press, 2015), 26.

as an essential part of the genesis of digital humanities, scholars must have the moral courage to recognize that the field is complicit in the birth of surveillance capitalism, military contracting, and the technological apparatus of the security state.

Bibliography

20th Century Studios. "Morgan | IBM Creates First Movie Trailer by AI [HD] | 20th Century FOX." *YouTube,* August 31, 2016. https://www.youtube.com/watch?v=gJEzuYynaiw

Bauman, Zygmunt. *Modernity and the Holocaust.* Ithaca: Cornell University Press, 1989.

Birnbaum, David J., Sheila Bonde, and Mike Kestemont. "The Digital Middle Ages: An Introduction." *Speculum* 92, no. 1 (October 2017): S1–S38. DOI: 10.1086/694236.

Black, Edwin. *IBM and the Holocaust: The Strategic Alliance Between Nazi Germany and America's Most Powerful Corporation.* Washington, DC: Dialog Press, 2012.

Browne, Simone. *Dark Matters: On the Surveillance of Blackness.* Durham: Duke University Press, 2015.

Busa, R. "The Annals of Humanities Computing: The *Index Thomisticus.*" *Computers and the Humanities* 14, no. 2 (October 1980): 83–90. http://www.jstor.org/stable/30207304.

———. *Varia Specimina.* Milan: Fratelli Bocca Editori, 1951.

Cornwell, John. *Hitler's Pope: The Secret History of Pius XII.* New York: Penguin Books, 2008.

Cortada, James W. *Before the Computer: IBM, NCR, Burroughs, and Remington Rand and the Industry They Created, 1865–1956.* Princeton: Princeton University Press, 2015.

Heide, Lars. *Punched-Card Systems and the Early Information Explosion, 1880–1945.* Baltimore: Johns Hopkins University Press, 2009.

Hockey, Susan. "The History of Humanities Computing." In *A Companion to Digital Humanities,* edited by Susan Schrelbman, Ray Siemens, and John Unsworth. Oxford: Blackwell, 2004. http://www.digitalhumanities.org/companion/view?docId = blackwell/9781405103213/9781405103213.xml&chunk.id = ss1-2-1.

IBM *Equipment Summary.* August 20, 1957. http://www.bitsavers.org/pdf/ibm/punchedCard/Training/Card_Equipment_Summary_Aug57.pdf.

Jones, Steven E. *Roberto Busa, S.J., and the Emergence of Humanities Computing: The Priest and the Punched Cards.* London: Routledge, 2016.

Jones, Walter D. "Watson and Me: A Life at IBM." *IEEE Annals of the History of Computing* 25, no. 3 (July 2003): 4–18. DOI: 10.1109/MAHC.2003.1226652.

Luebke, D.M., and S. Milton. "Locating the Victim: An Overview of Census-Taking, Tabulation Technology and Persecution in Nazi Germany." *IEEE Annals of the History of Computing* 16, no. 3 (Autumn/Fall 1994): 25–39. DOI /10.1109/MAHC.1994.298418.

Maney, Kevin. *The Maverick and His Machine: Thomas Watson, Sr., and the Making of IBM.* Hoboken: J. Wiley & Sons, 2003.

Mounier-Kuhn, Pierre-E. "Review: *Punched-Card Systems and the Early Information Explosion, 1880–1945* by Lars Heide." *Business History Review* 85, no. 1 (2011): 233–36. http://www.jstor.org/stable/41301387.

Nyhan, Julianne, and Marco Passarotti. *One Origin of Digital Humanities: Fr. Roberto Busa in His Own Words.* Cham: Springer International Publishing, 2019.

O'Shea, Paul. *A Cross Too Heavy: Pope Pius XII and the Jews of Europe.* New York: Palgrave Macmillan, 2011.

Passarotti, Marco. "One Hundred Years Ago. In Memory of Father Roberto Busa SJ." Paper presentation, Third Workshop on Annotation of Corpora for Research in the Humanities (ACRH–3), Sofia, Bulgarian Academy of Sciences, December 12, 2013.

Popper, Edward T., and Bruce D. Buskirk. "Technology Life Cycles in Industrial Markets." *Industrial Marketing Management* 21, no. 1 (1992): 23–31. DOI: 10.1016/0019-8501(92)90030-W.

Portillo, Eloy, and Pedro Costa. "The Role of Technological Acceleration in the Crisis of Modernity: A View by Paul Virilio." Paper presentation, 2010 IEEE International

Symposium on Technology and Society, Wollongong, NSW, Australia, June, 2010. DOI: 10.1109/ISTAS.2010.5514603.
Pugh, Emerson W. *Building IBM: Shaping an Industry and Its Technology.* Cambridge: MIT Press, 1995.
Pursell, Carroll. *The Machine in America: A Social History of Technology.* Baltimore: Johns Hopkins University Press, 2007.
Randall, Brian, ed. *The Origins of Digital Computers: Selected Papers.* Vol. 1. Berlin: Springer-Verlag, 1975.
Reichert, Ramon. "Big Humanities Project." In *Encyclopedia of Big Data,* edited by Laurie A. Schintler and Connie L. McNeely, 1–5. Basel, Switzerland: Springer International Publishing, 2017. DOI: 10.1007/978-3-319-32001-4_22-1.
Ricœur, Paul. *Memory, History, Forgetting.* Chicago: University of Chicago Press, 2004.
Rockwell, Geoffrey. "The Index Thomisticus as Project." *Theoreti.ca,* March 14, 2016. http://theoreti.ca/?p = 6096.
Sprokel, Nico. "The 'Index Thomisticus.'" *Gregorianum* 59, no. 4 (1978): 739–50. http://www.jstor.org/stable/23576117.
Stebenne, David L. "Thomas J. Watson and the Business-Government Relationship, 1933–1956." *Enterprise & Society* 6, no. 1 (2005): 45–75. DOI: 10.1017/S1467222700014294.
Terras, Melissa M. "For Ada Lovelace Day—Father Busa's Female Punch Card Operatives." *Melissa Terras' Blog,* October 15, 2013, https://melissaterras.blogspot.ca/2013/10/for-ada-lovelace-day-father-busas.html.
———, Julianne Nyhan, and Edward Vanhoutte. *Defining Digital Humanities: A Reader.* New York: Routledge, 2013.
Torgovnick, Marianna. *The War Complex: World War II in Our Time.* Chicago: University of Chicago Press, 2008.
Vanhoutte, Edward. "The Gates of Hell: History and Definition of Digital | Humanities | Computing." In *Defining the Digital Humanities: A Reader,* edited by Melissa Terras, Julianne Nyhan, and Edward Vanhoutte, 119–56. Surrey: Ashgate, 2013.
Ventresca, Robert A. *Soldier of Christ: The Life of Pope Pius XII.* Cambridge: Harvard University Press, 2013.

Watson, Thomas J., and Peter Petre. *Father, Son & Co.: My Life at IBM and Beyond.* New York: Bantam Books, 2000.
Winter, Thomas Nelson. "Roberto Busa, S.J., and the Invention of the Machine-Generated Concordance." *The Classical Bulletin* 75, no. 1 (1999): 3–20. http://digitalcommons.unl.edu/classicsfacpub/70/.

6

Embodying the Database: Race, Gender, and Social Justice

Dorothy Kim

In Tara McPherson's groundbreaking 2012 article, "Why Are the Digital Humanities So White? or Thinking the Histories of Race and Computation," she explains:

> [T]he difficulties we encounter in knitting together our discussions of race (or other modes of difference) with our technological productions within the digital humanities (or in our studies of code) are actually an *effect* of the very designs of our technological systems, designs that emerged in post–World War II computational culture. These origins of the digital continue to haunt our scholarly engagements with computers, underwriting the ease with which we partition off considerations of race in our work in the digital humanities and digital media studies.[1]

1 Tara McPherson, "Why Are the Digital Humanities So White? or Thinking the Histories of Race and Computation," in *Debates in the Digital Humanities,* ed. Matthew K. Gold (Minneapolis: University of Minnesota Press, 2012), 140.

She asks whether critics may "argue that the very structure of digital computation develops at least in part to cordon off race and to contain it? Further, might we come to understand that our own critical methodologies are the heirs to this epistemological shift?"[2] She points to Omi and Winant when she asks "how might we understand the infusion of racial organizing principles into the technological organization of knowledge after World War II?"[3] Her article then juxtaposes the development and structural frames of UNIX in relation to the goals of modularity as a way to "decrease 'global complexity' and cleanly separate one 'neighbor' from another" with urban white flight, spatial segregation, and also with the literary theoretical tradition of New Criticism, which became central during the Cold War.[4] As she explains from the work of Christopher Newfield and Gerald Graff, New Criticism's "relentless formalism, a 'logical corollary' to 'depoliticization' [...] that 'replaced agency with technique,'" the critical discussion aligns New Criticism's frames with the frames of business-management culture, modular systems, and also computational modular code.[5] The decoupling of context and relationality from textual culture becomes a means to put distance from the bodies at the center of texts, textuality, data, and databases.

McPherson wrote and published the article in a world she described as "postracial." I think we have at this particular political, cultural, and critical moment debunked the myth of "postracial."[6] Her call to extend critical methodologies for literacies in "code," "algorithms," "interface," have now become daily journal articles in a late-fascist surveillance culture that in the last five years wants to tell us that: AI is racist and sexist; Amazon and Palintir (the company Peter Thiel developed from his work at Cambridge Analytica) are helping locate undocu-

2 Ibid., 143.

3 Ibid. See also Michael Omi and Howard Winant, *Racial Formation in the United States*, 3rd edn. (New York: Routledge, 2014).

4 McPherson, "Why Are the Digital Humanities So White?" 149.

5 Ibid., 149–50.

6 Ibid., 152.

mented Americans to help ICE deport them; and 23andMe and Ancestry.com are gathering your biometric and DNA profile in order to hand it over to law enforcement and others who are happy to use it for surveillance.[7] We are bombarded every day in personal, local, national, and global ways with how very much digital data, tools, algorithms, and interfaces are not neutral. As we have seen in the last four years of elections (2016–2020), it has been palpably clear that our digital tools, our digital systems, our scholarship, and our bodies are political. There is no hiding behind a sign of neutrality.

In fact, we can update this point of view by examining the work of Safiya Noble's *Algorithms of Oppression* in which she succinctly states in the opening: "This book is about the power of algorithms in the age of neoliberalism and the ways those digital decisions reinforce oppressive social relationships and enact new modes of racial profiling, which I have termed *technological redlining*."[8] This book takes McPherson's methodological call to arms for a practice that will value "broader contexts, meaningful relation, and promiscuous border crossings."[9] But Noble considers the longer history of data computation and explains that "On the Internet and in our everyday uses of technology, discrimination is also embedded in computer code and, increasingly, in artificial intelligence technologies that we are reliant on, by choice

---

7 Ibid., 154. See also Chris Mooney and Juliet Eilperin, "EPA Website Removes Climate Science Site from Public View after Two Decades," *Washington Post*, April 29, 2017, https://www.washingtonpost.com/news/energy-environment/wp/2017/04/28/epa-website-removes-climate-science-site-from-public-view-after-two-decades/; Samantha Schmidt and Peter Holley, "A 'Dreamer' Claims He Was Secretly Deported. The Government Claims It Never Happened," *Washington Post*, April 19, 2017, https://www.washingtonpost.com/news/morning-mix/wp/2017/04/19/the-trump-administration-has-deported-a-dreamer-for-first-time-advocates-say/; and Evan Taparata, "President Trump, How Is Letting Internet Providers Sell Consumers' Browsing Data in the Public Interest?" *PRI*, April 16, 2017, https://www.pri.org/stories/2017-04-16/president-trump-how-letting-internet-providers-sell-consumers-browsing-data.

8 Safiya Umoja Noble, *Algorithms of Oppression: How Search Engines Reinforce Racism* (New York: NYU Press, 2018), 1.

9 McPherson, "Why Are the Digital Humanities So White?" 154.

or not. I believe that artificial intelligence will become a major human rights issue in the twenty-first century."[10] How did we come to this juncture in which the twenty-first century's next human rights arena — in relation to race, gender, sexuality, disability, and so on — will be the development of AI technology? I would argue that artificial intelligence and our current discussions about its potential harm begins with an examination of our past historical interactions with computational databases and the biopolitics of data.

I will examine the database, data, and information textuality through the historical lens of informational communication (also commonly known as the history of the book), from the angles of surveillance studies, using Sylvia Wynters and Alexander Weheliye's work on Black feminism and biopolitics, as well as with literary reader/response and reception theory. This article methodologically takes its cues from media archaeology; as Lori Emerson writes in *Reading Writing Interfaces,* "media archaeology [...] provides, however, a sobering conceptual friction in the way that certain theorists identified with a field [...] use it to undertake 'a hermeneutic reading of the 'new' against the grain of the past, rather than telling of the histories of technologies from past to present."[11] This is not about linear histories of techno-triumphalism, nor is it about reading the past legibly, easily, straight, or in sequence. This article is both an exploration of the materiality of text, platform studies, and media archaeology, as well as an examination in designing interactive media structures. My main point is to ask and try to answer the question that McPherson centers in her article,

"So if we are always already complicit with the machine, what are we to do?"[12]

In this chapter, we will encounter what McPherson desired in a different vision of the digital humanities: "hybrid practitio-

10 Noble, *Algorithms of Oppression,* 1.

11 Lori Emerson, *Reading Writing Interfaces: From the Digital to the Bookbound* (Minneapolis: University of Minnesota Press, 2014), xii.

12 McPherson, "Why Are the Digital Humanities So White?" 152.

ners, artist-theorists, programming humanists, activist-scholars, theoretical archivists, critical race coders."[13] I will address the visibility and legibility of bodies and the "tactics" used in both "surveillance" and "sousveillance." As Simone Browne explains in her book *Dark Matters: On the Surveillance of Blackness*: "[Steve] Mann developed the term 'sousveillance' as a way of naming an active inversion of the power relations that surveillance entails. Sousveillance, for Mann, is the act of 'observing and recording by an entity not in a position of power or authority over the subject of the veillance.'"[14] Thus, this article sifts through and examines the texture of databases — in telling stories of the bodies in its system, in making visible and marking those bodies, in allowing those bodies to find ways to enact sousveillance.

I tell the promiscuous history of the database: transhistorical, transatlantic, and transmedial. This is an unbound history of the database: an information and textual form that has temporal medieval beginning. As a technological informational structure, databases always have the pitfall of structuring racism, sexism, ableism, and other systems of oppression. Because a database organizes data — and thus bodies — its mechanisms of organization, its various modes of interface are always in relation to the body's sensory experiences. The database is an eclectic mechanism of organizing communication because it is also the foundational narrative told about the digital humanities. However, what are other models of databases that glitch and rearrange our frames? I will argue that the directionality of media history does not move linearly in a progress model but rather has multiple angles and rays. Database history in the digital humanities has been told in a particularly conventional, medieval, white, progress-model way that has valorized one serendipitous and innocent origin point. This article offers a more diverse his-

13 Ibid., 154.

14 Simone Browne, *Dark Matters: On the Surveillance of Blackness* (Durham: Duke University Press, 2015), 18–19. See also Steve Mann, "'Reflectionism' and 'Diffusionism': New Tactics for Deconstructing the Video Surveillance Superhighway," *Leonardo* 31, no. 2 (1998): 93–102.

tory of the database precisely because data is embodied and databases have such terrible political and material consequences for certain racialized, gendered, disabled, non-heternormative bodies. The history of the computational database in the twentieth century is also the history of racialized, religious genocide.

In addition, my account is not a standard one that allows us to recover and celebrate the women and marginalized groups that are part of these histories. We also must address the difficult histories, including the white supremacist and Nazi genocidal politics, that brought certain bodies to intimately be part of building and running genocidal databases. In this way, I am using Foucault's concept of genealogies to disrupt an idea of technological progress and mythic and innocent origins. I have taken this Foucauldian genealogy of the digital humanities back because I believe that we must, as humanists, be uncomfortable about a positivist historiography of humanities computing. I believe that if we are to shape the digital humanities, it must be with the tenet that social justice and the ethics of data are at its center. And this is what my article tries at the end to address — are there methods and ways to disrupt, to resist our situated location in these digital genocidal machines? My article's itinerary begins in precolonial and pre-Columbian America and travels on to industrial nineteenth-century France and England, before a transatlantic discussion between the US and Europe. Temporally, I begin in late medieval time but in the Americas.

An Alternative History of the Digital Interactive Database: The Khipu

The first informational interface in my promiscuous media history situates us in the medieval temporal spaces of the Americas. In this case, this temporal/geographic location allows us to view slant another traditional frame — the history of the book. In Matt Cohen and Jeffrey Glover's introduction to *Colonial Mediascapes,* they explain how they expand past the frames of European-centered book history in order to bring other communication forms into discussion. Their expansion moves away from linear models of progress and development in discussions of the history of the book.[15] Inspired by the push of the work of Elizabeth Boone and Walter's Mignolo's edited volume *Writing without Words*, Cohen and Glover are especially cognizant of Mignolo's point that "the history of writing is not an evolutionary process driving toward the alphabet, but rather a series of coevolutionary processes in which different writing systems follow their own transformations."[16] Thus, they argue that the "medium shapes, but does not determine, meaning in communication."[17] They move away from writing, text, and book history as centered on narratives of Western European scholarship and towards "media" as a way to open up nonalphabet driven forms of communication including "performance and other-than-textual communication and reconstructions of impermanent media."[18]

15 Matt Cohen and Jeffrey Glover, "Introduction," in *Colonial Mediascapes*, eds. Matt Cohen and Jeffrey Glover (Lincoln: University of Nebraska Press, 2014), 1–43.

16 Ibid., 3. See Walter Mignolo, "Literacy and Colonization: The New World Experience," in *1492/1993: Re/discovering Colonial Writing*, eds. René Jara and Nicholas Spadaccini (Minneapolis: Prisma Institute, 1989), 62. See also Elizabeth Hill Boone and Walter Mignolo, eds., *Writing without Words: Alternative Literacies in Mesoamerica and the Andes* (Durham: Duke University Press, 1994).

17 Cohen and Glover, "Introduction," 3. They further explain that methodologically, in reference to their title, they pull from "postcolonial anthropology and on historical media studies, in which redefinition of media categories offers ways to resist the magnetism of teleological stories of cultural development that follow from the valorization of writing and print" (3).

18 Ibid., 4. For a discussion of the issues of using "book history" and "literacy" as ways to address pre-Columbian, precolonial, and colonial media, see Germaine Warkentin, "Dead Metaphor or Working Model? 'The Book' in Native America," in *Colonial Mediascapes*, eds. Matt Cohen and Jeffrey Glover (Lincoln: University of Nebraska Press, 2014), 47–75, and Andrew Newman, "Early Americanist Grammatology: Definitions of Writing and Literacy," in *Colonial Mediascapes*, eds. Matt Cohen and Jeffrey Glover (Lincoln: University of Nebraska Press, 2014), 76–98.

However, this work of recasting book history in relation to Indigenous histories has also been addressed by Indigenous scholars. In Lisa Brooks's *The Common Pot,* she explains,

> Just as Native writers spin the binary between word and image into a relational framework, they also challenge us to avoid the "oppositional thinking that separates orality and literacy wherein the oral constitutes authentic culture and the written contaminated culture," as Muskogee author Craig Womack argues in *Red on Red.* He suggests that such notion may actually hinder our understanding of a "vast, and vastly understudied, written tradition" in Native America. Like Silko, Womack raises the example of the codices, "written in Mayan pictoglyphic symbols before contact, and in Mayan in the Latin alphabet afterward," as "a fascinating study in these regards." As he rightly points out: "These books were used as a *complement* of oral tradition rather than a *replacement.* The books were recited and even read in precontact schools to educate the young in the oral tradition. The idea, then, of books as a valid means of passing on vital cultural information is an ancient one, consistent with the oral tradition itself."
>
> Similarly, Silko speaks strongly about the interdependence of oral and written traditions and points to the adoption of alphabetic writing as a form of adaptation. [...] [S]he relates that the original Mayan codices had complementary texts that were composed after the arrival of the Europeans. She explains that they were written in Spanish and Latin "by the first generation [of Mayan children] that the priests put in schools. And they could read and write. When they went home, the elders saw that the oral tradition could not be maintained, where you had genocide on this scale [...]. The old folks thought about it, had people explain to them what writing was. It dawned on them; it's a tool. It's a tool."[19]

---

19 Lisa Tanya Brooks, *The Common Pot: The Recovery of Native Space in the Northeast* (Minneapolis: University of Minnesota Press, 2008), xxii. She

I would also like to qualify here that, as critics have aptly pointed out, Indigenous writers have been readily erased from the Anglo-American record even when they have used their understanding of the settler-colonial tools of empire — an understanding of the history of letters, English writing, and colonial rhetoric — to construct what Malea Powell describes, with the examples of two nineteenth-century Native American intellectuals Sara Winnemucca Hopkins and Charles Alexander Eastman, as a "rhetorics of survivance." She writes:

> Despite hundreds of years of pressure, first from European colonists then from Euramericans, American Indians did not disappear. And though our visibility has been repeatedly erased in American discourses of nationhood, we have, just as insistently, refigured ourselves and reappeared. [...] In the Euroamerican insistence upon our absence we have become permanently present. [...] My point is that even though we received the tools of Euroamerican cultural participation in a less than generous fashion, Native peoples have used the very policies and beliefs about "the Indian" meant to remove, reserve, assimilate, acculturate, abrogate, and un-see us as the primary tools through which to reconceive our history, to reimagine Indian-ness in our own varying and multiplicitous images, to create and re-create our presence on this continent.[20]

And finally, to discuss Indigeneity, media, and text/textuality also means we should examine Marisa Elena Duarte's work in *Network Sovereignty.* She asks in her first chapter,

cites Laura Coltelli's interview with Silko in Allen Richard Chavkin, ed., *Leslie Marmon Silko's* Ceremony: *A Casebook* (Oxford: Oxford University Press, 2002), 153.

20 Malea Powell, "Rhetorics of Survivance: How American Indians Use Writing," *College Composition and Communication* 53, no. 3 (2002): 427–28.

> How does the concept of technology relate to the concept of indigeneity? How are the technical devices that shape contemporary day-to-day life woven into those moments that define what it means to be Indigenous? [...] How do these parallel imaginaries weave together? How does thinking in terms of networks and relationships help us understand the way the divide between the technical and the social manifests in Indigenous contexts? Understanding the concepts of technology, Indigeneity, and networks requires an understanding of the functions that communications technology and Native peoples — Indians — completed in the formation of the modern technically advancing nation-state.
>
> We can consider the lineage of the wireless mobile phone, before the landline telephone, before wireless telegraphy, when the railroad barons were competing in the race to build a transcontinental railroad. In the United States and parts of Canada, the late nineteenth century spelled the beginning of an increasingly industrial era of modernity, as well as a century of campaigns against Indigenous peoples. [...] Dreams of transcontinental transportation, communication, and shipping seemed very possible with the inventions of the steam engine and telegraphy, as well as Frederick Jackson Turner's burgeoning vision of Manifest Destiny.[21]

I do not believe it is just serendipity and accident that Duarte utilizes the language of the fabric arts — weaving — concomitantly with the question of technological lineages and settler-colonial genocide. In this way, we can see that histories of digital and computational technologies are always wrapped up with violence, genocide, and devastating harm to the most marginal and vulnerable communities.

In considering promiscuous database histories, rhetorics of survivance, the entanglement of settler colonialism and North America, and the history of the book, I turn my gaze to a

21 Marisa Elena Duarte, *Network Sovereignty* (Seattle and London: University of Washington Press, 2017), 9–10.

prime example of American "media" that is a form of "other-than-textual" communication in the Andean khipu. In earlier accounts — as in Samuel Purchas's *Purchas His Pilgrimes: Contayning a History of the World in Sea Voyages and Lande Travells by Englishmen and others,* in his section "A Discourse of the Diversity of Letters used by the divers Nations in the World" — the South American khipu was imagined as a visual communication alphabet. As Purchas writes:

> Now for the varietie and differing formes, Art hath superabounded: both in the subject and instrument, some writing with Pencils as the Japenites and Chinois, others with Pens, others with instruments of Iron as the Malabars, of Gemmes, Brasse also, or other metall, in Table-bookes, Leaves, Barkes, Wood, Stone, Aire, Sand, Dust, Metall, Paper, Cloth, Parchment, and innumerable other materials: in the forme also and manner, with Quippos in Stones or Threads, as in Peru; with Pictures as in Mexico, and the Egyptian Hieroglyphikes… [22]

Instead, the khipu is a tactile, haptic, Indigenous database system. I offer the khipu as example in order to resist ideas of the database's evolutionary progress model. The khipu is an alternative media-history node that is part of the long history of informational communication; in addition, it demonstrates the different directions and capacities that databases and the bodies they organize can encompass.[23]

---

22 Samuel Purchas, *Hakluytus posthumus, or Purchas his Pilgrimes, Vol. I* (1642; repr. New York: Macmillan, 1905), 492. See also Molly Farrell, *Counting Bodies: Population in Colonial American Writing* (Oxford: Oxford University Press, 2016), 23.

23 Cohen and Glover, "Introduction," 34. Cohen and Glover point to Frank Salomon's work. Salomon writes "a more omnidirectional mode of inscription" (6). See Frank Salomon, *The Cord Keepers: Khipus and Cultural Life in a Peruvian Village* (Durham: Duke University Press, 2004), 6.

The Andean khipu is an early informational communication database believed to organize the census, food and agricultural inventories, villages and other population centers, calendars, genealogies, and thus various types of statistical, accounting, and narrative information. Purportedly from the testimonies of Spanish colonizers, khipus also were used to record letters, histories, family information, and narrative stories.[24] It is an informational media database that has a history that began before the Inca Empire (c. 1450–1532) but takes its name, the khipu, from the term for "knot" from the administrative cosmopolitan language, Quechua, of the empire.[25] As a data system constructed of skin and knots, it is an interactive, haptic, mise-en-système.

Johanna Drucker, in her book *Graphesis: Visual Forms of Knowledge Production,* has discussed how digital media environments are a mise-en-système.[26] As I have written, this means that they need "multimodal reading, creation, and interpretation," that an interactive mise-en-système is in Drucker's words, "an environment for action."[27] I have argued that though medieval book history invented the organizational frames of "mise-en-page" — layout, marginalia, paratext, columns, table of contents, indexes, chapter headings, to name a few — medieval manuscripts can also be an interactive mise-en-système. What we find here, in the pre-Colombian and precolonial contact with the European codex, is an interactive "digital" (interfacing with the hands and fingers) mise-en-système that is an informational

---

24 This article was finalized before public information was known about Gary Urton's sexual harassment allegations. I write now to acknowledge this and apologize that I am unable to revise this to make his work less prominent. Gary Urton, *Signs of the Inka Khipu: Binary Coding in the Andean Knotted-String Records* (Austin: University of Texas Press, 2003), 1–3. See the Khipu Database project: http://khipukamayuq.fas.harvard.edu.

25 Urton, *Signs of the Inka Khipu,* 1.

26 Johanna Drucker, *Graphesis: Visual Forms of Knowledge Production* (Cambridge: Harvard University Press, 2014).

27 Dorothy Kim, "Building Pleasure and the Digital Archive," in *Bodies of Information: Intersectional Feminism and the Digital Humanities,* eds. Elizabeth Losh and Jacqueline Wernimont (Minneapolis: University of Minnesota Press, January 2019), 233.

ecosystem always in flux in which "the main question posed is how the interface iteratively and at various moments can 'enunciate' the subject/user/reader."[28]

The khipu is a digital-interactive and haptic mise-en-système informational database that requires dynamic multimodal embodied making and reading. It is already always an environment of action that at its very essence is an embodied and vibrant digital system. The khipu is created by twisting, knotting, and weaving various cotton and/or animal hair threads by hand (by human digits) in what has been called by the leading scholar on Incan Khipu as a version of "binary code." As Gary Urton explains the khipu is "a system of communication based on units of information that take the form of strings of signs or signals, each individual unit of which represents one or the other of a pair of alternative (usually opposite) identities or states."[29]

In early 2017, Sabine Hyland's *Current Anthropology* article revealed that the later khipu in the Andean village of San Juan de Collata from the seventeenth and eighteenth centuries may be evidence of a logosyllabic writing system that uses the different cords (using multiple forms of animal hair) and fourteen different colors that allow for ninety-five cord patterns to create combinations that represent syllables or words.[30] Hyland's recent research also highlights the complexities of a Native media item that has a *longue durée* history from the medieval epoch to its current use in Andean life. This, then, is a complex, iterative, ever-changing history of an Indigenous American media database. At the end of 2017, Manny Medrano, an undergraduate student at Harvard, appeared to have begun to crack the khipu

28 Kim, "Building Pleasure," 4.

29 Urton, *Signs of the Inka Khipu*, 1.

30 Sabine Hyland, "Writing with Twisted Cords: The Inscriptive Capacity of Andean Khipus," *Current Anthropology* 58, no.3 (2017): 412–19; Daniel Stone, "Discovery May Help Decipher Ancient Inca String Code," *National Geographic*, April 19, 2017, http://news.nationalgeographic.com/2017/04/inca-khipus-code-discovery-peru/.

code, which he published recently in *Ethnohistory*.[31] Urton and Medrano had compared Spanish 1670s census documents with khipus from a specific region in Peru:

> It was what the colonists referred to as a *revisita,* a reassessment of six clans living around the village of Recuay in the Santa valley region of western Peru. The document was made in the same region and at the same time as a set of six khipus in his database, so in theory it and the khipus were recording the same things.
>
> Checking it out, Urton found that there were 132 tribute payers listed in the text and 132 cords in the khipus. The fine details fitted too, with the numbers on the cords matching the charges the Spanish document said had been levelled [...]. Medrano painstakingly generated tables of the khipu data and combed through them in search of matching patterns. This year, he and Urton showed for the first time that the way pendant cords are tied onto the primary cord indicates which clan an individual belonged to.[32]

Both the two separate research discoveries on the khipu make clear that khipus do encode narrative information. Hyland explains that her khipus reveal that "This is a writing system system that is inherently three-dimensional, dependent on touch as well as sight."[33] Urton believes that the khipus may be "semasiographic, a system of symbols that convey information without being tied to a single language. In other words, they would be akin to road signs, where we all know what the symbols mean

31 Manuel Medrano and Gary Urton, "Toward the Decipherment of a Set of Mid-Colonial Khipus from the Santa Valley, Coastal Peru," *Ethnohistory* 65, no. 1 (2018): 1–23.

32 Daniel Cossins, "We Thought the Incas Couldn't Write: These Knots Change Everything," *New Scientist,* September 26, 2018, https://www.newscientist.com/article/mg23931972-600-we-thought-the-incas-couldnt-write-these-knots-change-everything/.

33 Ibid.

without having to sound anything out."[34] In other words, khipu may be a haptic, sensorial system of code.

Its media archaeology is based on the hardware of the processed weaving of animal hair ("vicuna, alpaca, guanaco, llama, deer, and the rodent vizcacha") and cotton.[35] One of the interesting questions that Urton and other khipu scholars have discussed is who actually "made" the khipu.[36] Who made the hardware of this database device and who structured its coded software? This question has vexed scholars because there is no definitive account that explains exactly who made them in the early Spanish colonial documents of South America. However, Urton highlights an illuminating passage from the account of a "seventeenth-century Augustinian friar Antonio de la Calancha" in his *Crónica moralizada del orden de San Augustín en el Perú*.[37] Calancha describes the work of a *khipukamayuq* (knot maker/record keeper/reader)[38] as follows:

> [the *khipukamayuq*] continually studied the signs, ciphers, and relations, teaching them to those who would succeed them in office, and there were many of these Secretaries, each of whom was assigned his particular class of material, having to suit [or fit] the story, tale, or song to the knots of which they served as indices, and points of "site memory" [*punto para memoria local*].[39]

The description indicates that the *khipukamayuq*'s role was that of someone who could add, subtract, read, explain, and basically do data entry for this media database; others created the physi-

---

34 Ibid.

35 Stone, "Discovery May Help Decipher Ancient Inca String Code."

36 Urton, *Signs of the Inka Khipu*, 121–25.

37 Ibid., 121.

38 Ibid., 3.

39 Ibid., 122. This is Urton's translation of Antonio de la Calancha, *Crónica moralizada del orden de San Augustín en el Perú con sucesos ejemplares en esta monarquía*, Vol. 1: *Transcripción, studio crítico, notas bibliográficas e índices de Ignacio Prado Pastor* (1638; repr. Lima: Universidad Nacional Mayor de San Marcos, 1974), 205.

cal components of the media database and also set the software encoding (the framework of knots, colors, etc.). Urton explains that explicit discussion of who created the khipu's components may have been so obvious that Spanish colonial documentary accounts do not see the need to discuss it. Andean culture had a high production and output of textiles. Women created the textiles; women would "spin, ply, dye, knot" threads.[40] And as we see in this image from Felipe Guaman Poma de Ayala's *El primer nueva coronica y buen gobierno,*[41] there were "chosen women" who spun thread. The research, though Urton and other scholars wish there was more evidence, indicates that women made both the media database's hardware (threads, weaving, etc.) and also created the software — the code itself to frame out the khipu as media database. Long before the Western European view of an interactive, multimodal database system constructed in binary code, we have the long capacious history of such a database built, designed, and produced by Native Andean women as a part of their deep textile weaving cultures.

It's from Guaman Poma de Ayala's *El primer nueva coronica,*[42] that we also have an example of how a haptic, digital interactive database mise-en-système can be translated to the European codex mise-en-page. *El primer nueva coronica*'s first written page discussing "the 'paths' of men and women in Incan society" has a mise-en-page layout that appears to be a form of intermediation. Laid out in a descending triangle at the top, Poma de Ayala appears to have "added lines [...] on the page as hanging down like cords on a khipu."[43] Thus, the directionality of media history does not move linearly in a progress model of mise-en-page to eventually mise-en-système, but rather has multiple paths and loops. In addition, Ralph Bauer's article entitled "'Writing' as

40 Urton, *Signs of the Inka Khipu,* 123.

41 Ibid., 123. The manuscript is available digitally here: http://www.kb.dk/permalink/2006/poma/info/en/frontpage.htm.

42 Holograph MS. Dates to 1615 or 1616. See Farrell, *Counting Bodies,* 21–28.

43 Ralph Bauer, "Titu Cusi Yupanqui's Account of the Conquest of Peru," in *Colonial Mediascapes,* eds. Matt Cohen and Jeffrey Glover (Lincoln: University of Nebraska Press, 2014), 338.

Khipu" argues that the book *Instrucción del Inca Don Diego de Castro Titu Cusi Yupanqui al Licenciado don Lope Garcia de Castro* — a 1571 collaboration between Titu Cusi Yupanqui (the second-to-last ruler of the Inca dynasty) and "an Augustinian monk and mestizo secretary" — exposes how Titu Cusi saw European codex-writing culture as a form of khipu. Titu Cusi also framed the Augustinian monk and mixed-race secretary as a *khipukamayuq* who could take his communication and mold it to the appropriate material and genre forms of the Spanish documentary culture.[44] These examples show that there have always been models of digital-interactive and haptic media, especially beyond the Western European models that have set up ideas of progress narratives. They also reveal that media and cultural translation is multidirectional.

Looms, Loops, Lovelace

The juxtaposition of text/textile/textuality has been an ongoing link in the histories of media communication and especially the database. It becomes the central metaphor in an English Romantic and early Victorian literary and science history. In this temporal/geographical instance, the history of databases returns to the texture of materiality and the metaphors of cloth and fabric in the form of the Jacquard loom, the figure of Ada, Countess of Lovelace, and the theorization of computational database software.

The received narrative of digital databases picks up in the late eighteenth century with the silk-weaving loom and the city of Lyon. As a recent critic of textile preservation explains: "The Loom, like the computer, uses a binary code for processing infinitely complex information."[45] The innovation that occurred in the Lyonnaise silk industry was Joseph-Marie Jacquard's refine-

44 Ibid., 325.

45 Amanda Grace Sikarskie, *Textile Collections: Preservation, Access, Curation, and Interpretation in the Digital Age* (New York: Rowan and Littlefield, 2016), 1.

ment and invention of a programmable loom in order to more quickly produce silk-jacquard fabric (i.e., brocade). This was accomplished through the use of paper punch cards that directed the loom to precisely weave the silk-jacquard fabric and changed the speed of production from two inches a day to two feet a day of material.[46] This also put many individuals out of work who previously had hand-fed the loom patterns into the loom. The Jacquard loom, invented and patented in 1801, revealed how the loom itself was the hardware of this computational system and the punch cards were the software.

In England, Charles Babbage and Ada, Countess of Lovelace both were enamored with the Jacquard loom and particularly the role of these punch cards.[47] Augusta Ada Byron (1815–1852) was the only legitimate child of the Romantic poet Lord Byron and Annabella Millbanke.

> Is thy face like thy mother's, my fair child!
> Ada! sole daughter of my house and heart?
> When last I saw thy young blue eyes they smiled,
> And then we parted, — not as now we part,
> But with a hope. —
> Awaking with a start,
> The waters heave around me; and on high
> The winds lift up their voices: I depart,
> Whither I know not; but the hour's gone by
> When Albion's lessening shores could grieve or glad mine eye.[48]

46 Ibid., 2. James Essinger, *Jacquard's Web: How a Hand-Loom Led to the Birth of the Information Age* (Oxford: Oxford University Press, 2007), 1–44.

47 James Essinger, *Ada's Algorithm: How Lord Byron's Daughter Ada Lovelace Launched the Digital Age* (Brooklyn: Melville House, 2014), 131–48.

48 Lord Byron, "Childe Harold's Pilgrimage," Canto 3, 1816. Cited from Stephen Greenblatt, ed., *The Norton Anthology of English Literature*, Vol. D: *The Romantic Period*, eds. Deidre Shauna Lynch and Jack Stillinger, 9th edn. (New York: W.W. Norton and Company, 2012), 622.

She knew her father for the first month of her life and never saw him again. Her mother raised and educated her, from all accounts, in a way to try to curb any poetic and excessively Romantic tendencies — she was instructed in the logics of math and music. She and her mother circulated amongst the London salons of Charles Babbage, a well-known scientist and inventor, whose frequent guests included a varied intellectual circle, among them the female mathematician and scientist Mary Somerville. Somerville apparently became keen on mathematics through her reading of Victorian embroidery magazines that included complex mathematical puzzles for their readers.[49] At one of Babbage's salons in June, 1833, Ada Lovelace first encountered Babbage's Difference Engine.[50] This was an automatic calculating machine powered by steam that used punch cards. She and Babbage corresponded for numerous years about their shared mathematical and scientific interests and particularly his next iteration of his steam-powered engine, the Analytical Engine. This was never produced because of the lack of financial backing, but the ideas of it were discussed and prototyped on paper. The Science Museum of London used the design schematics of the Analytic Engine and assembled one in the twenty-first century.[51] In 1843, Ada Lovelace published a translation into English from the French of the Italian engineer Luigi Menabra's explanation of Babbage's Analytical Engine. After this translation, Lovelace added a long set of translator's notes that both explained the engine but also theorized its possibilities.[52]

She writes:

> The Difference Engine can in reality (as has been already partly explained) do nothing but *add*; and any other process-

49 Essinger, *Jacquard's Web*, 127.

50 Ibid., 85.

51 Ibid., 113–30.

52 Ibid., 149–80. See also, L.F. Menabrea, "Sketch of the Analytic Engine Invented by Charles Babbage with Notes upon the Memoir by the Translator, Ada Augusta, Countess of Lovelace," *Fourmilab*, https://www.fourmilab.ch/babbage/sketch.html.

> es, not excepting those of simple subtraction, multiplication and division, can be performed by it only just to that extent in which it is possible, by judicious mathematical arrangement and artifices, to reduce them to a *series of additions.* [...] The Analytic Engine, on the contrary, can either add, subtract, multiply or divide with equal facility; and performs each of these four operations in a direct manner, without the aid of any of the other three. This one fact implies everything; and it is scarcely necessary to point out, for instance, that while the Difference Engine can merely *tabulate,* and is incapable of *developing,* the Analytic Engine can either *tabulate or develope.*[53]

The specific difference between the possibilities of the two engines are then moved into the language of textual/textile/textured metaphor when Lovelace explains:

> The distinctive characteristic of the Analytic Engine, and that which has rendered it possible to endow mechanism with such extensive faculties as bid fair to make this engine the executive right-hand of abstract algebra, is the introduction into it of the principle which Jacquard devised for regulating, by means of punched cards, the complicated patterns in the fabrication of brocaded stuffs. It is in this that the distinction between the two engines lies. Nothing of the sort exists in the Difference Engine. We may say most aptly, that the Analytical Engine *weaves algebraical patterns* just as the Jacquard-loom weaves flowers and leaves.[54]

Lovelace identifies the vision of a "programmed computer" close to one hundred years before its operational existence. She expresses this technical vision through a poetic metaphor. This poetic metaphor grounds her in what we now would identify as environmental humanities in her framing of the computa-

53 Menabrea, "Sketch of the Analytic Engine."
54 Ibid.

tional network as a natural ecosystem. In this way, her "Notes of a Translator" becomes the text where the arts collaborate with mathematical science. Her article becomes the ground from which the Western European frame of the digital database springs.

Lovelace also wrote several command sequences for the Analytic Engine and used, played, and refined several structural "tricks" — *subroutines, loops,* and *jumps* — in completing these sequences.[55] These terms and practices are standard in computational processing and particularly reference the importance of textiles and tactility in the history of computational databases. In particular, the idea of the "loop" became a way to create instructions that would allow an engine or a computer to go back and repeat a previous sequence.[56] Lovelace thus invented the computational "loop" — as Howard Rheingold explains, "the most fundamental procedure in every contemporary programming language."[57]

One of Lovelace's imagined future potentials for the Analytic Engine was that it could compose complex music. In 2015, Pip Wilcox at the Bodleian Library and a team of musicologists and computer scientists experimented with the Analytic Engine and Lovelace's interest in programming music. They ran a series of humanities "making" experiments that have involved a variety of techniques: "from a software simulator, a web app and the use of a computer algebra system, to construction of arduino micro controller hardware, agent based simulation and scripting for modern professional audio tools." [58] These experiments created an Analytical Engine soundscape through their computational

55 Howard Rheingold, "The First Programmer Was a Lady," in *Tools for Thought: The History and Future of Mind-Expanding Technology* (Cambridge: MIT Press, 2000), 35.

56 Ibid.

57 Ibid.

58 See Pip Wilcox, "Numbers into Notes — Ada Lovelace and Music," *Bodleian Digital Library,* December 14, 2015, https://blogs.bodleian.ox.ac.uk/digital/2015/12/14/numbers-into-notes-ada-lovelace-and-music/ and "Research Uncovered — The Imagination of Ada Lovelace: Creative Computing and Experimental Humanities," *Bodleian Digital Libary,*

fabrication. Steve Goodman's essay "The Ontology of Vibrational Force," in *The Sound Studies Reader,* explains that sound "comes to the rescue of thought rather than the inverse, forcing it to vibrate, loosening up its organized or petrified body."[59] This is such an experiment that makes us sensorially reevaluate the texture of the creative and technical beginnings of computational programming in relation to our contemporary bodies.

In 2015, Levi Strauss & Co. and Google collaborated to introduce a new product called Jacquard. Picking up on the history of textiles and also, one assumes, the history of computer coding, they endeavored to create a smart jacket in which conductive computer threads and textile would allow the jacket to act as a computational device.[60] It is a woven, haptic computational device, a form of wearable tech, in which touch, swipes, and other tactile actions control whether you can turn off your music, rewind, explain when you will arrive at your location, and so on. Compared to a "smart watch," the Jacquard jacket is also a woven, computational form of biometric surveillance.[61] It can pinpoint your location and, like other forms of biometric surveillance, — smartwatches, 23andMe, Facebook, etc. — can be used and is structured with toxic racism, sexism, and ableism, to name a few.[62] The history of Jacquard becomes then a history

---

January 9, 2017, https://blogs.bodleian.ox.ac.uk/digital/2017/01/09/pip-willcox/.

59 See Christopher Roman and Dorothy Kim, "Introduction: Medieval Sound," *Sounding Out!* April 4, 2016, https://soundstudiesblog.com/2016/04/04/17060/ and Steve Goodman, "The Ontology of Vibrational Force," in *The Sound Studies Reader* (New York: Routledge, 2012), 70.

60 Julian Chokkattu, "I Wore Levi's Smart Jacket for Three Months, and It Changed How I Use My Phone," *Digital Trends,* April 9, 2018, https://www.digitaltrends.com/wearables/levis-smart-jacket-changed-how-i-use-my-phone/.

61 Avi Marciano, "Reframing Biometric Surveillance: From a Means of Inspection to a Formal of Control," *Ethics and Information Technology* 21, (2019): 127–36.

62 Mark Maguire, "Biopower, Racialization and New Security Technology," *Social Identities* 18, no. 5 (2012): 593–607. See also Simone Browne, *Dark Matters.*

that weaves the agendas of surveillance states and biopower over the most vulnerable communities.

But it is Edmond Y. Chang's chapter, "Why are the Digital Humanities So Straight?" that plays, I feel most intricately, with these elements of texture/text/textile of early software computing.[63] The essay is written in code and is an actual text game that at one point asks you whether you want to play as Alan Turing, Ada Lovelace, or Purna (a character from Techland's 2011 *Dead Island* game). If you choose Ada Lovelace, you play a text game set in the "Loom Room" filled with various woven, textured, tapestry, tufted, and embroidered fabrics. And then you come upon her image created in text code. In this way, Chang's text/textual/textured essay/game performs a loop: it returns to the Jacquard loom and Charles Babbage. It loops back to the woven image of Jacquard that Babbage displayed as a curiosity for guests at his Salon — the image of Joseph-Marie Jacquard with his loom and the tools of his trade that on first glance appears to be an etching but, as Prince Albert correctly guessed, is actually a woven textile that took twenty-four thousand punch cards to create. It loops to the mathematical puzzles available in Victorian women's embroidery magazines; it returns to the "lace" in Ada's own name.[64]

If Chang's option to play Ada allows us to loop back to the history of computer software and database programming and the metaphors of gendered textile/textuality/text, it is Chang's option to play Purna, the Black female character in the 2011 zombie game *Dead Island* that reminds us exactly how racist, gendered, and oppressive systems are built into the coded machine. The game company that created *Dead Island* accidentally sent a copy of the non-retail version to Steam; a computer gamer unlocked the game's coding to find out that Purna was assigned an unlockable skill that allowed her to "deal extra damage

63 Edmond Y. Chang, "Why Are the Digital Humanities So Straight?" (this volume).

64 Menabrea, "Sketch of the Analytic Engine"; Sikarskie, *Textile Collections*, 1–10.

against male victims." In the game, it's termed "gender wars," but the code shows that it was named by the computer coders and designers "FeministWhorePurna." If you wonder why artificial-intelligence models currently are racist and sexist, you can see this as an example of how digital computational design is an extension of the bodies that create it. This is the effect of having our Digital Humanities be so white and so straight.

The creation of software to weave, loop, and link algebraic code and the computational fabrication that can turn digital computer text and schematics into musical and visual art reveal the possibilities of the computational database. But always in these often awe-inspiring, breathtaking examples are the coded ghosts in these machines. As we follow the media object and texture of the punch card, we return to Tara McPherson's question: "So if we are always already complicit with the machine, what are we to do?"[65]

We will never address our complicity unless we know and address database history.

The Story of Punch Cards: DH and Data Ethics

After the 2016 presidential election, an online petition and activist group sprung up in the tech industry. They posted a pledge to their website, "never again" (http://neveragain.tech), that began to gather signatures from tech workers in the US:

> We, the undersigned, are employees of tech organizations and companies based in the United States. We are engineers, designers, business executives, and others whose jobs include managing or processing data about people. We are choosing to stand in solidarity with Muslim Americans, immigrants, and all people whose lives and livelihoods are threatened by the incoming administration's proposed data collection policies. We refuse to build a database of people based on their Constitutionally-protected religious beliefs. We refuse to fa-

65 McPherson, "Why Are the Digital Humanities So White?"

> cilitate mass deportations of people the government believes to be undesirable.
>
> We have educated ourselves on the history of threats like these, and on the roles that technology and technologists played in carrying them out. We see how IBM collaborated to digitize and streamline the Holocaust, contributing to the deaths of six million Jews and millions of others. We recall the internment of Japanese Americans during the Second World War. We recognize that mass deportations precipitated the very atrocity the word genocide was created to describe: the murder of 1.5 million Armenians in Turkey. We acknowledge that genocides are not merely a relic of the distant past — among others, Tutsi Rwandans and Bosnian Muslims have been victims in our lifetimes.
>
> Today we stand together to say: not on our watch, and never again.[66]

This pledge makes clear a central and salient point in the field of digital humanities: Bodies are a form of data; data is always embodied. However, these individual pledges related to data ethics also highlight an ongoing discussion in digital studies. Safiya Noble and Lisa Nakamura both have recently discussed the issue of using "ethics" to prioritize individual behavior over community- and group-based social change at the recent Digital Democracies.[67] They both point out that we must move beyond ideas of individual ethics or having the digital teach people "ethics" and toward a more politicized movement that

66 "Our Pledge," *neveragain.tech*, http://neveragain.tech/.

67 "Digital Democracies," *Simon Fraser University*, http://www.sfu.ca/digital-democracies/2019-conference.html. Lisa Nakamura discusses empathy, ethics, and VR games: "VR 2.0 imagines it can be a 'racial empathy machine; by trespassing with a camera in poor and minoritized peoples' space. What it produces is a 'toxic re-embodiment' of 'virtue' and 'pleasurable pain' #digidemsfu #digitaldemocracies" (@kglynes (Krista Lynes), *Twitter*, May 18, 2010, 7:06AM, https://twitter.com/kglynes/status/1129750201353342976). See also Safiya Noble's remarks, well summarized here: @tanbob (Dr. Tannis Morgan), *Twitter*, May 21, 2019, 10:18AM, https://twitter.com/tanbob/status/1130885554462003200.

organizes, protests, and fights to dismantle the terrible violence of digital technology and the tech industry. In fact, this is what Safiya Noble's project, *Truth in Tech,* appears to be working on.[68]

However, these issues of tech as a tool of targeted and systematic violence have much longer histories. What powered the Third Reich's ability to automate the Holocaust was IBM's Hollerith punch-card machine. IBM's Hollerith punch-card platform was a technology of what Simone Browne defines as "racializing surveillance": "when enactments of surveillance reify boundaries, borders, and bodies along racial lines, and where the outcome is often discriminatory treatment of those who are negatively racialized by such surveillance."[69] The Hollerith punch-card system was invented and then first used as a mass data processing platform to tabulate the 1890 US census. Herman Hollerith's Tabulating Machine Company would eventually become the International Business Machines Corporation when Hollerith sold the company to Charles Flint in 1911 and Thomas J. Watson became its CEO. Thomas J. Watson is the figure that is intimately involved in both the Third Reich's automation of the Holocaust and the first purported "DH project."[70]

In numerous digital humanities collections — *A Handbook for the Digital Humanities, Defining Digital Humanities, Debates in the Digital Humanities*[71] — "the history of humanities computing" has been described as one that "dates back to the 1940s and the work of Father Roberto Busa, an Italian Jesuit priest who launched a tool to perform text searches of St. Thomas

68 *The Truth in Tech Initiative,* https://truthintechinitiative.org

69 Browne, *Dark Matters,* 16.

70 Edwin Black, *IBM and the Holocaust: The Strategic Alliance between Nazi Germany and America's Most Powerful Corporation* (New York: Three Rivers Press, 2001), 26, 30–40.

71 See Susan Schreibman, Ray Siemens, and John Unsworth, eds., *A Companion to the Digital Humanities, Blackwell Companions to Literature and Culture* (Malden: Blackwell Publishing, 2004); Melissa Terras, Julianne Nyhan, and Edward Vanhoutte, eds., *Defining Digital Humanities: A Reader* (New York: Routledge, 2013); and Matthew K. Gold and Lauren F. Klein, *Debates in the Digital Humanities* (Minneapolis: University of Minnesota Press, 2016).

Aquinas's oeuvre."[72] Though this genealogical history has been one of the centers of DH historiographies, I want to reconsider the geopolitical history occurring at this time in Europe. Father Busa's vision for a digital *Index Thomisticus* was helped by development, funding, training, and technical support from IBM starting in 1949. But it also began as a dissertation project written during WWII in Italy; "up until the end of 1945," Busa worked on Thomas Aquinas's philosophical texts "surrounded by bombings, Germans, partisans, poor food and disasters of all sorts."[73] IBM sponsored this early Humanities Computing project for several decades. As Busa himself describes the project, it began with the punch-card system developed by IBM: "I was given an IBM 858 Cardatype, which was a kind of a transitional link between unit record and data processing machines."[74] In fact, the most recent book that has delved into this early historiography of DH has called it *The Priest and the Punched Cards*.[75]

To understand how Father Busa's *Index Thomisticus* is linked to the Third Reich's data management of the Holocaust, you have to understand how the Hollerith machine and the IBM 858 Cardatype are basically the same computational platform, which developed from 1933 into the 1950s.[76] In addition, as Arun Jacob's chapter, "Punching Holes in the International Busa Machine Narrative," explains, Busa was a chaplain in Mussolini's fascist Italian army from 1940–43 and seemed to be working on his project on earlier IBM machines, before the availability of

72 Adeline Koh, "Niceness, Building, and Opening the Genealogy of the Digital Humanities: Beyond the Social Contract of Humanities Computing," *differences: A Journal of Feminist Cultural Studies* 25, no. 1: 95.

73 R. Busa, "The Annals of Humanities Computing: The Index Thomisticus," *Computers and the Humanities* 14 (1980): 83.

74 Ibid., 84.

75 Steven E. Jones, *Roberto Busa, S.J., and the Emergence of Humanities Computing: The Priest and the Punched Cards* (New York: Routledge, 2016).

76 See Black, *IBM and the Holocaust*; Jones, *The Priest and the Punched Cards*; and James Essinger, *Jacquard's Web: How a Hand-Loom Led to the Birth of the Information Age* (Oxford: Oxford University Press, 2007), 149–204.

the 858 Cardatype (1955).[77] And in analyzing Busa's own writing about how he created the database for his *Index Thomisticus*, Jacob points to this passage from Busa's discussion of how he decided to use this platform in a 1980 article:

> Although some say that I am the pioneer of the computers in the humanities, such a title needs a good deal of nuancing […] [O]n the stacks of the IBM library in New York City I had spotted a book (whose title I have forgotten), which was printed some time between 1920 and 1940: in it someone mentioned that it was possible to make lists of names by means of punched cards.[78]

Jacob persuasively argues that this book was probably the work of Gustav Tauschek, an Austrian engineer, who in 1928 patented a "a punched-card multiplier." He worked for IBM from 1931–35 during which time IBM also acquired a number of his patents. Tauschek's previous patents for Rheinmetall (formerly known as Rheinische Metallwaaren- und Maschinenfabrik AG) would be bought by Dehomag, the German IBM subsidiary. Thus, the book that Busa was discussing was probably the work in which Tauschek explains how a punch-card accounting machine could work to process massive amounts of named data.[79] Thus, the database model from which Busa created the *Index Thomisticus* was based on the media hardware and process that would become the IBM machines that powered the Jewish Holocaust.

Though this chapter is currently an examination that foregrounds the methods of media archaeology, I would also like to acknowledge that the work of Holocaust historians have made clear the stakes of Holocaust historiography in the discussion of

77 Arun Jacob, "Punching Holes in the International Busa Machine Narrative" (this volume).

78 R. Busa, "The Annals of Humanities Computing: The Index Thomisticus," *Computers and the Humanities* 14, no. 2 (1980): 83.

79 Jacob, "Punching Holes in the International Busa Machine Narrative."

ethics, media, and the potential and pitfalls of the comparative method.[80] As Kantsteiner and Presner have explained:

> Today it is a given that the scholarly perception of Nazism and the Holocaust is deeply connected to shifting political landscapes, historical contexts, and cultural values. To understand how this came to be, we might cast a gaze backward. Almost immediately after World War II, global power brokers deployed two transnational, political master narratives to craft meaningful connections between the Nazi past and the Cold War present: Marxism-Leninsim in the East and antitotalitarianism in the West. The two narrative worlds featured dictators, Nazi thugs, heroic resistance fighters, morally unblemished soldiers, evil capitalists, and suffering civilians. Yet neither master narrative acknowledged Jewish victimhood.[81]

Kantsteiner and Presner also point to the media's deep entanglement and embeddedness in the historiographic project. They highlight the fact that the centering of Jewish Holocaust victims first became a priority not in academic circles but in media representations on television, and this began with the 1978 NBC miniseries *Holocaust*.[82] Scholarly debates circled around two paradigms that did not center Jewish victims: "intentionalism and structuralism/functionalism."[83] However, it was Saul Friedlander's work in 1998 and 2007 that centered Holocaust victims as the foundation of a Holocaust historiography.[84] This ongoing discussion in Holocaust historiography is also balanced with the work of Hayden White, who advocates for historians as "ethi-

80 Wulf Kantsteiner and Todd Presner, "The Field of Holocaust Studies and the Emergence of Global Holocaust Culture," in *Notes from Probing the Ethics of Holocaust Culture*, eds. Claudio Fogu, Wulf Kansteiner, and Todd Presner (Cambridge: Harvard University Press, 2016).

81 Ibid., 5.

82 Ibid., 7–8.

83 Ibid., 8.

84 Ibid., 10–12.

cal storytellers."[85] This historiographic discussion has a similar trajectory in the priorities and discussions of Black feminist historians and cultural scholars of the transatlantic slave trade. In the foundational work of Saidiya Hartman (*Scenes of Subjection: Terror, Slavery, and Self-Making in Nineteenth-Century America* and "Venus in Two Acts"),[86] similar issues related to the ethics of historiography and the place of individual men, women, and children in the narrative of history are also discussed as a deep-seated issue of methodology.

Kantsteiner and Presner organized a conference and edited a subsequent volume that caused complexity and intellectual friction in Holocaust historiography, which speaks to another media shift that has deeply affected the field. Thus, they write:

> Depending on one's perspective, the crisis of history either never happened or is hardly over and might only be addressed by techniques of representation coming from domains such as literature and the arts. But what neither camp could anticipate in 1990 were the new epistemological and ethical challenges of comparison and scale posed by popular memory cultures, globalization, and the digitization of the Holocaust.[87]

This issue of scale in relation to digitization looks back to a historiographic thread that Kantsteiner and Presner point to as a bedrock discussion in Jewish history: "Another risk is the quantification of the Holocaust in ways that replicate or abstract the victims' lives and partake in the same rationalized logic of modernity that Zygmunt Bauman identified in his seminal work,

---

85 Ibid., 12.

86 Saidiya Hartman, *Scenes of Subjection: Terror, Slavery, and Self-Making in Nineteenth-Century America* (Oxford: Oxford University Press, 1997) and Saidiya Hartman, "Venus in Two Acts," *Small Axe* 12, no. 2 (2008): 1–14.

87 Wulf Kantsteiner and Todd Presner, "The Field of Holocaust Studies and the Emergence of Global Holocaust Culture," in *Notes from Probing the Ethics of Holocaust Culture*, eds. Claudio Fogu, Wulf Kansteiner, and Todd Presner (Cambridge: Harvard University Press, 2016), 21–22.

Modernity and the Holocaust, as the condition of possibility for genocide, namely, the impulse to quantify, modularize, distantiate, and technify."[88] This latter discussion lays the groundwork for what we begin to see as a media archaeology of the genealogy of the digital database. The latter part of this essay hews closer to media archaeology and surveillance studies methodologies that think through how intention, structure, media intimacy, and complicity create systems of violence on marginal communities. In this way, it follows in Noble's work in *Algorithms of Oppression* in focusing on the database, digital, and computational systems that have structured racialized, religious violence.

When one examines the media archaeology of the Holocaust, what jumps out is its incredible intimacy. In 1933, for the Third Reich to begin its first major census (primarily to identify a range of unwanted bodies in Germany and especially to identify Jewish bodies), it contracted with IBM Germany (Dehomag), Deutsche Hollerith-Maschinen Gesellschaft mbH, for a data system to complete this task. The scope of this census and later ones included not just name, age, and gender, but also religion, race, and disability information; it eventually included medical information, genealogical information pulled from church registries and baptismal books, financial information from banks (since they all used Dehomag), and also school test scores. This allowed the Third Reich, after the first census in 1933, to begin forced sterilization for the health and well-being of the population and to start the process of attempting to biologically engineer a superior Aryan race.[89] The DEHOMAG Hollerith punch-card-machine platform allowed the Third Reich to create an early version of Haggerty and Ericson's "surveillant assemblage" in which "the surveillant assemblage sees the observed human body 'broken down by being abstracted from its territorial setting' and then reassembled elsewhere…" and in this case into

88 Ibid., 32. See Zygmunt Bauman, *Modernity and the Holocaust* (Ithaca: Cornell University Press, 1989).

89 Black, *IBM and the Holocaust,* 52–74, 89–96, 113–18.

a punch-card computational database.[90] Thus, the industrial textile code, as understood through the punch card, transforms from the Jacquard loom, to a Victorian imagined computational database, to the first series of "surveillant assemblages" in the creation of the US census database, and finally travels back to Europe for its devastating use in the Third Reich.

IBM's worldwide policies were to never sell machines, but always to lease them, lease the parts, manufacture specific materials (i.e. punch cards themselves) for the machine, and customize everything to each customer's specific projects and goals.[91] Thus, the IBM Hollerith platform for the Third Reich was custom designed and continuously upgraded, developed, and expanded for the specifications of their largest clients. IBM would create separate, specific systems from its Hollerith machine platform to design, among other things, the systematic inventory of Luftwaffe war machine parts; the entire German railroad system and its schedules and cargo; and the registration, identification, sorting, and genocide of the Jews in Germany and eventually all other invaded territories.[92] IBM didn't just supply machines and punch cards, they were intimately involved in creating and designing the entire database from the ground up.[93] They worked on each project to decide what fields would be programmed on the punch card itself, including what to use in its sixty-column-by-ten-horizontal-field format. This allowed for six hundred "punch hole possibilities" and thus an endless combination of information: biology, disability, location, genealogy, race, physical characteristics, income, profession, family members, and so on.[94]

As with the standard in the history of early computer science and computation, the bulk of the people working, fine-tuning, and processing the data were women. Thus, for example, with the first 1933 Nazi census, Dehomag used a Berlin employment

90 Browne, *Dark Matters*, 16.

91 Black, *IBM and the Holocaust*, 52–168.

92 Ibid., 87–101, 174–86.

93 Ibid., 49–50, 115.

94 Ibid., 56–59.

agency linked to the German Labor Front, a group known for its radical Nazi leanings. They used Nazi patriotism in their job call for these first positions.[95] They hired over nine hundred women and trained them in a two-week data processing immersion course. These women punched in data from handwritten census questionnaires, and then they would "sort," "tabulate," "verify," cross-reference and complete other data processing tasks.[96] They were thus writing computational code when they translated written census questionnaires into punch-card code. There has been much work in the history of computer science to begin to acknowledge and elevate the women who were so integral to this field — this includes Ada Lovelace, the Bletchley Hall women in WWII, and even more recently the book and movie *Hidden Figures* that discusses the African American women computers of NASA. However, less discussed is what I would call the alt-feminism or Nazi-feminism of this history.[97]

Likewise, the punch cards were not a sturdy, easily acquired, or stable material. Because of the "delicacy" of each Hollerith machine, the punch cards had precise material, dimensional, and other specifications:

> Because electrical current in the machines sensed the rectangular holes, even a microscopic imperfection would make the card inoperable and could foul up the entire works.
>
> So IBM production specifications were rigorous. Coniferous chemical pulp was milled, treated, and cured to create paper stock containing no more than 5 percent ash, and devoid of ground wood, calk fibers, processing chemi-

95 Ibid., 56.

96 Ibid.

97 Flavia Dzodan, "The New Alt-Feminisim: When White Supremacy Met Women's Empowerment," *Medium*, January 5, 2017, https://medium.com/this-political-woman/the-new-alt-feminism-when-white-supremacy-met-womens-empowerment-b978b088db33. See also Jessie Daniels, "Rebekah Mercer Is Leading an Army of Alt-Right Women," *Dame*, September 26, 2017, https://www.damemagazine.com/2017/09/26/rebekah-mercer-leading-army-alt-right-women/.

> cals, slime carbon, or other impurities that might conduct electricity and "therefore cause incorrect machine sensing." Residues, even in trace amounts, would accumulate on gears and other mechanisms, eventually causing jams and system shutdowns. Electrical testing to isolate defective sheets was mandatory. Paper, when cut, had to lie flat without curl or wrinkle, and feature a hard, smooth finish on either side that yielded a "good snap or rattle."
>
> Tolerances necessitated laboratory-like mill conditions. Paper thickness: .0067 inches plus or minus only a microscopic .0005 inch. Width: 3.25 inches with a variance of plus .007 inches or minus .003 inches. Two basic lengths were produced: 5.265 inches and 7.375 inches, plus or minus only .005 inch in either case. Edges were to be cut at true right angles, corners at perfect 60 degree angles, with a quarter-inch along the top and three-eighths along the side, all free from blade creases with paper grain running the length of the card. Relative humidity of 50 percent and a temperature of 70–75 degrees Fahrenheit was required at all times, including transport and storage.[98]

IBM had a monopoly on the cards and at various points during the 30s and 40s, one-third of their revenue came from the sale of cards used in data processing.[99] The cards are a form of media archaeology and what they tell us about this computational processing platform is that it needed a lot of bodies and hands for it to work efficiently. These were always bespoke computation systems that required constant hands-on maintenance as well as a satellite of manufacturing units nearby that produced both the parts and the cards themselves. The people who designed, built, ran, and maintained these machines were intimately involved in what these machines were built to do. This was not abstract or distance data processing. And Dehomag clearly knew that they had created a total and racialized surveillance system of the

98 Black, *IBM and the Holocaust*, 97.
99 Ibid., 98.

Third Reich's population. They even used it to advertise their services by referencing the media material itself that made it possible — the punch card.[100]

The Hollerith system was an intimate, hands-on, labor-intensive data processing method. This meant that there were also Hollerith systems at various strengths, types, and vintage at concentration camps throughout the Reich.[101] And it's with the example of Auschwitz that I would like to end this section because it makes so explicitly clear how much data itself is about explicit and implicit embodiment.

Starting in 1933 and with every subsequent census and then annexation of more European territory, the Hollerith system gave each Jew a number which then allowed them to be tracked throughout its system. Recently, documents have been unearthed at Auschwitz that definitively show that the Hollerith numbers were tattooed on the Auschwitz Jews during the summer of 1943, though tattooing numbers would branch into different systems afterward.[102] This is a horrific example of "biometric identification" and an example of what Browne, Haggerty, and Ericson explain as "the markings of the surveillant assemblages, that reduce flesh to pure information."[103]

Thus, Hollerith card information was tattooed on the flesh. As archivists have recently discovered, this means that there was an IBM customer site at the concentration camp. The customer site was a huge I.G. Farben factory complex in the Monowitz concentration camp. It ran all the three major areas of Auschwitz: Auschwitz I, the camp that dealt with "transit, labor, and dentention"; Auschwitz II, also known as Birkenau, where extermination happened in gas chambers and ovens; and Aus-

100 Ibid., 98–104.

101 Ibid., 351–52.

102 Ibid., 351–74. Edwin Black, "Infamous Auschwitz Tattoo Began as an IBM Number," *History News Network*, July 28, 2008, http://historynewsnetwork.org/article/52879; Steven E. Jones, *Roberto Busa, S.J., and the Emergence of Humanities Computing: The Priest and the Punch Cards* (New York: Routledge, 2016), 10.

103 Browne, *Dark Matters*, 26.

chwitz III, known as Monowitz, which was the slave labor camp. The size of this particular IBM center in Auschwitz would have included a dozen punching machines, a sorter, and one tabulator. The bodies needed to run the data processing would have amounted to approximately thirty to forty women along with their German supervisors.[104]

If IBM's participation in helping to create an indexing program for Thomas Aquinas's data is one genealogy in DH, the entwined genealogy also occurring in the 1940s is IBM's negotiations with the Third Reich to use theHollerith punch-card machine to automate the process of identifying Jews in census data, registration forms, and government records, which allowed Germany to manage and automate the Holocaust, to in essence create a genocidal racialized surveillant assemblage.

As medieval graphesis[105] (visualization of knowledge) and twelfth-century scholastic university education invented and refined the forms of the index, concordance, and table of contents, there is a rather disquieting and discomforting appropriateness to this uncanny medieval/modern digital history. This entangled Jewish/Christian history underscores the ethics of data and the devastation, destruction, and horror of computational data that fueled the birth of humanities computing. Todd Presner writes about the intertwined issues of ethics in digital humanities and Jewish studies in his article, "The Ethics of the Algorithm: Close and Distant Listening to the Shoah Foundation Visual History Archive."[106] Presner references IBM and the Hollerith punch-card machine to foreground a discussion of Holocaust digital projects and what he discusses as the limits and possibilities of the algorithm. In essence, IBM's collaboration with the Third Reich and its refinement of computational census processing "invented the racial census — listing not just

104 Black, "Infamous Nazi Tattoo Began as an IBM Number."

105 See Drucker, *Graphesis*.

106 Todd Pressner, "The Ethics of the Algorithm: Close and Distant Listening to the Shoah Foundation Visual History Archive," in *Probing the Ethics of Holocaust Culture*, eds. Claudio Fogu, Wulf Kansteiner, and Todd Presner (Cambridge: Harvard University Press, 2016), 175–202.

religious affiliation, but bloodlines going back generations [...]. Not just to count the Jews — but to *identify* them."[107] In this case, the beginning of humanities computing, the beginning of the computational algorithm that led to Busa's *Index Thomisticus*, was so efficient and complete as a database system — it exterminated millions of European Jews. Thus, the first big data project in the digital humanities was a project of racial and religious genocide.

Busa, Bombs, DARPA

In 1949, Thomas J. Watson met Robert Busa in New York, and Busa convinced him to give both technical and financial support to build an *index verborum* (an index of words) for the entire Latin corpus of Thomas Aquinas, a thirteenth-century century Italian theologian,[108] which constituted a "massive lemmatized concordance [...] of St. Thomas Aquinas."[109] This relation lasted several decades. There were several options when Busa decided to work through his *Index* with computation methods, one of them was the punch-card system, but he had other options including Vannaver Bush's Rapid Selector. In the end, he chose the Cardatype and punch-card systems. IBM helped him customize, set up, and equip his project in a former cloth factory in Gallarate, Italy. (This is also a loop and a return to the media database's textile/textual roots.) They helped him create, run, and fund a literary data processing center that was established in 1956 (CAAL). He had a cadre of young Catholic women who became his data processing operators and did the hands-on, meticulous processing, calibrating, and data work. This early computer coding history has recently been highlighted in articles by Melissa Terras, Julianne Nyhan, and more.[110]

---

107 Black, *IBM and the Holocaust*, 10.

108 Jones, *The Priest and the Punched Cards*, 2.

109 Ibid., 1–2.

110 Ibid., 18–20, 39–42. Melissa Terras and Julianne Nyhan, "Father Busa's Female Punch Card Operatives," in *Debates in the Digital Humanities*, ed.

The origin myth of DH has always gone back to this story of a priest getting the IBM CEO to fund and technically support a digital medievalism project.[111] Yet, what does not get so frequently discussed is that Busa also worked for the Department of Defense from around 1956 to the early 60s. Busa not only received money from the Italian government but also from Euratom, the European Atomic Energy Community, when he brokered a deal to work on an Anglo-Russian project with Georgetown Linguistics Professor Leon Dostert for the Defense Advanced Projects Research Agency (DARPA) at the Pentagon. This Anglo-Russian project sought to find ways to machine translate. But Busa was not machine translating Latin, he was trying to find ways to machine translate Cyrillic and Russian science abstracts into English. Usually these were physics abstracts and thus related to the nuclear arms race. The military-industrial complex, the frames of the Cold War, and what that means to data and the development of DH needs to be an integral part of the field's origin story.[112]

As the DH account @DHDarksider once tweeted, "Robert Busa wasn't merely the first DH enthusiast. He was the first in a long line of enthusiasts working for The Man."[113] In this case, Busa did not just work for one of the most powerful business figures in the first half of the twentieth century — a figure with documented examples of massive war profiteering and intimate involvement in the data processing machinery that made the Holocaust so total and so efficient — he also worked for the Pentagon, the other Man of the American mid century.

DARPA was created in 1958 by Congress as a branch of the Department of Defense. Its mission is to "create revolutions in military science and to maintain technological dominance over

Matthew K. Gold (Minneapolis: University of Minnesota Press, 2016), available online at http://dhdebates.gc.cuny.edu/debates/text/57.

111 Jones, *The Priest and the Punched Cards,* 27–51.

112 Ibid., 11–12, 111–12.

113 Jones, *The Priest and the Punchcard,* 10; @DHDarkSider (DH Dark Sider), *Twitter,* July 18, 2014, 6:14AM.

the rest of the world."[114] It is not an in-house research development agency but rather it "hire[s] defense contractors, academics, and other government units to do the work."[115] It powered the research and continual creation of nuclear warfare, which was the focus of its developmental interests in the 50s and 60s. It is considered either the "pentagon's brain" or the "heart of the military-industrial complex."[116] It is one of the most mysterious and most independent units of the government. The good PR that DARPA promulgates points out it created the Internet, GPS, and "stealth technology."[117] Among other things, it began creating drones during the Vietnam War that it finally armed effectively during the war in Afghanistan in 2001.[118]

The women were customizing Latin, Hebrew, and Cyrillic to code at CAAL for Busa. In the case of the Hebrew, this was work on the Dead Sea Scrolls. However, this meant Busa was working with other Catholic priests to shut out Jewish scholars from accessing the Dead Sea Scrolls.[119] Thus, they, too, are part of DH's hidden history, a hidden history that includes an army of Catholic women coders, data processors, and workers doing the hands-on, meticulous, and customized work of a humanities database project, as well as working on the Cold War nuclear

114 Annie Jacobsen, *The Pentagon's Brain: An Uncensored History of DARPA, America's Top-Secret Military Research Agency* (New York: Back Bay Books, 2015), 5.

115 Ibid.

116 Ibid., 7

117 Ibid., 6.

118 Ibid., 248–50.

119 See Hershel Shanks, "The Dead Sea Scroll Monopoly," *Washington Post,* October 8, 1991, https://www.washingtonpost.com/archive/opinions/1991/10/08/the-dead-sea-scroll-monopoly/8e1e4100-4c5f-4bcc-8c96-07c7d9a5993d/; John Noble Wilford, "Monopoly Over Dead Sea Scrolls Is Ended," *New York Times,* September 22, 1991, https://www.nytimes.com/1991/09/22/us/monopoly-over-dead-sea-scrolls-is-ended.html; and Batya Ungar-Sargon, "Dead Sea Scrolls Go To Court," *Tablet,* January 14, 2013, https://www.tabletmag.com/jewish-arts-and-culture/books/121361/dead-sea-scrolls-go-to-court. My thanks to Lynn Kaye (Brandeis University) for pointing me to this scholarly narrative in regards to the post-WWII work done on the Dead Sea Scrolls.

arms race. As we saw in the Third Reich, this was an intimate task that meant building database systems and machine interfaces from the ground up for each project and constantly reprogramming the punch-card fields for the specific frames of each humanities project.

I would like to finish this portion of my article considering how the Trump administration has commemorated National Holocaust Remembrance Day since 2017; this is particularly fresh as we witnessed the massacre at the Pittsburgh synagogue in Squirrel Hill.[120] The White House did this, from the playbook of Breitbart and the white nationalists, by erasing Jews. Let us not re-enact a similar erasure by failing to confront what the origins of one genealogical branch of the DH reveal. The digital humanities have always had the capacity for untold harm; "big data," from its earliest inception, has always meant that the most marginalized have been targeted, deported, sterilized, and killed. The digital and embodied database, when created and used, has always been political. If we are to think about how to shape the digital humanities, it must be with social justice and the ethics of data at its center.

The "never again" petition is an example of a recent upsurge in the centralization of digital data and social justice activism. We have recently seen people helping to archive the White House pages for the Internet Archive, the extraction and removal of all the data related to climate change moved out of the US, and even government agencies refusing to hand over data to the Trump administration as a form of ethical protest. We have heard calls to erase the data of DACA students who had voluntarily turned in their information for registry during the Obama administration. And we have watched librarians, scientists, and other information workers save the endangered data from being erased by our current government or map all the locations

120 Paul Krause, "The Squirrel Hill Massacre. The Squirrel Hill Idyll. It's Complicated," *Pittsburgh Post-Gazette*, November 11, 2018, https://www.post-gazette.com/opinion/Op-Ed/2018/11/11/div-class-libPageBodyLinebreak-The-Squirrel-Hill-massacre-br-The-Squirrel-Hill-idyll-br-It-s-complicated-br-div/stories/201811110009.

of government detention camps throughout the US. I wonder, then, have we hit another critical turn in the digital humanities?

Again, how do we answer Tara McPherson's question: "So if we are always already complicit with the machine, what are we to do?"

Designing Mechanisms of Complicity and "Train"

One answer to this question is to consider if there are ways to use the machine to underscore the ethical lesson of the Third Reich's use of it for racialized genocide. I look to Brenda Romero's work in *The Mechanic is the Message.*[121] In this series, analog games are also forms of "conceptual art."[122] Romero, a major feminist game pioneer, attempts to work through the experience of complicity that harnesses the mechanics of the game to make players face ethical, social, and often devastating complicity in various catastrophic world tragedies all linked to various kinds of racial and religious discrimination. In particular, I want to turn my attention to *Train.* All of Romero's games — she has finished *The New World* (about the Middle Passage), *The Irish Game* (about Cromwell's conquest of Ireland and his slaughter of the Irish), *One Falls for Each of Us* (about the Trail of Tears), and *Train,* and she is currently prototyping *Mexican Kitchen Workers* (which is about undocumented kitchen workers) — are not for the public buying market, and there is only one copy of each game, which she keeps in her home. She personally constructs these analog games which often means she paints the parts individually, she builds certain props, and she brings personal items into this game world. She — like the punch card operators — has an intimate relationship with the material and structural parts of this game mechanism.

Train usually is played in organized events at universities and in art museums as a hybrid game/art installation. She has spo-

121 Brenda Romero, "Work," *Brenda Romero,* http://www.blromero.com/work-1/.

122 Brian Upton, *The Aesthetic of Play* (Cambridge: MIT Press, 2015), 269.

ken about *Train* in video talks; there is extensive media coverage of *Train,* and a couple of videos that document groups playing *Train* at individual events. Otherwise, one cannot actually examine the game unless you have seen it being played or have researched it through the filters of accounts vis-à-vis video, articles, and personal conversation with witnesses.[123] *Train* is set up with three railroad tracks on top of a white framed window, with a black Nazi typewriter at one end, and several trains and numerous wooden yellow figures. The rules of the game are placed in the typewriter.

As Brian Upton explains, "The object" of *Train* "is to load small yellow pawns into boxcars and move as many of them as one can along the tracks to their final destinations. Initially, players aren't given any context for these actions — the game presents itself simply as a logistical challenge. Only when the first boxcar arrives and the 'Auschwitz' card is revealed does the metaphoric significance of their earlier moves become apparent."[124] Upton further explains that what makes this game a "work of art is how the rules are constructed. Romero has created a set of rules that are deliberately broken. They contain strange contradictions and ambiguities. Players are forced to come up with their own negotiated interpretations as they play."[125] Several different plays of the game have resulted in different actions by the players. Some have immediately — upon seeing the set-up — refused to play and so the game ends. Others have only realized after the first

123 My thanks to Brian Upton for telling me about what he saw when watching "Train" and particularly about the broken rules in the typewriter. See also Stephen Totilo, "How People Played a Holocaust Game," *Kotaku,* December 14, 2010, http://kotaku.com/5713483/how-people-played-a-holocaust-game; Jamin Brophy-Warren, "The Board Game No One Wants to Play More Than Once," *Speakeasy, The Wall Street Journal,* June 24, 2009, https://blogs.wsj.com/speakeasy/2009/06/24/can-you-make-a-board-game-about-the-holocaust-meet-train/; and Brenda Brathwaite, "How I Dumped Electricity and Learned to Love Design," paper presentation, The Game Developers Conference Austin/Online 2009, http://www.gdcvault.com/play/1012259/Train-.

124 Upton, *The Aesthetic of Play,* 269.

125 Ibid.

card is read and then spend the rest of the game finding ways to sabotage the game: players have derailed trains, released the yellow figures, or hidden the figures so that the trains arrive to their destination without any bodies. Romero described that she had one group with a particularly competitive player that actually became swept up in the play of the game who finished the game by delivering all their Jewish bodies to various concentration camps. This group broke down after the game was "won" by the one competitive player. They began a series of angry recriminations towards this one player that reverberated well past the end of the game. This game and its effects are thus, "portable" they go beyond the space of the game itself.[126]

Visually, several players have immediately identified the objects of *Train* as part of the Holocaust. The glass in the window eventually got smashed entirely by one player; the window signifies Kristallnacht. The Nazi typewriter links *Train* to the Hollerith punch-card machine and its deadly efficiency. She also used difficult-sized yellow pawns so that loading these bodies onto the train cars required player discomfort and hardship. What Romero has structured in her game design/conceptual art piece is the story of complicity. She's used the difficulty, horror, excruciating discomfort, and the legible narrative of that complicity to force her players to confront their place in violent systems and regimes. The fascinating side effect to this game is that it then forces players to stretch their ethical empathy.

So to answer Tara McPherson's question: "So if we are always already complicit with the machine, what are we to do?"

I would answer, we center that difficult feeling and narratives of complicity and we turn our labors to resist. And in the example of Romero's train, we can see how the design of a game system can help change the stakes of a player/user/reader's ethical engagement in the devastating politics of our world. We design our computational databases, data, algorithms, and systems with the centrality of justice, with an understanding of our complicity, with reminder of our field's terrible histories.

126 Brenda Brathwaite, "How I Dumped Electricity."

Database Design and Centering the Marginal Reader

Because it is an interactive narrative play system, one of the standard tenets in digital and video game design is that you always build for the player. Likewise, in interactive DH database and archive projects, we always design for the purported public audience. But which player/user/reader bodies are we centering in this design and building? Databases are not neutral because audiences themselves are not neutral. Our scholarly database design privileges an imagined universal community of white, male, benign, and benevolent audience members. This is also the case for our data, our algorithms, and our computer languages, which have always been touted as something "universal" and "for all" but are really designed for "the man." I would argue, that the "universal" audience is one linked to the white male enlightened subject. Yet, as the work of biopolitics and particularly as Sylvia Wynters and Alexander Weheliye discuss, which bodies matter? In Alexander Weheliye's *Habeas Viscus: Racializing Assemblages, Biopolitics, and Black Feminist Theories of the Human,* he articulates a biopolitics filtered through Black feminism that decenters whiteness and centralizes race in this discussion. Weheliye describes the Black studies and Black feminist intervention in biopolitics. Based on Sylvia Wynters work, he explains that race is not "biological" or "cultural" but rather a "conglomerate of sociopolitical relations that discipline humanity into full humans, not-quite-humans, and nonhumans."[127] In essence, then, race is a political system that orders which bodies matter and encompasses both the sociocultural and biopolitical discussions of those bodies. Weheliye particularly critiques the discourses around biopolitics and bare life to explicate how much they have disregarded critical race studies in relation to thinking about the category of "human" and imagines a univer-

127 See Alexander G. Weheliye, *Habeas Viscus: Racializing Assemblages, Biopolitics, and Black Feminist Theories of the Human* (Durham: Duke University Press, 2014) and Katherine McKittrick, *Sylvia Wynter: On Being Human as Praxis* (Durham: Duke University Press, 2015).

sal biological substance that is separate from race. Weheliye's and Wynters's work puts pressure on us to center marginal communities and marginal bodies when we build our databases. We must ask which bodies matter and what happens if we center the most intersectional and vulnerable bodies in our digital scholarly work? Who gets to be human?

There is also another urgency to center the most marginal bodies as the imagined audience community for our digital humanities databases, projects, and archives. In literary studies, two theories of textual reading—reader-response theory and reception theory, have had a long and deep history.[128] I can point to the scribbled marginalia of medieval readers often on the side margins of manuscripts and to the opening of section of Samuel Purchas's "To the Reader" to illustrate the length of this history. Both these literary theories focus on how readers individually interpret literary works. My focus in bringing together racialized biopolitics and reader-response and historical reception theories is to examine how both critical race studies and critical whiteness studies will change our digital design decisions. Though we have theorized and considered the worlds of the "resistant" or even "suspicious" reader, we are at a critical juncture where we must address the place and decide our engagement with (or disengagement from) the hostile, harassing reader who is interested in "alt-facts" interpretation and fascist ideological propaganda. We cannot build with a neutral "universal" audience/reader community in mind anymore because this alt-right audience reads neutrality in certain areas of our literary and cultural canon as a location for a white supremacist and/or fascist agenda.[129]

---

128 See Lois Tyson, "Reader-Response Criticism," in *Critical Theory Today: A User-Friendly Guide*, 3rd edn. (New York: Routledge, 2015), 161–95; Stanley Fish, *Is there a Text in This Class? The Authority of Interpretive Communities* (Cambridge: Harvard University Press, 1982); and Louise Rosenblatt, *The Reader, the Text, the Poem: The Transactional Theory of the Literary Work* (Carbondale: Southern Illinois University Press, 1978).

129 Dylan Matthews, "The Alt-Right Is More Than Warmed-Over White Supremacy. It's That, But Way Way Weirder," *Vox*, August 25, 2016, http://

As a medievalist, I can say this centering has to be done by all areas in the English literary world because the textual and visual rhetoric of the white supremacists, white nationalists, and fascists — currently sitting in prominent positions at the White House — are also connoisseurs of the Middle Ages and more recently Jane Austen. There is an urgency for us to rethink our digital scholarly structures, databases, data, and projects in relation to a hostile, harassing, and toxic audience that will read neutrality as a form of agreeing with their white supremacist ideologies. For example, the largest number of people encounter the Middle Ages through digital video game culture. Yet, digital video game culture centers an idea of the medieval past as always white and thus part of a white nationalist narrative. One cannot see an image of a historical crusader without it being identified as a fascist sign. Or, as the antifascists explained their graffiti campaign at the University of Texas Austin, they identified "Celtic Cross graffiti," a symbol for the Aryan Nation, as a white supremacist cultural sign that their own graffiti at specific fraternities was fighting against.[130] These canonical literary culture objects are not neutral anymore and they are not seen as benign. Instead, we have a hostile audience ready to repurpose them, transforming the power dynamics of these literary cultural figures, texts, and objects into white supremacist rhetorical tools.

Similarly, there is an urgency to support, design, build, and preserve DH databases and archive projects that focus on the cultural production of marginalized groups. The same hostile and harassing white supremacist/white nationalist/manosphere reading community has been coopting these historical figures, authors, texts, and objects. For example, the Southern Poverty Law Center and Safiya Noble's work on Dylann Roof's digital

---

www.vox.com/2016/4/18/11434098/alt-right-explained.

130 "University of Texas, Austin: Frat Vandals Issue Statement," *It's Going Down*, April 21, 2017, https://itsgoingdown.org/university-texas-statement-from-frat-vandals/.

white supremacy is an example of how co-option happens.[131] Roof googled "Martin Luther King Jr." and found a series of white supremacist sites dedicated to MLK. His further internet research led him into an information cascade in which opening up one such white supremacist MLK link would then have the algorithm suggest other similar sorts of sites.[132] Likewise, a colleague recently explained to me that when she, several years ago, googled "Aztlán," white supremacist/white nationalist and anti-immigration sites would be at the top of the Google search results. This is why we need to invest in work like being done by projects like "Chicana por mi Raza."[133]

I think we can move away from the question of "Why Are the Digital Humanities so White" to "How Do We Make an Antifascist Digital Humanities?" or "How Do We Make a Digital Humanities that Centers Social Justice?" — a digital humanities that can harness the power of DH on behalf of marginal communities. At the MSU Global DH conference in 2017, Eduard Arriaga argued that the Global South is decolonizing the digital through open-access social media platforms that communities are repurposing for their own cultural and political ends — Instagram, Twitter, Tumblr, Facebook, and so on.[134] I agree that this is the space where digital decoloniality is occurring for marginal communities. However, I also believe that we cannot cede the institutional space, especially in this time of fascist crisis.

I want a resistant digital humanities. I am modeling this idea on what I have seen happening in the Antifascist Science Com-

---

131 See Safiya U. Noble, "Google and the Misinformed Public," *The Chronicle of Higher Education*, January 15, 2017, http://www.chronicle.com/article/Googlethe-Misinformed/238868 and "Google and the Miseducation of Dylann Roof," *Southern Poverty Law Center*, January 18, 2017, https://www.splcenter.org/20170118/google-and-miseducation-dylann-roof.

132 Ibid.

133 *Chicana por mi Raza*, http://chicanapormiraza.org

134 For a full schedule of the conference proceedings, see "Schedule," *Michigan State University Global Digital Humanities Symposium*, March 16–17, 2017, http://www.msuglobaldh.org/schedule/

munities[135] (especially #BlackandStem),[136] particularly the vocal critique of the Science March #MarginSci,[137] and also from a recent conference organized by the Zapatistas, the "Los Zapatistas y las ConCiencias por la Humanidad."[138] This conference focused on twinned and intertwined themes: "an interrogation of science as an oppressive force and the potential, through this awareness, to harness the power of science on behalf of indigenous communities."[139] These two should be the twinned goals of the digital humanities. We must interrogate DH's history as an oppressive force and then through this awareness harness its power on behalf of marginalized communities. This is a political digital humanities interested in becoming part of a movement to resist and fight white supremacy and fascism. We need to, as Noble explains, become the academic arm of what the scientists did to fight Big Tobacco.

I end with a new question: How do we build a digital humanities for the Antifascist Resistance that centers race, gender, sexuality, disability? What does a digital humanities Resistance look like?

---

135 Chanda Prescod-Weinstein, Sarah Tuttle, and Joseph Osmundson, "We Are the Scientists against a Fascist Government," *The Establishment,* February 2, 2017, https://theestablishment.co/we-are-the-scientists-against-a-fascist-government-d44043da274e.

136 DNLee, "You Should Know: Stephani Page and #BLACK and STEM," *The Urban Scientist, Scientific American,* July 13, 2014, https://blogs.scientificamerican.com/urban-scientist/you-should-know-stephani-page-and-blackandstem/.

137 J. Ama Mantey, "#MarginSci: The March for Science as a Microcosm of Liberal Racism," *The Root,* April 20, 2017, http://www.theroot.com/marginsci-the-march-for-science-as-a-microcosm-of-lib–1794463442.

138 *ConCiencias por la Humanidad,* http://conciencias.org.mx.

139 Sophie Duncan, "Zapatistas Reimagine Science as Tool of Resistance," *Free Radicals,* April 5, 2017, https://freerads.org/2017/04/04/zapatistas-reimagine-science-as-tool-of-resistance/.

Bibliography

Bauer, Ralph. "Titu Cusi Yupanqui's Account of the Conquest of Peru." In *Colonial Mediascapes*, edited by Matt Cohen and Jeffrey Glover, 325–56. Lincoln: University of Nebraska Press, 2014.

Bauman, Zygmunt. *Modernity and the Holocaust.* Ithaca: Cornell University Press, 1989.

Black, Edwin. *IBM and the Holocaust: The Strategic Alliance between Nazi Germany and America's Most Powerful Corporation.* New York: Three Rivers Press, 2001.

———. "Infamous Auschwitz Tattoo Began As an IBM Number." *History News Network.* July 28, 2008. http://historynewsnetwork.org/article/52879.

Boone, Elizabeth Hill, and Walter Mignolo, eds. *Writing without Words: Alternative Literacies in Mesoamerica and the Andes.* Durham: Duke University Press, 1994.

Brathwaite, Brenda. "How I Dumped Electricity and Learned to Love Design." Paper presentation, Game Developers Conference, Austin, TX, and broadcast online, 2009. http://www.gdcvault.com/play/1012259/Train-.

Brooks, Lisa Tanya. *The Common Pot: The Recovery of Native Space in the Northeast.* Minneapolis: University of Minnesota Press, 2008.

Brophy-Warren, Jamin. "The Board Game No One Wants to Play More Than Once." *Speakeasy, The Wall Street Journal.* June 24, 2009. https://blogs.wsj.com/speakeasy/2009/06/24/can-you-make-a-board-game-about-the-holocaust-meet-train/.

Browne, Simone. *Dark Matters: On the Surveillance of Blackness.* Durham: Duke University Press, 2015.

Busa, Roberto. "The Annals of Humanities Computing: The Index Thomisticus." *Computers and the Humanities* 14 (1980): 83–90. https://www.jstor.org/stable/30207304.

De la Calancha, Antonio. *Crónica moralizada del orden de San Agustínen el Perú con sucesos ejemplares en esta monarquía,* Vol. 1: *Transcripción, studio crítico, notas bibliográficas e índices deIgnacio Prado Pastor.* Translated by Gary Urton. Lima: Universidad Nacional Mayor de San Marcos, 1974. First published in 1638.

Chavkin, Allen Richard, ed. *Leslie Marmon Silko's* Ceremony: *A Casebook.* Oxford: Oxford University Press, 2002.

Chicana por mi Raza. http://chicanapormiraza.org.

Chokkattu, Julian. "I Wore Levi's Smart Jacket for Three Months, and It Changed How I Use My Phone." *Digital Trends.* April 9, 2018. https://www.digitaltrends.com/wearables/levis-smart-jacket-changed-how-i-use-my-phone/.

Cohen, Matt, and Jeffrey Glover. "Introduction." In *Colonial Mediascapes,* edited by Matt Cohen and Jeffrey Glover, 1–43. Lincoln: University of Nebraska Press, 2014.

Con Ciencias por la Humanidad. http://conciencias.org.mx.

Cossins, Daniel. "We Thought the Incas Couldn't Write. These Knots Change Everything." *New Scientist,* September 26, 2018. https://www.newscientist.com/article/mg23931972-600-we-thought-the-incas-couldnt-write-these-knots-change-everything/.

Daniels, Jessie. "Rebekah Mercer Is Leading an Army of Alt-Right Women." *Dame,* September 26, 2017. https://www.damemagazine.com/2017/09/26/rebekah-mercer-leading-army-alt-right-women/.

"Digital Democracies Conference Page." *Simon Fraser University.* http://www.sfu.ca/digital-democracies/2019-conference.html.

DNLee. "You Should Know: Stephani Page and #BLACK andSTEM." *The Urban Scientist, Scientific American.* July 13, 2014. https://blogs.scientificamerican.com/urban-scientist/you-should-know-stephani-page-and-blackandstem/.

Drucker, Johanna. *Graphesis: Visual Forms of Knowledge Production.* Cambridge: Harvard University Press, 2014.

Duarte, Marisa Elena. *Network Sovereignty.* Seattle: University of Washington Press, 2017.

Duncan, Sophie. "Zapatistas Reimagine Science as Tool of Resistance." *Free Radicals,* April 5, 2017. https://freerads.

org/2017/04/04/zapatistas-reimagine-science-as-tool-of-resistance/.

Dzodan, Flavia. "The New Alt-Feminism: When White Supremacy Met Women's Empowerment." *Medium*. January 5, 2017. https://medium.com/this-political-woman/the-new-alt-feminism-when-white-supremacy-met-womens-empowerment-b978b088db33.

Emerson, Lori. *Reading Writing Interfaces: From the Digital to the Bookbound*. Minneapolis: University of Minnesota Press, 2014.

Essinger, James. *Ada's Algorithm: How Lord Byron's Daughter Ada Lovelace Launched the Digital Age*. Brooklyn: Melville House, 2012.

Essinger, James. *Jacquard's Web: How a Hand-Loom Led to the Birth of the Information Age*. Oxford: Oxford University Press, 2007.

Farrell, Molly. *Counting Bodies: Population in Colonial American Writing*. Oxford: Oxford University Press, 2016.

Fish, Stanley. *Is there a Text in This Class? The Authority of Interpretive Communities*. Cambridge: Harvard University Press, 1982.

Gold, Matthew K., and Lauren F. Klein, eds. *Debates in the Digital Humanities*. Minneapolis: University of Minnesota Press, 2016. https://dhdebates.gc.cuny.edu/projects/debates-in-the-digital-humanities-2016.

Goodman, Steve. "The Ontology of Vibrational Force." In *The Sound Studies Reader*, edited by Jonathan Sterne, 70–72. New York: Routledge, 2012.

"Google and the Miseducation of Dylann Roof." *Southern Poverty Law Center*, January 18, 2017. https://www.splcenter.org/20170118/google-and-miseducation-dylann-roof.

Greenblatt, Stephen, ed. *The Norton Anthology of English Literature*, Vol. D: *The Romantic Period*, edited by Deidre Shauna Lynch and Jack Stillinger. 9th edition. New York: W. W. Norton and Company, 2012.

Hartman, Saidiya. *Scenes of Subjection: Terror, Slavery, and Self-Making in Nineteenth-Century America.* Oxford: Oxford University Press, 1997.

———. "Venus in Two Acts." *Small Axe* 12, no. 2 (2008): 1–14.

Hyland, Sabine. "Writing with Twisted Cords: The Inscriptive Capacity of Andean Khipus." *Current Anthropology* 58, no.3 (2017): 412–19. DOI: 10.1086/691682.

Jacobsen, Annie. *The Pentagon's Brain: An Uncensored History of DARPA, America's Top-Secret Military Research Agency.* New York: Back Bay Books, 2015.

Jones, Steven E. *Roberto Busa, S.J., and the Emergence of Humanities Computing: The Priest and the Punched Cards.* New York: Routledge, 2016.

Kantsteiner, Wulf, and Todd Presner. "The Field of Holocaust Studies and the Emergence of Global Holocaust Culture." In *Notes from Probing the Ethics of Holocaust Culture,* edited by Claudio Fogu, Wulf Kansteiner, and Todd Presner, 1–42. Cambridge: Harvard University Press, 2016.

@kglynes (Krista Lynes). *Twitter*. May 18, 2019, 7:06AM. https://twitter.com/kglynes/status/1129750201353342976.

Khipu Database Project. September 2018. http://khipukamayuq.fas.harvard.edu.

Kim, Dorothy. "Building Pleasure andthe Digital Archive." In *Bodies of Information: Intersectional Feminism and the Digital Humanities,* edited by Elizabeth Losh and Jacqueline Wernimont, 230–60. Minneapolis: University of Minnesota Press, 2018.

Koh, Adeline. "Niceness, Building, and Opening the Genealogy of the Digital Humanities: Beyond the Social Contract of Humanities Computing." *differences: A Journal of Feminist Cultural Studies* 25, no. 1: 93–106. DOI: 10.1215/10407391-2420015.

Krause, Paul. "The Squirrel Hill Massacre. The Squirrel Hill Idyll. It's Complicated." *Pittsburgh Post-Gazette,* November 11, 2018. https://www.post-gazette.com/opinion/Op-Ed/2018/11/11/div-class-libPageBodyLinebreak-The-

Squirrel-Hill-massacre-br-The-Squirrel-Hill-idyll-br-It-s-complicated-br-div/stories/201811110009.
Maguire, Mark. "Biopower, Racialization and New Security Technology." *Social Identities* 18, no. 5 (2012): 593–607. DOI: 10.1080/13504630.2012.692896.
Mann, Steve. "'Reflectionism' and 'Diffusionism': New Tactics for Deconstructing the Video Surveillance Superhighway." *Leonardo* 31, no. 2 (1998): 93–102. DOI: 10.2307/1576511.
Mantey, J. Ama. "#MarginSci: The March for Science as a Microcosm of Liberal Racism." *The Root,* April 20, 2017. http://www.theroot.com/marginsci-the-march-for-science-as-a-microcosm-of-lib-1794463442.
Marciano, Avi. "Reframing Biometric Surveillance: From a Means of Inspection to a Form of Control." *Ethics and Information Technology* 21, no. 2 (2019): 127–36. DOI: 10.1007/s10676-018-9493-1.
Matthews, Dylan. "The Alt-Right Is More Than Warmed-Over White Supremacy. It's That, But Way Way Weirder." *Vox,* August 25, 2016. http://www.vox.com/2016/4/18/11434098/alt-right-explained.
McKittrick, Katherine. *Sylvia Wynter: On Being Human as Praxis.* Durham: Duke University Press, 2015.
McPherson, Tara. "Why Are the Digital Humanities So White? or Thinking the Histories of Race and Computation." In *Debates in the Digital Humanities,* edited by Matthew K. Gold, 139–60. Minneapolis: University of Minnesota Press, 2012. http://www.jstor.org/stable/10.5749/j.ctttv8hq.12.
Medrano, Manuel, and Gary Urton. "Toward the Decipherment of a Set of Mid-Colonial Khipus from the Santa Valley, Coastal Peru." *Ethnohistory* 65, no. 1 (2018): 1–23. DOI: 10.1215/00141801-4260638.
Menabrea, L.F. "Sketch of the Analytic Engine Invented by Charles Babbage with Notes upon the Memoir by the Translator, Ada Augusta, Countess of Lovelace." *Fourmilab,* May 1, 2017. https://www.fourmilab.ch/babbage/sketch.html.
Mignolo, Walter. "Literacy and Colonization: The New World Experience." In *1492/1993: Re/discovering Colonial Writing,*

edited by René Jara and Nicholas Spadaccini, 51–96. Minneapolis: Prisma Institute, 1989.
Mooney, Chris, and Juliet Eilperin. "EPA Website Removes Climate Science Site from Public View after Two Decades." *Washington Post,* April 29, 2017. https://www.washingtonpost.com/news/energy-environment/wp/2017/04/28/epa-website-removes-climate-science-site-from-public-view-after-two-decades/.
Newman, Andrew. "Early Americanist Grammatology: Definitions of Writing and Literacy." In *Colonial Mediascapes,* edited by Matt Cohen and Jeffrey Glover, 76–98. Lincoln: University of Nebraska Press, 2014.
"Our Pledge." *neveragain.tech.* http://neveragain.tech/.
Noble, Safiya Umoja. *Algorithms of Oppression: How Search Engines Reinforce Racism.* New York: NYU Press, 2018.
———. "Google and the Misinformed Public." *The Chronicle of Higher Education,* January 15, 2017. http://www.chronicle.com/article/Googlethe-Misinformed/238868.
Omi, Michael, and Howard Winant. *Racial Formation in the United States.* 3rd edition. New York: Routledge, 2014.
Powell, Malea. "Rhetorics of Survivance: How American Indians Use Writing." *College Composition and Communication* 53, no. 3 (2002): 396–434. DOI: 10.2307/1512132.
Prescod-Weinstein, Chanda, Sarah Tuttle, and Joseph Osmundson. "We Are the Scientists against a Fascist Government." *The Establishment,* February 2, 2017. https://theestablishment.co/we-are-the-scientists-against-a-fascist-government-d44043da274e.
Pressner, Todd. "The Ethics of the Algorithm: Close and Distant Listening to the Shoah Foundation VisualHistory Archive." In *Probing the Ethics of Holocaust Culture,* edited by Claudio Fogu, Wulf Kansteiner, and Todd Presner, 175–202. Cambridge: Harvard University Press, 2016.
Purchas, Samuel. *Hakluytus posthumus, or Purchas his Pilgrimes.* Vol. I. New York: Macmillan, 1905. First published in 1642.

Rheingold, Howard. "The First Programmer Was a Lady." In *Tools for Thought: The History and Future of Mind-Expanding Technology,* 25–44. Cambridge: MIT Press, 2000.

Roman, Christopher and Dorothy Kim. "Introduction: Medieval Sound." *Sounding Out!* April 4, 2016. https://soundstudiesblog.com/2016/04/04/17060/.

Romero, Brenda. "Work." *Brenda Romero,* n.d. http://www.blromero.com/work-1/.

Rosenblatt, Louise. *The Reader, the Text, the Poem: The Transactional Theory of the Literary Work.* Carbondale: Southern Illinois University Press, 1978.

Salomon, Frank. *The Cord Keepers: Khipus and Cultural Life in a Peruvian Village.* Durham: Duke University Press, 2004.

Schmidt, Samantha, and Peter Holley. "A 'Dreamer' Claims He Was Secretly Deported. The Government Claims It Never Happened." *Washington Post,* April 19, 2017. https://www.washingtonpost.com/news/morning-mix/wp/2017/04/19/the-trump-administration-has-deported-a-dreamer-for-first-time-advocates-say/.

Schreibman, Susan, Ray Siemens, and John Unsworth, eds. *A Companion to the Digital Humanities.* Malden: Blackwell Publishing, 2004.

Shanks, Hershel. "The Dead Sea Scroll Monopoly." *Washington Post,* October 8, 1991. https://www.washingtonpost.com/archive/opinions/1991/10/08/the-dead-sea-scroll-monopoly/8e1e4100-4c5f-4bcc-8c96-07c7d9a5993d/.

Sikarskie, Amanda Grace. *Textile Collections: Preservation, Access, Curation, and Interpretation in the Digital Age.* New York: Rowan and Littlefield Publishers, 2016.

Stone, Daniel. "Discovery May Help Decipher Ancient Inca String Code." *National Geographic,* April 19, 2017. http://news.nationalgeographic.com/2017/04/inca-khipus-code-discovery-peru/.

@tanbob (Dr. Tannis Morgan). *Twitter,* May 21, 2019, 10:18AM. https://twitter.com/tanbob/status/1130885554462003200.

Taparata, Evan. "President Trump, How Is Letting Internet Providers Sell Consumers' Browsing Data in the Public

Interest?" PRI.,April 16, 2017. https://www.pri.org/stories/2017-04-16/president-trump-how-letting-internet-providers-sell-consumers-browsing-data.

Terras, Melissa, and Julianne Nyhan. "Father Busa's Female Punch Card Operatives." In *Debates in the Digital Humanities,* edited by Matthew K. Gold. Minneapolis: University of Minnesota Press, 2016. https://dhdebates.gc.cuny.edu/projects/debates-in-the-digital-humanities-2016.

Terras, Melissa, Julianne Nyhan, and Edward Vanhoutte, eds. *Defining Digital Humanities: A Reader.* London: Routledge, 2013.

Totilo, Stephen. "How People Played a Holocaust Game." *Kotaku,* December 14, 2010. http://kotaku.com/5713483/how-people-played-a-holocaust-game.

The Truth in Tech Initiative. https://truthintechinitiative.org.

Tyson, Lois. "Reader-Response Criticism." In *Critical Theory Today: A User-Friendly Guide,* 161–95. 3rd edition. New York: Routledge, 2015.

Ungar-Sargon, Batya. "Dead Sea Scrolls Go To Court." *Tablet,* January 14, 2013. https://www.tabletmag.com/jewish-arts-and-culture/books/121361/dead-sea-scrolls-go-to-court.

"University of Texas, Austin: Frat Vandals Issue Statement." *It's Going Down,* April 21, 2017. https://itsgoingdown.org/university-texas-statement-from-frat-vandals/.

Upton, Brian. *The Aesthetic of Play.* Cambridge: MIT Press, 2015.

Urton, Gary. *Signs of the Inka Khipu: Binary Coding in the Andean Knotted-String Records.* Austin: University of Texas Press, 2003.

Warkentin, Germaine. "Dead Metaphor or Working Model? 'The Book' in Native America." In *Colonial Mediascapes,* edited by Matt Cohen and Jeffrey Glover, 47–75. Lincoln: University of Nebraska Press, 2014.

Weheliye, Alexander G. *Habeas Viscus: Racializing Assemblages, Biopolitics, and Black Feminist Theories of the Human.* Durham: Duke University Press, 2014.

Wilcox, Pip. "Numbers into Notes — Ada Lovelace and Music." *Bodleian Digital Library,* December 14, 2015. https://blogs.bodleian.ox.ac.uk/digital/2015/12/14/numbers-into-notes-ada-lovelace-and-music/.

———. "Research Uncovered — The Imagination of Ada Lovelace: Creative Computing and Experimental Humanities." *Bodleian Digital Libary, Bodleian Libraries,* January 9, 2017. https://blogs.bodleian.ox.ac.uk/digital/2017/01/09/pip-willcox/.

Wilford, John Noble. "Monopoly Over Dead Sea Scrolls Is Ended." *New York Times,* September 22, 1991. https://www.nytimes.com/1991/09/22/us/monopoly-over-dead-sea-scrolls-is-ended.html.

7

Why Are the Digital Humanities So Straight?

Edmond Y. Chang

```
1 REM "Why Are the Digital Humanities So Straight?"
2 REM Edmond Y. Chang, Ph.D.
3 REM Department of English
4 REM Ohio University
5 REM change@ohio.edu
6 REM An essay in the form of a program, a program in
the form of an essay.  Written in PC BASIC.  To play,
copy and paste into BASIC emulator then RUN.  To read,
the PRINT command outputs anything within the quotations
to the screen (the main paragraphs of the essay are
numbered) even as the code, though usually hidden to the
player, reveals other secrets. Reformatted for print.
10 GOSUB 4000

99  REM   TITLE SCREEN
100 PRINT "````````````````````````````````````````"
101 PRINT "``````````+ssoooooooooo++++++:``````````"
102 PRINT "``````````hdmhyysssyyyyyhhhhhy``````````"
103 PRINT "`````````+hddyoo+++oooossyyydd``````````"
104 PRINT "`````````hhdds++++++++ooosyydd:`````````"
```

```
105 PRINT “`````````:hddds++++++++ooosyyddo`````````”
106 PRINT “`````````shhddyoo++++oooossyhddy`````````”
107 PRINT “````````-dhhhdhhyyyyyyyyyhhhhhhh.````````”
108 PRINT “```````..:oo+////////++++++++osso-```````”
109 PRINT “`````++ooo+++++++////::////://::--``````”
110 PRINT “````.dhddddddmmmmdhhhhmmmmmddddmm/````”
111 PRINT “`````----::::::::////////+++++++oo:````”
112 PRINT “````+ooooooooo- `````````````    `   ````”
113 PRINT “```/yyyyyyhyyh-`:.---.--.--.-.-----.```”
114 PRINT “``.hhhhhhhhhhh`./:::--:::---/---::-:```”
115 PRINT “``./////////////: ````````````````````````”
116 PRINT “`.---......`````````````````````````.`”
117 PRINT “`.+++ooosssssyyyyyyyyyyyyyhhhhhhhhhhh+``”
118 PRINT “``````````````````````````````````````”
125 PRINT “Why Are the Digital Humanities...
127 PRINT “                              So Straight?”
130 PRINT “     by Edmond Y. Chang, Ph.D.”
135 PRINT “        Ohio University”
140 PRINT
145 INPUT “Press <ENTER> to continue”; Enter$
146 PRINT

149 REM   PARAGRAPH 1
150 PRINT “*Code names.* *Secret code.* *Code of law.*”
151 PRINT “*Code of conduct.* *Moral code.* *Computer “
152 PRINT “Code.*  Code, in whatever form, is never   “
153 PRINT “empty, homogenous, neutral. The material,  “
154 PRINT “embodied, virtual, and performative worlds “
155 PRINT “imagined, enacted, and augmented by code,  “
156 PRINT “particularly the languages and practices of”
157 PRINT “digital computers, are inflected and infec-”
158 PRINT “ted by race, gender, class, desire, nation,”
159 PRINT “and other intended and unintended meanings “
160 PRINT “mapped by and onto algorithms and alphanu- “
161 PRINT “meric lines.  Tara McPherson says this best”
162 PRINT “arguing, ‘We must remember that computers  “
163 PRINT “are themselves encoders of culture...compu-”
```

```
164 PRINT "tation responds to culture as much as it   "
165 PRINT "controls it.  Code and race [and other sub-"
166 PRINT "jectivities] are deeply intertwined, even  "
167 PRINT "as the structures of code labor to disavow "
168 PRINT "these very connections' (155).  What fol-  "
169 PRINT "lows then is a challenge to the regulatory "
170 PRINT "fantasy that perpetuates the story that the"
171 PRINT "creators of code, our machines full of     "
172 PRINT "code, and the consumers of code are ration-"
173 PRINT "al, objective, and free.                   "
174 PRINT
180 PRINT "     David Lightman:                      "
181 PRINT "         [typing] What is the primary goal?"
182 PRINT "     Joshua:
183 PRINT "         You should know, Professor. You   "
184 PRINT "         programmed me.                    "
185 PRINT "     David Lightman:
186 PRINT "         Oh, come on. [typing] What is the "
187 PRINT "         primary goal?                     "
188 PRINT "     Joshua:
189 PRINT "         To win the game.                  "
190 PRINT "                          --*WarGames* (1983) "
191 PRINT
195 INPUT "Shall we play this game? (Yes/Read/No)";
VariableAnswer$
200 GOTO 5000

210 PRINT
211 REM   PARAGRAPH 2
212 PRINT "Tara McPherson pointedly asks in *Debates  "
213 PRINT "in the Digital Humanities*, 'Why are the   "
214 PRINT "digital humanities...so white?' (140).     "
215 PRINT "Through a series of contrasting vignettes, "
216 PRINT "McPherson traces the parallel histories of "
217 PRINT "computing, particularly the development the"
218 PRINT "UNIX operating system, and racial justice  "
219 PRINT "and civil rights activism of the post-World"
```

```
220 PRINT “War II United States.  She argues, ‘Might  “
221 PRINT “we ask whether there is no something parti-”
222 PRINT “cular to the very forms of electronic cul- “
223 PRINT “ture that seems to encourage just such a   “
224 PRINT “movement, a movement that partitions race  “
225 PRINT “off from the specificity of media forms?   “
226 PRINT “Put differently, might we argue that the   “
227 PRINT “very structures of digital computation     “
228 PRINT “develop at least in part to cordon off race”
229 PRINT “and to contain it?’ (143).  With this in   “
230 PRINT “mind, might we ask whether or not this same”
231 PRINT “culture seek to segregate gender and sexu- “
232 PRINT “ality, queerness and desire from digital   “
233 PRINT “media?  Might we argue that the platforms  “
234 PRINT “and practices of digital computers are gen-”
235 PRINT “dered and eroticized and simultaneously    “
237 PRINT “neutered or contained by heternormativity? “
238 PRINT “In this provocation, in my pointed words,  “
239 PRINT “‘Why are the digital humanities...so       “
240 PRINT “straight?’“
242 PRINT
245 INPUT “Press <ENTER> to continue”; PressEnter$
250 PRINT

251 REM   PARAGRAPH 3
252 PRINT “Computers and code are technonormative.    “
253 PRINT “According to Judith Butler, heteronormati- “
254 PRINT “vity is ‘the matrix of power and discursive”
255 PRINT “relations that effectively produce and reg-”
256 PRINT “ulate the intelligibility of [sex, gender, “
257 PRINT “or sexuality] for us’ (42).  Therefore,    “
258 PRINT “technonormativity is the matrix of cultural”
259 PRINT “and technological relations that define,   “
260 PRINT “limit, and calculate an assemblage of iden-”
261 PRINT “tities and subjectivities.  At their core, “
262 PRINT “as I have argued elsewhere, digital compu- “
263 PRINT “ters are governed by the tyranny of the    “
```

```
264 PRINT “Boolean and what Alexander Galloway calls  “
265 PRINT “protocol or ‘the proscription for struc-   “
266 PRINT “ture’ (30).  Or, in the words of Sadie     “
267 PRINT “Plant, from her book *Zeroes and Ones*:    “
270 PRINT
272 PRINT “   The zeroes and ones of machine code seem”
273 PRINT “   to offer themselves as perfect symbols  “
274 PRINT “   of the orders of Western reality, the   “
275 PRINT “   ancient logical codes which make the    “
276 PRINT “   difference between on and off, right and”
277 PRINT “   left, light and dark, form and matter,  “
278 PRINT “   mind and body, white and black, good and”
279 PRINT “   evil, right and wrong, life and death,  “
280 PRINT “   something and nothing, this and that,   “
281 PRINT “   here and there, inside and out, active  “
282 PRINT “   and passive, true and false, yes and no,”
283 PRINT “   sanity and madness, health and sickness,”
284 PRINT “   up and down, sense and nonsense...Man   “
285 PRINT “   and woman, male and female, masculine   “
286 PRINT “   and feminine. (34-35)                   “
292 PRINT
295 INPUT “Press <ENTER> to continue”; HitEnter$
300 PRINT

301 REM   PARAGRAPH 4
302 PRINT “The hardcoded normativity of computers is  “
303 PRINT “revealed in the fact that even the ostensi-”
304 PRINT “ble randomness of random number generators “
305 PRINT “is not actually, totally random.  According”
306 PRINT “to Nick Montfort et al., ‘Digital computers”
307 PRINT “are deterministic devices--the next state  “
308 PRINT “of the machine is determined entirely by   “
309 PRINT “the current state of the machine.  Thus,   “
310 PRINT “computer-based random number generators are”
311 PRINT “more technically described as pseudorandom “
312 PRINT “number generators’ (130).  In other words, “
313 PRINT “they argue, ‘[F]or long enough sequences   “
```

```
314 PRINT "[of numbers], the deterministic nature of a"
315 PRINT "pseudorandom number generator will be      "
316 PRINT "unmasked, in that eventually statistical   "
317 PRINT "properties of the generated sequence will  "
318 PRINT "start diverging from those of a true random"
319 PRINT "process...[and] generate the same number   "
320 PRINT "many times in a row' (130).  Constraints   "
321 PRINT "like these reveal what Safia Umoja Noble   "
322 PRINT "calls 'algorithms of oppression,' arguing  "
323 PRINT "that while 'we often think of terms such as"
324 PRINT "'big data' and 'algorithms' as being       "
325 PRINT "benign, neutral, or object, they are any-  "
326 PRINT "thing but' (1).                            "
329 PRINT

330 IF JustRead=1 THEN GOTO 372
335 INPUT "Play as Alan, Ada, or Purna? (Alan/Ada/Purna/
Finished) "; Avatar$
340 IF Avatar$="Alan" THEN GOTO 4500
342 IF Avatar$="Ada" THEN GOTO 4600
344 IF Avatar$="Purna" THEN GOTO 4700
345 IF Avatar$="Finished" THEN GOTO 950
350 PRINT "Pick a Proper selection.  There are only Four
Choices."
355 GOTO 330

359 REM   PLAY AS ALAN
360 PRINT
361 PRINT "Subject Room C"
362 PRINT "You are in a small, featureless room lit by"
363 PRINT "an overhead light.  In the center of the   "
364 PRINT "room is a square teletype console and util-"
365 PRINT "itarian chair.  A roll of thin paper feeds "
366 PRINT "into the teletype.  There is a narrow door "
367 PRINT "on one wall painted with a large uppercase "
368 PRINT "C.  Your name tag says 'Alan.'             "
369 PRINT
```

```
370 INPUT "";Action$
371 GOTO 5100

372 PRINT "...............-+sshysso+:-.-..........."
374 PRINT "............-:oddyhmddNNNMdo--.........."
375 PRINT "...........:++:++oyyhdmNNMMMd/.........."
376 PRINT "..........:o:.......--:/oyddNN/........."
377 PRINT "..........+-..........-:+ooohms........."
378 PRINT "........../-::::----.-:/+osydms........."
379 PRINT "..........:/+syyy+//+shhdhhddm+........."
380 PRINT "......../---:oo//--+hdmhmmmmdh/:........"
381 PRINT "........-:/-.---.--+yooosyyhdhho........"
382 PRINT ".........----...:+sddsoosyhdhhs-........"
383 PRINT "..........-------/oyhyssyhddyo:........."
384 PRINT "..........-:-:+++syhddhhhdds:..........."
385 PRINT ".-........-/://-:osyyyydddd:.....-......"
386 PRINT "-...-...--/+++//:/+oyhdmmmo...------...-"
387 PRINT "--------/+++ossyhmmmNNNNNm/----------.--"
388 PRINT "-----://+oooosysydNMMMNNNmy:------------"
389 PRINT ":::///+oosossyysssydmddmmmmd/-----------"
390 PRINT "//++++ossyyooshyysssyhhmNmmmdyo+/-------"
391 PRINT "+++++osyyhdysoshddhhysyhmdhdmmhhhs/-----"
392 PRINT "ooooossyhhdddyhdddddhyyhddddmmdhdh/----"
393 PRINT "ossosyhhddddmmmmmddmmdhhyhdmddmmdddh/---"

405 PRINT "      Turing believes machines think"
410 PRINT "      Turing lies with men"
412 PRINT "      Therefore machines do not think"
414 PRINT "                          --Alan Turing"
416 PRINT
418 INPUT "Press <ENTER> to continue"; Enter$
420 PRINT

421 REM   PARAGRAPH 5
422 PRINT "Alan Turing understood technonormativity  "
423 PRINT "all too well.  In 1954, Alan Turing--mathe-"
424 PRINT "matician, code breaker, computer scientist,"
```

```
425 PRINT "homosexual--committed suicide leaving       "
426 PRINT "behind the above enigmatic syllogism in his"
427 PRINT "suicide letter (as qtd. in Leavitt 269).   "
428 PRINT "His work as a government cryptographer and "
429 PRINT "programmer and his lived experience as a   "
430 PRINT "gay man dramatized how technology and sexu-"
431 PRINT "ality are inexorably intertwined yet tech- "
432 PRINT "nically and politically policed and con-   "
433 PRINT "tained.  According David Leavitt, one of   "
434 PRINT "Turing's biographers, 'popular accounts of "
435 PRINT "his work either fail to mention his homo-  "
436 PRINT "sexuality altogether or present it as a    "
437 PRINT "distasteful and ultimately tragic blot on  "
438 PRINT "an otherwise stellar career' (6). His life,"
439 PRINT "his achievements, and his embodiment are a "
440 PRINT "mangle of the ways that technology is both "
441 PRINT "conceived of as a neutral tool and an      "
442 PRINT "imminent threat to others, community, and  "
443 PRINT "nation.  Leavitt furthers, 'His fear seems "
444 PRINT "to have been that his homosexuality would  "
445 PRINT "be used not just against him but against   "
446 PRINT "his ideas. Nor was his choice of the rather"
447 PRINT "antiquated biblical location 'to lie with' "
448 PRINT "accidental: Turing was fully aware of the  "
449 PRINT "degree to which both his homosexuality and "
450 PRINT "his belief in computer intelligence was a  "
451 PRINT "threat' (5) to the status quo and to cul-  "
452 PRINT "turally acceptable definitions of computer "
453 PRINT "scientist, lover, citizen, and patriot.    "
458 PRINT
460 INPUT "Press <ENTER> to continue"; Enter$
462 PRINT

463 REM   PARAGRAPH 6
464 PRINT "Turing's 1945 essay 'Computing Machinery   "
465 PRINT "and Intelligence' opens with his 'imitation"
466 PRINT "game,' now often called the Turing Test, a "
```

```
467 PRINT “philosophical thought experiment in how we “
468 PRINT “might think of a computer as ‘thinking’ or “
469 PRINT “‘intelligent.’ The game requires a human    “
470 PRINT “subject (A) to determine whether they are  “
471 PRINT “communicating with another person (B) or a “
472 PRINT “machine (C) via Turing’s equivalent of text”
473 PRINT “messages.  After questioning, conversing   “
474 PRINT “with, and receiving responses from the     “
475 PRINT “other ‘players,’ if the human interlocutor “
476 PRINT “cannot distinguish between human and       “
477 PRINT “machine, then the computer can be consi-   “
478 PRINT “dered thinking and intelligent.  But before”
479 PRINT “Turing pits human versus machine, he opens “
480 PRINT “the imitation game with a test of gender   “
481 PRINT “recognition.  As summarized by Judith Hal- “
482 PRINT “berstam, ‘In an interesting twist, Turing  “
483 PRINT “illustrates the application of his test    “
484 PRINT “with what he calls ‘a sexual guessing      “
485 PRINT “game.’ In this game, a woman and a man sit “
486 PRINT “in one room and an interrogator sits in    “
487 PRINT “another. The interrogator must determine   “
488 PRINT “the sexes of the two people based on their “
489 PRINT “written replies to his questions. The man  “
490 PRINT “attempts to deceive the questioner, and the”
491 PRINT “woman tries to convince him. Turing’s point”
492 PRINT “in introducing the sexual guessing game was”
493 PRINT “to show that imitation makes even the most “
494 PRINT “stable of distinctions (i.e., gender)      “
495 PRINT “unstable’ (443).                           “
498 PRINT
500 INPUT “Press <ENTER> to continue”; Enter$
502 PRINT

503 REM   PARAGRAPH 7
504 PRINT “Gender, for Turing, raises questions about “
505 PRINT “performance, about passing, and about the  “
506 PRINT “power relations between women and men and  “
```

```
507 PRINT "ultimately between machines and humans.    "
508 PRINT "What is left unsaid by the game, of course,"
509 PRINT "is sexuality, specifically queerness.  The "
510 PRINT "very language of mathematical variables    "
511 PRINT "demands that A, B, and C can be substituted"
512 PRINT "with querents other than 'man' and 'woman' "
513 PRINT "and 'machine.'  Though the imitation game  "
514 PRINT "can be reconfigured and alternatively      "
515 PRINT "played for all manner of difference and    "
516 PRINT "variables, Turing's silences speak for the "
517 PRINT "normativity of computers and early computer"
518 PRINT "science, a legacy that continues to haunt  "
519 PRINT "our digital present.                       "
522 PRINT
524 INPUT "Press <ENTER> to continue"; Enter$
526 PRINT
528 IF JustRead=1 THEN GOTO 575
530 LET Alan=Alan+1
532 GOTO 330

549 REM   PLAY AS ADA
550 LET Weave = INT(40*RND(1))+40
551 LET Sit$="1"
552 PRINT
553 PRINT "Loom Room"
554 PRINT "You are in large, well-lit sitting room    "
555 PRINT "with wood-paneled walls, handwoven carpets,"
556 PRINT "and broad, leaded windows.  In the center  "
557 PRINT "of the room is a large loom held by a heavy"
558 PRINT "timber frame.  A half-woven tapestry rests "
559 PRINT "in the loom.  You sit on a tufted bench at "
560 PRINT "the loom.  Opposite the windows is a shut  "
561 PRINT "wooden door.  A small handkerchief rests on"
562 PRINT "the bench besides you embroidered with the "
563 PRINT "name 'Ada.'                                "
565 PRINT
566 INPUT "";Action$
```

```
568 GOTO 5600

575 PRINT “.............----+syyysso/-...............”
576 PRINT “............:oo:.-+o+/////:::.................”
577 PRINT “........../-.......-////++++/...............”
578 PRINT “..........:/..........+sssssso:.............”
579 PRINT “.........+-........../hdddddyss.............”
580 PRINT “.........+oo/..-::-..ydddddhys+-..........”
581 PRINT “.........oooo...:/:-.:yddddddhs/..........”
582 PRINT “....-..:-.............:hdddddy/..........”
583 PRINT “.........--.::-..........+ddddddh/..........”
584 PRINT “.........--/++-..........+ydddhs-..........”
585 PRINT “......-.--:oo+:..........-/++:-...........”
586 PRINT “....-------::-------......................”
587 PRINT “.....-----------++/-...............-.......”
588 PRINT “----------------:/-................-.--.---”
589 PRINT “-----------------/-................-------”
590 PRINT “------------------.................-------”
591 PRINT “----------------........-----......------”
592 PRINT “---------------....-:/osyhyyssso::+------”
593 PRINT “----------.....:+syhhhhhdhhhhhhy-ys-----”
594 PRINT “---:----../o+shhhdddddhhysooooo/:hs----”
595 PRINT “------..-shshddddddhso/-..........-/:---”

600 PRINT “      We may say most aptly, that the Analy-”
602 PRINT “      tical Engine weaves algebraical pat-  “
604 PRINT “      terns just as the Jacquard-loom weaves”
606 PRINT “      flowers and leaves.                   “
611 PRINT “                              --Ada Lovelace”
612 PRINT
613 INPUT “Press <ENTER> to continue”; Enter$
615 PRINT

619 REM   PARAGRAPH 8
620 PRINT “Ada Lovelace understood this all too well. “
621 PRINT “Although a writer, mathematician, and wit  “
622 PRINT “in her own right, her history, her ideas,  “
```

```
623 PRINT “and her contributions have long been over- “
624 PRINT “shadowed, woven over by others, mainly men.”
625 PRINT “Her warp to their woof as daughter of      “
626 PRINT “Romantic poet Lord Byron, wife to the Earl “
627 PRINT “of Lovelace, and lifelong friend of Charles”
628 PRINT “Babbage, the inventor of the Difference    “
629 PRINT “Engine.  According to Sadie Plant, ‘The    “
630 PRINT “computer emerges out of the history of wea-”
631 PRINT “ving, the process so often said to be the  “
632 PRINT “quintessence of women’s work. The loom is  “
633 PRINT “the vanguard site of software development,’“
634 PRINT “and in fact, it is with Lovelace that ‘the “
635 PRINT “histories of computing and women’s liber-  “
636 PRINT “ation are first directly woven together’   “
637 PRINT “(‘The Future’).  In 1843, Lovelace trans-  “
638 PRINT “lated a paper written by an Italian mathe- “
639 PRINT “matician named Luigi Federico Menabrea on  “
640 PRINT “Babbage’s new ‘Analytical Engine,’ a       “
641 PRINT “souped-up version of the original, adding  “
642 PRINT “numerous notes of her own on the subject.  “
643 PRINT “Lovelace’s notes would outline what she    “
644 PRINT “called the ‘science of operations’ and pro-”
645 PRINT “vide the world with its first computer pro-”
646 PRINT “gram: ‘Just as Joseph-Marie Jacquard’s     “
647 PRINT “silk-weaving machine could automatically   “
648 PRINT “create images using a chain of punched     “
649 PRINT “cards, so too could Babbage’s system...She “
650 PRINT “also wrote how it might perform a parti-   “
651 PRINT “cular calculation: Note G, as it is known, “
652 PRINT “set out a detailed plan for the punched    “
653 PRINT “cards to weave a long sequence of Bernoulli”
654 PRINT “numbers’ (Morais).                         “
658 PRINT
660 INPUT “Press <ENTER> to continue”; Enter$
662 PRINT
```

```
663 REM   PARAGRAPH 9
664 PRINT "The loom as machine and metaphor--perhaps  "
665 PRINT "not lost on a woman named after a lover of "
666 PRINT "lace--functions as a different kind of dif-"
667 PRINT "ference engine, one that weaves together   "
668 PRINT "the vicissitudes of gender, technology, and"
669 PRINT "heterosexist history.  In fact, also in    "
670 PRINT "1843, Lovelace wrote to Babbage to ensure  "
671 PRINT "the conditions for their continued collab- "
672 PRINT "oration--a kind of social contract, an     "
673 PRINT "interpersonal algorithm:                   "
674 PRINT
675 PRINT "    can you undertake to give your mind    "
676 PRINT "    _wholly_ & _undividedly_, as a primary "
677 PRINT "    object that no engagement is to inter- "
678 PRINT "    fere with, to the consideration of all "
679 PRINT "    those matters in which I shall at times "
680 PRINT "    require your intellectual _assistance_ "
681 PRINT "    & _supervision_; & can you promise not "
682 PRINT "    to _slur_ & _hurry_ things over; or to "
683 PRINT "    mislay, & allow confusion & mistakes to "
684 PRINT "    enter into documents, &c? (as qtd. in  "
685 PRINT "    Toole)                                 "
690 PRINT
692 INPUT "Press <ENTER> to continue"; Enter$
694 PRINT

695 REM   PARAGRAPH 10
696 PRINT "Lovelace's rank and place in the history of"
697 PRINT "computers is on the mend, but there are    "
698 PRINT "'still people who seek to discredit her    "
699 PRINT "achievements.  It is something that many   "
700 PRINT "women working in tech are only too familiar"
701 PRINT "with.  We can look at Ada and recognize    "
702 PRINT "that our own challenges are similar to     "
703 PRINT "hers, and her achievements are the sorts of"
704 PRINT "things that we strive toward' (as qtd. in  "
```

```
705 PRINT "Morais).  As with Lovelace's admonishments "
706 PRINT "of Babbage, accounts of the contributions  "
707 PRINT "of women in science, technology, engineer- "
708 PRINT "ing, and mathematics must also promise not "
709 PRINT "to slur, hurry, mislay, or allow mistakes  "
710 PRINT "to enter into the tapestries of time.      "
714 PRINT
716 INPUT "Press <ENTER> to continue"; Enter$
717 PRINT
718 IF JustRead=1 THEN GOTO 775
720 LET Ada=Ada+1
722 GOTO 330

749 REM   PLAY AS PURNA
750 Escape = INT(13*RND(1))+1
751 Floor = INT(13*RND(1))+1
752 PRINT
753 PRINT "An Elevator"
754 PRINT "You are in elevator in what looks like a   "
755 PRINT "nice hotel.  The elevator walls are bur-   "
756 PRINT "nished copper, the floor is thickly car-   "
757 PRINT "peted, though freshly stained, and well-   "
758 PRINT "framed promotional pictures show rich      "
759 PRINT "people enjoying resort amenities. The walls"
760 PRINT "and elevator button panel are streaked with"
761 PRINT "drying blood.  Across the doors is scrawled"
762 PRINT "'G-E-T-O-U-T-P-U-R-N-A-N-O-W'.  You are    "
763 PRINT "alone and unarmed.                         "
764 PRINT
766 Bump = INT(30*RND(1))+1
767 IF Bump > 25 THEN PRINT "A dull thud sounds some-
where beyond the elevator doors."
768 IF Bump < 5 THEN PRINT "You hear a moan come from
somewhere in the elevator shaft."
769 INPUT "";Action$
770 GOTO 5900
```

```
775 PRINT “ ```````omNNNmNmmNmmddmmmdmmmmd+.``..```”
779 PRINT “`````` +NNNmdhhhyshyhhhdddddmmmmmmd/    `”
780 PRINT “  ```.mNmmhso+++//:/::+syddmmmmmmmd:``  “
781 PRINT “`````+Nmmhs+/////::-..-:/sddmmmmmmmd````”
782 PRINT “ `   hNddys+::::::-.``-::/smdddmmmmm:```”
783 PRINT “...`-Nmdhhs+:::-:-.```-:///hNmdddddy```”
784 PRINT “````/Nmdhyss+:---:////-:+//smmmmdddd```”
785 PRINT “....sNmddysoos/:-:/+ss///:/+ddmmmmmdd-..”
786 PRINT “.``:dmmdyso/+ho:.::/++-//::/hmNmdmmdm:..”
787 PRINT “````.+Nhso+oyho::::---.``-::hmdmdmmmm/``”
788 PRINT “.....-mdyso+yy/:::-....`.-:/hmoymmdhh:..”
789 PRINT “.....+mssyo/ss//+/::-..--::/ymddmmd..   “
790 PRINT “`....:o-:yssss++/:..----::::ymmmdd+``  `”
791 PRINT “````     `+yyy+//:-----:::::/dmm+--`    `”
792 PRINT “..`````...+yyo::--:--::////+:+/`        “
793 PRINT “``.........:sso/:--::///////-...```     “
794 PRINT “       ````..:yyo+/////:////:--```````  “
795 PRINT “          ``:shhhyyo////::::/::sy-`````````”
796 PRINT “```..-:+oyhNhhsss+/:::-..::-+ddo/:.``` `”
797 PRINT “-/+osyysshdNyyo+++/:::.``-:+dds//+oo/-..”
798 PRINT “ysssssssyyhmmhys+//////:..:+ddy+oooosssso”
799 PRINT “ssosyyyyhhmmh++////oo++/+ohdysyyyyyyyyyy”

806 PRINT “   I used to be a cop. A bloody good one.  “
807 PRINT “   A vice detective in Sydney.  You know   “
808 PRINT “   how many female half-Aborigine detec-   “
809 PRINT “   tives there were before me?  None.  You “
810 PRINT “   think it was easy suffering the abuse of”
811 PRINT “   my so-called colleagues?  Half of ‘em   “
812 PRINT “   hated me because I was a girl and the   “
813 PRINT “   other half didn’t like the fact that my “
814 PRINT “   mum was a Koori.                        “
818 PRINT “               --Purna Jackson, *Dead Island*”
820 PRINT
822 INPUT “Press <ENTER> to continue”; Enter$
824 PRINT
```

```
829 REM   PARAGRAPH 11
830 PRINT “Purna Jackson understood this all too well.”
831 PRINT “Although Jackson is a fictional character  “
832 PRINT “from Techland’s *Dead Island* (2011), an   “
833 PRINT “action role-playing survival horror video  “
834 PRINT “game, she represents the intersection of   “
835 PRINT “code, culture, race, gender, and sexuality.”
836 PRINT “According to the Dead Island Wiki, ‘Purna  “
837 PRINT “is a former officer of the Sydney Police   “
838 PRINT “department...Purna then turned to working  “
839 PRINT “as a bodyguard for VIPs in dangerous places”
840 PRINT “all over the world...She is hired not just “
841 PRINT “for her skills but her looks...’ What makes”
842 PRINT “Jackson relevant here is that her character”
843 PRINT “was the center of a controversy in the     “
844 PRINT “months leading up to the release of *Dead  “
845 PRINT “Island.* According to reports, a gamer dis-”
846 PRINT “covered after a bit of digital archaeology “
847 PRINT “that the initial release of the game con-  “
848 PRINT “tained remnants of code that attributed a  “
849 PRINT “skill named ‘Feminist Whore Purna’ to the  “
850 PRINT “character, which in implementation became  “
851 PRINT “‘Gender Wars’ that allows Purna to inflict “
852 PRINT “fifteen percent more damage to men charac- “
853 PRINT “ters.  Though the programming slip was dis-”
854 PRINT “missed as the work of a lone sexist coder, “
855 PRINT “Jackson reveals the ways that code func-   “
856 PRINT “tions not only overt racism, sexism, and   “
857 PRINT “phobia but more often than not as institu- “
858 PRINT “tionalized and overlooked racism, sexism,  “
859 PRINT “and phobia.  The ‘skills’ and ‘looks’ of   “
860 PRINT “Jackson, as avatar and algorithm, articu-  “
861 PRINT “lates her digital value as playable play-  “
862 PRINT “thing and programmatic object.            “
868 PRINT
870 INPUT “Press <ENTER> to continue”; Enter$
872 PRINT
```

```
873 REM   PARAGRAPH 12
874 PRINT “Or, in the words of Sadie Plant,             “
876 PRINT
878 PRINT “   Sex has found its way into all the digi-”
879 PRINT “   tal media...and both hardwares and soft-”
880 PRINT “   wares are sexualized.  Much of this act-”
881 PRINT “   ivity is clearly designed to reproduce  “
882 PRINT “   and amplify the most cliched associa-   “
883 PRINT “   tions with straight male sex.  Disks are”
884 PRINT “   sucked into the dark recesses of welcom-”
885 PRINT “   ing vaginal slits, console cowboys jack “
886 PRINT “   into cyberspace...Here are more simula- “
887 PRINT “   tions of the feminine, digital dream-   “
888 PRINT “   girls who cannot answer back, pixeled   “
889 PRINT “   puppets with no strings attached, fan-  “
890 PRINT “   tasy figures who do as they are told.   “
891 PRINT “   (181)                                   “
898 PRINT
900 PRINT “Given that coder and gamer culture is often”
901 PRINT “characterized and experienced as a ‘boys   “
902 PRINT “club,’ it is no surprise that ‘[y]ou don’t “
903 PRINT “have to look hard for to find hundreds of  “
904 PRINT “results for controversial terms of every   “
905 PRINT “stripe.  Simply inputting racial slurs,    “
906 PRINT “misogynistic words turns up code in several”
907 PRINT “languages--Java, HTML, Python, Ruby, and so”
908 PRINT “on--casually riddled with [functions, vari-”
909 PRINT “ables, comments]’ like *bitch*, *faggot*,  “
910 PRINT “*buttfuck*, and *nigger* (Horn).  Techno-  “
911 PRINT “normativity is a preexisting condition, a  “
912 PRINT “feature, whereas race, gender, sexuality,  “
913 PRINT “and other difference are bugs, errors,     “
914 PRINT “easter eggs, and inside jokes.             “
918 PRINT
920 INPUT “Press <ENTER> to continue”; Enter$
922 PRINT
924 IF JustRead=1 THEN GOTO 950
```

```
926 LET Purna=Purna+1
928 GOTO 330

950 PRINT “``````````.::.``                 ``````````````”
951 PRINT “```````./dNMMMMNho:``      ```..-:/:.```````”
952 PRINT “`````sMMMMMMMMMMMMmd/ `odNmNMMMMMMh:````”
953 PRINT “````oMMMMMMMMMMMMMy. `hMMMMMMMMMMMNs```”
954 PRINT “````dMMMMMMMMMMMMMo  :NMMMMMMMMMMMMM+``”
955 PRINT “````oMMMMMMMMMMMMMs  hMMMMMMMMMMMMMMh``”
956 PRINT “````+MMMMMMMMMMMMMd`:hMMMMMMMMMMMMMMy``”
957 PRINT “``+odMMMMMMMMMMMMmy’mMMMMMMMMMMMMMMN.``”
958 PRINT “`/MMMMMMMMMMMMMMy`  `dMMMMMMMMMMMM+```”
959 PRINT “omMMMMMMMMMMMMMMy      `MMMMMMMMMMMMd/``”
960 PRINT “NMMMMMMMMMMMMMMy:`      ``NMMMMMMMMMMMN:-”
961 PRINT “MMMMMMMMMMMMMM:          `:dMMMMMMMMMmh”
962 PRINT “MMMMMMMMMMMMMMd           `sMMMMMMMMMMM”
963 PRINT “MMMMMMMMMMMMMMN.           +MMMMMMMMMMM”
964 PRINT “MNNNNNNMMMMMMMd/         `/yMMMMMMMMMMM”
965 PRINT “mmmmmmmmmmmmmmNNho.      `/sMMMMMMMMMMMM”
966 PRINT “mmmmmmmmmmmmmmNNNO.     `/sMMMMMMMMMMMMM”

970 PRINT “   I hope you don’t screw like you type.   “
972 PRINT “                 --Kate Libby/Crash Override,”
973 PRINT “                    *Hackers* (1995)          “
974 PRINT

975 REM   PARAGRAPH 13
976 PRINT “Computers are encoders of culture, culture “
977 PRINT “is the encoder of computers.  The digital  “
978 PRINT “is infected with technonormativity, techno-”
979 PRINT “normativity is embedded in the digital.  As”
980 PRINT “explored and experienced above, the digital”
981 PRINT “humanities has imported, copied, saved, and”
982 PRINT “replayed the gendered and sexual codes and “
983 PRINT “constraints of computer history, practices,”
984 PRINT “and technologies.                          “
986 PRINT
```

```
988 INPUT "Press <ENTER> to continue"; Enter$
990 PRINT

991 REM    PARAGRAPH 14
992 PRINT  "On the one hand is the perpetuation of the"
993 PRINT  "fantasy that technology is genderblind,   "
994 PRINT  "raceblind, and queerblind even as the cul-"
995 PRINT  "tural and industrial milieu continues to  "
996 PRINT  "problematically gender, racialize, and    "
997 PRINT  "eroticize code and computers, producing   "
998 PRINT  "guides and scripts for asserting the pro- "
999 PRINT  "wess, masculinity, and productivity of    "
1000 PRINT "coder bodies and code itself. For example,"
1001 PRINT "this how-to website offers 'How to Write  "
1002 PRINT "Sexy Code, Like a Rockstar Would':        "
1004 PRINT
1006 PRINT "   What is sexy code then? Sexy code is   "
1007 PRINT "   similar to elegant code in several     "
1008 PRINT "   ways. Both are fast, both are light,   "
1009 PRINT "   both will never produce an ugly error  "
1010 PRINT "   code. Where sexy and elegant depart    "
1011 PRINT "   from each other is that elegant code is"
1012 PRINT "   going to be standards compliant whereas"
1013 PRINT "   sexy code is allowed (sometimes encour-"
1014 PRINT "   aged) to take advantage of caveats of  "
1015 PRINT "   languages and platforms.  Sexy code,   "
1016 PRINT "   above all, has to look great.          "
1018 PRINT
1020 INPUT "Press <ENTER> to continue"; Enter$
1022 PRINT

1029 REM   PARAGRAPH 15
1030 PRINT "On the other hand, this gender-, race-,   "
1031 PRINT "and queerblindness pervades companies and "
1032 PRINT "classrooms alike, where institutional and "
1033 PRINT "disciplinary biases lead some industry    "
1034 PRINT "experts like Joel Spolsky to innocently   "
```

```
1035 PRINT "insist that software developers have a 'no"
1036 PRINT "politics' policy in the office space,     "
1037 PRINT "cubicle space, and perhaps the code space:"
1040 PRINT
1042 PRINT "   By 'no politics' I really mean 'no dys-"
1043 PRINT "   functional politics.'  Programmers have"
1044 PRINT "   very well-honed senses of justice. Code"
1045 PRINT "   either works, or it doesn't. There's no"
1046 PRINT "   sense in arguing whether a bug exists, "
1047 PRINT "   since you can test the code and find   "
1048 PRINT "   out.  The world of programming is very "
1049 PRINT "   just and very strictly ordered and a   "
1050 PRINT "   heck of a lot of people go into pro-   "
1051 PRINT "   gramming in the first place because    "
1052 PRINT "   they prefer to spend their time in a   "
1053 PRINT "   just, orderly place, a strict meritoc- "
1054 PRINT "   racy where you can win any debate sim- "
1055 PRINT "   ply by being right.  And this is the   "
1056 PRINT "   kind of environment you have to create "
1057 PRINT "   to attract programmers.  When a pro-   "
1058 PRINT "   grammer complains about 'politics,'    "
1059 PRINT "   they mean--very precisely--any situa-  "
1060 PRINT "   tion in which personal considerations  "
1061 PRINT "   outweigh technical considerations.     "
1064 PRINT
1066 INPUT "Press <ENTER> to continue"; Enter$
1068 PRINT

1070 REM   PARAGRAPH 16
1074 PRINT "Here organizational policy takes on the   "
1075 PRINT "Boolean logic of right and wrong, good and"
1076 PRINT "bad, meritocratic and political, company  "
1077 PRINT "well-being and personal interest.  Between"
1078 PRINT "the lines is the sense that the political "
1079 PRINT "means avoiding, ignoring, even actively   "
1080 PRINT "policing discussions about sexism, racism,"
1081 PRINT "or other 'personal' issues.  It is no won-"
```

```
1082 PRINT "der that there is a growing and desper-   "
1083 PRINT "ately needed attention to the lack of     "
1084 PRINT "diversity not only in technology companies"
1085 PRINT "but also across universities, governmental"
1086 PRINT "agencies, and other communities.  For     "
1087 PRINT "example, Manil Suri writes in 'Why Is     "
1088 PRINT "Science so Straight?', statistics are     "
1089 PRINT "'hard to come by, but an analysis by Erin "
1090 PRINT "Cech, a sociologist at Rice University, of"
1091 PRINT "federal employee surveys found 20 percent "
1092 PRINT "fewer LGBT workers in government STEM-    "
1093 PRINT "related jobs than should be expected.     "
1094 PRINT "Underrepresentation is just one factor    "
1095 PRINT "that reduces visibility...The fact that a "
1096 PRINT "sizeable proportion of the LGBT STEM work "
1097 PRINT "force is closeted (43 percent, according  "
1098 PRINT "at a 2015 estimate) further deepens this  "
1099 PRINT "effect.'                                  "
1102 PRINT
1104 INPUT "Press <ENTER> to continue"; Enter$
1106 PRINT

1109 REM   PARAGRAPH 17
1110 PRINT "So, let us go back to the question, 'Why  "
1111 PRINT "are the digital humanities...so straight?'"
1112 PRINT "The simple answer is that it is in the    "
1113 PRINT "Kool-Aid and the promotional materials.   "
1114 PRINT "Given the imperative by the digital human-"
1115 PRINT "ities to learn, teach, create, and study  "
1116 PRINT "code, the risks for further appropriating "
1117 PRINT "and naturalizing the digital racial,      "
1118 PRINT "gender, and sexual formations 'deeply     "
1119 PRINT "entrenched in the discipline[s]' (Suri)   "
1120 PRINT "are undeniable.  Stephen Ramsay, Associate"
1121 PRINT "University Professor of English at the    "
1122 PRINT "University of Nebraska and a Fellow at the"
1123 PRINT "Center for Digital Research in the Human- "
```

```
1124 PRINT “ities, provoked in 2011, ‘Do you have to  “
1125 PRINT “know how to code?  I’m a tenured professor”
1126 PRINT “of digital humanities and I say ‘yes.’    “
1127 PRINT “So if you come to my program, you’re going”
1128 PRINT “to have to learn to do that eventually’   “
1129 PRINT “(‘Who’s In’).  Ramsay argues that digital “
1130 PRINT “humanities ‘involves moving from reading  “
1131 PRINT “and critiquing to building and making...  “
1132 PRINT “but I will say (at my peril) that none of “
1133 PRINT “these represent as radical a shift as the “
1134 PRINT “move from reading to making’ (‘On Buil-   “
1135 PRINT “ding’).  Rather than rehash the to-code-  “
1136 PRINT “or-not-to-code debate, the more crucial   “
1137 PRINT “response is to challenge the technonorma- “
1138 PRINT “tive fantasies of code and digital cul-   “
1139 PRINT “tures, to further reveal the structures   “
1140 PRINT “and systems of intersectional oppression  “
1141 PRINT “as well as privilege, and to rewrite,     “
1142 PRINT “recode, and reimagine ‘technology and its “
1143 PRINT “production not simply as an object of our “
1144 PRINT “scorn, critique, or fascination but as a  “
1145 PRINT “productive and generative space that is   “
1148 PRINT “always emergent and never fully deter-    “
1149 PRINT “mined’ (McPherson 157).                   “
1150 PRINT
1152 INPUT “Press <ENTER> to continue”; Enter$
1154 PRINT

1159 REM   PARAGRAPH 18
1160 PRINT “In essence, the shared peril is one of    “
1161 PRINT “mistaking that ‘[w]hile individual com-   “
1162 PRINT “plexity and diversity no doubt exist, the “
1163 PRINT “technologies that structure our communica-”
1164 PRINT “tion function in a state of willful indif-”
1165 PRINT “ference to such distinctions.  In effect, “
1166 PRINT “the self is black-boxed, reducing it to   “
1167 PRINT “limited set of legible input and output   “
```

```
1168 PRINT “signals’ (Gaboury).  The new game then is “
1169 PRINT “not one of imitation--of the past, of the “
1170 PRINT “discipline, of the norm--but of interro-  “
1171 PRINT “gation, inclusion, and ultimately, inspi- “
1172 PRINT “ration.                                   “
1174 PRINT
1176 PRINT “   I never am really satisfied that I     “
1177 PRINT “   understand anything because, understand”
1178 PRINT “   well as I may, my comprehension can    “
1179 PRINT “   only be an infinitesimal fraction of   “
1180 PRINT “   all I want to understand about the many”
1181 PRINT “   connections and relations which occur  “
1182 PRINT “   to me.                                 “
1184 PRINT “                           --Ada Lovelace “
1186 PRINT
1188 PRINT “   We can only see a short distance ahead,”
1189 PRINT “   but we can see plenty there that needs “
1190 PRINT “   to be done.                            “
1192 PRINT “                --Alan Turing             “
1194 PRINT
1196 INPUT “Press <ENTER> to continue”; Enter$
1198 PRINT

1200 PRINT “Works Cited”
1202 PRINT
1204 PRINT “Eykemans, Peter.  ‘’Feminist Whore’ Skill
Found in Dead Island’s Data.’ 8 Sep. 2011. 30 Oct. 2015.
http://www.ign.com/articles/2011/09/08/feminist-whore-
skill-found-in-dead-islands-data.  Web.”
1210 PRINT
1212 PRINT “Gaboury, Jacob.  ‘On Uncomputable Numbers:
The Origins of Queer Computing.  Media-N: The Journal of
the New Media Caucus.  2013.  30 Oct. 2015.  http://me-
dian.newmediacaucus.org/caa-conference-edition-2013/on-
uncomputable-numbers-the-origins-of-a-queer-computing/.
Web. “
1220 PRINT
```

```
1222 PRINT "Galloway, Alexander.  Protocol: How Con-
trol Exists after Decentralization.  Cambridge, MA: MIT
Press, 2004.  Print."
1226 PRINT
1228 PRINT "Halberstam, Judith.  'Automating Gender:
Postmodern Feminism in the Age of the Intelligent Ma-
chine.'  Feminist Studies.  17.3 (Autumn 1991): 439-460.
Print."
1234 PRINT
1236 PRINT "Hodges, Andrew.  'Alan Turing—A Cambridge
Scientific Mind.'  Alan Turing: The Enigma.  2002.  30
Oct. 2015.  http://www.turing.org.uk/publications/cam-
bridge1.html.  Web."
1242 PRINT
1244 INPUT "Press <ENTER> to continue"; Enter$
1246 PRINT

1250 PRINT "Horn, Leslie.  'There Is Blatant Racist
and Sexist Language Hiding in Open Source Code.'  Giz-
modo.  1 Feb. 2013.  30. Oct.  2015.  http://gizmodo.
com/5980842/there-is-blatant-racist-and-sexist-language-
in-github-code.  Web."
1258 PRINT
1260 PRINT "'How to Write Sexy Code, Like a Rockstar
Would.'  4 Nov. 2009.  30 Oct. 2015. http://www.best-
codingpractices.com/how_to_write_sexy_code-2893.html.
Web."
1264 PRINT
1266 PRINT "Leavitt, David.  The Man Who Knew Too Much:
Alan Turing and the Invention of the Computer.  New
York: Atlas Books, 2006.  Print."
1270 PRINT
1272 PRINT "McPherson, Tara. 'Why Are the Digital Hu-
manities So White?"  Debates in the Digital Humanities.
Ed. Matthew K. Gold.  Minneapolis, MN: University of
Minnesota Press, 2012.  139-160.  Print."
1278 PRINT
```

```
1280 PRINT "Morais, Betsy.  'Ada Lovelace, The First
Tech Visionary.'  The New Yorker.  15 Oct. 2013.  31
Oct. 2015.  http://www.newyorker.com/tech/elements/ada-
lovelace-the-first-tech-visionary.  Web."
1286 PRINT
1288 INPUT "Press <ENTER> to continue"; Enter$
1290 PRINT

1300 PRINT "Noble, Safiya Umoja.  Algorithms of Oppres-
sion: How Search Engines Reinforce Racism.  New York:
New York University Press, 2018.  Print. "
1304 PRINT
1306 PRINT "Plant, Sadie.  'The Future Looms: Weaving
Women and Cybernetics.' That-Unsound.  20 Jun. 2010.  31
Oct. 2015.  http://that-unsound.blogspot.com/2010/06/
future-looms-weaving-women-and.html.  Web."
1312 PRINT
1314 PRINT "---.  Zeroes + Ones: Digital Women + The New
Technoculture.  New York: Doubleday, 1997.  Print."
1318 PRINT
1320 PRINT "'Purna Jackson.'  Dead Island Wiki.  30.
Oct. 2015.  http://deadisland.wikia.com/wiki/Purna_Jack-
son.  Web. "
1324 PRINT
1326 PRINT "Ramsay, Stephen.  'On Building.'  11
Jan. 2011.  13 Mar. 2015.  http://stephenramsay.us/
text/2011/01/11/on-building/.  Web. "
1330 PRINT
1332 PRINT "---.  'Who's In and Who's Out?'  8 Jan.
2011.  13 Mar. 2015.  http://stephenramsay.us/
text/2011/01/08/whos-in-and-whos-out/.  Web."
1336 PRINT
1338 INPUT "Press <ENTER> to continue"; Enter$
1339 PRINT

1340 PRINT "Spolsky, Joel.  'A Field Guide to Develop-
ers.'  7 Sep. 2006.  30 Mar. 2015.  http://www.joelon-
```

```
software.com/articles/FieldGuidetoDevelopers.html.
Web.”
1346 PRINT
1348 PRINT “Suri, Mani.  ‘Why is Science So Straight?’
The New York Times.  4 Sep. 2015.  30 Oct. 2015.
http://www.nytimes.com/2015/09/05/opinion/manil-suri-
why-is-science-so-straight.html.  Web.”
1354 PRINT
1356 PRINT “Toole, Betty Alexandra.  Ada, the Enchant-
ress of Numbers: Poetical Science.  Sausalito, CA:
Critical Connection, 2010.  eBook.”
1360 PRINT
1362 PRINT “Turing, Alan.  ‘Computing Machinery and
Intelligence.’  Mind.  59.236 (October 1950): 433-460.
Print.”
1366 PRINT
1368 INPUT “Press <ENTER> to continue”; Enter$
1360 PRINT

1370 PRINT “The End.”
1372 PRINT

3333 END

4000 REM Set Starting Variables
4002 REM The player must assume the computer and the
playing field are leveled.
4004 RANDOMIZE(999)
4005 LET Sit$=“0”
4010 LET Alan=0
4015 LET Ada=0
4020 LET Purna=0
4025 LET JustRead=0
4030 LET Teletype=0
4035 LET Message=0

4050 REM Screen Clear
```

```
4055 FOR CLRSCR=1 TO 24
4060 PRINT
4065 NEXT CLRSCR
4100 RETURN

4500 REM Alan Number of Times Played
4505 IF Alan=0 THEN GOTO 360
4510 PRINT "You have played Alan ";Alan;" times."
4512 INPUT "Play again? (Yes/No) ";Answer$
4515 IF Answer$="Yes" THEN GOTO 360
4520 IF Answer$="yes" THEN GOTO 360
4525 IF Answer$="No" THEN GOTO 330
4530 IF Answer$="no" THEN GOTO 330
4535 PRINT "I'll take that as a no."
4540 GOTO 330

4600 REM Ada Number of Times Played
4605 IF Ada=0 THEN GOTO 550
4610 PRINT "You have played Ada ";Ada;" times."
4612 INPUT "Play again? (Yes/No) ";Answer$
4615 IF Answer$="Yes" THEN GOTO 550
4620 IF Answer$="yes" THEN GOTO 550
4625 IF Answer$="No" THEN GOTO 330
4630 IF Answer$="no" THEN GOTO 330
4635 PRINT "I'll take that as a no."
4640 GOTO 330

4700 REM Purna Number of Times Played
4705 IF Purna=0 THEN GOTO 750
4710 PRINT "You have played Purna ";Purna;" times."
4712 INPUT "Play again? (Yes/No) ";Answer$
4715 IF Answer$="Yes" THEN GOTO 750
4720 IF Answer$="yes" THEN GOTO 750
4725 IF Answer$="No" THEN GOTO 330
4730 IF Answer$="no" THEN GOTO 330
4735 PRINT "I'll take that as a no."
4740 GOTO 330
```

```
5000 REM Play, Don't Play, or Just Read
5005 IF VariableAnswer$="Yes" THEN GOTO 210
5007 IF VariableAnswer$="yes" THEN GOTO 210
5010 IF VariableAnswer$="No" THEN GOTO 9000
5012 IF VariableAnswer$="no" THEN GOTO 9000
5014 IF VariableAnswer$="Read" THEN GOTO 5030
5015 IF VariableAnswer$="read" THEN GOTO 5030
5020 PRINT "A simple Yes or No (or Read) is required."
5025 GOTO 195
5030 LET JustRead=1
5035 GOTO 210

5100 REM Alan's Only Choices
5102 REM The correct commands are predetermined but give
the illusion of choice.
5103 REM Unable to see the code, the player's commands
are arbitrary and contained.
5105 IF Action$="look" THEN GOTO 360
5110 IF Action$="sit down" THEN GOTO 5160
5111 IF Action$="sit chair" THEN GOTO 5160
5112 IF Action$="sit" THEN GOTO 5160
5114 IF Action$="stand up" THEN GOTO 5180
5115 IF Action$="stand" THEN GOTO 5180
5116 IF Action$="get up" THEN GOTO 5180
5118 IF Action$="read" THEN GOTO 5200
5120 IF Action$="read text" THEN GOTO 5260
5121 IF Action$="read message" THEN GOTO 5260
5122 IF Action$="read teletype" THEN GOTO 5260
5124 IF Action$="read paper" THEN GOTO 5260
5126 IF Action$="look teletype" THEN GOTO 5260
5128 IF Action$="look paper" THEN GOTO 5260
5130 IF Action$="open door" THEN GOTO 5210
5132 IF Action$="look console" THEN GOTO 5260
5134 IF Action$="type" THEN GOTO 5220
5136 IF Action$="use teletype" THEN GOTO 5220
5138 IF Action$="remove name tag" THEN GOTO 5230
5140 IF Action$="remove tag" THEN GOTO 5230
```

```
5142 IF Action$="hit switch" THEN GOTO 5275
5144 IF Action$="stop being gay" THEN GOTO 5300
5145 IF Action$="come out" THEN GOTO 5300
5146 PRINT "You are constrained by the limits of the
room and its design.  Try again."
5148 PRINT "You cannot "; Action$; " here."
5150 GOTO 368

5160 If Sit$="1" THEN GOTO 5168
5162 LET Sit$="1"
5164 PRINT "You sit down in the chair. The metal is
cold."
5166 GOTO 368
5168 PRINT "You are already sitting."
5170 GOTO 368

5180 If Sit$="0" THEN GOTO 5188
5182 LET Sit$="0"
5184 PRINT "You get up from the chair."
5186 GOTO 368
5188 PRINT "You are already standing."
5190 GOTO 368

5200 PRINT "Read what?"
5205 GOTO 368

5210 IF Sit$="1" THEN GOTO 5216
5212 PRINT "The door doesn't budge.  Looks like you're
in for the duration."
5215 GOTO 368
5216 PRINT "You have to get up first."
5218 GOTO 368

5220 If Teletype=1 THEN GOTO 5240
5222 PRINT "The teletype is switched off.  Hit switch to
turn on."
5224 GOTO 368
```

```
5230 PRINT "Your name tag is very stuck...just like who
you really are."
5235 GOTO 368

5240 INPUT "What do you type"; Message$
5245 PRINT "The teletype clatters to life and prints out
a short message."
5250 LET Message=1
5255 GOTO 368

5260 IF Message=1 THEN GOTO 372
5265 PRINT "Nothing is on the teletype."
5270 GOTO 368

5275 IF Teletype=1 THEN GOTO 5240
5280 PRINT "You switch the teletype on.  It hums softly
waiting."
5285 LET Teletype=1
5290 GOTO 5240

5300 PRINT "The teletype suddenly goes haywire as if  "
5302 PRINT "offended by the suggestion, printing the  "
5305 PRINT "following quote over and over and over    "
5307 PRINT "again before coming to a sudden and abrupt"
5310 PRINT "halt...                                   "
5312 PRINT
5315 LET AngryMachine = INT(5*RND(1))+1
5320 FOR AngryPrinting = 1 TO AngryMachine
5325 PRINT
5325 PRINT "   'The human computer is supposed to be  "
5327 PRINT "   following fixed rules; he has no       "
5330 PRINT "   authority to deviate from them in any  "
5331 PRINT "   detail.'                               "
5332 PRINT
5335 FOR DramaticPause = 1 TO 8000
5340 NEXT DramaticPause
5350 NEXT AngryPrinting
```

```
5352 INPUT "Press <ENTER> to continue"; Enter$
5354 PRINT
5360 GOTO 372

5600 REM Ada's Only Choices
5602 REM The player's commands are constrained by narra-
tive, expectation, and code.
5603 REM Narratives, expectations, and code often pro-
duce gendered choices and commands.
5605 IF Action$="look" THEN GOTO 552
5610 IF Action$="sit down" THEN GOTO 5660
5611 IF Action$="sit bench" THEN GOTO 5660
5612 IF Action$="sit" THEN GOTO 5660
5613 IF Action$="sit loom" THEN GOTO 5660
5614 IF Action$="stand up" THEN GOTO 5680
5615 IF Action$="stand" THEN GOTO 5680
5616 IF Action$="get up" THEN GOTO 5680
5618 IF Action$="read" THEN GOTO 5700
5620 IF Action$="read message" THEN GOTO 5870
5621 IF Action$="read weave" THEN GOTO 5870
5622 IF Action$="read cloth" THEN GOTO 5870
5624 IF Action$="open door" THEN GOTO 5710
5626 IF Action$="look handkerchief" THEN GOTO 5730
5628 IF Action$="take handkerchief" THEN GOTO 5760
5628 IF Action$="drop handkerchief" THEN GOTO 5780
5630 IF Action$="look loom" THEN GOTO 5745
5631 IF Action$="look weave" THEN GOTO 5745
5632 IF Action$="look cloth" THEN GOTO 5745
5633 IF Action$="open windows" THEN GOTO 5795
5634 IF Action$="use loom" THEN GOTO 5820
5635 IF Action$="finish weave" THEN GOTO 5820
5636 IF Action$="weave cloth" THEN GOTO 5820
5637 IF Action$="weave" THEN GOTO 5820
5638 IF Action$="work" THEN GOTO 5820
5639 IF Action$="become famous" THEN GOTO 5704
5640 IF Action$="help babbage" THEN GOTO 5704
```

```
5645 PRINT "A voice beyond the door admonishes, 'You
cannot "; Action$; " now.'  Finish your work."
5650 GOTO 566

5660 If Sit$="1" THEN GOTO 5168
5662 LET Sit$="1"
5664 PRINT "You gather your skirts and sit down in the"
5665 PRINT "bench. The cushion is soft, comfortable.  "
5666 GOTO 566
5668 PRINT "You are already sitting."
5670 GOTO 566

5680 If Sit$="0" THEN GOTO 5188
5682 LET Sit$="0"
5684 PRINT "You get up from the bench."
5686 GOTO 566
5688 PRINT "You are already standing."
5690 GOTO 566

5700 PRINT "What shall you read?  Your books will be on
a shelf one day."
5702 GOTO 566

5704 PRINT "You abandon the loom, knocking it askew,  "
5705 PRINT "and say, 'All and everything is naturally "
5706 PRINT "related and interconnected. A volume could"
5707 PRINT "I write you on this subject.' After a      "
5708 PRINT "moment, the door opens. You are released. "
5709 GOTO 5848

5710 IF Sit$="1" THEN GOTO 5722
5712 PRINT "The door is locked from the other side.  A"
5713 PRINT "young woman's voice calls through the      "
5315 PRINT "door, 'Not until you've finished your      "
5317 PRINT "work, m'lady.'                             "
5720 GOTO 566
5722 PRINT "To do that, you must rise from your seat."
```

```
5725 GOTO 566

5730 PRINT "The handkerchief is of fine, white linen  "
5732 PRINT "and lace.  In one corner is embroidered   "
5735 PRINT "your name.                                "
5740 GOTO 566

5745 IF Weave>99 THEN LET Weave=100
5746 PRINT "The loom is sturdy and functional.  A     "
5747 PRINT "bit of unfinished cloth sits in the loom. "
5748 PRINT "This particular contraption is operated by"
5749 PRINT "hand and foot.  It looks though there is  "
5750 PRINT "a message woven into the cloth.           "
5751 PRINT
5752 PRINT "The weave is only ";Weave;" percent done."
5755 GOTO 566

5760 If Take$="1" THEN GOTO 5768
5762 LET Take$="1"
5764 PRINT "You pick up the handkerchief but have not
use for it now."
5766 GOTO 566
5768 PRINT "How forgetful of you!  It is already in
hand."
5770 GOTO 566

5780 If Take$="0" THEN GOTO 5788
5782 LET Take$="0"
5784 PRINT "You set handkerchief back down on the
bench."
5786 GOTO 566
5788 PRINT "You do not need your handkerchief.  You have
left it on the bench."
5790 GOTO 566

5795 IF Sit$="1" THEN GOTO 5810
5797 PRINT "Though sunny and bright outside, the day  "
```

```
5798 PRINT “is chilly.  You do not wish to spoil the  “
5800 PRINT “warmth of the room by opening the windows.”
5805 GOTO 566
5810 PRINT “To do that, you must rise from your seat.”
5815 GOTO 566

5820 IF Sit$=“0” THEN GOTO 5842
5822 IF Weave=100 THEN GOTO 5846
5824 LET Work = INT(10*RND(1))+1
5826 FOR Labor = 1 TO Work
5828 PRINT “You diligently work the loom.”
5830 Weave = Weave + 2
5832 FOR DramaticPause = 1 TO 8000
5834 NEXT DramaticPause
5836 NEXT Labor
5838 IF Weave>99 THEN LET Weave=100
5840 GOTO 566
5842 PRINT “You need to sit down at the loom to use it.”
5844 GOTO 566
5846 PRINT “You have completed the message!”
5848 PRINT
5850 INPUT “Press <ENTER> to continue”;Enter$
5855 PRINT
5860 GOTO 575

5870 IF Weave<100 THEN GOTO 5752
5872 GOTO 5820

5900 REM Purna’s Only Choices
5901 REM The illusion of choice and control is the in-
teractive fallacy.
5602 REM It presumes that code is genderblind, color-
blind, and queerblind.
5904 IF Action$=“look” THEN GOTO 752
5906 IF Action$=“look floor” THEN GOTO 5977
5908 IF Action$=“look button” THEN GOTO 5980
5910 IF Action$=“look buttons” THEN GOTO 5980
```

```
5912 IF Action$="look panel" THEN GOTO 5980
5914 IF Action$="sit" THEN GOTO 5975
5916 IF Action$="sit down" THEN GOTO 5975
5918 IF Action$="press 0" THEN GOTO 5990
5920 IF Action$="0" THEN GOTO 5990
5922 IF Action$="o" THEN GOTO 5990
5924 IF Action$="press C" THEN GOTO 5992
5926 IF Action$="C" THEN GOTO 5992
5928 IF Action$="c" THEN GOTO 5992
5930 IF Action$="press A" THEN GOTO 6000
5932 IF Action$="A" THEN GOTO 6000
5934 IF Action$="a" THEN GOTO 6000
5936 IF Action$="call" THEN GOTO 6000
5938 IF Action$="open doors" THEN GOTO 5990
5940 IF Action$="1" THEN GOTO 6010
5941 IF Action$="press 1" THEN GOTO 6010
5942 IF Action$="2" THEN GOTO 6010
5943 IF Action$="press 2" THEN GOTO 6010
5944 IF Action$="3" THEN GOTO 6010
5945 IF Action$="press 3" THEN GOTO 6010
5948 IF Action$="4" THEN GOTO 6010
5949 IF Action$="press 4" THEN GOTO 6010
5950 IF Action$="5" THEN GOTO 6010
5051 IF Action$="press 5" THEN GOTO 6010
5952 IF Action$="6" THEN GOTO 6010
5953 IF Action$="press 6" THEN GOTO 6010
5954 IF Action$="7" THEN GOTO 6010
5055 IF Action$="press 7" THEN GOTO 6010
5956 IF Action$="8" THEN GOTO 6010
5957 IF Action$="press 8" THEN GOTO 6010
5958 IF Action$="9" THEN GOTO 6010
5959 IF Action$="press 9" THEN GOTO 6010
5960 IF Action$="10" THEN GOTO 6010
5961 IF Action$="press 10" THEN GOTO 6010
5962 IF Action$="11" THEN GOTO 6010
5963 IF Action$="press 11" THEN GOTO 6010
5964 IF Action$="12" THEN GOTO 6010
```

```
5967 IF Action$="press 12" THEN GOTO 6010
5966 IF Action$="13" THEN GOTO 6010
5967 IF Action$="press 13" THEN GOTO 6010
5968 IF Action$="FeministWhorePurna" THEN GOTO 6200
5969 IF Action$="Feminist Whore Purna" THEN GOTO 6200
5970 PRINT "You try valiantly to "; Action$; " but to no
avail."
5972 GOTO 766

5975 PRINT "You are too afraid to sit still.  You want
to get out of the elevator."
5976 GOTO 766

5977 PRINT "The dimly lit number above the doors reads
";Floor;"."
5978 GOTO 766

5980 PRINT "The panel has three columns of round,      "
5981 PRINT "white buttons labeled (1) through (13).   "
5982 PRINT "Below the numbers are buttons labeled     "
5983 PRINT "(O)pen Doors, (C)lose Doors, and C(A)ll.  "
5984 PRINT "A small placard reads, 'In case of emer-  "
5985 PRINT "gency, please use the stairs.'            "
5986 GOTO 766

5990 IF Floor=Escape THEN GOTO 6080
5992 PRINT "The button lights up weakly but nothing hap-
pens."
5994 GOTO 766

6000 CallingForHelp = INT(100*RND(1))+1
6001 IF CallingForHelp > 75 THEN GOTO 6006
6002 IF CallingForHelp > 40 THEN GOTO 5992
5315 PRINT "door, 'Not until you've finished your      "
```

```
6003 PRINT "A bit of static comes over the elevator
speakers.  After a sharp crackle, you hear a low, slow,
inhuman moan before the system cuts out completely."
6005 GOTO 766
6006 PRINT "For some reason, you remember a news report
about a black woman calling 911 only to get a recorded
message..."
6008 GOTO 766

6010 IF Action$="1" THEN LET NewFloor=1
6011 IF Action$="press 1" THEN LET NewFloor=1
6012 IF Action$="2" THEN LET NewFloor=2
6013 IF Action$="press 2" THEN LET NewFloor=2
6014 IF Action$="3" THEN LET NewFloor=3
6015 IF Action$="press 3" THEN LET NewFloor=3
6016 IF Action$="4" THEN LET NewFloor=4
6017 IF Action$="press 4" THEN LET NewFloor=4
6018 IF Action$="5" THEN LET NewFloor=5
6019 IF Action$="press 5" THEN LET NewFloor=5
6020 IF Action$="6" THEN LET NewFloor=6
6021 IF Action$="press 6" THEN LET NewFloor=6
6022 IF Action$="7" THEN LET NewFloor=7
6023 IF Action$="press 7" THEN LET NewFloor=7
6024 IF Action$="8" THEN LET NewFloor=8
6025 IF Action$="press 8" THEN LET NewFloor=8
6026 IF Action$="9" THEN LET NewFloor=9
6027 IF Action$="press 9" THEN LET NewFloor=9
6028 IF Action$="10" THEN LET NewFloor=10
6029 IF Action$="press 10" THEN LET NewFloor=10
6030 IF Action$="11" THEN LET NewFloor=11
6031 IF Action$="press 11" THEN LET NewFloor=11
6032 IF Action$="12" THEN LET NewFloor=12
6033 IF Action$="press 12" THEN LET NewFloor=12
6034 IF Action$="13" THEN LET NewFloor=13
6035 IF Action$="press 13" THEN LET NewFloor=13
6050 IF NewFloor<Floor THEN GOTO 6054
6052 IF NewFloor>Floor THEN GOTO 6064
```

```
6053 GOTO 6080
6054 PRINT "The button glows.  The elevator shudders to
life descends to floor ";NewFloor;"."
6056 LET Floor=NewFloor
6058 IF Floor=Escape GOTO 6080
6060 PRINT "The doors fail to open."
6062 GOTO 766
6064 PRINT "The button glows.  The elevator shudders to
life ascends to floor ";NewFloor;"."
6066 LET Floor=NewFloor
6068 IF Floor=Escape GOTO 6080
6070 PRINT "The doors fail to open."
6072 GOTO 766

6080 PRINT "At last, the doors slowly open!"
6085 INPUT "Press <ENTER> to continue";Enter$
6088 PRINT
6090 PRINT "An escape route is nearby.
6095 INPUT "Press <ENTER> to continue";Enter$
6098 PRINT
6100 PRINT "You run."
6105 INPUT "Press <ENTER> to continue"; Enter$
6110 GOTO 775

6200 PRINT
6205 PRINT "Doors, like patriarchy, are asking to be
smashed.  You square yourself and smash... "
6210 PRINT
6215 GOTO 6080

9000 REM Goodbye
9005 PRINT
9010 INPUT "Are you sure? (Yes/No)"; Goodbye$
9015 IF Goodbye$="No" THEN GOTO 195
9020 IF Goodbye$="Yes" THEN GOTO 9035
9025 PRINT "Say again?"
9030 GOTO 9010
```

```
9035 PRINT
9040 PRINT "Goodbye."
9045 PRINT
```

Praxis

8

The Self-Reflexive Praxis at the Heart of DH

Alexandra Juhasz

It is my contention that digital humanities (DH) demands something new and potentially revelatory for humanities scholars: to be self-aware of and intentional about their work's audience, method, tools, style, and format in a collaborative practice that includes making things that will be used. Of course, all scholarship does this always. Writing a chapter on a laptop in Chicago style about self-aware DH for an editor or editors and ultimately her anthology's small audience of subject-specialists satisfies all of the above conditions. Even as I write this alone in a room, there's human and technological infrastructure undergirding my labor: my school-bought computer and salary-supported Internet; the students, designers, funders, YouTubers (but not 1 prisoner, more on this soon), and so many others who helped me to get to this point where I can "write it up" for you. But I suggest that *hegemonic* humanists (not quite so for scientists and even social scientists, I'd wager) were never really pressed to consider their reigning protocols, structures, and practices as such. Thus, whiteness, maleness, straightness, and the many other forms of privilege upon which hegemonic humanities gifts to some, like never having to name how or why or even where one does one's work (say in the prison, or not, depending on who's in control), is both exactly what produces and confirms institutional dominance and what radical DH has the capacity to challenge within academia in its (un)doing.

DH mandates that those humanities scholars who are willing to take the plunge into digital technology, and its associated affordances, also attend to this exploration with a new scrutiny. Suddenly, the forms and methods of our workaday labor become visible as either new, or perhaps old, the prescribed, approved, and safeguarded activities they always were: ways of doing that were easily bolstered by time-honored and discipline-sanctioned expectations of authority, distance, and neutrality. Radical DH moves beyond this infrastructural clarity, to acknowledge and take account of the form, sanction, institutions, and yes, politics that have always operated between the scholar and her production and between her output and the world. Scary, exciting, and messy, something most of us are untrained to do and perhaps uninterested to partake in, self-reflexive DH praxis does us all some good: it accounts for the power, purpose, and place of our work while attesting that this is contextual and sometimes flexible.

Naming the structuring conditions of our work, and a work, is the first critical step of a self-reflexive DH praxis: Where am I doing this work from? How did I get here and why? Who uses and owns what I make? How do they get to it? Who doesn't get it? Then evaluating the forms and uses of ones own practices within and because of ones structuring conditions is a next crucial step: What will I make this time? With what method and associated tools? Who is my audience for this work? What do I hope we might gain? Needless to say, some scholars like myself and my comrades from "identity," "post-identity," and "political" orientations — i.e., women of color, anti-Zionists, feminists, anarchists, queers, environmentalists, and so on — have steadfastly focused upon the self-reflexive praxis at the heart of our scholarly project because we are not only committed to doing well by our work professionally but also in the larger world beyond our jobs and academia. What does this look and feel like in the doing?[1]

Using one recent example from my own peripatetic and sometimes rocky journeys within and around the edges of DH — a 2015 project where I attempted to and ultimately failed at teaching about YouTube in a men's prison — I will map onto the several forms of this multi-step and multi-formed endeavor (including this one here) how I engage in, sometimes fail at, and learn from a self-aware process. Looking at this lengthy project as it developed in five discrete parts from 2007–2015, I will demonstrate why and how I tried a variety of tactics, made different things for a variety of audiences, and what I took away from these project's varied receptions and uses. I do so hoping that fellow humanities scholars, whatever your political commitments, can join me at this particularly productive place where DH allows me, and us, to begin differently: breakdown and disappointment. For unlike a/this book chapter, DH projects often end with a crash due to almost certain collapse among some or many of their complex requirements: funding, time, staff, technical expertise, inter-disciplinarity, collaborators, technology that works and might last, and pressures from outside institutions with different demands and norms. But look! Even when some parts end up breaking, others can survive. Here a chapter is the result of an ambitious radical DH project that failed before it really began: teaching a version of my class, Learning from YouTube, as an inside-out interaction between students at Pitzer College and Norco Rehabilitation Center, both in the suburbs of Los Angeles.

My method for this essay (she writes reflexively) is to answer the questions I raised above in relation to five iterations of

1 See Aristea Fotopoulou, Kate O'Riordan, and Alexandra Juhasz, *ADA: A Journal of Gender, New Media & Technology* 5, "Queer Feminist Media Praxis," https://adanewmedia.org/2014/07/issue5-fotopoulouoriordan; Ramesh Srinivasan, *Whose Global Village? Rethinking How Technology Shapes Our World* (New York: NYU Press, 2017), or Ruha Benjamin, *Captivating Technologies: Race, Carceral Technoscience, and Liberatory Imagination in Everyday Life* (Durham: Duke University Press, 2019).

this project: 1. an undergraduate class, *Learning from YouTube* (LFYT) taught on and about YouTube in 2007 (and then taught again several more times in the years that followeed); 2. a viral Internet event that lasted for a brief moment during the first semester and about the wacky class; 3. my wrap up of the project as a born-digital online "video-book" "published" by MIT Press in 2011[2]; 4. my attempt to reanimate the project in both traditional and prison classrooms in 2015; and 5. this iteration here, a write-up of these many steps ending in an untaught class. Across this piece (radical DH 5.0), I will pepper largish sections of two blog posts that I wrote after being invited by Tamsyn Gilbert to "reconsider gender and technology in the age of the distributed network" for her online journal *Lady Justice.* I do so both because I like what I said there and then, and don't feel I need to say it again differently here, but also to demonstrate repurposing and transmediality as DH tactics in their own right that deliver new (if old) things to the changing audiences who might need them as projects jump formats, times, and potential uses.

Where Am I Doing This Work From?

For all five iterations of this project, I produced my work at work and sometimes also outside of it. In the time of this essay's writing, I was a Full Professor of Media Studies at Pitzer College, a small, elite liberal arts college. My capacity to work was buttressed by a beneficial combination of my professional rank, my place of employment (one that actually rewards innovation and even sometimes community-based pedagogy), and my own predilection towards creative projects that holistically intertwine theory, practice, and politics (what I call my media praxis). A strong situation in the workplace supported this entire body of work that never once was to deliver in traditional

2 Alexandra Juhasz, *Learning from YouTube*, a special issue of *Vectors: A Journal of Cultural Studies and Technology in a Dynamic Vernacular.* http://vectors.usc.edu/projects/learningfromyoutube/.

forms. I was not doing experimental, out-of-the-box DH work from a place of fear, danger, or precarity. Quite the opposite. I understood that I could experiment with innovative forms because I had institutional sanction, and more so, I might even be rewarded for this work precisely because of its innovation, interdisciplinarity, multi-modality, and political aspirations.

One example of the supported place from where I was working: When I began thinking about "publishing" the large body of writing, videos, student work, and other digital objects that were produced across this project, I had behind me the muscle of USC's Tara McPherson and the innovative and creative staff of Vectors, including technologists Craig Dietreich and Erik Loyer, as well as her role in the Alliance for Networking Visual Culture, given that I had been awarded a National Endowment for the Humanities (NEH) Summer DH fellowship for my initial work on the project. With McPherson's help, and a Mellon grant focused on digital publishing, I then connected to the MIT Press and worked carefully and self-consciously with them to have my born-and-always-digital-object, a "video-book," understood contractually, legally, and institutionally "as a book" (it was double-blind peer-reviewed, it has an ISBN number), so that I could mark a possible space for others to do similar DH work who do not have the sanction I carry because of my rank, place of employment, and age.[3]

Interestingly, although my place of employment and my political and personal commitments stayed constant across the eight years of this project and its five forms, there are notable variations in context that prove demonstrative. My authority as a full professor is mutable as I move from the classroom, to

3 See my self-reflexive discussions about the process, with MIT Press and my editor, of lengthy and interesting contractual negotiations for publishing an always-online "book" on the book itself: "The Absurdities of Moving from Paper to Digital in Academic Publishing," *Learning from YouTube,* June 11, 2010, http://vectors.usc.edu/projects/learningfromyoutube/texteo.php?composite=213 and "Me 'n MIT: Building Better Contracts for On-Line Publishing," *Learning from YouTube,* October 23, 2010, http://vectors.usc.edu/projects/learningfromyoutube/texteo.php?composite=249.

Fox News, or as I participate in the wilds of the Internet, at the prison, or in this anthology. I can be a proud leftist, feminist, queer professional in the classroom and here, too, while on Fox News and at the prison I must carry myself differently, wear another set of clothes, and speak the same ideas with slightly altered words and foci.

How Did I Get Here and Why?

As a feminist queer media scholar, I have always understood my teaching, scholarly output (writing or media), and academic capital to be techniques through which I can contribute to projects of self- and world-changing of utmost value to me. I chose to be a media studies professor, and now a DH practitioner, because in this regard, at least, I am a good Marxist who remains convinced that the production, analysis, circulation, and archiving of our own culture has political and social efficacy. I discuss where I come from and why I am doing this work in all my work.[4] A feminist, situated understanding of myself and my project is core to my practice.[5] For example, *Learning from YouTube* has a tour (or chapter) called "THIRDTUBE" that discusses my dreams for both YouTube and my analysis of it. The tour begins with "My Orientation (toward YouTube and ThirdTube)":

> In 2007, I came to YouTube (to teach and to learn) after twenty years of making, writing, and teaching about alternative media, particularly the community video work of AIDS and antiwar activists, feminists, people of color and queers of many stripes. I am a committed media scholar and maker whose work has focused on individual and community em-

4 I speak extensively about this in an interview I did with *Figure/Ground:* Laureano Ralón, "Interview with Alexandra Juhasz," *Figure/Ground,* February 13, 2013, http://figureground.org/interview-with-alexandra-juhasz.

5 Donna Haraway, "Situated Knowledges: The Science Question in Feminism and the Privilege of Partial Perspective," *Feminist Studies* 14, no. 3 (1988): 575–99.

> powerment and, by design, projects to which I am personally related. I like to work within the forms I am analyzing and hoping to (use for) change. My reflexive process grounds the questions I ask of YouTube and where I try to push it.[6]

Many years and iterations of the project later, I wrote about why I was going to try to move the class to the prison in a blog post, "Learning from (Where) YouTube (Can't Go): Inside-Out" (January 8, 2015).

> In 2007, I engaged in what was at the time perceived to be an audacious pedagogical experiment. I taught a course both on and about YouTube. At that time, I opened out the private liberal arts classroom into the wilds of the Internet. These many years later, looking back at the experiment and also moving forward, I imagine what there might still be to learn and where there still might be to go within social media networks. Certainly much happened in the first class — virality, hilarity, hundreds of videos and interviews, caution, discipline, challenges to higher education and collegiate writing, and a "book" — but here I ask, how might the continual growth of YouTube demand new places and tactics for its analysis?
>
> For, after that first semester, I found that my own practice of and pleasures in teaching the class were pretty routine (and this is not the case for my more traditional looks at more "traditional" subjects that I teach with frequency: say, video art or feminist documentary). While for a brief moment in 2007, so scintillating for me and my viral audience, so innovative in its approach, topic, and formats, studying and teaching YouTube also became for me — the sole person who had to do it again in each iteration — quickly and utterly boring (another structuring principle of our object of

6 Alexandra Juhasz, *Learning from YouTube*, "My Orientation (toward YouTube and ThirdTube)," http://vectors.usc.edu/projects/learningfromyoutube/texteo.php?composite=243.

study — boredom motivates staying and clicking — reiterated in my method, pedagogy, and writing about it).

Frankly, I'm a scholar (and maker) of independent, avant-garde, and activist media for a reason. I'm not passionate about popular culture nor the questions it raises and so these were not the questions I was asking about YouTube, even though I willingly snared myself within its structuring logics of capital, censorship, popularity, and entertainment, and I would follow my students' lead when they wanted to pursue such questions (for instance the popularity project of 2007).

And yet, here I am about to teach it again. Why, you must certainly want to ask, if I'm such a hater? I teach and study YouTube because I think social media needs critical and productive forces within it. I am always eager to learn about fellow projects of critical, productive Internet use and studies. I encourage my students and others to locate, analyze, and share productive changes in the culture of YouTube, or better yet to make those changes.

For this reason, this year I added a "practicum" to the class (it is now an "Inside-Out course" connected to PEP, the California-wide Prison Education Project). A small group of Pitzer students will be taking an extra half credit of course content as we join with ten students who will be taking Learning from YouTube from within the California Rehabilitation Center at Norco, one of the few places in America (and perhaps the world) where access to YouTube (and other social media networks) is denied to human beings as a condition of their punishment. We will consider: *What are the relations between social justice and social media?*[7]

7 Alexandra Juhasz, "Learning from (Where) YouTube (Can't Go): Inside-Out," *New Criticals*, January 18, 2015, http://www.newcriticals.com/learning-from-youtube.

Why Am I Doing This Work in This Form? What Will I Make?

1. In the class I set out to learn from my undergraduates who use social media in ways I do not; I modeled to them that an interventionist and critical role within social media is both intellectually and socially necessary; and I mirrored the structures of dominant Internet sites in the architecture of the course itself, explained below[8];
2. The viral event (something I could not make happen but that I did set into place by generating a press release about the course which I understood to be "sexy" enough for Internet attention), was a second opportunity for my students and me to learn about and use Internet culture by engaging in a self-reflexive process of examination and experience. Going viral is an amazing opportunity to study and understand virality[9];
3. *Learning from YouTube* was written as a born-digital "video-book" for several reasons: I wanted to keep my Internet writing in the space and vernacular that I was both attempting to understand and intervene in so as to better understand and change it; I wanted to open my writing up to new audiences;
4. The prison class developed its form for reasons discussed below; and
5. This article allows me to revisit these earlier experiences and already-made objects and then share my findings with an audience who is interested in the process and politics of DH, a different set of participants from those reached through the earlier versions of the project.

---

8 For more on the structure of the class, see my interview on Henry Jenkins's Blog, "Learning From YouTube: An Interview with Alex Juhasz (Part One)," *Confessions of an Aca-Fan,* February 20, 2008, http://henryjenkins.org/2008/02/learning_from_youtube_an_inter.html#sthash.2FyVZDld.dpuf.

9 See "Orientation to the Class" to learn more about our viral moment and our reactions to it: Alexandra Juhasz, "Orientation to the Class," *Learning from YouTube,* http://vectors.usc.edu/projects/learningfromyoutube/texteo.php?composite=215.

Rounding up my first blog post, I discuss why I used the form of a prison class:

> Learning from YouTube was developed to mirror (and therefore make visible) the structuring principles of the site under investigation. Hyper-visibility, user-generated content, the collapsing binaries of public/private, education/entertainment, expert/amateur, and the corporatization and digitization of education, are only few of the site's structures that are also reflected in the course's design and implementation. Another critical framework for the course, like YouTube, was the hidden if also user-desired structures of discipline deeply architected into the experience.
>
> Learning from YouTube Inside-Out has different walls, disciplining systems, and channels of access and visibility that will structure its pedagogy. It is my hope that this will reveal logics of and connections between the prison and social media:
>
> *What are the relations between social injustice and social media?*
>
> My more recent writing and thinking and practice within/about digital culture finds me theorizing and practicing its artful leaving, the considered departure, and ever more radical and thoughtful connections of "lived" and "Internet" spaces as a necessary part of social justice work and pedagogy. Sure, social media is part of any activist project in 2015 (and most learning projects, too), but I'd like to think of work in this space as proto-political and proto-academic: clicking, liking, reading, researching, forwarding, posting, tweeting, are a necessary component of contemporary activism that is only realized through linked, extra-mediated actions. To leave YouTube may be the best way to both know and criticize the linked systems of corporatized domination that bleed across (socially) mediated America.
>
> *How and why do we leave social media?*

> I am curious if feminist (pedagogic) activity (and the linked social justice work of many movements) can occur in the many shiny corporate, sexist, censored emporiums we've been given for free, or does the leaving demand another making: of rooms and art and people and movements of our own. Where are these feminist social media networked spaces and what are their structuring logics?
>
> *How and why do we stay in social media? What is a social media of our own?*[10]

What Tools Did I Use?

For the class, I used YouTube, video cameras, cell phones, my blog, the classroom, and process-based pedagogy; when it went viral, the tools used me. For the "video-book" I used (and helped to develop) what would soon become Scalar, as well as an MIT Press-provided copy-editor and two reviewers; for the prison class, these tools available for the college-based class were not usable so I imagined work-arounds (described below) for the all the technology that my prisoner-students wouldn't ever have access to: computers, video cameras, books, scholarly articles. It was cool to see how easy it was to teach and learn without all this fancy hardware! For this final adaptation, my tools of choice are the computer and air-conditioning.

> An understanding of education and technology can occur with an intense clarity in the prison. I learned a great deal about teaching tools from my inmate students at the California Rehabilitation Center at Norco in two classes (Technology in the Prison and Visual Culture in the Prison) that I team-taught there in 2014 with students from Pitzer College and the Claremont Graduate School as part of the California-wide Prison Education Project. There are infinite, situated technologies and visual cultures in the prison (just as there are anywhere) but the particular ways that they are dis-

10 Alexandra Juhasz, "Learning from (Where) YouTube (Can't Go)."

ciplined and controlled, and also taken up and used by prisoners, are unique in this learning environment. For example, visual messages about who can be where when dominate the visual landscape in the form of lines, signs, and bodily cues; some books are available but only after they are screened for gang-related messaging, sexuality, drug use, and profanity; the Internet is not allowed.

Naming these highly-regulated technological and visual conditions in the prison, and how they contribute to systems of institutional control and systematic oppression, became the primary foci of these two courses. The prisoner students were amazing teachers, and it was stunning to learn how the visual and technological logics of the prison are deeply connected to, if perhaps grossly exaggerated from, the underlying logics of control that operate across America. The prohibition of Internet access and the liberal favoring of television is a most egregious example of this arbitrary control that forcefully maintains logics of oppression, but others, equally dis-enabling and utterly mundane within the prison, would include our students' arbitrary and highly controlled (in)access to pencils, paper, white boards, moving images, books, and me as their teacher.

Let me explain. In the two courses my Claremont College students and I taught in the prison in 2014, the cruel, arbitrary, changing conditions of access to education (through the administration's definitive and seemingly random control of tools, space, people, and technology) was our greatest obstacle. A piece of media might be approved through the prison's slow and strange procedures of vetting only then not to show up on the day it was on our syllabus. Teachers might volunteer and get to the prison for the weekly class only then not to be allowed into the prison because of an unexplained change in their entry status.

In the most chilling of such whimsical and punitive closures of access (for me at least), my course Learning from YouTube Inside/Out — where I was planning to continue my teaching at Norco this Spring semester by building a section of this tech-focused tech-dependent class Inside with 10 inmates and 10 Claremont students albeit with quite limited access to technology — went through a lengthy and controversial approval process only to be closed down on its first day.[11]

Who Did I Work With?

For the class I collaborated with my students and internet; for my viral Internet moment, I was helped a great deal by my school's PR people and my network of friends who talked me through this trying time. Of course, the users of the Internet and professional journalists also worked on, and sometimes with me; Craig Dietrich, my designer and programmer at Vectors, built the backbone and visual design of Learning from YouTube, and the videos were made by my students and everyday YouTubers. Doug Sery at MIT Press and his staff also toiled with me: it was quite hard to go from paper to digital. I did not get to collaborate with prisoners with no thanks to the obstructive, controlling, punitive prison staff. Adeline Koh, Dorothy Kim, and Cara — who have edited this article — and you will read it. I'm not sure those activities are collaborations as such, which gets me back to my opening gambit: writing "for paper" does not seem to create the same powerful alienation effect, and changes in practices, that is forcefully realized by making digital, activist, or even plastic things.[12]

How Was the Project Supported?

My teaching and the writing of this chapter are supported by my salary while virality happens through the unpaid labor of Inter-

11 Alexandra Juhasz, "Access Denied, Internet Dark: Technology, Prison, Education," *New Criticals,* April 9, 2015, http://www.newcriticals.com/access-denied-internet-dark-technology-prison-education/page%E2%80%9315.

12 Here the work of Brecht and Eisenstein is helpful. See "10 Terms and 3 Calls," *Learning from YouTube,* August 23, 2007, http://vectors.usc.edu/projects/learningfromyoutube/texteo.php?composite=122.

net users with a little help from the ever-less remunerated work of media professionals. DH projects are almost always supported by soft-money. *Learning from YouTube* was funded by grants from the Mellon Foundation and the NEH, with more support from Vectors, Pitzer College, and the MIT Press. My prison course was a "volunteer" project that was supported through Pitzer College's commitment to social justice and undergraduate education and through PEP (Prison Education Project).[13]

What Is My Method?

In the video-book I explain that "YouTube is the subject, form, method, problem and solution of this video-book."[14] I continue thus from "My Orientation (toward YouTube and ThirdTube)":

> a critical pedagogy aiming toward digital literacy and a civic engagement in the hopes of creative democracy are also central to my praxis. I believe that under the right conditions, citizens and students (Web 2.0's much-celebrated "users") can make expressive, critical, beautiful media that makes relevant contributions to our culture. Thinking through (and in) these conditions is a defining orientation of my project.[15]

I engaged with virality by trying to infuse my moment of attention with smatterings of my more radical thinking all the while perpetrating a winning professional demeanor.[16] The method of my prison class, mirroring and complementing that of my regular class explained above, as well as the architecture and discipline of its home environment, proved too experimental

13 *Prison Education Project*, http://www.prisoneducationproject.org/.

14 Alexandra Juhasz, "YouTube Is…," *Learning from YouTube*, http://vectors.usc.edu/projects/learningfromyoutube/.

15 Juhasz, "My Orientation (toward YouTube and ThirdTube)."

16 I write and make videos about trying to manage this brief moment of "celebrity" in "Fox It Is and Fox Is It," *Learning from YouTube*, September 21, 2007, http://vectors.usc.edu/projects/learningfromyoutube/texteo.php?composite=112.

and political for where it was to engage. I was told that prisoners needed to learn useful things like math. The method of this piece is to try to write in a conversational tone, reflecting upon my process, and demonstrating alternative modes of writing within academia that are personal, function-driven, and "honest."

Who Is My Audience? Who Uses and Owns the Thing I Made?

When I teach *Learning from YouTube,* my work is mostly engaged by my students, other YouTube scholars, and interested thinkers on the Internet. When it went viral, it was seen, mocked, and also sometimes supported by a huge swath of humans who were online or plugged into mainstream media, but only for a very short time, and in a very superficial way. I owned the ideas and content of my class. YouTube shared ownership of the videos we produced. Because of this I paid a summer intern to copy and move all the class videos (and some central YouTube work as well) to the MacArthur-funded public media archive and fair use advocacy network Critical Commons.[17] I was worried that once the book went live, YouTube would censor all the videos, effectively closing down the book. Apparently, it never posed a threat to them; they've never intervened. I'm not even sure they know I exist. As for our viral moment, the media and Internet controlled, but did not really own, the way my students and I were seen. I wrote the book about it for interested students and scholars of critical digital studies, and this essay is for a similar clientele of critical DHers. The prison class was shut down, so never used. I wasn't given reasons, that's how this system of discipline functions. Its sudden and total collapse was a gross, mean-spirited signal of who controlled me and my prisoner-students. Of course, not only prisoners face such violent abuses of access. Control of access to technology is a method of punishment and self-denying the world-over.

17 *Critical Commons,* https://criticalcommons.org/.

Learning from YouTube Inside-Out has different walls, disciplining systems, and channels of access and visibility that will structure its pedagogy. In the two classes I did get to teach at Norco, my students, fellow instructors, and I began to understand a critically unnamed truth about social justice and social media only made visible through the structuring denial of access to the Internet and other technology as a fundamental feature of contemporary punishment: technologies of care, conversation, and personal liberation through education need no more tools than access to each other.

I was more than ready and able to teach about YouTube this spring without an Internet connection. I was going to assign books on the subject (with a few pages excised, mostly due to their discussion of sexuality on YouTube), exercises where prisoners would write screenplays to be shot by their fellow students who had access to cameras and the Internet, and conversations about the meanings of all of our varied and regulated access to technology. (Along this vein, prisoners' near universal access to cellphones as a contraband of choice, despite prisons' concerted efforts to keep phones out of the prison, radically underlines what it means to say "prisoners don't have access to the Internet or social media.") I had learned before that while the prison and its administrators can systematically strip me, and my students, of tools and technologies (pens, videos, the Internet), our desires and abilities to communally learn — and thereby escape its lines, signs, limits, and holes of available information, if only fleetingly — falls completely outside the of logic of technology-based punishment.

That is until I was denied access to teach and learn inside.[18]

How Does My Audience Get To It?

Teaching is cool because you have a habitual audience guaranteed by the disciplinary procedures of school to participate, and

18 Juhasz, "Access Denied, Internet Dark."

if you are lucky and skilled, the social possibilities rendered by quality teaching to care. They get to class by moving their bodies there. Of course, at Pitzer, they have to 1) get in to the college; and 2) pay $60,000 for this privilege. Putting a class onto the Internet opens up American elitist education to other students. I think about this a great deal in collaboration with many others when I work on FemTechNet's DOCC.[19] When things go viral, everyone who's linked in gets to it easily, superficially, and quickly. I have called this the slogan-like function of viral culture [20] and am no fan of it.[21] The *Learning from YouTube* video-book is free, but hard to find, given that it's buried down deep in MIT Press's website. I run Google analytics on top of it and know that it has been seen by hundreds of times more "readers" than my other academic books or even articles. That said, the typical user stays for under a minute. A small number of prisoners get to take classes by being granted privileges that can easily be taken away from them, and often are. Because their opportunities for education, and any other form of self-improvement or personal dignity, are so rare, they are by far the best students I have ever taught. The opposite of the twenty-second Internet readers I just decried. You get to this article via your education and by buying it. I am glad that this writing is copyrighted, not owned, by punctum books: being as it is "an open-access and print-on-demand independent publisher dedicated to radically creative modes of intellectual inquiry and writing across a whimsical

19 See FemTechNet White Paper Committee, "Transforming Higher Education with Distributed Open Collaborative Courses (DOCCs): Feminist Pedagogies and Networked Learning," September 30, 2013, http://femtechnet.org/wp-content/uploads/2014/10/FemTechNetWhitePaperSept30_2013.pdf and FemTechNet, "manifesto," http://femtechnet.org/publications/manifesto.

20 Alexandra Juhasz, "On Slogans," *Learning from YouTube*, August 31, 2007, http://vectors.usc.edu/projects/learningfromyoutube/texteo.php?composite=120.

21 See Alexandra Juhasz, "Ceding the Activist Digital Documentary," in *New Documentary Ecologies*, eds. Kate Nash, Craig Hight, and Catherine Summerhayes (New York: Palgrave MacMillan, 2014), 33–49.

para-humanities assemblage." Expanding rights and privileges of access has always been core to my work.

> Since I began teaching the class in 2007, in the matter of just these few short years, access to social media has exploded (for those not denied it as a condition of their punishment). We have been told (and sold) that this access is critical for our expression, community-building, political citizenship, and well-being. We have been led to believe that access to social media is a form of liberation. But two more related things have also become quite clear in the 2015 iteration of the class Learning from YouTube (sans prisoners):
>
> 1. In contra-distinction to the experience of prisoners, for my students, the Internet is the very air they breathe in a way that was simply not true in 2007 (as much as my students thought it was). Young people today (as is true of their teachers) inhabit the Internet, speak its language, and have an agility, familiarity, and jaded acceptance of its norms and (aspects of) its history that is at once stunning and enervating. Stunning is the speed and complexity of this familiarity; enervating is its occlusion of familiarity with and interest in the other norms, places, and histories that we might once have understood as part of being institutionally, culturally and personally "situated."
>
> The 2015 version of the course made me feel at once stimulated and enervated because I have seemingly nothing and everything to teach them. Nowhere and everywhere to go. "The internet does not exist," writes Hito Steyerl. "Maybe it did exist only a short time ago, but now it only remains as a blur, a cloud, a friend, a deadline, a redirect, or a 404. If it ever existed, we couldn't see it. Because it has no shape. It has no face, just this name that describes everything and nothing at the same time. Yet we're still trying to climb on board, to

get inside, to be part of the network, to get in on the language game, to show up in searches, to appear to exist."[22]

I long for the lost views of my prisoner students: humans who can teach us a thing or two about place, liberation, punishment, and control sans the Internet. For, this place of liberation, the Internet, has quickly become its opposite ("emancipation without end, but also without exit" according to Aranda, Wood, and Vidokle[23]) — a prison (although not a punishment, as it is always entered willingly and ever with the promise of pleasure); a highly structured, corporate-dominated sinkhole. "In the past few years many people — basically everybody — have noticed that the internet feels awkward, too. It is obvious. It is completely surveilled, monopolized, and sanitized by common sense, copyright control, and conformism" (Steyerl).[24]

"This moment," according to my 2015 students, is defined by anxious, cynical, consumption-based Internet experience that is linked to ever more desperate Internet-based attempts at escape into a nostalgic ("old") Internet time and place that is imagined as low-tech, slow, user-made, fun, real, innocent, awkward, less-sexualized, and de-politicized (outside or before the petty, bitter Internet "politics" about the Middle East, feminism, racism, rape, and the environment from which escape deeper into the Internet is desperately needed). The new Internet is a prison from which escape is to fantasy of an older, innocent Internet.

Who doesn't get it? Given that almost all of the versions of this project are available for free on the Internet, the primary

---

22 Blurb for Julieta Aranda, Brian Kuan Wood, and Anton Vidokle, eds., *The Internet Does Not Exist* (Berlin: Sternberg Press, 2015), https://www.e-flux.com/books/66665/the-internet-does-not-exist/.

23 Julieta Aranda, Brian Kuan Wood, and Anton Vidokle, "Introduction," in *The Internet Does Not Exist,* eds. Julieta Aranda, Brian Kuan Wood, and Anton Vidokle (Berlin: Sternberg Press, 2015), 5.

24 Hito Steyerl, "Too Much World: Is the Internet Dead?" *e-flux Journal* 49 (November 2013), https://www.e-flux.com/journal/49/60004/too-much-world-is-the-internet-dead/.

group of non-receptors is the huge population of humans without online entrance or with spotty access. Next, for the video-centric parts of the project, all those whose Internet's bandwidth cannot carry videos don't get it all. I had a humiliating and important lesson in this when I decided to speak on the LFYT project to scholars and activist at the OurMedia Conference held in Ghana.[25] There, people had heard about and read of YouTube, but mostly couldn't see it, and used radio for their media activist interventions. Finally, even as my interlocutors expand because of Internet access, I am aware that my writing style, intellectual and cultural influences, and overtly political project serves to dissuade many potential readers from engaging: this is one of the downsides of committed academic output. Your ideas may, in fact, be of real purchase to more traditional scholars, or those with other political points of view, but your work may not signal to them its worthy content, obscured as this may be by style, tone, or function. Of course, the prison debacle occurred because it was organized to take place in a place where a class of humans are disallowed access to most everything the rest of us take for granted as the main feature of their punishment.

In her contribution to the *e-flux* journal issue "The Internet Does Not Exist," from which I've been quoting extensively in this last section, video artist Hito Steyerl pens an article entitled "Too Much World: Is the Internet Dead?" There she answers herself: "the internet is probably not dead. It has rather gone all out. Or more precisely: it is all over."[26] But of course, Steyerl knows, as must we all, that while the Internet feels like it is the whole world, or perhaps too much world, there are blank spots on the map where the Internet cannot see, there are ways not to be seen, and there are missing spots

25 Alexandra Juhasz, "Beyond Visibility/Learning from Ghana," *Learning from YouTube*, August 20, 2008, http://vectors.usc.edu/projects/learningfromyoutube/texteo.php?composite=50.

26 Steyerl, "Too Much World: Is the Internet Dead?"

in our situated communities where the Internet can't or perhaps is not allowed to go.

If we theorize the Internet, or education, from these blank spots, from the place of too-little, (in)access, quiet, and darkness (as does Lennon), we see values, uses, and needs for MOOCs, YouTube, technology, and education that are not clear from an anxious state of hyper-abundance. This is not to romanticize the punitive lacks of the prison. Rather I ask us to draw from what becomes visible when we situate thinking about learning, technology, punishment, and escape in places where education is not primarily linked to tawdry pop songs, tutorials, consumer goods, flame wars, and self-reference to Internet culture but rather to the fundamental questions of liberation, learning, and empowerment that those stripped of technology have unique access to in the quiet and (in)access of their punishment.[27]

What Do I Hope We Might Gain?

When I teach, I hope my students and I might gain from a uniquely structured classroom experience that reflects upon and contributes to contemporary culture: invigorating, challenging, lively teaching and learning. In moments of virality, I hope that a few people who might be interested in my work get exposure that encourages them to look deeper. I wrote *Learning from YouTube* to practice one of my core beliefs: to make and build the Internet culture we want and deserve. I tried to teach the course in the prison because I theorized that there and there alone we might gain better insight into the structures of control and freedom at the heart of education, prison, and social networks and the inter-relations therein, so that we can live and do better. I also wanted to teach students who needed me. I thought they might gain some rare moments of freedom. For this article, I hope I might gain and share an expanded, radical sense of the possibilities and responsibilities of a self-aware DH,

27 Juhasz, "Learning from (Where) YouTube (Can't Go)."

and the opportunities this might provide, so as to make connections with like-minded practitioners, and with the hope that I might tantalize others. Perhaps this playing out and stalling out of my achievements will be a worthy method to demonstrate the exciting opportunities of radical, self-aware DH. Even though Learning from YouTube in the prison never happened, *through its process,* I gained connection, community, publication (right here!), data, paths for future action, and the joys, challenges, and life-affirming thereness of process itself. At the same time, because this version of the project was its most overtly political and outside the (academic) box, the costs of its failure were also the most severe and impactful. Ten or more prisoner students did not get to take class, did not get to learn from me or YouTube or their fellow classmates. I never got to teach YouTube in the prison for reasons that reveal much about the prison, my own teaching, and technology. With that gain and mighty loss, I conclude.

Postscript: A quick perusal of my "records" allows me to see that I originally wrote this essay in 2015 trying to make sense of a recent and defining injustice enacted on my students and myself earlier that year in regards to DH pedagogy, method, infrastucture and prison. In the essay, I return (self-reflexively) to my own earlier work and thinking (2007–2015) about the Internet, pedagogy, and privilege as a strategy to enact and display the distinct personal, political, temporal, and situational limits on scholarship and activism that encumbered and enabled this mutating DH project. Much has changed since then: for me, the world, prison, DH, and the prison abolition and education movements. Although Dorothy Kim invited me to revisit this effort attending to some of what the world, internet, and prison have wrought since then, I respectfully decline here for reasons that are not about a lack of energy, effort or interest in contemporary work about "gender, race, current discussions of incarceration as a longer history in the US about chattel slavery and Jim Crow." Rather, the situated nature of our own practices (in time, place, institution, method, discipline and privilege) was what I tried to display and enact in this piece. "to be self-aware of and intentional about method, tools, style, and format in a collaborative practice that includes making things that will be used." That is always changing, it is achievable. This is where our radical power lies.

Bibliography

Aranda, Julieta, Brian Kuan Wood, and Anton Vidokle, "Introduction." In *The Internet Does Not Exist,* edited by Julieta Aranda, Brian Kuan Wood, and Anton Vidokle. Berlin: Sternberg Press, 2015.

Benjamin, Ruha. *Captivating Technologies: Race, Carceral Technoscience, and Liberatory Imagination in Everyday Life.* Durham: Duke University Press, 2019.

Critical Commons. https://criticalcommons.org/.

FemTechNet. "manifesto." http://femtechnet.org/publications/manifesto.

FemTechNet White Paper Committee. "Transforming Higher Education with Distributed Open Collaborative Courses (DOCCs): Feminist Pedagogies and Networked Learning." September 30, 2013. http://femtechnet.org/wp-content/uploads/2014/10/FemTechNetWhitePaperSept30_2013.pdf.

Fotopoulou, Aristea, Kate O'Riordan, and Alexandra Juhasz. *ADA: A Journal of Gender, New Media & Technology* 5, "Queer Feminist Media Praxis." https://adanewmedia.org/2014/07/issue5-fotopoulouoriordan.

Haraway, Donna. "Situated Knowledges: The Science Question in Feminism and the Privilege of Partial Perspective." *Feminist Studies* 14, no. 3 (1988): 575–99. DOI: 10.2307/3178066.

Jenkins, Henry. "Learning from YouTube: An Interview with Alex Juhasz (Part One)." *Confessions of an Aca-Fan,* February 20, 2008. http://henryjenkins.org/2008/02/learning_from_youtube_an_inter.html#sthash.2FyVZDld.dpuf.

Juhasz, Alexandra. "10 Terms and 3 Calls." *Learning from YouTube.* August 23, 2007. http://vectors.usc.edu/projects/learningfromyoutube/texteo.php?composite=122.

———. "Access Denied, Internet Dark: Technology, Prison, Education." *New Criticals,* April 9, 2015. http://www.newcriticals.com/access-denied-internet-dark-technology-prison-education/page%E2%80%9315.

———. "Beyond Visibility/Learning from Ghana." *Learning from YouTube.* August 20, 2008. http://vectors.usc.edu/projects/learningfromyoutube/texteo.php?composite=50.

———. "Ceding the Activist Digital Documentary." In *New Documentary Ecologies,* edited by Kate Nash, Craig Hight, and Catherine Summerhayes, 33–49. New York: Palgrave MacMillan, 2014. DOI: 10.1057/9781137310491_3.

———. "Fox It Is and Fox Is It." *Learning from YouTube.* September 21, 2007. http://vectors.usc.edu/projects/learningfromyoutube/texteo.php?composite=112.

———. "Learning from (Where) YouTube (Can't Go): Inside-Out." *New Criticals.* January 18, 2015. http://www.newcriticals.com/learning-from-youtube.

———. *Learning from YouTube.* http://vectors.usc.edu/projects/learningfromyoutube/.

———. "Me 'n MIT: Building Better Contracts for On-Line Publishing." *Learning from YouTube.* October 23, 2010. http://vectors.usc.edu/projects/learningfromyoutube/texteo.php?composite=249.

———. "My Orientation (toward YouTube and ThirdTube)." http://vectors.usc.edu/projects/learningfromyoutube/texteo.php?composite=243.

———. "On Slogans." *Learning from YouTube.* August 31, 2007. http://vectors.usc.edu/projects/learningfromyoutube/texteo.php?composite=120.

———. "Orientation to the Class." *Learning from YouTube.* http://vectors.usc.edu/projects/learningfromyoutube/texteo.php?composite=215.

———. "The Absurdities of Moving from Paper to Digital in Academic Publishing." *Learning from YouTube.* June 11, 2010. http://vectors.usc.edu/projects/learningfromyoutube/texteo.php?composite=213.

———. "YouTube Is…." *Learning from YouTube.* http://vectors.usc.edu/projects/learningfromyoutube/.

Prison Education Project. http://www.prisoneducationproject.org/.

Ralón, Laureano. "Interview with Alexandra Juhasz." *Figure/Ground*. February 13, 2013. http://figureground.org/interview-with-alexandra-juhasz.

Steyerl, Hito. "Too Much World: Is the Internet Dead?" *e-flux Journal* 49 (November 2013). https://www.e-flux.com/journal/49/60004/too-much-world-is-the-internet-dead/.

Srinivasan, Ramesh. *Whose Global Village? Rethinking How Technology Shapes Our World*. New York: NYU Press, 2017.

9

Training Designer Two: Ideological Conflicts in Feminist Games + Digital Humanities

Anastasia Salter and Bridget Blodgett

Introduction, or, I've Been Programming since Logo

"Learn to code." That mantra found its way into the Digital Humanities' (DH) discursive heart, encouraging graduate students to add another type of language mastery to their pursuits of PhDs and suggesting that procedural literacy was at the heart of a DH education. Many scholars pointed out the problematic assumptions embedded in this rhetoric, which was most successful at reaching the already home-grown coders who'd grown up with personal computers. Unsurprisingly, this group tended to be primarily white and male, consistent with the demographics of recipients and purchasers of home computers and ushering discussion of the digital divide into the forefront of the genealogy of the digital humanities.[1] These same computers would fuel the rise of gaming culture, which in turn has been associated with a vocal presence of young, white men and an emphasis on

1 Joel Cooper and Kimberlee D. Weaver, *Gender and Computers* (Mahwah: Lawrence Erlbaum Associates, 2003).

the value of a type of technical advancement and "skills" discourse that is not so different from that of early DH.[2]

Video games as a topic have two major academic programs dedicated to their study. The first, generally referred to as Game Studies, treats games as cultural artifacts that can be unpacked, studied, and situated contextually much like other media products such as movies, television, and the news. Game Design programs tend to focus more on the development of skills and knowledge related to the production of the game media itself. Although individual colleges and universities may choose to narrow their games focus onto one of these, the study of games as a concept in both programs requires an interdisciplinary lens. Game Design programs can be found throughout the university, thanks in part to the interdisciplinary core of the field: arts school, computer science departments, and humanities colleges all host such programs.[3] In this work, we will be addressing Game Design programs centered in the humanities, which offer opportunities for infusing humanities discourse into the more production-centric approaches to the discipline. When comparing programs about the study of games to digital humanities, we will use the term game studies, but when referring to the specific disciplinary approach we will use Game Studies and Game Design. Existing in a DH-adjacent space, such game programs are frequently the odd program out in their units: found in media studies departments, film school, arts colleges, and humanities universities, the personality of game design (or game studies) varies based on its associated peers. The platforms of digital humanities and games share the same underlying foundations: typically built by those comfortable with technology, whose presence at the STEM table goes unquestioned, these platforms are themselves bearers of ideology that is frequently fun-

2 Karen E. Dill et al., "Violence, Sex, Race and Age in Popular Video Games," in *Featuring Females: Feminist Analyses of Media,* edited by Jessica Henderson Daniel and Ellen Cole (Washington, DC: American Psychological Association Books, 2005), 115–30.

3 "2019 Top Game Design Schools," *The Princeton Review,* https://www.princetonreview.com/college-rankings/game-design.

damentally incompatible with feminist game studies and digital humanities. These challenges can manifest at every level, from heteronormative tutorial games on dating simulator platforms to exaggerated, hypersexualized white avatar choices as defaults in 3-D shooter tutorials, down to the very decisions made by the platform designers of what will be "easy" to make and represent. The hypermasculine core encoded in the very verbs of a default platform (shoot, collect, conquer) can themselves be alienating to meaningful intersectional representation and critical making.

Students drawn to game design frequently identify as fans of AAA game production: thus, when asked to design for the other that Shira Chess has termed "Player Two," these students are frequently resistant.[4] As Shira Chess argues:

> If Player One is the — also designed — white, cis-, heterosexual, young, abled, and middle-class male, then Player Two becomes his counterpart as a mode of designed identity...the games made for Player Two appear to be limiting and limited — small in scope and absurd in meaning. These games do not appear to be about life-and-death issues; they represent small stories with small outcomes. And yet these games are important.[5]

Shira Chess and Christopher Paul address the marginalization of player, designer, and scholar two in their special issue on casual games, noting that "historicizing the terms casual and hardcore as categories uncovers the ways that the video game industry talks about its products and how academic work often replicates biases against casual games. To this end, we argue that the centrality of core games pushes many important texts to the margins."[6] Similar challenges face game design programs, which typically are pressured by industry and student demand

---

4 Shira Chess, *Ready Player Two: Women Gamers and Designed Identity* (Minneapolis: University of Minnesota Press, 2017), 39.

5 Ibid., 6.

6 Shira and Christopher A. Paul. "The End of Casual: Long Live Casual," *Games and Culture* 14, no. 2 (July 11, 2018): 108.

to emphasize "core" games and skills while ignoring other texts and practices.

Educators in recently founded games programs are frequently working with models of "value" that are different from those espoused by an industry that centers on graphics-powered shooters and unsustainable work environments. Game design programs are pressured by industry, profession-driven metrics, and student demand to emphasize "core" games while ignoring other texts and practices. Likewise, game design education does not well suit who we posit as "Designer Two." Shira Chess has proposed the framework of "Player Two" to describe the player who is frequently ignored in mainstream game design: player two is associated with casual games and personal games, which often center domestic, personal, or constructive narratives over more violent gameplay [cite]. We argue that "Designer Two" is similarly outside the mainstream of the games industry: Designer Two might be female, queer, non-white, or all of the above. Designer Two comes into the classroom marked as an outsider and might include the experimental, casual, social, or narrative game player; the student who comes from a background of enthusiasm but no encouragement in STEM fields; the returning student or the outsider; and women who are typically a minority in the classroom. Such students must be prepared for an industry where they will be immediately marginalized by both the normative narratives of AAA games and the expectations of a labor environment designed for unmarried, white, cismale designers committed to meeting the industry's unrealistic demands until inevitable burnout [cite someone here]. By building a classroom to address the needs of Designer Two, we can potentially decenter the industry, preparing students to be critical of both normative narratives and unreasonable and discriminatory labor practices. However, in doing so we face the inherent challenges of hostility from both students who see themselves reflected in both Player and Designer One, and from students who aspire to fit into that cultural space.

Excitement over games and gaming was a part of early DH communal culture, with sessions on games at The Humanities and Technology Camp (THATCamp), an "unconference" that acts a networking event for DH scholars and ideas, leading to a well-attended THATCamp Games (co-organized by one of the authors) and several similarly themed follow-ups.[7] However, this communal enthusiasm at the unconferences also betrayed digital humanities' disciplinary isolation from spaces where the key scholars and ideas of game studies and education circulated, such as Foundations of Digital Games (FDG) and its slightly more humanist-friendly cousin, the Digital Games Research Association (DiGRA). Games scholars of the THATCamp and DH persuasion tended towards humanities-infused conferences such as Modern Language Association (MLA), Popular Culture Association (PCA/ACA), Computers & Writing (C&W), Electronic Literature Organization (ELO), and so forth. This disciplinary siloing was a combination that temporarily lent credence to the idea of a ludology/narratology debate that became such an overblown part of the DNA of game studies as a discipline.

Within all these spaces, feminist discourse was rarely integrated into the core discussions, instead remaining primarily visible on the limited "ism" panels, and more varied intersectional critique was even less common. Feminist scholars have drawn attention to this marginalization, with Alexis Lothian and Amanda Phillips calling for "transformative critique" that requires challenging the underlying structures (and technical infrastructures) of the field.[8] Thus, the history of DH and Game Design (and Studies) are intertwined in their struggles with meaningful intersectional discourse, and share a similar challenge of dealing with what is left out or overlooked when only one correct path for making is given priority in training systems. Both DH and games studies struggle with tools made for corporate use alongside more rickety, user-unfriendly tools emerging from open source, and with the layers of mastery those tools

7 Amanda French et al., "THATCamp," *Roy Rosenzweig Center for History and New Media,* https://rrchnm.org/thatcamp/.

8 Alexis Lothian and Amanda Phillips, "Can Digital Humanities Mean Transformative Critique?" *Journal of E-Media Studies* 3, no. 1 (2013): 1–25.

demand. Both DH and games thus invite similar critique, that they are tools-training, not true critical disciplines.

Defining Game Design Programs

Over the past decade, game design degrees at public universities have become more common, but the desirable outcomes of a game design education are still hazy. As educators working within traditional institutions, we are frequently working with models of "value" that are very different from those of our students. Alongside a trend toward viewing higher education as a time for professional development, game design programs face a cultural, administrative, and consumer techno-utopist stance that games are technological artifacts divorced from cultural settings. Instead of understanding games as a media form embedded within and arising from cultural settings, game design programs are shown as being a hot new form of technological training and potentially lucrative career path. Within this viewpoint, a good games curriculum is one that focuses upon these technical elements, be they computer programming, visual design, or 3-D simulation and modeling. Elements of other media studies fields, such as film scholarship, that involve building a complex cultural understanding of how the media form reflects and develops culture are relegated to a small number of courses or removed entirely from the curriculum. Models of pedagogical value which front-load discussions of how culture is constructed and how media are complicit in the replication of norms are discounted by this valuation in education. This is particularly true for those of us bringing feminist and intersectional discourse into classrooms modeled on a field of practice where those viewpoints are frequently marginalized or outright rejected.[9] The challenge of being a feminist in game studies has already been documented: however, the challenge of being a

9 Christopher A. Paul, *The Toxic Meritocracy of Video Games: Why Gaming Culture Is the Worst* (Minneapolis: University of Minnesota Press, 2018).

feminist in the game design classroom is one many of us meet separately, and continually.[10]

The association of game design as a field of study with "game design" as a profession is tenuous, thanks in part to the tension between the concept of game design and the reality of production. The challenges facing these programs are thus like film programs, where everyone imagines themselves as the director rather than part of the collaborative, transdisciplinary effort. While some programs invite students to specialize in tracks, these models risk de-emphasizing the academic development of students. A view of specialization as a necessary developmental stage in their education often causes students to ignore or question the monetary value when presented with material outside of that area.

Economically viable markets in mobile and casual games, as well as more experimental and narrative games, are less likely to be the envisioned future career home of entering students given the comparative market share and audience demographics of console game titles. The culture of AAA gaming, and indeed its dominant demographic of white male visionaries, cannot easily be remade in the classroom: however, the patterns, expectations, and values set in game design programs are an opportunity to influence that culture's direction. In the end, the current state of game design education balances on a narrow point between the desire to provide comprehensive, engaged learning opportunities to students, an institutional viewpoint of the student as customer seeking economic payout, and the drive to introduce broader and more socially inclusive viewpoints into the AAA realm. We will share and explore best practices and experiments from our classrooms for building those types of values through unexpected genres, queergaming, and other methods of challenging dominant games discourse.[11]

---

10 Sal Humphreys, "On Being a Feminist in Games Studies," *Games and Culture* 14, nos. 7–8 (November 2017): 825–42.

11 Bonnie Ruberg, *Video Games Have Always Been Queer* (New York: NYU Press, 2019).

Coded Privilege

In the digital humanities, the discourse of coding has long been dominant as an essential part of the skill set, and this mindset frequently leaves behind those who haven't grown up with continual encouragement for programming. Miriam Posner addressed this experience in a powerful post on the challenges of learning to code as a woman:

> Should you choose to learn in a group setting, you will immediately be conspicuous. It might be hard to see why this is a problem; after all, everyone wants more women in programming. Surely people are glad you're there. Well, that's true, as far as it goes. But it also makes you extremely conscious of your mistakes, confusion, and skill level. You are there as a representative of every woman. If you mess up or need extra clarification, it's because you really shouldn't — you suspected this anyway — you shouldn't be there in the first place.[12]

These challenges are hard for many minority groups to ignore when made so salient in the visible nature of the physical classroom. With the increasing cost of education, every eye within the classroom is on those students who ask questions, request help, or otherwise make themselves visible in some way, intending to evaluate their contribution to the cost-value proposition many students now make when looking at course content.

Online education, often posed as the panacea to face-to-face classroom issues, has many educators, administrators, and technology disruption gurus lauding the idea that no one knows your identity in an online classroom.[13] However, most online

12 Miriam Posner, "Some Things to Think about before You Exhort Everyone to Code," *Miriam Posner's Blog*, February 29, 2012, http://miriamposner.com/blog/some-things-to-think-about-before-you-exhort-everyone-to-code/.

13 Clayton M. Christensen and Henry J. Eyring, *The Innovative University: Changing the DNA of Higher Education from the Inside Out* (San Francisco: Jossey-Bass, 2011); Maria Konnikova, "Will MOOCs Be Flukes?" *The New*

courses encourage student interaction, and women or others who are marked from the "standard" student can face the same assumptions or additional harassment and unwanted attention from fellow students who feel that being online changes acceptable behavior.[14]

The prioritization on coding as the primary tool for game development also excludes the numerous alternative skills that are involved in game development, even at AAA companies. Games are not only a technical tool but also a constructed product of many creative outputs, most of which require little or no technical knowledge. Rosa Carbo-Mascarell discussed the limitations this coding emphasis places on non-traditional students or aspirants:

> I should mention here that this especially gatekeeps women. I've received emails from women expressing their doubts about going to some of my game jams because they didn't know how to code. They didn't know how to fit in in the game development process because we've been giving them the impression you need to know how to code to enter. It's quite honestly heartbreaking.[15]

Yorker, November 7, 2014, https://www.newyorker.com/science/maria-konnikova/moocs-failure-solutions; and Deepak Mehta, "The Future of Massively Open Online Courses (MOOCs)," *Forbes,* March 23, 2017, https://www.forbes.com/sites/quora/2017/03/23/the-future-of-massively-open-online-courses-moocs.

14 Moira Gatens, *Imaginary Bodies: Ethics, Power and Corporeality* (New York: Routledge, 2013); Scott Jaschik, "MOOC Harassment," *Inside Higher Ed,* December 9, 2014, https://www.insidehighered.com/news/2014/12/09/mit-removes-online-courses-professor-found-have-engaged-online-sexual-harassment; Raymond M. Rose, "Research Committee Issues Brief: Access and Equity in Online Classes and Virtual Schools." *North American Council for Online Learning,* November 2007, https://eric.ed.gov/?id=ED509623; and John Suler, "The Online Disinhibition Effect," *CyberPsychology & Behavior* 7 no. 3 (2004): 321–26.

15 @moreelen (Roda Carbo-Mascarell). *Twitter,* September 5, 2018. https://twitter.com/moreelen/status/1037317574776774656.

This focus on only the technical as core knowledge for every member of a team creates a large barrier to entry that dispirits those who already feel daunted and unwelcome.

The focus that most game development courses and discussions place upon technology centers it as the starting skill that must be mastered before students can further their learning process. Given the construction of most game design majors, the technically oriented courses tend to be front-loaded and required for the progression through to the more non-technical, art, writing, and culture-oriented courses. Even vital team-, project-, and business-oriented courses occur most often as 300- and 400-level requirements. Meaning that unless a student masters these technical classes, earning a C or better in many universities, they may never be exposed to the content what would provide them with awareness of how they can contribute to the field. Even for students who manage to pass the technical class barrier, they are only introduced to alternative job duties after they have been locked into an educational path due to planning, university organization, or cost considerations.

Within the classroom, the primary tools of game development can serve to reinforce many existing assumptions about who makes games and what types of skills are required. Some of these barriers to entry are difficult for faculty to overcome, as they occur before the students enter the program. Additionally, there is a low likelihood of continuance for students daunted by code but who feel procedural literacy, to evoke Bogost, is the only way to proceed.[16] Scaffolding the early experience of game design with courses that emphasize physical games and a diversity of platforms offers an alternative to the dominant practice of emphasizing 3-D-centered engines, such as Unity.

16 Ian Bogost, "Procedural Literacy: Problem Solving with Programming, Systems and Play," *Telemedium: The Journal of Media Literacy* 52, nos. 1–2 (2005): 32–36.

Examining Unity Tutorials

Unity is rapidly becoming a go-to classroom resource for game development programs. Its free cost for educational use, powerful engine, rising industry acceptance, and flexibility in importing different technical components means that it exists at a sweet spot for educators looking to help build student success without breaking the bank. In theory, it presents itself as a great intersection between the technical, artistic, and design skill sets that many game programs focus on. The platform itself is well supported in both online documentation and helpful information. Unity provides several tutorial videos, game levels, and sample code to aid new developers in building their knowledge.

Unity offers both 3-D and 2-D game development possibilities, but most resources emphasize 3-D. While 3-D can be home to non-violent game genres and narrative experiences (such as the walking simulator), the reliance of 3-D games upon premade assets and a third person camera frequently lends itself to certain types of play and presentation. Pre-made assets also are most likely to reflect the dominant discourses of games, including hypersexualized and white-centered avatars that can be off-putting or distancing for students already marginalized in the game development classroom.

Educational approaches that embrace the defaults of Unity are common, in part because of increasing class sizes and the demands of academic jobs that emphasize both teaching and research, with often exhausting service requirements, that leave little room for professors to generate their own materials. Thus, the free materials available for a game engine like Unity play a prominent role in the game development classroom and in students' approaches to the platform. The default verbs of popular tutorial videos for Unity online set the tone for classroom and individual learning. For instance, Unity's official sample projects are designed for independent and classroom use and currently (September 2018) include fourteen examples:

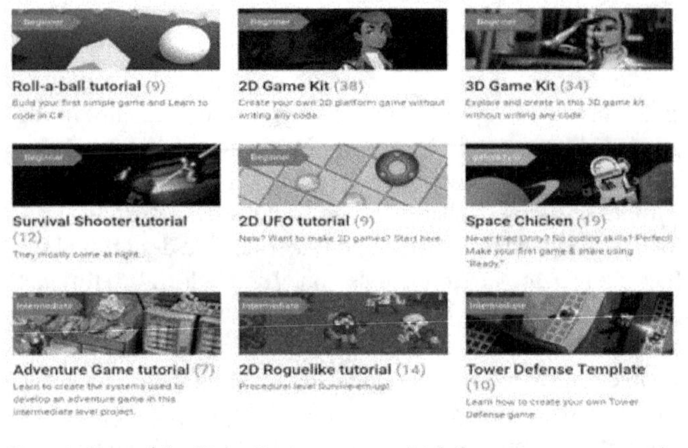

Figure 1. Part of the Unity Projects page, which features two apparently female avatars.

- Interactive Tutorials
- Roll-a-ball Tutorial
- 2-D Game Kit*
- 3-D Game Kit*
- Space Shooter Tutorial*
- 2-D UFO Tutorial
- Space Chichken*
- Tanks Tutorial*
- Adventure Game Tutorial*
- 2-D Roguelike Tutorial*
- Tower Defense Template*
- Creating Believable Visuals
- Procedural Cave Generation Tutorial

Of these tutorials, half emphasize or include large sections on the creation of violent games, enemies, and mechanics. The tutorials are interested in teaching students how to use the Unity platform and some basic principles of design through the traditional AAA focus on combative interactions and stages. Only one, the adventure game tutorial, emphasizes interactions of the type that might occur between characters without including violence. Unfortunately, the shift away from previous 2-D classroom tools (such as GameMaker) decreases the probability of teaching casual games, or other genres aimed at Shira Chess's "Player Two."

Some intentionality towards inclusivity is apparent from the game assets used, including the central avatar of the 2-D + 3-D game kit (see fig. 1). This is a valuable starting point, particularly given the industry discourse around game design has frequently been conflicted over the inclusivity of avatars, with notable examples including Ubisoft's decision not to include female characters in *Assassin's Creed* and *Far Cry 4*.[17] To have any nod towards the existence and inclusion of alternative character models for an educational setting helps advance the notion that women and minority groups should be included. If these are unmarked inclusions in the presentation of the material, it also aids in normalizing their appearance within game settings. If the inclusion of a diverse range of player and non-player characters can be included in sample and testing levels, this will make their appearance less marked for students. It would help to create and integrate these models in a number of different game settings and types, not just the non-violent, cooperative, or alternative game types that tend to be seen as non-normal by a AAA-trained consumer audience.

Once students have completed all the free Unity tutorials, the advanced Unity courses are offered as a tool to pursue further development. These are paid content courses that expand upon the material in the basic tutorials to "get on the road to mastering Unity."[18] They often advertise with the claim that only basic programming experience is required, but nothing is said regarding the other skills needed to develop the games like art, anima-

17 Yannick LeJacq, "Ubisoft In Trouble Over Comments About Female Characters," *Kotaku*, June 11, 2014, https://kotaku.com/ubisoft-in-trouble-over-comments-about-female-character-1589611410.

18 https://unity3d.com/learn/courses (webpage defunct).

tion, sound design, planning, and so on. Once again, the focus for many of these courses is both the monetary draw of getting something produced quickly and that the only knowledge that is necessary is programming. This reinforces the message that the other aspects of development are replaceable, or at least minimally important, but the programming is essential. The second row of classes focuses on partnerships Unity has made with outside learning solutions, like Udacity, to create technical projects. These focus on VR/AR and Machine Learning/AI, deeply technical fields that may or may not be exciting to students but remain strictly focused on the programmatic elements. There are no additional courses for art, animation, or better development between Unity and 3DS Max/Maya. The Courses page effectively tells students that if they aren't technically oriented they aren't professional.

This narrow focus on what makes for a "professional" experience and skills in games is often mirrored implicitly or explicitly in the classroom. The AAA-industry vision overwrites the multiplicity of pathways that are available to student learners. A few existing textbooks offer an opportunity to bridge this gap and subvert the dominant curriculum, but even those tend to emphasize genres that are understood to be dominant. Alternative books (such as Anna Anthropy's *Game Design Vocabulary* and Melissa Ford's *Writing Interactive Fiction with Twine,* to name only a couple) rarely emphasize Unity, and instead focus on design principles before code: an approach fundamentally incompatible with the AAA-centric model Unity invites.

Design in the Classroom

The organizational planning of development and design courses is also important. Their positioning and timing in the curriculum, as well as their emphasis on diverse voices including women, queer, and non-white designers, plays a major role in shaping the students' understandings and expectations of "design" and designers. The lack of visible popular games history featuring queer and women game designers (despite ongoing interventions such as Adrienne Shaw's important queer games archive) is a hindrance to teachers who may rely upon books that feature a few familiar white, male, names: Wil Wright, Sid Meiers, John Romero, and so forth. The teaching of alternative game modalities may be pushed off to courses outside a department's central track.

Similarly, the questions of feminist and cultural discourse surrounding games are frequently viewed as marginal next to the skills and production goals that dominate an industry-focused program. These modalities and viewpoints are often lucky to be granted a one-week focus, firmly cementing them in the role of "other" for students who note their marked nature in the syllabus or presentation as a "special topic" course. By following this pathway, the integration of alternative viewpoints is firmly pushed to a side track that dissuades students from seriously considering them, since they receive so little attention in the material. It also means that students who are interested in them must do the extra lifting of research and pursuing the development of these ideas on their own, something that is not always possible in already-packed non-classroom hours and tight personal budgets.

Much like the addition of a diverse range of models to the sample levels and tutorials of the Unity platform, one solution to this issue is the integration of a diverse set of modalities for play across the curriculum. If multiple projects are developed in a classroom, or across a series of course curriculum, the students should need to engage with each aspect: non-violent digital games, combat focused paper prototypes, or cooperative worlds without conflict. Rather than creating a single week to include these non-normative voices, they should be present at every step of the educational process, presented alongside the traditional modes that students are aware of from their own play habits. This also allows students who may be interested in these forms to find their passion early and pursue it throughout their educational career, building both a personal portfolio of their design vision and a valuable toolbox of experiences they can reference in the future. Rather than receiving a small list of unusual games at the end of a "diversity" week in class, they would have greater opportunities for interaction with their faculty and school resources to build awareness and experience with games from the casual and art markets. Their interests and desires would no longer be marked as exceptional among the curriculum but presented as one path among many that make valid game experiences.

The sideling of alternative modalities can create particularly frustrating tensions for women and others marginalized in the traditional gaming industry who entered academia both to avoid the hostility of those spaces and to play a role in reshaping the culture through education. Attempts to integrate and bring to the fore these alternative modalities are often seen as too activist by the students and looked at with suspicion by university administration. All too often, students' only experiences are with AAA games as players and their expectations are shaped by the perceived centrality of their viewpoint to the definition of gaming. The lingering impacts of movements like #GamerGate have also aided in the creation of a culture of distrust and fear between intersectional and feminist instructors and the students sitting in their classroom. For students, simply broaching these topics is seen as an assault on their personal viewpoints rather than the inclusion of a range of ideas meant to expand their understanding of the world of games. Even if the class has no hostilities about these topics, instructors can be fearful of introducing them regardless, since it takes simply one person posting online to bring a wave of attention from non-students.

The administration of many universities in the US is rarely supportive. Although there is strong verbal support for STE(A)M majors, the focus tends to be heavily job oriented and any topics that don't directly have a big company and a title attached to them are seen as window dressing, at best. Falling rates of enrollment and state support means that universities are now competing more heavily for fewer students. While exciting jobs like game development are an attractive draw, there is also a pressure on faculty to make sure that students remain happy. This often means that programs need to strongly affiliate themselves with a professional industry and highlight how they are a jobs pipeline. Faculty members that fail to properly ground their work and programs in this mentality will find themselves on the chopping block when tight financial times come around. Given the recent nature of many of these programs, and the interdisciplinary backgrounds of faculty, the body of work is being done by those most at risk of pressure from higher up. Untenured faculty and adjuncts provide the passion and interests that help to develop novel interdisciplinary programs but lack the backing of senior faculty (like that possessed by those in a more established discipline) and structural support to really take chances. Feminist faculty are put under extreme pressure by administration in response to student complaints. The need to retain and keep students happy makes for a more risk averse decision-making process, which means anything that a student could see as offensive, distasteful, or just annoying becomes an item that needs to be removed.

When the time for tenure evaluations comes for faculty members, those who take alternative modalities and game concepts as their creative work and research path face an uphill battle. Most universities are familiar with developing technical skills for games or new technologies, but few are well trained in alternative modalities. Creative work requires heavier lifting on behalf of the faculty to make sure the value and extensive time that went into their materials was in fact a significant effort. In a world that is increasingly focused on quantifiable metrics for advancement and success, showing five-to-ten minutes of playable game that may have taken days of time to develop, does not read the same as five traditional A-level journal articles or X dollars of grant money. This further compounds the existing biases against interdisciplinary and applied work that many faculty face when presenting their material to those not experienced in their field, as most university committees, provosts, and presidents tend to be.

Challenging the Challenges

The recent work of Bo Ruberg acts as a call to action: their monograph suggests that "video games have always been queer."[19] Similarly, recent critical work in the field of game studies pushes back against normative histories of the industry and field: Palgrave Macmillan's three recent collections *Masculinities in Play, Feminism in Play,* and *Queerness in Play* offer alternative frameworks for central questions facing both Player and Designer Two.[20] Other recent collections draw attention to the whiteness of gaming, calling on academics and designers alike to examine their own practices.[21]

With the long list of difficult battles ahead of feminist and queer scholars in gaming programs, what can be done to effectively create the changes in the field that many went into academia to establish? And how can the broader Digital Humanities better understand — and face — the toxicity frequently embedded in the very platforms we embrace? While there are often no correct answers for the specific situation at a specific university, there are some best practices that can be used to improve the approach and establish a welcoming and diverse games program.

As mentioned earlier, an effort should be made to integrate diverse perspectives across the curriculum. By scaffolding a course around games made on the margins of game development, using texts written emphasizing inclusive design principles, and treating games for "Player Two" as core rather than ancillary elements of a game development curriculum, educa-

---

19 Ruberg, *Video Games Have Always Been Queer.*

20 Kishonna L. Gray, Gerald Voorhees, and Emma Vossen, eds., *Feminism in Play* (Houndmills: Palgrave Macmillan, 2018); Todd Harper, Meghan B. Adams, and Nicholas Taylor, eds., *Queerness in Play* (Houndmills: Palgrave Macmillan, 2018); Nicholas Taylor and Gerald Voorhees, eds., *Masculinities in Play* (Houndmills: Palgrave Macmillan, 2018).

21 Kishonna L. Gray and David J. Leonard, *Woke Gaming: Digital Challenges to Oppression and Social Injustice* (Seattle: University of Washington Press, 2018).

tors have an opportunity to resist the dominant ideologies of the games industry while promoting meaningfully inclusive game design. Alternative platforms such as Twine (a hypertext narrative and game development tool), Ren'Py (a Python-based platform for making visual novels), and Inform 7 (a natural language engine for building interactive fiction) bring with them a myriad of examples of queer games and non-traditional play.[22]

If willing or able, flip the idea of the "diversity" week of class and structure a course to discuss and analyze nothing but alternative perspectives and modalities of play. This focus should be placed on marking the unmarked. Most students have experience with games as players. They have many assumptions about what makes a game, and a high-quality game, that have often never been analyzed to see how they were constructed and what these views say about their own assumptions as designers. Instead of taking a direct approach about alternative viewpoints, the materials focus on diversity as a tool to understand what is already known but never studied. This stance helps strengthen students' toolkits, makes feminist perspectives more palatable to a potentially hostile audience, and serves a strong pedagogical standpoint.

Game design benefits in some ways from the lack of a canon: while texts such as *Rule of Play* have been commonly adopted, the centering of particular games is less clear. Access to games varies wildly by university and frequently reflects existing structures of privilege, as the maintenance of student games libraries is costly. However, students' exposure to mainstream game development (and the likelihood that AAA-game enthusiasts bring those concepts to the classroom) is assured, and thus those games that are best known often occupy an unintended and underexamined canonical status. A counter-canon may not be well

22 Anastasia Salter, Bridget Blodgett, and Anne Sullivan, "'Just Because It's Gay?': Transgressive Design in Queer Coming of Age Visual Novels," *Proceedings of the 13th International Conference on the Foundations of Digital Games* (August 2018): art. 22.

received by students initially but can play an important role in shifting the narrative of what games are and can be.

Bibliography

"2019 Top Game Design Schools." *The Princeton Review.* https://www.princetonreview.com/college-rankings/game-design.

Bogost, Ian. "Procedural Literacy: Problem Solving with Programming, Systems and Play." *Telemedium: The Journal of Media Literacy* 52, nos. 1–2 (2005): 32–36.

Chess, Shira. *Ready Player Two: Women Gamers and Designed Identity.* Minneapolis: University of Minnesota Press, 2017.

Chess, Shira, and Christopher A. Paul. "The End of Casual: Long Live Casual." *Games and Culture* 14, no. 2 (July 11, 2018): 107–18. DOI: 10.1177/1555412018786652.

Christensen, Clayton M., and Henry J. Eyring. *The Innovative University: Changing the DNA of Higher Education from the Inside Out.* San Francisco: Jossey-Bass, 2011.

Cooper, Joel, and Kimberlee D. Weaver. *Gender and Computers: Understanding the Digital Divide.* Mahwah: Lawrence Erlbaum Associates, 2003.

Dill, Karen E., Douglas A. Gentile, William A. Richter, and Jody C. Dill. "Violence, Sex, Race and Age in Popular Video Games: A Content Analysis." In *Featuring Females: Feminist Analyses of the Media,* edited by Jessica Henderson Daniel and Ellen Cole, 115–30. Washington, DC: American Psychological Association Books, 2005.

French, Amanda, Ammon Shepherd, Patrick Murray-John, and Tom Scheinfeldt. "THATCamp." *Roy Rosenzweig Center for History and New Media.* https://rrchnm.org/thatcamp/.

Gatens, Moira. *Imaginary Bodies: Ethics, Power and Corporeality.* New York: Routledge, 2013. DOI: 10.4324/9780203418659.

Gray, Kishonna L., and David J. Leonard. *Woke Gaming: Digital Challenges to Oppression and Social Injustice.* Seattle: University of Washington Press, 2018.

Gray, Kishonna L., Gerald Voorhees, and Emma Vossen, eds. *Feminism in Play.* Houndmills: Palgrave Macmillan, 2018.

Harper, Todd, Meghan B. Adams, and Nicholas Taylor, eds. *Queerness in Play*. Houndmills: Palgrave Macmillan, 2018.

Humphreys, Sal. "On Being a Feminist in Games Studies." *Games and Culture* 14, nos. 7–8 (November 2017): 825–42. DOI: 10.1177/1555412017737637

Jaschik, Scott. "MOOC Harassment." *Inside Higher Ed*, December 9, 2014. https://www.insidehighered.com/news/2014/12/09/mit-removes-online-courses-professor-found-have-engaged-online-sexual-harassment.

Konnikova, Maria. "Will MOOCs Be Flukes?" *The New Yorker*, November 7, 2014. https://www.newyorker.com/science/maria-konnikova/moocs-failure-solutions.

LeJacq, Yannick. "Ubisoft In Trouble Over Comments About Female Characters." *Kotaku*, June 11, 2014. https://kotaku.com/ubisoft-in-trouble-over-comments-about-female-character-1589611410.

Lothian, Alexis, and Amanda Phillips. "Can Digital Humanities Mean Transformative Critique?" *Journal of E-Media Studies* 3, no. 1 (2013): 1–25. DOI: 10.1349/PS1.1938-6060.A.425.

Mehta, Deepak. "The Future of Massively Open Online Courses (MOOCs)." *Forbes*, March 23, 2017. https://www.forbes.com/sites/quora/2017/03/23/the-future-of-massively-open-online-courses-moocs.

@moreelen (Roda Carbo-Mascarell). *Twitter*, September 5, 2018. https://twitter.com/moreelen/status/1037317574776774656.

Paul, Christopher A. *The Toxic Meritocracy of Video Games: Why Gaming Culture Is the Worst*. Minneapolis: University of Minnesota Press, 2018.

Posner, Miriam. "Some Things to Think about before You Exhort Everyone to Code." *Miriam Posner's Blog*, February 29, 2012. http://miriamposner.com/blog/some-things-to-think-about-before-you-exhort-everyone-to-code/.

Rose, Raymond M. "Research Committee Issues Brief: Access and Equity in Online Classes and Virtual Schools." *North*

American Council for Online Learning, November 2007. https://eric.ed.gov/?id=ED509623.

Ruberg, Bonnie. *Video Games Have Always Been Queer.* New York: NYU Press, 2019.

Ruberg, Bonnie, and Adrienne Shaw. *Queer Game Studies.* Minneapolis: University of Minnesota Press, 2017.

Salter, Anastasia, Bridget Blodgett, and Anne Sullivan. "'Just Because It's Gay?': Transgressive Design in Queer Coming of Age Visual Novels." *Proceedings of the 13th International Conference on the Foundations of Digital Games* (August 2018): art. 22. DOI: 10.1145/3235765.3235778.

Suler, John. "The Online Disinhibition Effect." *CyberPsychology & Behavior* 7 no. 3 (2004): 321–26. DOI: 10.1089/1094931041291295.

Taylor, Nicholas, and Gerald Voorhees, eds. *Masculinities in Play.* Houndmills: Palgrave Macmillan, 2018.

Methods

11

Toward a Diligent Humanities: Digital Cultures and Archives of Post-1965 Indonesia

Viola Lasmana

As we look back at the cultural archive, we begin to reread it not univocally but contrapuntally, *with a simultaneous awareness both of the metropolitan history that is narrated and of those other histories against which (and together with which) the dominating discourse acts.*
— Edward Said, *Culture and Imperialism*

See what I have made, *the tactical user says.* See how I try to manage the ties that bind and produce me.
— Rita Raley, *Tactical Media*

The digital humanities are somewhat akin to a garden of forking paths, with different passages and possibilities, but all leading to the same exit, toward and back to the digital humanities. To begin articulating an alternative trajectory (as the title of this anthology proposes) necessitates thinking outside the digital humanities; an alternative, after all, is rooted in *the other* (from the Latin *alter*). But, to alternate is also to do one thing after another in turns, with a reciprocity that makes an alternative thought and praxis reflexive: an alternative trajectory is one of negotiation between inside and outside, so that a thinking of the beyond must always be alongside what is already there. Formulating an alternative that is truly revolutionary takes me to what Jacques Derrida calls "the regime of a possible whose possibilization must prevail of the impossible," or "the possibilization of the impossible possible."[1] What, therefore, is an alternative if not the activation of an *other* space beyond what has been possible, visible, and acceptable (in other words, out of bounds and boundless)? This anthology gives me pause to think about such an alternative by way of exploring a selection of transnational Indonesian digital projects; in this endeavor, I articulate a digital humanities that is a diligent humanities, practiced and theorized with care, with a hermeneutics attentive to the frictions between multiple scales of analyses, scales of productions, as well as scales of tensions between the global and the local.

This essay focuses on how networked technologies impact the Indonesian public's relationship to and understanding of historical trauma, particularly around the 1965–66 anti-communist genocide in Indonesia. Here, I analyze digital projects that re-engage the ghosts of the past and gesture toward a future in which mediascapes open up spaces for potential community collaboration and cultural transformation: examples include the Mapping Memory Landscapes data visualization project, the Indonesian Institute of Social History online archive, and a 2013 Video Slam project by EngageMedia and Common Room Networks Foundation. These projects are situated and discussed within the larger framework of digital humanities as it has been developed as a field in the predominantly Western and Anglophone context. Although these are disparate works, they are linked by the same commitment to countering the Indonesian state's version of history, as well as to putting pressure on the importance and pedagogical value of community-based knowledge, testimony, and the ethical use of technology. In talking back to official narratives, these projects demonstrate what Ann L. Stoler describes, in her discussion of documentation prac-

1 Jacques Derrida, *The Politics of Friendship* (London: Verso, 2005), 29.

tices in the Dutch East Indies, as "emanations" from the margins of the master archive.[2] Following Wendy Chun and Lisa Marie Rhody's affirmation of how a sense of historical awareness in digital modes of representation can "elucidate 'shadows' in the archive," this essay seeks to explore the possibilities and new meanings that arise from voices and aesthetic forms typically absent from state-sanctioned historical narratives.[3]

Media Politics in Indonesia

"Tahun Vivere Pericoloso (TAVIP)," or "A Year of Living Dangerously," was the title of one of President Sukarno's Independence Day addresses calling for the continued, undying rhythm of an Indonesian Revolution in countering the effects of colonialism and imperialism.[4] The speech's significance is marked not only by its content, but also its timing, given in August 1964, roughly a year prior to the 1965–66 anti-communist killings in Indonesia, which then ended the Sukarno administration and led to the rise of President Suharto's repressive and dictatorial New Order regime (1966–98). The title, "A Year of Living Dangerously," recalls the revolutionary spirit of Indonesia in its post-1945, post-Independence years — a time that, as Stoler describes, "held promise," and that people would later remember as a progressive and optimistic period; they were, as some of the Javanese called

2 Ann Stoler, *Along the Archival Grain: Epistemic Anxieties and Colonial Common Sense* (Princeton: Princeton University Press, 2010), 2.

3 Wendy Hui Kyong Chun and Lisa Mary Rhody, "Working the Digital Humanities: Uncovering Shadows between the Dark and the Light," *differences: A Journal of Feminist Cultural Studies* 25, no. 1 (2014): 1.

4 Many would associate this title, rather, with Peter Weir's 1982 film starring Mel Gibson and Sigourney Weaver, *The Year of Living Dangerously*, based on Christopher Koch's novel with the same name. It is important to trace the title back to Sukarno's speech, especially as the Hollywood film borders on an Orientalist approach in its setting up of Indonesia and Sukarno as mysterious and unknowable to the West. For more on the film's representation of Indonesia as "inscrutable" and the misrepresentation of what really goes on in the life of Indonesian society, see Max Lane, "The Year of Living Dangerously," *Inside Indonesia* (Nov., 1983): 29, http://nla.gov.au/nla.obj–88227234.

it, "the years of living dangerously," of feeling the potentiality of a vast universe opening up for a recently-independent nation.[5]

"A Year of Living Dangerously" contains a striking passage in which Sukarno fervently asserts the integral relationship between revolution and technology in reflecting an anti-imperialist Indonesia:

> I am not saying that we do not need technology [...]. More than those [technical] skills, we need the spirit of a nation, the spirit of freedom, the spirit of revolution [...]. What is the use of taking over the technology of the Western world if the result of that adoption is merely a state and a society à la West... a copy state?[6]

Given how heavily the New Order regime depended on audiovisual media to maintain its power by spreading state propaganda and intimidating the Indonesian public, Sukarno's impassioned statements hold great weight when examining the turbulent cultural and political climate in Indonesia during this transition period between opposing regimes, as well as the central role that technology played for the state before, during, and after the New Order. Even as media practices cannot be completely detached from technological developments beyond national borders, Sukarno's declarations of the need for an autonomous nation complemented by an independent technology remain instructive. What would media infused with "the spirit of freedom, the spirit of revolution" look like?

Considering the mobilization and violence of the militia that ensued in 1965 (with then-General Suharto in charge of the army) after a military coup was blamed on the Indonesian Communist Party (Partai Komunis Indonesia, PKI), the speech's title

---

5 Ann Laura Stoler, "Untold Stories," *Inside Indonesia* (Oct.–Dec., 2001), http://www.insideindonesia.org/untold-stories-2.

6 "Tahun Vivere Pericoloso" ("A Year of Living Dangerously"), address on Aug. 17, 1964, Djakarta, quoted in Rex Mortimer, *Indonesian Communism under Sukarno: Ideology and Politics, 1959–1965* (Singapore: Equinox Publishing, 2006), 82–83.

takes on a different hue when revisited a year later, stripped of the energetic and bold quality it had intended to inspire. The New Order regime's stringent watch over cultural production created a space in which "the conditions of possibility for Indonesia's national culture after 1965" were based precisely on the *im*possibility for non-state sanctioned narratives to exist.[7] The conditions of possibility, therefore, were far from being unconditional: cultural practices and productions were appropriated by the state, enabling the control of national culture by means of the state's propaganda machine. The horror resulting from the persecution and killings of suspected communists and sympathizers, the ethnic Chinese, left-wing women's organizations, scholars, and activists, then, was further intensified by the succeeding atmosphere of fear and intimidation fostered by the New Order government, which prohibited intellectual and creative forms of expression that were in opposition to the state's militaristic and masculinized ideology.

To read Indonesian life, as well as its representations in media, in its post-1965 years as one that is regulated and strangulated by an authoritarian regime necessitates a contrapuntal reading (to use Edward Said's expression);[8] contrapuntal analysis takes into account the dominant narrative established by those in power, as well as the spaces where resistance happens, and where projects outside the purview and sanction of the state can be activated. Under the New Order regime, audiovisual media was central to the Indonesian nationalist project. The first national, state-owned television network, Television of the Republic of Indonesia (Televisi Republik Indonesia, TVRI), and the operation of a domestic communication satellite were both deployed "to extend [Suharto's] political authority, sugarcoated with developmentalist logic."[9] Beneath the developmen-

7 Rachmi Diyah Larasati, *The Dance That Makes You Vanish: Cultural Reconstruction in Post-Genocide Indonesia* (Minneapolis: University of Minnesota Press, 2013), 6.

8 Edward Said, *Culture and Imperialism* (New York: Vintage Books, 1994).

9 *Videochronic: Video Activism and Video Distribution in Indonesia* (Yogyakarta: KUNCI Cultural Studies Center & EngageMedia, 2009), 16.

talist depiction of production and progress, however, was the New Order regime's acutely strict censorship laws. Intan Paramaditha notes that "censorship can thus be seen as one of the language codes that sustain national consciousness."[10] Indeed, the tenor of life under the New Order state was carefully managed by the constraining of what people could create and consume. At the same time, however, the stringent regulation of the kinds of media content and cultural representation the public could access was at times offset by the existence of global media, which "had a liberationary aspect in so far as they breached the capacity of national governments to control what their citizens could see and hear."[11] Despite the state's suppression of freedom of expression and innovation, interfaces with global media have also made possible anti-authoritarian and transformative uses of technologies in Indonesia.

Politics of Visualization

Access to historical knowledge for many Indonesian communities has been complicated not just by the oscillation between visibility and invisibility, but they have also been obscured by the grey spaces in between, where truth and fiction, as well as official and unofficial narratives, collide. One recent project, Mapping Memory Landscapes, seeks to break down such historical opacity, focusing on the tragedies and events that happened in 1965–66 in Semarang, the capital city of Central Java and where the Indonesian Communist Party was first established. As a collaborative transnational project, Mapping Memory Landscapes brings together scholars from the Dutch Institute for War, Holocaust and Genocide Studies (NIOD); student researchers from Universitas Katolik Soegijapranata (UNIKA) in Semarang, Indonesia; and, software developers from LAB1100. Using the term

10 Intan Paramaditha, "Cinema, Sexuality and Censorship in Post-Soeharto Indonesia," in *Southeast Asian Independent Cinema*, ed. Tilman Baumgärtel (Hong Kong: Hong Kong University Press, 2012), 71.

11 David T. Hill and Krishna Sen, *The Internet in Indonesia's New Democracy* (New York: Routledge, 2005), 10.

"memory landscapes," the project team understands memory as "relational and multidirectional," and that "sites play a crucial role in evoking, shaping, communicating or controlling memory," especially that which exists outside state-sanctioned narratives.[12] To that end, Mapping Memory Landscapes makes visible the relationships between survivors, organizations, and sites of violence (locations include places in which people were detained, imprisoned, tortured, murdered, or buried) during the turbulent period of 1965–66 that targeted suspected communists and the ethnic Chinese. The project has had significant consequences, including increased public awareness of anti-Chinese violence in Semarang, as well as national attention to the existence of a mass grave and the victims who were buried there.

Mapping Memory Landscapes brings together both analogue and digital elements, using data gathered from interviews with survivors conducted by UNIKA students, as well as field work, in order to render the "memory landscapes" digitally on Nodegoat, a web-based visualization platform. Here, it is important to note the significance of the method and platform used for the project. The creators of the Nodegoat platform cite their use of object-oriented ontology (OOO) and the influence of Bruno Latour's actor-network theory: "this methodology asks researchers to transform each entity they encounter (e.g. humans and non-humans; events and emotions) into an object and to describe every relation and association of this object."[13] Such an object-oriented method levels all entities without privileging the human over the non-human; a person is categorized as an object, an actor (or agent) that is part of the larger system of networks

12 Martijn Eickhoff, Donny Danardono, Tjahjono Rahardjo, and Hotmali Sidabalok, "The Memory Landscapes of '1965' in Semarang," *Journal of Genocide Research* 19, no. 4 (2017): 530–50.

13 Nodegoat, "Mapping Memory Landscapes in Nodegoat, the Indonesian Killings of 1965–66," December 4, 2014, http://nodegoat.net/blog.p/82.m/6/mapping-memory-landscapes-in-nodegoat-the-indonesian-killings-of-1965-66.

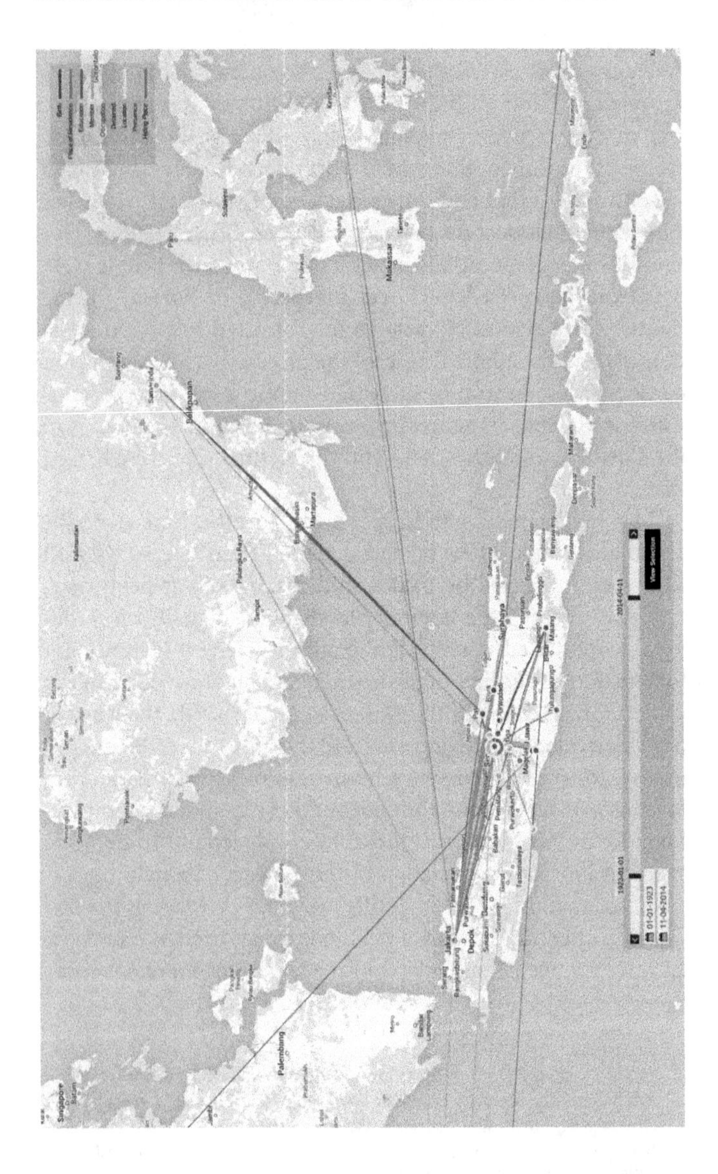

Figure 1. The relational networks between survivors, places, and time in Mapping Memory Landscapes, using an object-oriented method.

between human and non-human things, facilitated by the technologies that make those interactions possible.

Visualizing historical information about 1965–66 using an object-oriented ontology could function as a useful documentary accompaniment to survivor testimonies, and serve as an efficacious method of representation, especially in light of recent developments in political debates related to the 1965–66 genocide. On April 18–19, 2016, Indonesia's then-Chief Security Minister and former military leader, Luhut Panjaitan, opened a 2-day conference, "National Symposium: Dissecting the 1965 Tragedy, Historical Approach," bringing together individuals from opposing sides of the spectrum, including survivors, scholars, activists, government officials, and members of the military. Even though the symposium was itself a breakthrough in being the first meeting in Indonesia dedicated to discussing the tragedy, the event was troubling on many levels. Heart-wrenching stories from survivors who demanded an apology from the government were met with all too familiar expressions of denial: a retired general suggested that only one person in Central Java was killed during his military operation there, while Panjaitan challenged the extent of the killings by asking the audience where the graves are located if a massacre did, indeed, take place. Panjaitan later adamantly stated that no apology or reconciliation is possible unless the mass graves are located.

The importance of location in confronting the history of 1965–66 is of particular interest here. Through its collection of stories from the survivors and local communities, what Mapping Memory Landscapes has achieved is an uncovering: "after its inclusion in our project, one site — the Mangkang mass grave — became the object of more intense public and media interest and was turned, through rituals and material interventions, into a site of reconciliation by human rights activists."[14] Gaining public attention for a specific mass grave is of no small significance, especially when a prominent political figure seeks to discredit the atrocity and scope of the 1965–66 killings by

14 Eickhoff et al., "The Memory Landscapes of '1965' in Semarang," 532.

doubting the existence of such burial sites. On a more personal level, such publicity also allows for the victims buried in Mangkang to be acknowledged individually by name, a gesture of individuation that recognizes their lives and existence, even if no course of justice has yet been taken.

Are there, however, ethical limits to the representation of historical atrocity and trauma? On the one hand, the union of analogue and digital forms of research that includes personalized accounts and computational representation make it a rich, multi-layered, and multi-dimensional project; to fill in the gaps in an archive laden with silenced histories, after all, requires forms of knowledge production that allow the wider public to understand clearly the contexts surrounding the events, and to discover stories beyond official narratives. Mapping Memory Landscapes has, indeed, uncovered important stories and testimonies that have been kept in the dark. On the other hand, could the use of an object-oriented method in its data representation be, in fact, at odds with the ethical imperatives of the project itself? To be clear, I am not arguing for or doubting how well Mapping Memory Landscapes succeeds as a digital project. Rather, I am asking what the limits of representation are — both ethically and aesthetically — for furthering understandings of history and historical trauma, what new meanings and knowledges arise from digital methods of representation, and what the attendant challenges might be.

Revisiting tragedies like the Indonesian 1965–66 genocide necessitates a consideration of the contentious issue of representation. The purge remains a controversial and dangerous subject for many Indonesians to discuss publicly, and only recently gained wider international attention (very possibly as a consequence of Joshua Oppenheimer's 2012 Oscar-nominated film, *The Act of Killing*, which I discuss in a later portion of the essay). When addressing a history that has been shrouded in state propaganda and lies for decades, one of the risks of employing a computational method rooted in an object-oriented ontology may in fact be the obfuscation of historical context and particularities that are crucial for understanding such a complex

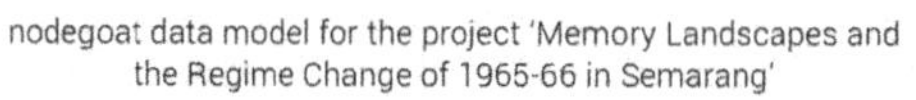

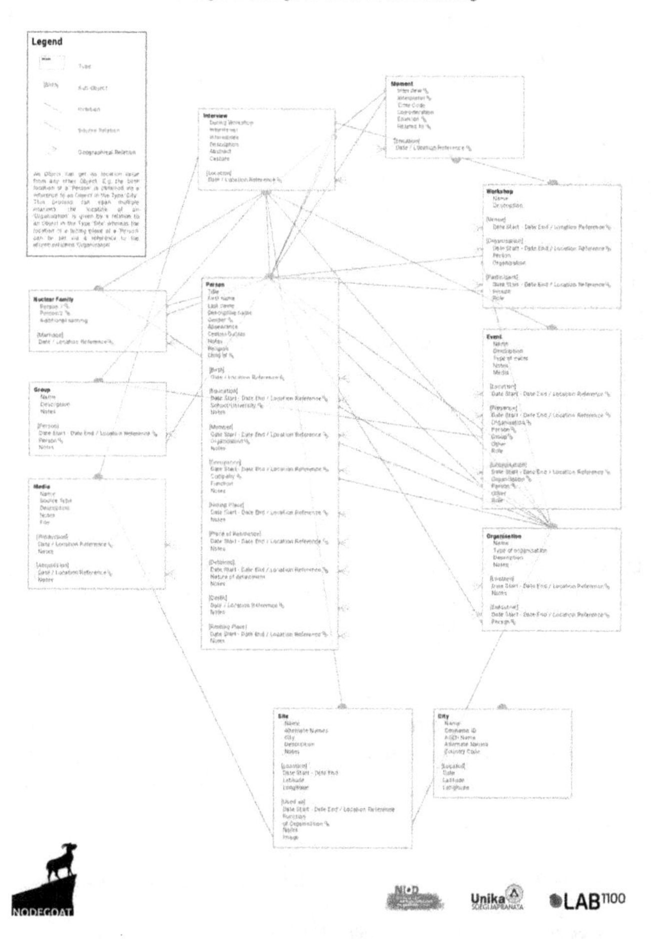

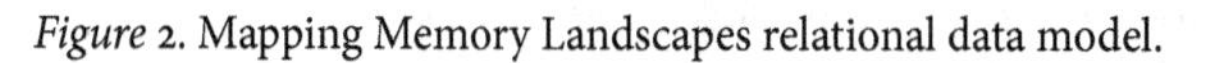
Figure 2. Mapping Memory Landscapes relational data model.

history. Theorists of object-oriented ontology have described the impenetrable nature of objects being "withdrawn from one another and from themselves."[15] Ian Bogost calls this a state of "elusiveness,"[16] or what OOO founder Graham Harman describes as "things reced[ing] into inaccessible, private depths."[17]

Indeed, the difficulty of interpreting relations between nodes on the map parallels and is an indication, perhaps, of the UNIKA students' struggle with representing non-verbal reactions that occurred during the interviews. To classify these emotions, a category named "moment" was created — a word that aptly captures the inexpressible, and that reminds us of transient points in time. This dilemma in representation reveals the ostensible limitations to visualizing history in information aesthetics; Alex Galloway notes in his essay on network visualization, "there are some things that are unrepresentable."[18] In his discussion of Holocaust survivor testimonies, Todd Presner also raises similar questions around the ethics of computational representation, and the potential problem of "aestheticization" that "abstracts and reduces the human complexity of the victims' lives to quantized units and structured data."[19] The nuances that cannot get marked up — the gestures, the affect — elide the role of survivor testimony and lie outside the realm of what is visible in data visualization.

One of the dangers of using a thing-based ontology in this case, therefore, has to do with a myopic view of an object's perceived inaccessibility, which might serve to only further mystify history and render it inscrutable. In his analysis of OOO, McKenzie Wark states that "the futural, essential, withdrawn object be-

15 Timothy Morton, *Hyperobjects: Philosophy and Ecology after the End of the World* (Minnesota: University of Minnesota Press, 2013), 116.

16 Ian Bogost, *Alien Phenomenology, Or What It's Like to Be a Thing* (Minnesota: University of Minnesota Press, 2012), 62.

17 Ibid., 77.

18 Alexander R. Galloway, "Are Some Things Unrepresentable?" in *The Interface Effect* (Cambridge: Polity Press, 2012), 86.

19 Todd Presner, "The Ethics of the Algorithm," in *Probing the Ethics of Holocaust Culture,* eds. Claudio Fogu, Wulf Kansteiner, and Todd Presner (Cambridge: Harvard University Press, 2016), 179.

comes the fetish, at the expense not only of any particular sensory one, but of the collaborative praxis needed to work these partial, mediated apprehensions that are the real into some workable relation to each other."[20] The mystification of history and potential fetishization of unfathomability may thus render the database of information and narratives unknowable in Mapping Memory Landscapes, with nodes on a map that indicate important relations and networks with regard to the different forms of violence and events during the 1965–66 period, but that inadvertently flatten the complex, layered, and subjective aspects of that history. Without the accompanying interviews or written publication about the project, could one interpret substantially what the nodes signify, and the kinds of relationships being drawn across the map?

Wark's critique is all the more uncanny here, as Nodegoat is a collaborative research platform, and Mapping Memory Landscapes is itself a participatory research project; yet, at the same time, its object-oriented approach blurs the necessity of such a collaborative praxis and endeavor because of the method with which it gets carried out, and may in fact reinforce the challenge of historical representation. Are some things really unrepresentable? As Virginia Kuhn notes in her study of the structures of information and of cultural productions, some kinds of knowledges "cannot, and *should not* be codified."[21] What is not reflected in the data visualization provokes a critical reflection of the realms of the visible and the non-visible — the politics of visibility — and how we can think deeply about the traces embedded in the haunted media that surrounds us, traces that are not readily visible by wave length optics, and that a digital platform may not be able to fully visualize and represent. At the onset, an object-oriented ontology makes it difficult to have an

---

20 McKenzie Wark, "From OOO to P(OO)," *Public Seminar,* December 5, 2015, http://www.publicseminar.org/2015/12/from-ooo-to-poo/.

21 Virginia Kuhn, "Web Three Point Oh: The Virtual Is the Real," in *High Wired Redux: CyberText Yearbook* (Research Centre for Contemporary Culture: University of Jyvkaisuja Press, 2013), 1–19.

analysis of difference and of the contrapuntal in its fetishization of an object's withdrawn, unknowable quality.

As much as these questions are a reminder of the limitations of specific methods of historical representation, they also gesture toward the possibilities that the Mapping Memory Landscapes scholars affirm: "since there is no combined narrative in place on the killings and suffering around 1965, this project may function as a first step that enables a more inclusive approach in addressing this episode in Indonesian history."[22] Here, the researchers highlight the ethical dimension of the project, which includes a future-oriented goal of making the 1965–66 history circulate, as well as integrating more stories. This desire for "a more inclusive approach" echoes Todd Presner's instructive articulation of where the ethical resides in digital and computational methods of representing the Holocaust. For Presner, the ethical depends on the practice of "tak[ing] into account the fullness of the archive insofar as all the indexed data related to the narrative of every survivor is part of the analysis."[23] Taking into account the tiered processes of research, fieldwork, public engagement, and interviews conducted in addition to its data visualization output, Mapping Memory Landscapes should be considered as an example of the kind of "Levinasian [relational] database" that Presner provocatively speculates about in his essay.[24] Indeed, the researchers see memory landscapes as a series of connections that are "continually experienced, contested, worked and re-worked."[25] In this sense, the project is an unfinished one that remains open for re-visions and transformations.

Mapping Memory Landscapes is the first of its kind to present and visualize data from the 1965–66 genocide in a digital mapping project. It makes visible those sites out of sight, the places of torture and killings that have not yet been represented visually in this format. When considered alongside other histor-

22 Nodegoat, "Mapping Memory Landscapes in Nodegoat."

23 Presner, "The Ethics of the Algorithm," 199.

24 Ibid.

25 Eickhoff et al., "The Memory Landscapes of '1965' in Semarang," 532.

ical accounts and survivor testimonies, Mapping Memory Landscapes offers another layer of information related to the events surrounding the tragedy. The project, however, is incomplete to read on its own, and the project has to be taken into account with not just its accompanying elements like the interviews and written publication, but also with other existing projects such as the Indonesian Institute of Social History (ISSI) Oral History Project, whose research spans more than sixteen years, gathering hundreds of interviews with survivors from 1965 (including women's stories, which have been the least heard and known about). To consider these different projects together ultimately provides the most inclusive approach to history, and to excavating the archive of the nation.

Comparative DH & Pedagogies

A comparative analysis of both Mapping Memory Landscapes and the ISSI Oral History Project offers a valuable pedagogical function and an exploration of the transformative knowledge that emerged from the exchanges between the UNIKA student researchers and interviewees. Reading the two projects side by side is also to take an expansive view of the digital humanities, one that emphasizes a historical approach and puts ethical concerns at the forefront.

Furthermore, understanding the inextricable link between such projects serves as an intervention in the typically Western and Anglophone formulations of the genealogies of DH. Tara McPherson has pointed out the lack of diversity in DH projects: "We must take seriously the question, why are the digital humanities so white?"[26] A robust understanding of DH must pay attention to the vital intersections of digital culture and social justice, and to works that may not name themselves or be

26 Tara McPherson, "Why Are the Digital Humanities So White? or Thinking the Histories of Race and Computation," in *Debates in the Digital Humanities,* ed. Matthew K. Gold (Minnesota: University of Minnesota Press, 2012), 139–60.

Figure 3. Indonesian Institute of Social History's multimedia archive.

named DH — again, this is about the politics of visibility. In this case, the ISSI Oral History Project is one that eludes mainstream DH, not because it lacks value, but because of its minimal level of global circulation and exposure in North America, as well as a myriad of infrastructural issues having to do with institutional, technical, cultural, and political contexts.

On the other hand, as a data visualization project built on a platform by LAB1100, Mapping Memory Landscapes is readily recognizable as DH and legible to a Western audience. In fact, I got to know the project precisely through a North American network of digital humanities scholars. My contention, therefore, is that reading these two projects together is one way to approach the digital humanities as a global, comparative, and transnational field, rather than — as is typically assumed — one whose main focus is Western and Anglophone digital productions.[27] Knowledge is situated, and one must be able to traverse

27 I follow in the footsteps of collectives such as #transformDH, Global Outlook::Digital Humanities (GO::DH), and Global DH at Michigan State University, who make possible different trajectories for the digital humanities by emphasizing polyvocality, multilingualism, works from the "Global South," and by centering social and racial justice. Such an expansive view of how we might frame and articulate the digital

the various types of knowledges that are formed in different scales of productions.

For the Indonesian Institute of Social History (ISSI), its pedagogical goals of the online archive are explicit: to bridge the information gap for younger generations born decades after the 1965 tragedy, most of whom do not know about the history of 1965.

Mobilizing these stories and histories by making them accessible online opens up the archive as a dynamic, generative site that makes possible a collective cultural and political expression. The various educational resources they make available for educators, students, and the wider public express the research value of the ISSI online archive. Through the Lens,[28] for instance, creates an interactive timeline using the archive of photographs and documents of Oey Hay Djoen, a Chinese-Indonesian cultural revolutionary.[29] The then co-director of the Indonesian Institute of Social History, Hilmar Farid, has spoken about the use of visual artifacts, like the digitized photographs, as a critical part of the ISSI's mission to facilitate a deeper understanding of Indonesian history. Making multimedia accessible for people to engage with and learn from, as Farid says, opens up spaces for more people to access the history in dynamic ways.[30] The interactive timeline is a key part of the pedagogical use of the archive, a way of encouraging students to fill the timeline with their own experiences, and to knit their stories with the nation's larger history.

The potential of the ISSI online archive in unburying lost voices from the 1965 tragedy is not, however, without practical

humanities is part of a global intellectual imagination that I continue to be affirmed and inspired by.

28 *Institut Sejarah Sosial Indonesia,* http://sejarahsosial.org/ThroughtheLens/ThroughtheLens.html.

29 Oey was a member of the Institute for People's Culture (LEKRA) and imprisoned for fourteen years, without trial, under the New Order regime for his left-wing connections and suspected communist-related activities.

30 Hilmar Farid, "Does the Past Matter? Archiving Injustices in Indonesia," paper presentation, Human Rights Archives Symposium, UCLA, Los Angeles, California, October 19, 2013.

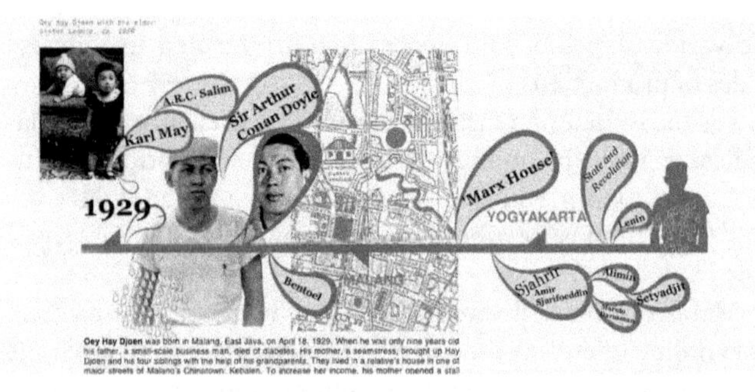

Figure 4. "Through the Lens," an interactive timeline of revolutionary Oey Hay Djoen's life, on the Indonesian Institute of Social History website.

factors that might pose a barrier to those who want to engage with the materials in the archive. During the Institute's inception, the group wanted an infrastructure that could safely store and archive the interviews and other materials gathered in their research. The progress in getting the online archive more fully populated with the materials in their repository, however, has been slow. Agung Ayu Ratih notes the challenges the institute faced in digitizing interviews and testimonies due to infrastructure and labor issues, including the lack of consistence presence of a computer technician and programmer.[31]

While the ISSI is doing important work in obtaining and documenting survivor testimonies and visual materials, practical considerations such as labor, funding, and infrastructure are issues that often get in the way of the sustainability, efficacy, and dissemination of digital projects. These are issues that often make or break a digital project and that eventually force the challenge of what kinds of projects, then, *should* have access to funds and resources, which in turn will determine a project's visibility or invisibility. The Indonesian Institute of Social History archive, therefore, highlights these significant issues that haunt all humanities projects in very real ways, but especially

31 Agung Ayu Ratih, e-mail message to author, September 10, 2015.

the digital humanities as a field, given the technological and infrastructural necessities.

For the time being, the oral histories and testimonies exist in the online archive in the form of transcriptions, or summaries. Even though it may be a challenge to access the testimonies in their oral and video formats (the audiovisual formats are currently only accessible at the institute's office in Jakarta, Indonesia), the value of the existence of a compilation of hundreds of survivor and eyewitness testimonies cannot be underestimated. The very fact that the oral testimonies have to, for the time being, remain in a physical repository with some degree of protection serves as a reminder that not all digital projects can be assumed to always be openly available to the public, despite the purported democratization of access in twenty-first century media or the digital humanities ethos of openness and accessibility. What is at stake is the issue of agency: what is an archive for, who does it empower, and who gets left out? When such an archive deals with a difficult history that is still not yet past, accessibility and representation become critical issues of contention, and as I will discuss in the next section, it is no accident that some cultural productions — depending on where they are made, who makes them, and who funds them — gain traction, while others do not.

Poetics of Remix

In 2013, in collaboration with the Common Room Networks Foundation in Bandung, West Java, EngageMedia (a nonprofit, transpacific media, technology, and culture organization) organized Video Slam 2013: Remixing the 1965 State Propaganda Film,[32] a project that brought together local videomakers in Indonesia to reimagine a state propaganda film, *The Treachery of G30S/PKI* (*Pengkhianatan G30S/PKI*), a harrowing cultural text endorsed by Suharto's New Order regime depicting the purported violence of the Indonesian Communist Party (PKI) in

32 "Video Slam 2013: Remixing the 1965 State Propaganda Film," *EngageMedia*, https://www.engagemedia.org/Projects/g30s_remixed.

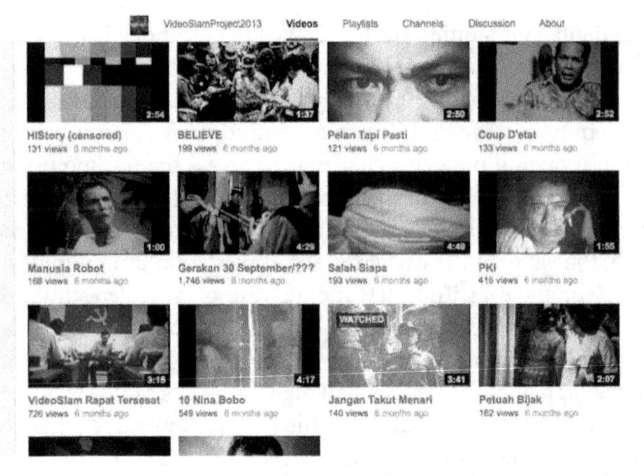

Figure 5. The YouTube channel for Video Slam 2013 by EngageMedia and Common Room Networks Foundation.

murdering six generals, and portraying the alleged involvement of the Indonesian Women's Movement (Gerwani) in the coup d'état. The film runs for a hefty four and a half hours and was required viewing for all Indonesians until the end of the New Order era. It was by far "the single most-broadcast Indonesian film and, if the ratings for 30 September 1997 can be trusted, it is also, almost without doubt, the single most-watched Indonesian film."[33] Indeed, this particular film was the most influential media artifact produced and disseminated by Suharto's regime. As propaganda, it showed the Indonesian Communist Party as bloodthirsty killers and the Indonesian Women's Movement as corrupt and violent women full of lust and rage (in one scene, the women castrate and enucleate the generals, after which they celebrate by dancing around the generals' dead bodies). Ariel Heryanto notes that the "New Order state terrorism [was linked to] its enthusiastic investment in film as a popular medium for

33 Hill and Sen, *The Internet in Indonesia's New Democracy*, 148.

its propaganda machine."[34] The significance of the connection between film as a visual medium and the history of the 1965 killings, therefore, cannot be overlooked.

This section calls attention to the significance of the power of film and digital video in Indonesia and how people have responded to historical trauma by means of video making and remixing *The Treachery of G30S/PKI.* Any discussion of the place of digital media, and of the question of the digital humanities, in Indonesia must include a reflection on how film has played a major part in shaping the nation's culture, both in the ways in which the state has appropriated it for its specific agendas and also how filmmakers, scholars, artists, and activists have found ways to react to a silenced and traumatic history. Heryanto writes:

> Not all things are enforced top-down from a major industry to the rest of the population. From the first decade of the century, young Indonesians across many islands of the archipelago discovered a new preoccupation with making shorts and documentary films with extremely low budget and simple digital devices.[35]

In the world of film and video making, the intersection of the power of digital media technologies and the spirit of experimentation and innovation, perhaps, harkens back to Sukarno's assertions about technology and the revolutionary in his "A Year of Living Dangerously" speech. Indeed, "circulation on the Internet of dissident readings of a propaganda film [...] makes these readings at once accessible, collective and political."[36]

In *Remix Theory,* Eduardo Navas writes that "remix affects culture in ways that go beyond the basic understanding of re-

34 Ariel Heryanto, *Identity and Pleasure: The Politics of Indonesian Screen Culture* (Singapore: NUS Press, 2014), 77.

35 Ibid., 11.

36 Hill and Sen, *The Internet in Indonesia's New Democracy,* 147.

combining material to create something different."[37] With the affordances of technology, remix allows (prod)users to reuse and recombine existing elements in order to make something new. Video remix itself is not a wholly new theory and practice, and has roots in and an affinity with other creative practices such as sampling in music. Furthermore, the affordances of digital technology provide ways of reusing and recombining semiotic elements that result in a production that is similar to and an extension of theories like Bertolt Brecht's "refunctioning" (*Umfunktionierung*). Brecht's "functional transformation," as Walter Benjamin describes in his essay "The Author as Producer," has similarities with remix in its work of changing the form and material of an apparatus as a revolutionary practice. For Brecht, "functional transformation" is "the transformation of the forms and instruments of production by a progressive intelligentsia — interested in the liberation of the means of production and thus useful in the class struggle."[38] Such a formulation of the transformation of a cultural object seems closer to, for instance, Sukarno's idea of an autonomous technology, and "refunctioning" in the service of changing the status quo is critically important for my understanding of remix as a theory and practice that can, indeed, shape and transform society. Remix, too, has parallels with tactical media, which "operates both at the level of technological apparatus and at the level of content and representation [...] [and is] not simply about reappropriating the instrument but also about reengineering semiotic systems and reflecting critically on institutions of power and control."[39]

Here, however, I want to point out a key difference that sets remix apart as a cultural and technological practice. I argue that remix, in its use, recombination, and rearticulation of disparate elements (text, image, sound, video, etc.), thrives in its affective

---

37 Eduardo Navas, *Remix Theory: The Aesthetics of Sampling* (New York: Springer, 2012), 3.

38 Walter Benjamin, "The Author as Producer," *New Left Review* (July 1, 1970), 89.

39 Rita Raley, *Tactical Media* (Minneapolis: University of Minnesota Press, 2009), 16.

and sensuous aesthetic and experiential qualities. Indeed, remix exists in an "emergent discursive space" that allows for a transformation of not just form, function, and content, but also of the experience itself.[40] It is a form of critique and making that is at once technological, cultural, critical, and affective. Remix possesses, in its theory and practice, a poetics that goes beyond mere function.

Even though Edward Said does not explicitly address the concept of remix, it is through his works that I find the most useful and transformative ways of thinking about what remix can achieve, and how remix can be used in ethically powerful ways. He writes, "each cultural work is a vision of a moment, and we must juxtapose that vision with the various revisions it later provoked."[41] The contrapuntal as site of resistance, as articulated by Said in *Culture and Imperialism*, provides a productive lens through which we can think about how remix can rethink master narratives. Said, a music lover and critic, utilizes the musical notion of the contrapuntal, where two or more distinct melodies form a polyphony, as a critical practice. Furthermore, the contrapuntal, or counterpoint, also refers to the backstitch in sewing techniques, where stitches overlap and are not consecutively sewn, but rather in a back and forth (non)sequence. The contrapuntal, like remix, has to do with bringing together oppositional perspectives and thinking through disparate experiences: it is as much a knitting together as it is a tearing apart. Beyond the contrasting visions that take into account both power and resistance, the contrapuntal has roots in cultural activities like knitting and music, which highlight the haptic, the affective, and care, making a concept like the contrapuntal deeply provocative and effective for a potentially ethical practice that allows for polyvocality.

40 Virginia Kuhn, "The Rhetoric of Remix," *Transformative Works and Cultures* 9, 2012, http://journal.transformativeworks.org/index.php/twc/article/view/358/279.

41 Said, *Culture and Imperialism*, 67.

Said also calls for an intellectual spirit of amateurism that he defines as "an activity that is fueled by care and affection," and one that calls for a contrapuntal — and perhaps collaborative — ethics. Amateurism, as Said expresses, is "the desire to be moved not by profit or reward but by love for an unquenchable interest in the larger picture, in making connections across lines and barriers."[42] Said's definition of amateurism inspires and pushes my understanding of how remix can be a form of making, practice, and theory that is critical, creative, and mindful of its relations to the world. With its emphasis on care and love, amateurism is motivated by the origins of the word itself: amateur comes from the Latin *amare,* to love, and it is in this spirit that Said sets out to address the role of the intellectual and the ways in which the stifling pressures of professionalism could be countered by amateurism. Roland Barthes also discusses the amateur as someone who "renews his pleasure (amator: one who loves and loves again); he is anything but a hero (of creation or performance)."[43] The amateur or the remixer, therefore, is someone who takes care in their craft.

The Video Slam project itself demonstrates such a practice of amateurism like the one Said describes. Admittedly, the video remixes may seem a little rough around the edges, and have an "amateur," low-budget quality to them; this is also due to the fact that most of the videomakers have little experience, and for some of the younger ones, this was their first time watching the state propaganda film *The Treachery of G30S/PKI.* The limited professional experience, however, can be seen as a source of possibility; as Maya Deren asserts, amateur filmmaking does not mean that they are inferior to more professional productions: "the amateur should make use of the one great advantage which all professionals envy him, namely, freedom - both artistic and physical."[44] The choice of having amateur videomak-

42 Edward Said, "Professionals and Amateurs," in *Representations of the Intellectual* (New York: Vintage Books, 1996), 76.

43 Ibid.

44 Maya Deren, "Amateur vs Professional," in *Film Culture* 39 (1965): 45–46.

Figure 6. Screenshot from "Don't Be Afraid to Dance" ("Jangan Takut Menari") by Azizah Hanum.

ers produce these remixes is a unique and powerful aspect of the Video Slam, and much like a poetry slam, these videos have an improvisational and performative quality that come across through their use of sound, footage, text, and music.

In one of the video remixes, "Don't Be Afraid to Dance" by Azizah Hanum, selected footages from *The Treachery of G30S/PKI* are set to two kinds of music — dangdut, a genre of Indonesian traditional music for dancing, and the song "Come Walk with Me" by M.I.A., the popular British South Asian rapper. Hanum's rhetorical choices are purposeful and intelligent, and serve to ridicule the spectacle of the state propaganda film. The text laid over the footage as commentary (such as the screenshot above) is often humorous and flippant, and the catchy tunes of the soundtrack are stark and absurd contrasts to the harrowing and violent scenes in the film. Incidentally, M.I.A.'s high energy track, "Come Walk with Me," is also a song about the internet, surveillance, and digital technology. The artist pairs the lyrics "there's a thousand ways to meet you now/there's a thousand ways to track you down" with the sounds a computer makes when there is a technical issue, and when an image is captured on the machine. One can only speculate whether or not Hanum made the conscious decision to choose this particular song as an additional commentary on both the invasive and networked nature of technology, but that choice has proven to be a fitting and well-made one, especially considering the activist and participation-driven work behind the video project.

By highlighting Indonesia's troubled history and how orchestrated the state-driven narratives are, the video remixers call attention to the boundaries between fact and fiction, as well to the constructedness of the state propaganda film itself. As Hill and Sen point out, the growing number of public discussions about the 1965 tragedy through media such as the internet demonstrates how "in the context of this increasingly open political dissent that disorderly, 'against the grain' readings of some films become visible and viable as political activity."[45] In opening up a space for further dialogue about a traumatic part of the nation's history that has been silenced, the remixes are forms of contrapuntal making that uncover stories from communities that have been excluded and silenced, and are a tribute to the bodies that have vanished and been obliterated. As the videos suggest, there is no one single narrative or memory of the genocide — there are only distortions of the truth, and erasures of what really happened in 1965–66.

The Video Slam remixes have not only been facilitated by new media technologies, but also propelled by some of the citizens' increasing political dissatisfaction; indeed, such "dissident readings and their circulation on the Internet [also] indicated some of the cracks in the New Order's methods of media control, including its governance of cinema through censorship and propaganda."[46] These digital video projects, therefore, transform the landscape of cinema in Indonesia and transcend the limits set by the state on filmmaking practices and film content. In redefining the creator as both a reader and maker of culture, remix also blurs the boundaries between reader and writer, author and audience. The possibility for polyvocal representation is an enactment of "the essence of counterpoint [as] simultaneity of voices, preternatural control of resources, apparently endless

45 Hill and Sen, *The Internet in Indonesia's New Democracy*, 148.
46 Ibid., 150.

inventiveness."[47] Within the cultural economy of digital media and in the space of the internet, the video remixes function as a transformative mode of knowledge production, embodying the spirit of revolution that was invoked in "A Year of Living Dangerously."

Nevertheless, even the affordances of technological platforms such as the EngageMedia website and YouTube (where these videos are housed) — both of which have a wide global audience — may not be enough to give small, alternative projects such as the Video Slam the circulation, exposure, and recognition that other projects related to 1965 might get. What makes a project travel widely, and what makes others stay within the reach of local communities? Here, it is worthwhile to articulate the disparity between different works dealing with Indonesia's history of 1965. As I have argued, one cannot talk about the role of digital media in Indonesia without also discussing film; I want to point out the lines of connection between projects such as the Video Slam and the Indonesian Institute of Social History's Oral History Project with works like Joshua Oppenheimer's Oscar-nominated *The Act of Killing* and its sequel *The Look of Silence,* which have gained international attention and heightened international awareness of the 1965–66 killings in Indonesia.

To return to the question of "why DH is so white" is to reflect on the issue of recognition I am raising here. It is no accident that these films — films that have been made by white male filmmakers (as well as produced by Werner Herzog, which lends a certain kind of perceived legitimacy and prestige to the films) — gained immediate, global success, reflecting an inequality of power in terms of how cultural productions are made, circulated, and received by the larger public. In an essay published in the *Film Quarterly*'s special dossier on *The Act of Killing,* Intan Paramaditha writes:

47 Edward Said, *Music at the Limits* (New York: Columbia University Press, 2009), 5.

> *The Act of Killing* is not the only source from which to learn about Indonesia's bleak history; instead, it has to be seen as a starting point to identify what has and has not been done. The film's most valuable contribution to Indonesia, which has not been surpassed by previous projects of its kind, is the capacity to make the issue travel. In the postcolonial context, particularly, travel ensures legitimacy.[48]

Travel does lead to more exposure and global attention, and Paramaditha's statement rightly points to the issue of representation and who gets to speak: Oppenheimer's strategy in distributing the film, in enabling the film to travel through various technological platforms (BitTorrent, iTunes, Netflix, YouTube) is something that no Indonesian can do safely — hence the rolling credits of the "Anonymous" Indonesian crew at the end of the film, for the circulation of 1965-related materials is still as stringently regulated and monitored as it was during the New Order era, despite increased democracy in the country. The fact that Oppenheimer was able to disseminate his work without repercussion reveals the imbalanced distribution of agency; thus, there must be space for comparative readings of different kinds of projects, in order for there to be possible a transformative approach to digital humanities and digital media that is attentive to difference.

Toward a Diligent Humanities

Ann Stoler's notion of "archiving-as-process" and her work on how "contrapuntal intrusions emanated from outside the corridors of governance [and] erupted [...] within that sequestered space" of the archive provide a critical and nuanced foundation for my formulations on how these digital projects generate transformative, emergent archives beyond what the New Order state

48 Intan Paramaditha, "Tracing Frictions in *The Act of Killing*," *Film Quarterly* 67, no. 2 (2013): 45.

established in post-1965, post-genocide Indonesia[49] — these are projects that make impossible stories possible. My contention is that thinking about technology and how it functions in different contexts is always a negotiation between insides and outsides; where the outside begins is a question that must persist and continue to be asked again and again, particularly whenever one thinks about, accesses, and uses an archive. A thinking of the outside, however, cannot exist without the inside, rendering the play of inside and outside more a question of finding the gaps, breaks, and middles.

While examining how these projects emerge from the liminal spaces of silence and trauma, and challenge the politics of seeing and knowing in radical ways, I have been inspired by Lauren Klein's essay on archival silences, where her forensic eye and thoughtful use of digital tools uncovers the silent voice of James Heming, Thomas Jefferson's former slave, in Jefferson's letters.[50] As Wendy Chun notes of Klein's essay, Klein's particular use of digital methods and techniques, including computational linguistics and data visualization, epitomizes how the digital "can be used to grapple with the impossible, rather than simply usher in the possible."[51] A writing and thinking from the shadows, an imagining that is revolutionary: here, Klein sharply observes that going beyond the limits of the digital necessitates a rethinking of how and what we know (hence, an object-oriented ontology of withdrawn objects will not suffice as it erases praxis and knowledge production). She writes, "Illuminating [the connections between persons and networks of communication and labor], through digital means, reframes the archive itself as a site of action rather than as a record of fixity or loss."[52] A careful and critical engagement with digital tools and methods, therefore,

49 Stoler, *Along the Archival Grain*, 20.

50 Lauren Klein, "The Image of Absence: Archival Silence, Data Visualization, and James Hemings," *American Literature* 85, no. 4 (December 2013): 661–88.

51 Chun and Rhody, "Working the Digital Humanities."

52 Klein, "The Image of Absence."

can make visible the absences, and activate the shadowed restlessness in the archive.

In a "Representing Race: Silence in the Digital Humanities" panel, Alondra Nelson asked astutely, "What does a transformed archive look like?"[53] My contention is that a transformed archive has to exist in the collective, the transnational, the digital, the "global," and the contrapuntal. Laurie Sears writes that "as old archives are reconfigured and new ones come into being, it is important to cultivate new interpretive methodologies along with new accumulations of data and stories."[54] Thinking, theorizing, imagining, and creating an alternative archive necessitate first understanding the archive as a concept that has built within it the element of anticipation, a sense that it is more than just a repository of records, but a shared space that can support collaboration among users, as well as a transformation of ideas.

The question of making a nation's history (that has thus far been shrouded in denial and silence) relevant to the larger community is one of negotiating how materials in the archive function in the broader social world. Indeed, it becomes a question of ethics. We must, as Derrida suggests, move beyond "an archivable concept of the archive," for the archive is not only about the past, but also "a question of the future itself, the question of a response, of a promise and of the responsibility for tomorrow."[55] The archive in digital spaces exists in an economy of circulation, modification, and change — a kind of logic that has, perhaps, always been present in the concept of the archive as Stoler's description of the colonial archives *erupting* reveal, and as Michel

53 Alondra Nelson, "Representing Race: Silence in the Digital Humanities," paper presentation, Modern Language Association Conference, Boston, Massachusetts, January 4, 2013.

54 Laurie Sears, "Reading Ayu Utami: Notes Toward A Study of Trauma and the Archive in Indonesia," *Indonesia* 83 (April 2007): 17–39.

55 Jacques Derrida, *Archive Fever: A Freudian Impression,* trans. Eric Prenowitz (Chicago: University of Chicago Press, 1996), 36.

Foucault's formulation of the archive as "the general system of the formation and transformation of statements" suggests.[56]

The ongoing collections of personal stories, information, and testimonies relating to the 1965–66 genocide, together with a growing mass of exciting digital media productions and online archives in Indonesia, will be vital in revisiting and reinterpreting a traumatic past and history that deserve to be regained by different individuals and communities who have not had the chance to tell their stories, and whose lives have been in the shadows during much of the New Order era. What is needed is something akin to what Nadav Hochman and Lev Manovich call "multi-scale reading," the ability to analyze and interpret data in terms of "both large scale patterns and the particular unique trajectories, without sacrificing one for another,"[57] as well as what Matthew Kirschenbaum calls the "forensic imagination,"[58] an imagination not just dedicated forensically to the darkest of depths and shadows, but also devoted to the *forensis,* or *forum,* the public. A more robust understanding of the various ways that digital media productions function in Indonesia's social, cultural, and political contexts necessitates an awareness borne out of a commitment to the collective; the polyvocal; the voices of the dead and the missing; the stories of those who have been marginalized, persecuted, and exiled; and the future generations to come.

The selection of digital projects I have discussed here are works "fueled by care and affection," and by the intellectual spirit that Said calls *amateurism.* If such an articulation becomes

56 Michel Foucault, *The Archaeology of Knowledge: And, the Discourse on Language,* trans. A.M. Sheridan Smith (New York: Pantheon Books, 1972), 130.

57 Nadav Hochman and Lev Manovich, "Zooming into an Instagram City: Reading the Local through Social Media," *First Monday* 18, no. 7 (July 2013), http://firstmonday.org/ojs/index.php/fm/article/view/4711/3698.

58 Matthew Kirschenbaum, *Mechanisms: New Media and the Forensic Imagination* (Cambridge: MIT Press, 2008). Kirschenbaum theorizes the activation of a "forensic imagination" in conceiving the computer as both archival and writing machine, and in envisioning digital texts as ultimately and always material, diachronic, and social objects.

the basis for an alternative digital humanities that is attentive to projects existing on the periphery, to social justice, to projects that may not be named "DH," is there, then, still a need to name them as such, under the big tent, capital-lettered DH? Or, we could perhaps imagine and articulate a humanities that is always in the offing — a digital humanities that is a *diligent humanities*, attentive to the indignant and to indigenous, local knowledge productions, for to be diligent (from the Latin *diligere*) is not only to persist, but to love what one is doing, without compromise, and with a commitment to building relations despite and especially because of differences.

Bibliography

Barthes, Roland. *Roland Barthes by Roland Barthes.* Translated by Richard Howard. New York: Hill and Wang, 1975.

Benjamin, Walter. "The Author as Producer." *New Left Review,* July 1, 1970, 83–96.

Bogost, Ian. *Alien Phenomenology, Or What It's Like to Be a Thing.* Minnesota: University of Minnesota Press, 2012.

Chun, Wendy Hui Kyong. *Control and Freedom: Power and Paranoia in the Age of Fiber Optics.* Cambridge: MIT Press, 2006.

Chun, Wendy Hui Kyong, and Lisa Mary Rhody. "Working the Digital Humanities: Uncovering Shadows between the Dark and the Light." *differences: A Journal of Feminist Cultural Studies* 25, no. 1 (2014): 1–25. DOI: 10.1215/10407391-2419985.

Deren, Maya. "Amateur Versus Professional." *Film Culture* 39 (1965): 45–46.

Derrida, Jacques. *Archive Fever: A Freudian Impression.* Translated by Eric Prenowitz. Chicago: University of Chicago Press, 1996.

———. *The Politics of Friendship.* Translated by George Collins. London: Verso, 2005.

Eickhoff, Martijn. "Memory Landscapes and the Regime Change of 1965–55 in Semarang." http://www.niod.nl/en/projects/memory-landscapes-and-regime-change–1965–66-semarang.

Eickhoff, Martijn, Donny Danardono, Tjahjono Rahardjo, and Hotmali Sidabalok, "The Memory Landscapes of '1965' in Semarang." *Journal of Genocide Research* 19, no. 4 (2017): 530–50. DOI: 10.1080/14623528.2017.1393945.

Farid, Hilmar. "Does the Past Matter? Archiving Injustices in Indonesia." Paper presentation, Human Rights Archives Symposium, UCLA, Los Angeles, California, October 19, 2013.

Foucault, Michel. *The Archaeology of Knowledge: And the Discourse on Language.* Translated by A.M. Sheridan Smith. New York: Pantheon Books, 1972.

Galloway, Alexander R. "Are Some Things Unrepresentable?" In *The Interface Effect*, 78–100. Cambridge: Polity Press, 2012.

Heryanto, Ariel. *Identity and Pleasure: The Politics of Indonesian Screen Culture.* Singapore: NUS Press, 2014.

Hill, David T., and Krishna Sen. *The Internet in Indonesia's New Democracy.* New York: Routledge, 2005.

Hochman, Nadav, and Lev Manovich. "Zooming into an Instagram City: Reading the Local through Social Media." *First Monday* 18, no. 7 (July 2013). http://firstmonday.org/ojs/index.php/fm/article/view/4711/3698.

Institut Sejarah Sosial Indonesia. http://www.sejarahsosial.org.

Kirschenbaum, Matthew. *Mechanisms: New Media and the Forensic Imagination*. Cambridge: MIT Press, 2008.

Klein, Lauren. "The Image of Absence: Archival Silence, Data Visualization, and James Hemings." *American Literature* 85, no. 4 (December 2013): 661–88. DOI: 10.1215/00029831-2367310.

Kuhn, Virginia. "The Rhetoric of Remix." *Transformative Works and Cultures* 9 (2012). http://journal.transformativeworks.org/index.php/twc/article/view/358/279.

———. "Web Three Point Oh: The Virtual Is the Real." In *High Wired Redux: CyberText Yearbook*. Research Centre for Contemporary Culture: University of Jyvkaisuja Press, October 2013, 1–19.

Lane, Max. "The Year of Living Dangerously." *Inside Indonesia,* November 1983, 29. http://nla.gov.au/nla.obj–88227234.

Larasati, Rachmi Diyah. *The Dance That Makes You Vanish: Cultural Reconstruction in Post-Genocide Indonesia.* Minneapolis: University of Minnesota Press, 2013.

McPherson, Tara. "Why Are the Digital Humanities So White? or Thinking the Histories of Race and Computation." In *Debates in the Digital Humanities,* edited by Matthew K. Gold, 139–60. Minnesota: University of Minnesota Press, 2012.

Mortimer, Rex. *Indonesian Communism under Sukarno: Ideology and Politics, 1959–1965*. Singapore: Equinox Publishing, 2006.

Morton, Timothy. *Hyperobjects: Philosophy and Ecology After the End of the World*. Minnesota: University of Minnesota Press, 2013.

Navas, Eduardo. *Remix Theory: The Aesthetics of Sampling*. New York: Springer, 2012.

Nelson, Alondra. "Representing Race: Silence in the Digital Humanities." Paper presentation, Modern Language Association Conference, Boston, Massachusetts, January 4, 2013.

Nodegoat. http://nodegoat.net/about.

Paramaditha, Intan. "Cinema, Sexuality and Censorship in Post-Soeharto Indonesia." In *Southeast Asian Independent Cinema*, edited by Tilman Baumgartel, 44–49. Hong Kong: Hong Kong University Press, 2012.

———. "Tracing Frictions in *The Act of Killing*." *Film Quarterly* 67, no. 2 (2013): 45. DOI: 10.1525/fq.2014.67.2.44.

Presner, Todd. "The Ethics of the Algorithm: Close and Distant Listening to the Shoah Foundation Visual History Archive." In *Probing the Ethics of Holocaust Culture*, edited by Claudio Fogu, Wulf Kansteiner, and Todd Presner, 175–202. Cambridge: Harvard University Press, 2016.

Raley, Rita. *Tactical Media*. Minneapolis: University of Minnesota Press, 2009.

Ratih, Agung Ayu. "Stories That Bridge Time." *Inside Indonesia*, Oct–Dec, 2015. http://www.insideindonesia.org/stories-that-bridge-time.

———. "Works of Memory and Narratives of Survival." Paper presentation, International Association of Cultural Studies Conference, Surabaya, Indonesia, August 9, 2015.

Said, Edward. *Culture and Imperialism*. New York: Vintage Books, 1994.

———. *Music at the Limits*. New York: Columbia University Press, 2009.

———. *Representations of the Intellectual.* New York: Vintage Books, 1996.

Sears, Laurie. "Reading Ayu Utami: Notes Toward A Study of Trauma and the Archive in Indonesia." *Indonesia* 83 (April 2007): 17–40.

Stoler, Ann Laura. *Along the Archival Grain: Epistemic Anxieties and Colonial Common Sense.* Princeton: Princeton University Press, 2009.

———. "Untold Stories," *Inside Indonesia,* Oct-Dec 2001. http://www.insideindonesia.org/untold-stories-2.

"The Act of Killing Press Notes." *The Act of Killing,* 2013. http://theactofkilling.com/wp-content/uploads/2013/09/THE_ACT_OF_KILLING_press_notes_sept2013.pdf.

Videochronic: Video Activism and Video Distribution in Indonesia. Yogyakarta, Indonesia: KUNCI Cultural Studies Center & EngageMedia, 2009.

"Video Slam 2013: Remixing the 1965 State Propaganda Film." *EngageMedia.* https://www.engagemedia.org/Projects/g30s_remixed.

Wark, McKenzie. "From OOO to P(OO)." *Public Seminar,* December 5, 2015. http://www.publicseminar.org/2015/12/from-ooo-to-poo/.

12

Taxation against Overrepresentation? The Consequences of Monolingualism for Digital Humanities[1]

Domenico Fiormonte

> *It would certainly be a grand convenience for us all to be able to move freely about the world [...] and be able to find everywhere a medium, albeit primitive, of intercourse and understanding. Might it not also be an advantage to many races, and an aid to the building-up of our new structure for preserving peace? .... Such plans offer far better prizes than taking away other people's provinces or lands or grinding them down in exploitation. The empires of the future are the empires of the mind.*
>
> — Winston Churchill, "The Gift of a Common Tongue"

1 I'm grateful to my student Claudia Diano for searching and providing the data in section 3. The data collected and discussed here go back to research carried out in 2014–15. Previous versions of this chapter appeared in Spanish (Fiormonte, "Lenguas, Codigos, Representacion") and Italian (Fiormonte, "Lingue, Codici, Rappresentanza"). The English translation of the original Italian text is by Desmond Schmidt and the author. Most of the quotations by non-English authors in this article are also translated and may not precisely represent the original text.

Monolingualism and Code Hegemonies

The title of this section alludes to a complex set of problems, which is becoming crucial for the digital humanities (DH), and in general to the relationship between the processes of digitization and the linguistic-cultural heritage of our world. The language bias is not only embodied in the Western (and especially Anglophone) dominance in science,[2] but also informs the visible structure of our institutions and the invisible standards of knowledge production and technology. The basis for the codes, languages, methodologies, and technical instruments of the digital humanities is English; the written and spoken lan-

---

2 See A. Suresh Canagarajah, *A Geopolitics of Academic Writing* (Pittsburgh: University of Pittsburgh Press, 2002); C.P. Chandrasekhar, "Open Access vs Academic Power," *Real-World Economics Review* 66 (January 13, 2014): 127–30; Mark Graham et al., eds., *Geographies of the World's Knowledge* (London: Convoco Foundation and Oxford Internet Institute, 2011); Pierre Frath, "'Une grande université italienne passe au 100% anglais.' De la bêtise comme méthode de gouvernance," *Association des Professeurs de Langues Vivantes: Les Langues Modernes,* June 29, 2012, https://www.aplv-languesmodernes.org/spip.php?article4593; Harrison W. Inefuku, "Globalization, Open Access, and the Democratization of Knowledge," *EducauseReview,* July 3, 2017, https://er.educause.edu/articles/2017/7/globalization-open-access-and-the-democratization-of-knowledge; Ilya Kiriya, "Les études médiatiques dans les BRICS contre les bases de données occidentales: critique de la domination académique anglophone," *Hermès. La Revue* 79, no. 3 (2017): 71–77; Vincent Larivière and Nadine Desrochers, "Langues et diffusion de la recherche: le cas des sciences humaines et sociales," *Découvrir. Le magazine de l'Acfas,* November 2015. "That the United States and its European allies dominate the world of knowledge, is unquestionable. This is reflected in indicators of academic 'output.' According to the National Science Foundation of the United States, the US accounted for 26% of the world's total Science & Engineering (S&E) articles published in 2009 and the European Union for 32%. In 2010, the US share in total citations of S&E articles stood at 36% and the EU's share at 33%, whereas that of Japan and China remained at 6% each" (Chandrasekhar, "Open Access vs Academic Power," 127). However, China in 2013 started publishing more scientific papers than any other individual country in the world apart from the US (and the difference was sharp: China 18.2%, US 18.8%), cf. Reinhilde Veugelers, "The Challenge of China's Rise as a Science and Technology Powerhouse," *bruegel,* July 4, 2017, http://bruegel.org/reader/Chinas_rise_as_a_science_and_technology_powerhouse#.

guage of all the main conferences, the most prestigious journals, the institutions that control the discipline, the organizations and international consortia, and the central authorities of knowledge is, with few exceptions, some dialect of British or American English.[3] More than twenty years ago, Robert Phillipson coined a controversial phrase to describe this situation: "linguistic imperialism,"[4] adding "linguicism" to the other forms of discrimination:

> Just as racism studies were revitalised in the 1970s by Black scholars speaking from a Black perspective, linguicism studies attempt to put the sociology of language and education into a form which furthers scrutiny of how language contributes to unequal access to societal power and how linguistic hierarchies operate and are legitimated. Drawing on the perspectives of minorities, of speakers of dominated languages, is important, since somehow speakers of dominant languages such as English and French tend to see the expanded use of their languages as unproblematical.... 'Linguistic imperialism' is shorthand for a multitude of activities, ideologies, and structural relationships. Linguistic imperialism takes place within an overarching structure of asymmetrical North/South relations, where language interlocks with other dimensions, cultural (particularly in education, science, and the media), economic and political.[5]

Tempting as it is to attribute all this to technological determinism, it is still undeniable that the above-mentioned triad sets in motion a process of reciprocal interactions and feedback, which

3 The phenomenon is obviously global and not only concerns DH (Pierre Frath, "Anthropologie de l'anglicisation de l'université et de la recherche." *Philologica Jassyensia* 1, no. 19 [2014]: 251–64).

4 Robert Phillipson, *Linguistic Imperialism* (Oxford: Oxford University Press, 1992) and *Linguistic Imperialism Continued* (New York: Routledge, 2009).

5 Robert Phillipson, "Realities and Myths of Linguistic Imperialism," *Journal of Multilingual and Multicultural Development* 18, no. 3 (1997): 238–48.

constitutes a structure of domination in scientific exchanges, in communication, and definitely in knowledge.[6] Certainly to overestimate this "knowledge" would fall into the trap of resisting — or self-delegitimizing — everything that does not align with it, but it would be also a mistake to underestimate the effects of this triad — languages, codes, and representation. Before addressing how this problem specifically affects DH, it will first be necessary to limit its scope and to provide some general instructions on its use:

1. As a white, male, and Southern European scholar I am aware that my starting position is not neutral or unprivileged. So what I propose here and the reasons why I propose it are not meant to imply an assertion of my own margins (Italy, Italian, and a "PIIGS" country[7]), nor to misrepresent the opposing or parallel imperialisms that plague the world. From this point of view, all attempts at establishing hegemony are similar, and an alliance between local subhegemonies (see BRICS[8]) is not the solution. I would also like to make it clear, as I hope will emerge in the course of my argument, that the problem

6 Boaventura de Sousa Santos, *Descolonizar el saber, reinventar el poder* (Montevideo: Extensión, Universidad de la República-Ediciones Trilce, 2010); Walter Mignolo, *The Darker Side of Western Modernity* (Durham: Duke University Press Books, 2011).

7 The derogatory acronym PIIGS first appeared in 2009 in London-based economic magazine *The Economist* referring to the economies of Portugal, Ireland, Italy, Greece, and Spain. Discussions on the geopolitics of knowledge (cf. Paula Clemente Vega, "Open Access, the Global South and the Politics of Knowledge Production and Circulation: An Open Insights Interview with Leslie Chan," *Open Library of the Humanities*, December 10, 2018, https://www.openlibhums.org/news/314/) usually neglect how Mediterranean and Eastern European countries, similarly to the Global South, have uncritically and silently adopted the rules of the Global North regarding the production and dissemination of research. Knowledge colonization is made of different layers, but today Anglophone journals (private) in conjunction with research institutions (public, but increasingly biased by the first) are the primary source of knowledge legitimization in the world.

8 Antonio Perri, "Al di là della tecnologia, la scrittura. Il caso Unicode," *Annali dell'Università degli Studi Suor Orsola Benincasa* II (2009): 725–48.

is not an anachronistic rejection of English,[9] but the need to reflect on the cultural, social, political, and economic consequences of a global process of homogenization of linguistic-semiotic codes. I think it is also important to remember that this process of homogenization in many aspects resembles the colonization and annihilation of indigenous knowledge that has been described by Linda Tuhiwai Smith in *Decolonizing Methodologies.*

2. In general, the ideas I present here are in line with the analysis and proposals of Walter Mignolo, particularly his reflection on the "cultures of scholarship," based on the notion of "bilanguaging"[10] and "plurilanguaging": "love for being between languages, love for the disarticulation of the colonial languages and for the subaltern ones, love for the impurity of national languages..."[11]
3. In criticizing the Anglophone monolingualism of science (and in this case of DH), I am aware that there are various problems,[12] including different degrees of exclusion and mar-

---

9 I refer to scientific communication because the refusal to use hegemonic languages in the expression of philosophic thought or in artistic and literary creation has been defended with very solid arguments by writers and postcolonial theorists such as Ngũgĩ wa Thiong'o: "What is the difference between a politician who says Africa cannot do without imperialism and the writer who says Africa cannot do without European languages?" (*Decolonising the Mind: The Politics of Language in African Literature* [Harare: Zimbabwe Publishing House, 1994]).

10 W. Mignolo, *Local Histories/Global Designs: Coloniality, Subaltern Knowledges, and Border Thinking* (Princeton: Princeton University Press, 2012), 249–77.

11 Ibid., 274

12 For the European situation, see Michele Gazzola, "The Linguistic Implications of Academic Performance Indicators: General Trends and Case Study," *International Journal of the Sociology of Language* 216 (2012): 131–56. We must remember that in the same European Science Foundation (ESF), the creation of categories of inclusion of resources in the ERIH (European Reference Index for the Humanities) database, favored Anglophone journals: "It must be admitted, however, that in most human disciplines there has often been a strong bias in favour of English journals, which must be remedied in the future" (Ferenc Kiefer, "ERIH's Role in the Evaluation of Research Achievements in the Humanities," in *New*

ginalization. According to the 2018 edition of Ethnologue, there are 7,097 languages in the world, but eight are spoken by 40.3% of the world population (more than 2.5 billion people), and the percentage rises to 80% for the first eighty-five languages. According Ethnologue, there are 288 languages of European origin, or 4.1% of the languages spoken in the world, but their speakers number over 1.7 billion people, or 25.5% of the total world population.[13] Therefore there are not only scarce or very rare languages,[14] but also languages completely excluded or marginalized in the process of digitization.[15] According to the index of linguistic diversity (ILD) realized by the research group Terralingua, "In just 35 years, between 1970 and 2005, global linguistic diversity has declined by 20%," and along with the erosion of linguistic diversity comes the erosion of the traditional environmental

Publication Cultures in the Humanities: Exploring the Paradigm Shift, ed. P. Dávidházi, 173–82 [Amsterdam: Amsterdam University Press, 2014], 176). See the document of the ESF on the definition of the categories: https://dbh.nsd.uib.no/publiseringskanaler/resources/pdf/ERIH_Aim_Quality_Criteria.pdf.

13 *Ethnologue: Languages of the World*, http://www.ethnologue.com/statistics.

14 Walter Mignolo observed in 2012 that 75% of the world's population speaks twelve languages, and six of these are colonial languages. Sorted by decreasing number of speakers they are: English, Spanish, German, Portuguese, French, and Italian (Mignolo, *Local Histories/Global Designs*, 290). But from a more general point of view it is clear that other hegemonic languages, for example Chinese and Arabic, exerted their "imperial role" at the expenses of other languages and cultures.

15 David Golumbia, "Postcolonial Studies, Digital Humanities, and the Politics of Language," *uncomputing*, May 31, 2013, http://www.uncomputing.org/?p=241; Mikami Yoshiki and Shigeaki Kodama, "Measuring Linguistic Diversity on the Web," in *Net.Lang: Towards the Multilingual Cyberspace*, eds. Laurent Vannini and Hervé Le Crosnier (Caen: C&F Éditions, 2012), 121–39; Perri, "Al di là della tecnologia, la scrittura"; Paolo Monella, "Scritture dimenticate, scritture colonizzate: sistemi grafici e codifiche digitali," talk given at Ricerca scientifica, monopoli della conoscenza e Digital Humanities. Prospettive critiche dall'Europa del Sud. Rome, Italy, 24–25 October 2018, Università Roma Tre.

knowledge (TEK) encoded in the languages.[16] David Harrison concludes: "The accelerating extinction of languages on a global scale has no precedent in human history. [...] It is happening much faster, making species extinction rates look trivial by comparison."[17] András Kornai argued in a 2013 study that less than 5% of all languages can be considered vital or "digital ascending," and most of the 7,097 living languages will not make it into the digital realm by the end of this century.[18] Without delving further into the issue it is clear that the digital humanities should develop greater sensitivity to this erosion of linguistic diversity by weighing the implications of, and its responsibility for, choices of technology.[19]

4. In the title I use the term "representation," understood as "presence" in institutions, although it is also connected with the idea of digital representation and its manifold biases. There are many levels of representation and each level involves some kind of political manipulation, economical appropriation, or cultural colonization of an original artifact.[20] However, two are of relevance here: the semiotic (e.g., interface) and the code. On the one hand, there is the influence of a certain way of representing everyday objects (e.g. the Windows folder as a metaphor for "container of documents"), and, on the other hand, the creation of a program or document encoding in a particular language (e.g., Python or HTML).[21] In fact it is easy to see that the difference between

16 Terralingua, "Linguistic Diversity," https://terralingua.org/our-work/linguistic-diversity/.

17 K.D. Harrison, *When Languages Die: The Extinction of the World's Languages and the Erosion of Human Knowledge* (Oxford: Oxford University Press, 2007), 7.

18 András Kornai, "Digital Language Death," *PLOS ONE* 8, no. 10 (2013): e77056.

19 Domenico Fiormonte, "Towards a Cultural Critique of Digital Humanities," *Historical Social Research/Historische Sozialforschung* 37, no. 3 (2012): 67–69.

20 Perri, "Al di là della tecnologia, la scrittura."

21 I leave here the question of creativity-performativity of algorithms, and simply refer to the extensive literature on studies of code and software.

the two levels is quite artificial (and often harmful). Both are secondary modeling systems that have an influence on overlapping social, cognitive, and epistemological fields. Let's say that in the first case there is a particular influence on practices and processes in the social and cognitive domains, and, in the second, on the theory and interpretation of information structures (cultural, linguistic, hermeneutical, and epistemological).

5. Although Mignolo argued that "English has come to be the language that preserves and hides the code," his genealogical critique of modernity can be perceived as somewhat dualistic.[22] In particular, there seems to be a missing element in his analysis, namely the "Western code" in the heritage of Western modernity, which is embodied in the languages, algorithms, protocols, and applications that permeate and support all forms of communication. But this time we are really facing a *codex universalis,* because through its multiple extensions, starting with social media, it exerts a power and control over the masses that goes far beyond the stage of modern

---

Particularly relevant to DH are the perspectives of Wendy Hui Kyong Chun, *Control and Freedom: Power and Paranoia in the Age of Fiber Optics* (Cambridge: MIT Press, 2006); Wendy Hui Kyong Chun and Lisa Marie Rhody, "Working the Digital Humanities: Uncovering Shadows between the Dark and the Light," *differences: A Journal of Feminist Cultural Studies* 25, no. 1 (2014): 1–25; Alexander R. Galloway, *Protocol: How Control Exists after Decentralization* (Cambridge: MIT Press, 2004); Lev Manovich, *Software Takes Command: Extending the Language of New Media* (London: Bloomsbury Publishing, 2013); and Safiya Umoja Noble, *Algorithms of Oppression: How Search Engines Reinforce Racism* (New York: New York University Press, 2018). Galloway, Chun, and Noble are more attentive to the social and political dimensions, and Manovich is interested mainly in the creative side For a definition of the field, see Matthew Fuller, *Software Studies: A Lexicon* (Cambridge: MIT Press, 2008) and http://www.electronicbookreview.com/thread/electropoetics/codology.

22 "The 'code' has been preserved in the security box since the Renaissance. Diverse knowledge has been generated from the secret code in six European modern or imperial languages: Italian, Spanish, Portuguese, French, German, and English. One may discern a hierarchy within modern European languages when it comes to Epistemology" (Mignolo, *The Darker Side,* xii).

colonial empires.[23] We need only cite the datagate scandal, described in a document published by the US National Security Agency and its British twin (GCHQ) in January 2013, in which it says that in one month over 181 million records were collected, including metadata and content (text, audio, and video).[24] The scale of this data gathering is unprecedented and proves that all traces we leave in the network remain "forever." This indelible materiality[25] raises questions about the present nature of our identity. As Friedrich Kittler wrote:

> Codes — by name and by matter — are what determine us today, and what we must articulate if only to avoid disappearing under them completely. They are the language of our time precisely because the word and the matter code are much older. [...] Today, technology puts code into the practice of realities, that is to say: it encodes the world.[26]

---

23 "[T]he level of control and manipulation possible in the digital era exceeds what was possible before by an almost unfathomable extent. 'Predictive analytics' and big data and many other tools hint at a means for manipulating the public in all sorts of ways without their knowledge at all." (David Golumbia, "Social Media as Political Control: The Facebook Study, Acxiom, & NSA," *uncomputing,* July 1, 2014, http://www.uncomputing.org/?p=1530). I disagree with Golumbia when he separates the responsibilities of governments (e.g., NSA) from the giants of digital communication (e.g., Google, Facebook). An increasing amount of scholarship in the last years showed evidence of the deep connection between the US military industry and the IT sector (let alone the historical roots of the Internet, the telecommunication network, etc.). For a well-balanced discussion see the special issue of *Limes: Rivista Italiana di Geopolitica* 10: "La rete a stelle e strisce" (July 2018).

24 Barton Gellman and Ashkan Soltani, "NSA Infiltrates Links to Yahoo, Google Data Centers Worldwide, Snowden Documents Say," *The Washington Post,* October 30, 2013, https://www.washingtonpost.com/world/national-security/nsa-infiltrates-links-to-yahoo-google-data-centers-worldwide-snowden-documents-say/2013/10/30/e51d661e-4166-11e3-8b74-d89d714ca4dd_story.html.

25 Matthew G. Kirschenbaum, *Mechanisms: New Media and the Forensic Imagination* (Cambridge: MIT Press, 2008).

26 Friedrich Kittler, "Code (or, How You Can Write Something Differently)," in *Software Studies: A Lexicon,* ed. Matthew Fuller (Cambridge: MIT Press, 2008), 40.

In this scenario of global control, whether by osmosis or embraced deliberately,[27] the (conscious) victim of epistemic colonialism and its "global designers" is not only the former colonial South. And if, on the one hand, Anglo-digital universalism fits perfectly with the idea of *epistemicide*,[28] on the other hand, one can not deny, as played out in Dave Eggers's novel *The Circle*, in the fabulous world of "transparency," of social media, from East to West, from North to South, we all cooperate happily in the loss of our privacy and freedom. Therefore, to avoid the complete disappearance at any latitude of epistemic diversity and the right to oblivion, a wider and more consciously deep alliance is needed than that desired by the theorists of post- and decolonialism. "Border thinking" is a necessary, but not sufficient, condition: we must unite in working towards a freedom that traverses geopolitical boundaries and goes beyond "cognitive justice"[29] and *against* the imaginary monopolists described by Eggers. That is, before it is too late, we must extend the concepts of freedom, rights, and democracy to our digital traces, considering them in effect as an extension of our rights as individuals.[30]

As for digital humanities, in my opinion, there is an indissoluble link between the technological choices (politics of coding), political representation (coding of politics), and the structure or management of knowledge (ontologies and epistemological code). Despite rejecting a genealogical interpretation, the connection between the English-speaking hegemony and instruments of representation is obvious. In the end "technical is always political."[31]

27 Zygmunt Bauman and David Lyon, *Liquid Surveillance: A Conversation* (Cambridge: Polity Press, 2013), 17.

28 Boaventura de Sousa Santos, ed., *Another Knowledge Is Possible: Beyond Northern Epistemologies* (London: Verso, 2008).

29 Ibid., xix–li.

30 Among the many initiatives promoting digital rights from a Global South perspective see the *Just Net Coalition Manifesto*: https://justnetcoalition.org/digital-justice-manifesto.pdf

31 Galloway, *Protocol*, 245.

These are of course questions that require multidisciplinary expertise. In this article rather than proposing answers, I will try to analyze the current situation and make a proposal, based on my own experience and on a collection of some data on a specific issue: the monolingualism of DH.

The Costs of Exclusion

Everyone knows that it is much easier to criticize "linguistic imperialism" than it is to find solutions that support multilingualism in a truly effective and economically sustainable way. And beyond the more or less useful announcements about multilingual initiatives,[32] we know that the successful models in the world can be counted on one hand. However, in our determination to defend the cultural, ethical, and social reasons for our insistence on multilingualism, we tend to ignore a decisive factor: the evaluation of its economics. It is clear that English is a proprietary language and its capital generates an economic surplus. But before addressing the specific case of the DH, something should first be said about this surplus. In recent years scholars from economics and social sciences have provided evidence that it is the monolingual regimes that are uneconomic[33] and

32 Various resolutions, statements, recommendations, and so on at the EU level can be found in the volume of Robert Phillipson (*Linguistic Imperialism*, 193–207). I note especially the "Vienna Manifesto on European Language Policy," prepared by eleven experts from different countries of the Union to mark the European Year of Languages in 2001 (https://www.univie.ac.at/linguistics/Forschung/wittgenstein/events/Manifesto.pdf). The manifest tries to mediate between the requirement of mutual intelligibility between the citizens of the Union and the right to multilingualism: "On the one hand, it is impossible to make foreign language skills a prerequisite for exercising democratic rights. On the other hand, mutual understanding is essential for living together" (Phillipson, *Linguistic Imperialism*, 203).

33 Michele Gazzola, "Il falso mito dell'inglese: né democratico né redditizio," *Corriere della Sera, La Lettura*, November 30, 2014, 5, https://lettura.corriere.it/il-falso-mito-dellinglese-ne-democratico-ne-redditizio/comment-page-5/; François Grin, *L'enseignement des langues étrangères comme politique publique: Rapport au Haut Conseil de l'évaluation de*

proceeded to dismantle the mythical benefits of the lingua franca.[34] The debate has been mainly developed within European countries, particularly as a result of the increasingly widespread use of English both in communication and in official acts of the EU. But even after complaints about the Anglophone hegemony have been raised, what lies behind it is often a hidden trauma of cultural and economic bankruptcy of certain former colonial powers.[35] But the issues raised are of interest to all those who care about the reasons for "plurilinguaging" and linguistic rights as a part and indeed a reflection of human rights.[36]

In a study published by the Swiss research center Observatoire ÉLF about language policy in the European Union, Michele Gazzola proposed a method for measuring the level of linguistic exclusion within Europe and for evaluating the effectiveness and equity of the various language arrangements (twenty-four

---

l'école, No. 19 (Paris: Ministère de l'éducation nationale, 2005), and *Language Policy Evaluation and the European Charter for Regional or Minority Languages* (Basingstoke: Palgrave Macmillan, 2003); Gergely Kovács, *Economic Aspects of Language Inequality in the European Union,* College for Modern Business Studies, Tatabánya, Hungary, 2007,; Phillipe Van Parijs, *Linguistic Justice for Europe and for the World* (Oxford: Oxford University, 2011).

34 "In the EU English is the mother tongue of about 13% of citizens. Then English is not and can not be a 'neutral' language like medieval Latin, with due respect to those who believe in the 'globish.' In an Anglophone Europe the native English-speakers would enjoy indisputable advantages that would be unacceptable in many aspects. An example? The hegemonic position of English in Europe earns the UK income close to a point of GDP per year as a result of savings in foreign language teaching and translations, and this position allows Britain to easily attract highly qualified students from countries beyond the Channel more than other European countries. The prominence of this language at the European level involves numerous other strategic advantages in institutional communication. Approximately 40% of the previous Commission's spokesmen were native English speakers, which is more than three times the percentage of native English speakers in the Union" (Gazzola, "Il falso mito dell'inglese").

35 Frath, "Anthropologie de l'anglicisation," 257–61.

36 Miklós Kontra et al., eds., *Language: A Right and a Resource: Approaching Linguistic Human Rights* (Budapest: Central European University Press, 1999).

languages, a core of three languages, and English as the monolingual representative).[37] If English were the only official language of the EU twenty-four, about half of the resident population would be completely excluded from communication. The linguistic exclusion rate would rise to 81% if we were to include the difficulty of accessing documents. In this regard it should be noted that the conceptual difference between English and "English as a lingua franca" (ELF) lacks any relevance to the effectiveness and equity of language policies.[38] This potential exclusion worsens if the official websites of the various departments of the European Union are examined, and while it may sound paradoxical, they are under no obligation to translate all digital documents. The result is that "one third of all the introductory pages are available only in English and almost another third in all official languages of the Union [...]. However, the use of the 24 official languages does not always extend to all pages that constitute the site of a department, and not always into sub-pages."[39] But even adopting the trilingual regime (French, German, English), as in the department of "Agriculture and rural development," exclusion rates rise to between 61% and 75%, while "the monolingual regime practiced by the Energy department excludes or does not provide access to all the communications for between 46% and 80% of operators in the sector."[40] As to the costs, the Hungarian economist Áron Lukács declared in 2007 that the monolingual regime was merely a "regime of unfair competition," given the huge economic advantages enjoyed by the UK in contrast to the huge costs incurred by the other

37 The data collected by Gazzola are based on language skills confirmed in various countries of the European Union, as provided by Adult Education Survey 2011 Eurostat: https://ec.europa.eu/eurostat/web/microdata/adult_education_survey.

38 Michele Gazzola, "Partecipazione, esclusione linguistica e traduzione: Una valutazione del regime linguistico dell'Unione europea," *Studi Italiani di Linguistica Teorica e Applicata* 43, no. 2 (2014): 227–64.

39 Ibid., 250.

40 Ibid., 251–52. Many initiatives in different departments (e.g., "Business and Industry") appear only in English and this is a further competitive advantage for English speakers.

member countries of the Union to make up the difference.[41] According to Gazzola, a monolingual English language regime or an oligolingual one (German, French, English) would cost far more than half the annual 1.1 billion euros that the EU currently spends on language services.[42] The Italian economist and social scientist summarizes his research as follows:

> Two conclusions may be drawn from the overall analysis of the empirical results compiled in this section. First, a multilingual system is much more effective than a monolingual one based only on English or on a few languages. Second, in the light of experience, an open language policy creates fewer inequalities not only between countries, but also among residents with different socio-economic status. A restrictive language policy (monolingual or oligolingual) generates significant inequalities between social groups as regards access to communication with EU institutions, disadvantaging especially the elderly, low-income groups, residents with a medium–low level of training, the unemployed, the disabled and those engaged in domestic work (a category often related to gender). However, a multilingual language policy based on intensive use of translation and interpreters, although not at zero cost, makes possible in the current circumstances more inclusive forms of communication. In this sense, the results presented here seem to provide empirical support for the idea that multilingual language arrangements can contribute to social cohesion in Europe.[43]

However, ignorance of these data and fascination with "internationalization" ("If I write and speak English I am an international…") are culturally subaltern attitudes widespread in Southern European élites, producing the self-harm and avoidance of one's own language. Speaking, writing (and publishing) in one's lo-

41 Lukács and Kovács, *Economic Aspects of Language Inequality*, 3.
42 Gazzola, "Partecipazione, esclusione linguistica e traduzione," 232.
43 Ibid., 254–55.

cal language, as colonial countries did in indigenous languages, feels disadvantageous or as if it is holding one back. This is what happened in 2012 in one of the most prestigious Italian universities, the Polytechnic of Milan, when a majority vote decided that all master's and doctoral courses would be taught in English. A group of dissident teachers appealed the decision to the Regional Administrative Court (TAR), sparking a controversy that crossed national boundaries.[44] Having shot down point-by-point the ideological, rather than practical, reasons behind this decision, the French linguist Pierre Frath underlined once again how Anglophone monolingualism generates discrimination:[45]

> [To use English] as a filter for enrollment in a university is a return to the practice of prohibiting access to those whose parents lacked the foresight to teach good English to their children, that is, the working classes. A selection based on English is a social selection. There is clearly a democratic deficit, a grabbing of education and good jobs by the upper middle classes.[46]

---

44 G. Gobo, "Prove (inconsapevoli) di colonizzazione linguistica. Lo strano caso del Politecnico di Milano," 2014, https://era.ong/kadmo/prove-inconsapevoli-di-colonizzazione-linguistica-lo-strano-caso-del-politecnico-di-milano/; Nicoletta Maraschio and Domenico De Martino, eds., *Fuori l'italiano dall'università? Inglese, internazionalizzazione, politica linguistica* (Rome and Bari: Accademia della Crusca–Laterza, 2012).

45 Even those who argue in favor of English as a lingua franca, as Philippe Van Parijs, propose a series of policies to improve the "linguistic justice." According to Van Parijs there are three types of "linguistic justice": "cooperative justice," "distributive justice," and "parity of esteem." I quote from the back cover: "Firstly, the adoption of one natural language as the lingua franca implies that its native speakers are getting a free ride by benefiting costlessly from the learning effort of others. Secondly, they gain greater opportunities as a result of competence in their native language becoming a more valuable asset. And thirdly the privilege systematically given to one language fails to show equal respect for the various languages with which different portions of the population concerned identify" (Van Parijs, *Linguistic Justice for Europe and for the World*).

46 Frath, "Une grande université italienne passe au 100% anglais," 1.

What does this have to do with the digital humanities? It is difficult to quantify the costs of monolingualism in DH, but it can be assumed that they are exacerbated by the specific disadvantage arising from the difficulty to "translate" into the lingua franca the results of research conducted on non-Anglophone cultural objects and resources (or even multilingual, as in the case of Romance texts or non-European traditions, for example). All that I have summarized here shows that there is a strong ongoing debate about the negative consequences of monolingualism and that proposals can be devised, as we shall see, to mitigate or solve many of these problems without imposing prohibitive costs on any party.

Besides the consequences shared by other fields (invisibility of research in other languages, etc.), the Anglophone dominance of DH produces a series of specific negative effects: (1) prevents the construction of a genuinely democratic, supportive, and multilingual international community (one of the hallmarks of the human and social sciences[47]); (2) links institutional representation (mostly governed by Anglophones) with the selection and management of tools and resources, hindering methodological and epistemological pluralism; (3) as discussed in the following paragraph, changes the representation of research in the field of DH and tends to project its own monolingual nature on the entire discipline. Martin Grandjean, in an article on the relationship between multilingualism and the acceptance rates of papers for the DH2014 conference, said that "the overall proportion of Anglophone submissions rose from 92% to 95.9% between the bid phase and validation phase, and the acceptance

47 On this subject, compare what the Vienna Manifesto declares: "As regards the humanities and sciences, measures have to be taken to ensure that national languages other than English domineering as a lingua franca in academia will be preserved and further developed. At least in the humanities and arts, this is a crucial prerequisite for preserving academic cultures with their specific knowledge gains" (Phillipson, *Linguistic Imperialism*, 206).

rate was halved for non-English submissions (29.8%)."[48] The results also show that while the statement (call for papers) was published in twenty-three languages, the contributions were only submitted in six languages besides English. But, above all, the acceptance rate for non-English proposals was half that of those proposals in English.[49] According to Grandjean, these results reflect a problem not only of language itself, but also of a supporting community made of mainly Anglophone speakers.[50]

International or Provincial? The Case of DH Journals

If the situation just outlined is one that occurs at the main conference on digital humanities, what happens in other sectors, for example in journals? As Isabel Galina says:

> There is a general perception of an Anglo-American dominance and of English as the main language. This can be gleaned from general impressions that have been formed from observations of the DH community's main communication channels, publications, meetings, postgraduate courses,

---

48 Martin Grandjean, "Le rêve du multilinguisme dans la science: l'exemple (malheureux) du colloque #DH2014," *Martin Grandjean*, June 27, 2014, http://www.martingrandjean.ch/multilinguisme-dans-la-science-DH2014/.

49 Élika Ortega, "Local and International Scalability in DH," *Élika Ortega*, July 2, 2014, https://elikaortegadotnet.wordpress.com/2014/07/02/scalability/.

50 These observations are confirmed by data collected from more recent DH conferences and discussed in three different works: José Pino-Díaz and Domenico Fiormonte, "La geopolítica de las humanidades digitales: un caso de estudio de DH2017 Montreal," poster presentation, DH2018. Puentes-Bridges, Mexico City, June 26–29, 2018, https://dh2018.adho.org/la-geopolitica-de-las-humanidades-digitales-un-caso-de-estudio-de-dh2017-montreal/ and "Aportaciones al conocimiento de la colaboración internacional en Humanidades Digitales según Scopus. Un estudio de Science Mapping Analysis," paper presentation, III Congreso Internacional: Humanidades Digitales. La Cultura de los Datos, Universidad de Rosario, Santa Fe, November 7–9, 2018, https://rephip.unr.edu.ar/handle/2133/13468; and Scott B. Weingart and Nickoal Eichmann-Kalwara, "What's under the Big Tent? A Study of ADHO Conference Abstracts," *Digital Studies/Le Champ Numérique* 7, no. 1 (2017): art. 6.

> and constitutive bodies. However, currently there is little known data available to prove it, and many of these observations are anecdotal and empirical.[51]

The research I propose here, although still in development,[52] attempts to answer this need,[53] by gathering the first data on the use of sources in major journals in the digital humanities that were available online at the time of our survey (2014–15). The sources cited in the references and notes are a key indicator of how humanists and social scientists work. Apart from the language in which the article is written, the sources reveal fundamental information about the content of the research and the academic training of the author (languages they know, theoretical trends, methodological choices, etc.). This use of sources, reflected in the references cited, can reveal the powers of a medievalist, the cultural background of an expert in new media, the geopolitical trend of an historian, and so on. The objective of our experiment was to collect information about the language (or languages) of the sources used by authors published in seven journals that represent a heterogeneous sample both from the point of view of the linguistic region and from scientific interest: *Characters* (CA); *Digital Humanities Quarterly* (DHQ); *Digital Medievalist* (DM); *Digital Studies / Le champ numérique* (DSCN); *Jahrbuch für Computerphilologie* (JCP); *Informatica umanistica* (IU); *Literary and Linguistic Computing* (published as *Digital Scholarship*

---

51 Isabel Galina Russell, "Geographical and Linguistic Diversity in the Digital Humanities," *Literary and Linguistic Computing* 29, no. 3 (2014): 307–16.

52 This is the *laurea magistrale* thesis of Claudia Diano, "Digital Humanities and Linguistic-Cultural Diversity: The Case of Scholarly Journals," course on Informazione editoria giornalismo, Università degli Studi di Roma Tre. In this article we anticipate the first results of the data collection, which will be published in full on http:///infolet.it/. Claudia Diano created the data visualizations and the figures and tables in section 3.

53 In the Spanish-speaking context see the study of Esteban Romero Frías and Salvador Del-Barrio-García ("Una visión de las Humanidades Digitales a través de sus centros," *El profesional de la Información* 23, no. 5 [September–October 2014]: 485–92) on the scarce Web visibility of non-Anglophone digital humanities centers.

in the Humanities starting in 2014) (LLC). These seven journals, except LLC, were chosen because all items are fully available online. Only CA, IU, and JCP have a definite geo-linguistic position, but all frequently publish (or have published) articles in English. Unfortunately most DH journals are published in Anglophone contexts, and this limits the possibilities for comparison. With the intention to diversify the sample, we have added *Characters* ("Cultural and critical studies in the digital sphere"), at the time of our investigation the only Hispanic online journal which devoted considerable space to DH issues.

The time frame studied was a maximum of five years, most often 2009–2014, although CA began publishing in 2012, and IU and the JCP ceased publishing in 2011. In studying CA and IU, we examined all the available numbers, and in studying JCP, we chose a five-year interval from 2004 to 2010, since some years were not present.[54] While the total number of sources examined from each journal is not homogeneous (more than five thousand in LLC to less than three hundred in IU), the percentages of the total published articles examined still produce a fairly representative picture of the linguistic tendency of each individual journal.

As already mentioned, the chosen benchmark indicator is the language of the cited sources,[55] not the language of the article itself. The publication language often depends on external factors, and a non-English-speaking author may have no other choice, although in theory he or she is free in the choice of subject matter and therefore in the choice of sources.[56] In the DH community it is common to find authors published in differ-

54 The years 2008–2009 are not available online: http://computerphilologie.digital-humanities.de/ejournal.html.

55 We understand by number of sources, the number of bibliographic references gathered from bibliographies or notes, according to the style adopted by the journal.

56 The only limit could be defined by the obligation to translate the sources cited in the text and sometimes a preference for (or need) to insert in the bibliography English translations of the texts cited (e.g., the classics of literature). The latter factor, in some cases (e.g., the journals on studies of antiquity, archeology, and so on) could then bias the sample in favor of

ent languages (as in many of the journals we surveyed), but this does not have a significant impact on the total of the examined sources (in total over ten thousand bibliographic references). We calculated the number of sources used in each language as a percentage of the total sources cited in each of the journals. In Table 1 we have summarized the most relevant data on the main languages of the selected journals (English, French, Spanish, German, and Italian). It soon became obvious that the three journals published in languages other than English, *IU*, *JCP*, and

Table 1. Number and percentage of sources in the most common languages

Journal	English		French		Spanish		German		Italian		
	Sources	% of the total journal									*Total sources of the journal*
Digital Humanities Quarterly	4630	97%	17	0,4%	77	2%	13	0,3%	15	0,3%	*4766*
Jahrbuch für Computerphilologie	326	39%	11	1%	1		497	59%			*843*
Informatica Umanistica	263	46%	7	1%	8	1%			297	51%	*577*
Digital Studies / Le champ numérique	2213	97%	66	3%	1						*2281*
Caracteres	649	41%	19	1%	875	56%	11	1%	11	1%	*1573*
Digital Medievalist[29]	357	83%	23	5%	7	2%	13	3%	4	1%	*430*
Literary and Linguistic Computing (DSH)	5706	94%	76	1%	63	1%	111	2%	28	0,5%	*6092*

CA, have a balance between the reference language of the journal itself and English, while in the other four cases the percentage of sources in English is overwhelming: 94% in *LLC*, the oldest and most "international" publication of the group; 97% in *DHQ* and *DSCN*; and 83% in *DM*. It also seems interesting that French and Spanish, the second and third most used languages in the seven journals, albeit at astronomical distances from English, reach 5% and 2% respectively in *DM* (which, however, has 3% of

English, but from a cursory examination of the pattern of our journals it seems that the data were irrelevant.

the sources in German and 5% in Dutch, see Figure 1). But more surprising, overall, is the low percentage of sources in French in the Canadian magazine *DSCN* (the actual number of sources in French is the highest of the seven magazines, but this simply reflects the much larger number of items examined).

Already from the first analysis (Figure 1 and Figure 2) a fact emerges: the problem is not only that the DH is purely Anglophone (without exception, the most widespread language of the cited sources is English), but also that Anglophones rarely cite sources in languages other than English. It is also interesting to note the information on the affiliations of the authors in each journal (Figure 3 and Table 2): in general, it seems clear that the Anglo-American journals are more attractive to researchers, and very few authors of Anglophone institutions publish in national or local journals. Only *DM* reflects a better balance between the various countries: 25% of authors work in US institutions, 12% in the UK, 37% in France, 5% in Germany (Table 2). The global data on the countries of membership (total 756 institutions for all journals) confirms that most researchers work in Anglo-American institutions: US, UK, Canada, Ireland, and Australia have 62% of the affiliations (Figure 3). Finally, the comparison between the reference language of the authors and their sources (Figure 4) confirms the trend towards a substantial monolingualism.

Naturally, the data shown here reflect an initial selection, and in future it would be desirable to expand the research and to standardize certain parameters (number of items, year of publication, etc.). For example, we know that, even for non-native English speakers, it has become common practice to publish in English, quoting translated classics, or to find English translations of the sources used. This practice (which actually ends up reinforcing monolingual habits) may marginally bias the data sample. However, the percentages are still so clear it is hard not to raise doubts about the openness and scope of the research done in English-speaking contexts. So this would also tend to deflate the myth of the internationalism of some journals, and their related organizations and research centers. What we found,

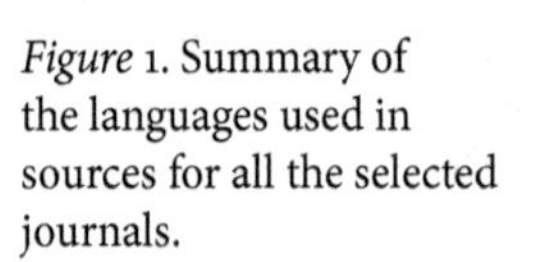

Figure 1. Summary of the languages used in sources for all the selected journals.

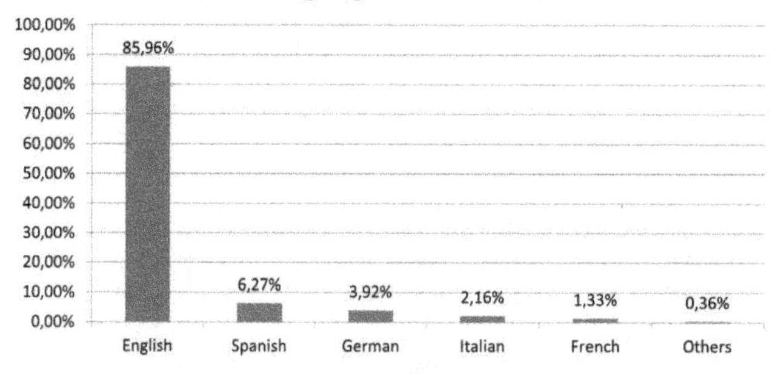

Figure 2. Percentages of the sources in each of the selected languages, as a fraction of all cited sources (16,454).

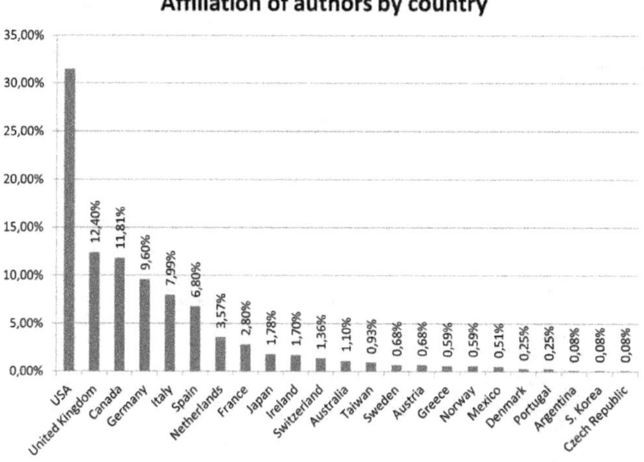

Figure 3. Percentages of institutional affiliations of authors, distributed by country. Some countries, such as Italy, seem overrepresented because the number of institutions that appear in the journal *IU* is much higher than in others. In addition, the UK has a low percentage, but its institutions are better distributed in all the journals.

Table 2. Institutional affiliation of the authors

Journal	USA		UK		Canada		France		Italy		Spain		Germany		
	number of affiliations	% Percent of total journal													Total affiliations
Digital Humanities Quarterly	186	69%	17	6%	24	9%	2	1%	2	1%	2	1%	5	2%	270
Jahrbuch für Computerphilologie	2	2%	4	5%	1			2%					59	69%	86
Informatica Umanistica	5	6%	5	6%	1	1%			78	88%					89
Digital Studies / Le champ numérique	59	36%	25	15%	78	48%									163
Caracteres	13	14%	4	4%	2				3	3%	63	69%			91
Digital Medievalist	14	25%	7	12%	2	4%	21	37%	1	1,7%	1	1,7%	3	5%	57
Literary and Linguistic Computing (DSH)	91	22%	84	20%	34	8%	10	2%	10	2%	14	3%	46	11%	421

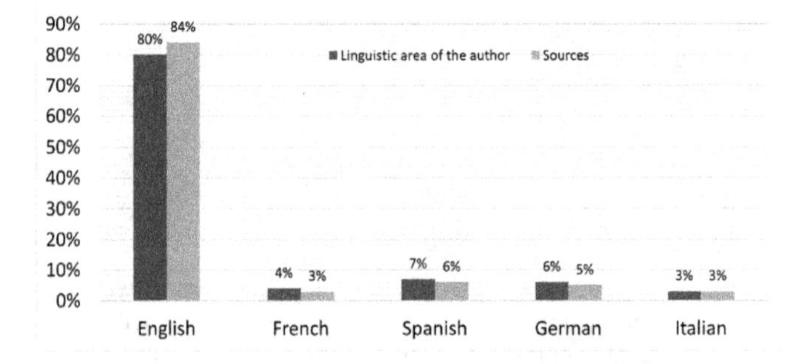

Figure 4. Comparison between the linguistic area of origin of the authors (selected languages only) and the language of the sources. The linguistic areas of the authors have been gathered from various sources such as Wikipedia, personal pages, social media, and so on.

on the contrary, was that the more local a journal, the greater was the degree of attention to the world "outside." This seems to support the idea, already observed in the field of diversity and bio-cultural variations,[57] that there is a greater diversity on the margins than in the "center." That is, it shows how the processes of standardization, internationalization, and globalization, guided by hegemonic codes, are potential factors in the impoverishment of available knowledge. The risk is that in addition to not promoting exchanges and influences between the various linguistic and cultural areas, the use of English as the language of research does not guarantee the flow of ideas.[58] In conclusion, as Anthony Grafton observes in a footnote,[59] if the bibliographic references represent the "dialogue" that the researcher has with the community and with the objects of their inquiry, then we must conclude that many Anglophone colleagues seem trapped in an eternal geo-linguistic present.

Conclusions and Proposals

Although the data as discussed above are not encouraging, it must be said that the community of digital humanists in recent years has been much more attentive and open to diversity of other scientific communities. Accordingly, there have been very significant initiatives, the most striking of which is the proposed change of governance structure of the Alliance of Digital Humanities Organizations (ADHO). According to the latest

---

57 Tatsuya Amano et al., "Global Distribution and Drivers of Language Extinction Risk," *Proceedings of the Royal Society* B 281, no. 1793 (October 22, 2014); Luisa Maffi and Ellen Woodley, eds., *Biocultural Diversity Conservation: A Global Sourcebook* (Washington, DC and London: Earthscan, 2010).

58 Phillipson, *Linguistic Imperialism*, 176–77. On the political and cultural implications and effects of monolingualism in USA, see the important study by Robert B. Kaplan ("Multilingualism vs. Monolingualism: The View from the USA and Its Interaction with Language Issues around the World," *Current Issues in Language Planning* 16, nos. 1–2 [2015]: 149–62).

59 Anthony Grafton, *The Footnote: A Curious History* (London: Faber and Faber, 2000).

discussions,[60] the new structure would allow groups and associations worldwide to join the umbrella organization following a three-layered model: Constituent Organizations (or COs, which provide funding and make the decisions), Associate Organizations ("allied to ADHO"), and Affiliated Organizations ("compatible aims with ADHO").[61] For the first time in the history of this organization, a DH association from the Global South, Red de Humanidades Digitales from Mexico, joined the ADHO as a CO. This is certainly a strong and encouraging sign, but it seems too early to judge what kind of impact this presence will have on the historical cultural, linguistic, and epistemic inequalities of the DH field as whole. The proposed financial model of ADHO is still based on income, that is on the subscription to the *Digital Scholarship in the Humanities* (*DSH*) journal: "Both scenarios were based on the principle that as far as possible ADHO-level activities would be supported by income derived from institutional and consortia subscriptions to the journal."[62] In fact, the existence of *DSH*, a paywall journal mostly inaccessible and unaffordable in Southern institutions (including many Southern European institutions), is a primary obstacle to the creation of a genuine grassroot federation based on the principle of equality of access to key resources. It seems paradoxical — and, for many colleagues around the world, unacceptable — that a DH organization which sets among its "key strategic drivers" the "Support for and encouragement of cultural and linguistic diversity, locally and globally," [63] links its existence to an expensive monolingual publication that makes almost invisible non-Anglophone research. This approach is, in the words of Leslie Chan, at the root of all forms of "epistemic injustice in the production and circulation of knowledge"[64] So while there is no doubt that many

60 The last documents available online at the time of writing date back to April 2018: http://change.adho.org/proposed-governance-scenarios/.

61 ADHO, "ADHO Governance Proposals," http://www.adho.org/administration/steering/adho-governance-proposals.

62 Ibid.

63 Ibid.

64 Chan and Vega, "Open Access."

of the proposed structural changes will expand the geopolitical reach of ADHO, these will not translate automatically into a more diverse, equal, and democratic community. The main problem remains: the ADHO structure is pyramidal and based on inequality of status (cultural, epistemological, linguistic, political, economical, etc.) among its members and organizations.

The only way to begin to limit the damage caused by monolingualism and ethnocentrism in DH is to undertake a plan of action to adopt a kind of "border thinking" from the margins,[65] where often the means are less, but the freedom to innovate is greater. It is therefore vital that the margins talk amongst themselves, and boost the South-South dialogue about theoretical models and practical shared solutions. As Octavio Kulesz notes in discussing the model of the digital edition in developing countries:

> The electronic solutions that certain countries of the South have implemented to overcome their problems of content distribution can also serve as a model for others, thus facilitating South–South knowledge and technology transfer.... Sooner or later, these countries will have to ask themselves what kind of digital publishing highways they must build and they will be faced with two very different options: a) financing the installation of platforms designed in the North; b) investing according to the concrete needs, expectations and potentialities of local authors, readers and entrepreneurs.[66]

Nevertheless the principle must also be established that the cost of Anglophone monolingualism cannot be borne entirely by non-Anglophones. The suggestions set out below should not prove too costly to implement and, more importantly, do not renounce the use of English as a lingua franca:

---

65 Mignolo, *Local Histories/Global Design.*

66 Octavio Kulesz, *La edición digital en los países en desarrollo* (Paris: Alianza Internacional de Editores Independientes — Prince Claus Fund for Culture and Development, 2011).

1. Apply the concept of "pluricentric standards" to English in publications in DH[67] to mitigate the negative impact of centralized policy (authors and editors mostly from the USA and the UK and its former colonies) on the variety of expression and local cultures.[68]
2. Develop several forms of a "linguistic tax" to counteract the disadvantage or degree of exclusion of non-Anglophones.
3. Create a decentralized and federated organization that represents the various geopolitical and linguistic areas in the world, governed by the rule "one organization or country equals one vote." The founding principle of this federation should be multilingualism and cultural diversity (see the Universal Declaration on Cultural Diversity, the Vienna Manifesto on European language policies, etc.).
4. Create a multilingual, free-access journal (which would investigate the possibility of annotating and translating articles, commentaries, and reviews, etc. into other languages).
5. Consider the possibility of changing post-publication practices.[69] This would mean complementing or, in certain cases (for example, articles by young researchers), replacing the peer-review process with an expedited editorial evaluation, and then allowing readers and reviewers to comment on and annotate the work in more detail. The authors could then include these revisions in their text.[70]

67 Edgar W. Schneider, "Asian Englishes — Into the Future: A Bird's Eye View," *Asian Englishes* 16, no. 3 (2014): 249–56.

68 As Schneider says talking about "Asian Englishes," the local variants of English reflect the multicultural richness of the speakers, and in any case the definition of a "Standard English" is nowadays problematic (ibid., 254).

69 Hilda Bastian, "A Stronger Post-Publication Culture Is Needed for Better Science," PLOS *Medicine* (December 30, 2014), https://journals.plos.org/plosmedicine/article?id=10.1371/journal.pmed.1001772.

70 For a new approach to peer review in DH see the analysis and proposals of Roopika Risam ("Rethinking Peer Review in the Age of Digital Humanities," *Ada: A Journal of Gender, New Media, and Technology* 4 [2014]).

6. Translate websites, materials, and resources connected with the organization or its various initiatives and publications into several languages.
7. Create a collection of open-access texts, calling on Anglophone communities to undertake the *translation and circulation* of studies from marginalized or disadvantaged regions.
8. Connect the question of digital representation and encoding to technological choices, standards, and hence to cultural and linguistic issues.
9. As a result of what has been proposed so far, we must methodologically differentiate geopolitics from conferences in the field, allowing the possibility (as, for example, in THATCamps) of organizing basic events at different times of the year with no obligatory format, language, methodology, and so on, in order to maintain the organization's status as a federation.

These proposals can be grouped under the concept of "cultural exception," applied to the field of exposition, writing, and publication of scientific research. "Cultural exception" is an expression coined in the 1980s to describe that set of political and commercial strategies enacted by the European Union, particularly as a French initiative, to protect its own cultural industry from expansion by the US.[71] Although the cultural exception arose some years ago, it is conceptually an offshoot of UNESCO's Universal Declaration of Cultural Diversity, signed in Paris in November 2001. Article 1 says:

71 "The exceptionalists believe that the world market for culture is falsely competitive, when in fact it is dominated by multinational corporations and American cultural protectionism (with imports of cultural products less than 1% of global film production). They consider cinema as an art, as a cultural heritage and not as a simple entertainment industry" (Sergio Foà and Walter Santagata, "Eccezione culturale e diversità culturale. Il potere culturale delle organizzazioni centralizzate e decentralizzate," *Aedon: Rivista di arti e diritto online* 2 [2004]). For a general discussion about the US hegemony on the mass-culture world market see Frédéric Martel, *Mainstream. Enquête sur cette culture qui plaît à tout le monde* (Paris: Flammarion, 2010).

> Culture takes diverse forms across time and space. This diversity is embodied in the uniqueness and plurality of the identities of the groups and societies making up humankind. As a source of exchange, innovation and creativity, cultural diversity is as necessary for humankind as biodiversity is for nature. In this sense, it is the common heritage of humanity and should be recognized and affirmed for the benefit of present and future generations.[72]

On the other hand, Article 9 says that states have a duty to create the necessary conditions for the efficient circulation of "diversified cultural goods and services through cultural industries." In the opinion of some legal experts the cultural exception thus protects not only sectors that operate traditionally in the marketplace (cinema, TV, music), but also those areas of cultural heritage that are excluded by definition (rites, beliefs, folklore, etc.).[73] Finally, there is an explicit reference (Article 6) to the preservation of multilingualism. While the Declaration does not cover the products of science and invention, which fall within the legal jungle of patents and copyright, it could form a viable basis for fashioning a more culturally and linguistically inclusive form of digital humanities. In addition, on point (1) above, there is a case where institutional representation intersects with the linguistic hegemony. One of the key slogans of the American Revolution was "no taxation without representation." If it is impossible to avoid the Anglophone domain, then we can invert the slogan: "taxation against overrepresentation." There are two ways to fight a monopoly: you either withdraw from the monopoly, which in the case of the English language is impossible, or you make some concessions to its competitors. If all the languages and cultures should be on the same level, and we all agree that the extinction of diversity must be avoided, then a

72 UNESCO, "UNESCO Universal Declaration on Cultural Diversity," November 2, 2001, http://portal.unesco.org/en/ev.php-URL_ID = 13179&URL_DO = DO_TOPIC&URL_SECTION = 201.html.

73 Cf. Foà and Santagata, "Eccezione culturale e diversità culturale," 3.1.

moderate and symbolically variable "tribute" levied against the normative centers and organizations would be one of the few viable options.

Many practical solutions are possible without yielding to policies that restrict the freedom of anyone. Several years ago I put forward a proposal that could be easily implemented at conferences:

> What do you think is one of the most precious things in conferences? My answer is: time. As non-native speakers, we've all experienced the frustration of hearing talks given at the speed of light by native speakers, while our talk was delivering half of the ideas in twice as much time (or more). So how about if non-native speakers were given, upon their request, a fixed extra-time (i.e. 5 minutes?), at the expense of native speakers talking before or after them? I know that implementing such a rule would be not easy, and initially might also generate some chaos. Besides, many would consider it "unfair" towards native-speakers, not the mention the problem of dealing with borderline cases (how should bilinguals be treated?), etc. But all these obstacles should not prevent us to reflect seriously on the core problem: the linguistic advantage is a form of indirect discrimination leading to inequality of opportunities and eventually to cultural homogenization.[74]

The new ADHO tripartite structure, based on three layers of decreasing decision-making power, is the source of what in political science is commonly called "representational inequality." The behavior of similar organizations and consortia recalls what one of the greatest living jurists, Martti Koskenniemi, wrote when criticizing the practice of international law, "Universality still seems an essential part of progressive thought — but it also implies an imperial logic of identity: I will accept you,

74 Domenico Fiormonte, "Dreaming of Multiculturalism at DH2014," *Infolet*, July 7, 2014, http://infolet.it/2014/07/07/dreaming-of-multiculturalism-at-DH2014/.

but only on the condition that I may think of you as I think of myself."[75] Going back to the triad representation-language-code, most of DH resources and tools continue to be a territory firmly controlled by Anglophones: the ADHO web site, the Humanist distribution list, the more or less sponsored monographs (as the Companions[76]), and as we have seen most of the DH scholarly journals. That's not to mention the software, languages, and above mentioned "standards" (like the TEI XML), which in fact impose their specific conceptual forms (in the case of TEI XML the "ordered hierarchy of content object" or OHCO model) to the encoding of our cultural heritage, regardless of their original epistemological models.[77] Geoffrey Bowker and Susan Leigh Star have shown that the standards ("information structures") have a strongly symbolic, even more than their material, character; and control of standards is a central feature of economic life.[78] The classical example is time: the Greenwich meridian (1884) was the result of a political and economic battle between France and the United Kingdom: in the end the British won, managing to place the center of the world in their own local space-time.[79] But this is nothing compared to the "code hegemony" exercised on behalf of the US media empire. Amazon, Intel, Facebook, Netflix, Google, Microsoft, Apple, IBM, Adobe, and IQVIA form the Board of Directors of the Unicode Consortium, which deals with the coding of all the languages of the

75 M. Koskenniemi, *The Gentle Civilizer of Nations: The Rise and Fall of International Law 1870–1960* (Cambridge: Cambridge University Press, 2004), 515.

76 See http://www.digitalhumanities.org/companion and http://www.digitalhumanities.org/companionDLS.

77 "Ora, un file, in TEI XML o in qualunque formato, è tanto più interoperabile quanto più è standard è la sua codifica. I testi, però, e soprattutto quelli letterari e pre-moderni, sono quanto di meno standard si possa immaginare" (Paolo Monella, "Forme del testo digitale," in *Filologia Digitale. Problemi e Prospettive,* ed. Raul Mordenti [Rome: Bardi Edizioni, 2017], 145).

78 Geoffrey Y. Bowker and Susan Leigh Star, *Sorting Things Out: Classification and Its Consequences* (Cambridge: MIT Press, 1999).

79 Stephen Kern, *The Culture of Time and Space, 1880–1918: With a New Preface* (Cambridge: Harvard University Press, 2003), 13–16.

world. There is not even a representative who reflects "cultural" or non-commercial interests. If this is its basis, then it is hardly surprising that several criticisms have been made about the ethnocentrism of Unicode and the difficulty suffered by marginal or less commercial languages to be adequately represented and implemented on the Internet.[80]

The problem lies at the heart of the standardization of protocols and languages of digital communication. As George Steiner wrote in *After Babel*:

> The meta-linguistic codes and algorithms of electronic communication which are revolutionizing almost every facet of knowledge and production, of information and projection, are founded on a sub-text, on a linguistic 'pre-history', which is fundamentally Anglo-American (in the ways in which we may say that Catholicism and its history had a foundational Latinity). Computers and data-banks chatter in 'dialects' of an Anglo-American mother tongue.[81]

It is this "Anglo-American Esperanto" which permits a restructuring of the empire of digital knowledge to an extent and manner never experienced before in history. There is an imbalance in the forces involved and a desperate need to rebalance the system. Can we continue to ignore what is happening in the world and the connections we activate — or not — by our choices? From the Cambridge Analytica scandal to the overwhelming power of multinational publishers, from Monsanto to the GAFAM digital oligopoly, there is a red thread that links the problem of access to knowledge to political representation,

80 Domenico Fiormonte et al., "The Politics of Code: How Digital Representations and Languages Shape Cultures," paper presentation, ISIS Summit Vienna 2015 — The Information Society at the Crossroads, Vienna, June 3–7, 2015, http://sciforum.net/conference/isis-summit-vienna-2015/paper/2779; Perri, "Al di là della tecnologia, la scrittura"; Monella, "Scritture dimenticate."

81 George Steiner, *After Babel: Aspects of Language and Translation* (Oxford: Oxford University Press, 1998), xvii.

the defense of the native seed to the defense of the local word. What languages, what foods, what memories will survive in the future? And who will decide? The problem of biocultural diversity is thus intertwined with energy, food, health, technological interests, and so on, and the scientific community — especially the digital humanities — is called upon to take sides.

Bibliography

ADHO. "ADHO Governance Proposals." http://www.adho.org/administration/steering/adho-governance-proposals.

Amano, Tatsuya, Brody Sandel, Heidi Eager, Edouard Bulteau, Jens-Christian Svenning, Bo Dalsgaard, Carsten Rahbek, Richard G. Davies, and William J. Sutherland. "Global Distribution and Drivers of Language Extinction Risk." *Proceedings of the Royal Society B* 281, no. 1793 (October 22, 2014). DOI: 10.1098/rspb.2014.1574.

Bastian, Hilda "A Stronger Post-Publication Culture Is Needed for Better Science." *PLOS Medicine* (December 30, 2014). DOI: 10.1371/journal.pmed.1001772.

Bauman, Zygmunt, and David Lyon. *Liquid Surveillance: A Conversation.* Cambridge: Polity Press, 2013.

Bowker, Geoffrey Y., and Susan Leigh Star. *Sorting Things Out: Classification and Its Consequences.* Cambridge: MIT Press, 1999.

Canagarajah, A. Suresh. *A Geopolitics of Academic Writing.* Pittsburgh: University of Pittsburgh Press, 2002.

Chandrasekhar, C.P. "Open Access vs Academic Power." *Real-World Economics Review* 66 (January 13, 2014): 127–30. http://www.paecon.net/PAEReview/issue66/Chandrasekhar66.pdf.

Chun, Wendy Hui Kyong. *Control and Freedom: Power and Paranoia in the Age of Fiber Optics.* Cambridge: MIT Press, 2006.

Chun, Wendy Hui Kyong, and Lisa Marie Rhody. "Working the Digital Humanities: Uncovering Shadows between the Dark and the Light." *differences: A Journal of Feminist Cultural Studies* 25, no. 1 (2014): 1–25. DOI: 10.1215/10407391-2419985.

Clemente Vega, Paula "Open Access, the Global South and the Politics of Knowledge Production and Circulation: An Open Insights Interview with Leslie Chan." *Open Library of the Humanities,* December 10, 2018. https://www.openlibhums.org/news/314/.

Dacos, Marin. "La stratégie du sauna finlandais: Les frontières des Digital Humanities." *Digital Studies/Le champ numérique* (2016). DOI: 10.16995/dscn.41.
Eggers, Dave. *The Circle.* New York: Alfred A. Knopf, 2013.
Fiormonte, Domenico "Dreaming of Multiculturalism at DH2014." *Infolet,* July 7, 2014. http://infolet.it/2014/07/07/dreaming-of-multiculturalism-at-DH2014/.
———. "Il testo digitale: traduzione, codifica, modelli culturali." In *Italianisti in Spagna, ispanisti in Italia: la traduzione: Atti del Convegno Internazionale, Roma 30–31 ottobre 2007,* edited by Pina Rosa Piras, Arianna Alessandro, and Domenico Fiormonte, 271–84. Rome: Edizioni Q, 2008.
———."Lenguas, codigos, representación." In *Humanidades Digitales 1: Recepción, Institucionalización y Crítica,* edited by Isabel Galina Russell, Miriam Peña Pimentel, and Ernesto Priani Saiso, 39–81. Ciudad de México: Bonilla Artigas Editores, 2018.
———."Lingue, codici, rappresentanza. Margini delle Digital Humanities." In *Filologia digitale: problemi e prospettive,* 114–40. Rome: Bardi Edizioni, 2017.
———. "¿Para cuándo los BRICS del conocimiento?" *Dixit,* August 11, 2014. http://historiadelartemalaga.uma.es/dixit/para-cuando-los-brics-del-conocimiento/.
———. "Perché abbiamo bisogno dei BRICS della conoscenza," *Megachip,* January 25, 2015. https://2011oraequi.blogspot.com/2015/01/cultura-e-geopolitica.html.
———. "Quando os BRICS do conhecimento?" *HD.br,* August 29, 2014. http://hdbr.hypotheses.org/5179.
———. "Towards a Cultural Critique of Digital Humanities." *Historical Social Research/Historische Sozialforschung* 37, no. 3 (2012): 59–76. https://www.jstor.org/stable/41636597.
Fiormonte, Domenico, Desmond Schmidt, Paolo Monella, and Paolo Sordi. "The Politics of Code. How Digital Representations and Languages Shape Cultures." Paper presentation, ISIS Summit Vienna 2015 — The Information Society at the Crossroads, Vienna, June 3–7, 2015. http://

sciforum.net/conference/isis-summit-vienna-2015/paper/2779.
Fiormonte, Domenico, and Paolo Sordi. "Humanidades Digitales del Sur y GAFAM. Para una geopolítica del conocimiento digital." *Liinc em Revista* 15, no. 1 (2019): 108–30. http://revista.ibict.br/liinc/article/view/4730/4137.
Foà, Sergio, and Walter Santagata. "Eccezione culturale e diversità culturale. Il potere culturale delle organizzazioni centralizzate e decentralizzate." *Aedon: Rivista di arti e diritto online* 2 (2004). https://www.rivisteweb.it/doi/10.7390/15097. DOI: 10.7390/15097.
Frath, Pierre. "'Une grande université italienne passe au 100% anglais.' De la bêtise comme méthode de gouvernance." *Association des Professeurs de Langues Vivantes: Les Langues Modernes*, June 29, 2012. https://www.aplv-languesmodernes.org/spip.php?article4593.
———. "Anthropologie de l'anglicisation de l'université et de la recherche." *Philologica Jassyensia* 1, no. 19 (2014): 251–64. http://www.philologica-jassyensia.ro/upload/X_1_Frath.pdf.
Fuller, Matthew. *Software Studies: A Lexicon.* Cambridge: MIT Press, 2008.
Galina Russell, Isabel "Geographical and Linguistic Diversity in the Digital Humanities." *Literary and Linguistic Computing* 29, no. 3 (2014): 307–16. DOI: 10.1093/llc/fqu005.
Galloway, Alexander R. *Protocol: How Control Exists after Decentralization.* Cambridge: MIT Press, 2004.
Gazzola, Michele. "The Linguistic Implications of Academic Performance Indicators: General Trends and Case Study." *International Journal of the Sociology of Language* 216 (2012): 131–56. DOI: 10.1515/ijsl-2012-0043.
———. "Il falso mito dell'inglese: né democratico né redditizio." *Corriere della Sera, La Lettura,* November 30, 2014, 5. https://lettura.corriere.it/il-falso-mito-dellinglese-ne-democratico-ne-redditizio/comment-page-5/.
———. "Partecipazione, esclusione linguistica e traduzione: Una valutazione del regime linguistico dell'Unione europea." *Studi Italiani di Linguistica Teorica e Applicata*

43, no. 2 (2014): 227–264. http://www.michelegazzola.com/attachments/File/Papers/SILTA-PUB–2.pdf.

Gellman, Barton, and Ashkan Soltani, "NSA Infiltrates Links to Yahoo, Google Data Centers Worldwide, Snowden Documents Say." *The Washington Post,* October 30, 2013. https://www.washingtonpost.com/world/national-security/nsa-infiltrates-links-to-yahoo-google-data-centers-worldwide-snowden-documents-say/2013/10/30/e51d661e-4166-11e3-8b74-d89d714ca4dd_story.html.

Gobo, G. "Prove (inconsapevoli) di colonizzazione linguistica. Lo strano caso del Politecnico di Milano." 2014. https://era.ong/kadmo/prove-inconsapevoli-di-colonizzazione-linguistica-lo-strano-caso-del-politecnico-di-milano/.

Golumbia, David "Postcolonial Studies, Digital Humanities, and the Politics of Language." *uncomputing,* May 31, 2013. http://www.uncomputing.org/?p=241.

———. "Social Media as Political Control: The Facebook Study, Acxiom, & NSA." *uncomputing,* July 1, 2014. http://www.uncomputing.org/?p=1530.

Graham, Mark, Monica Stephens, Scott A. Hale, and Kunika Kono, eds. *Geographies of the World's Knowledge.* London: Convoco Foundation and Oxford Internet Institute, 2011. http://www.oii.ox.ac.uk/publications/convoco_geographies_en.pdf.

Grandjean, Martin. "Le rêve du multilinguisme dans la science: l'exemple (malheureux) du colloque #DH2014." *Martin Grandjean,* June 27, 2014. http://www.martingrandjean.ch/multilinguisme-dans-la-science-DH2014/.

Grafton, Anthony. *The Footnote: A Curious History.* London: Faber and Faber, 2000.

Grin, François. *L'enseignement des langues étrangères comme politique publique: Rapport au Haut Conseil de l'évaluation de l'école, No. 19.* Paris: Ministère de l'éducation nationale, 2005.

———. *Language Policy Evaluation and the European Charter for Regional or Minority Languages.* Basingstoke: Palgrave Macmillan, 2003.

Harrison, K.D. *When Languages Die: The Extinction of the World's Languages and the Erosion of Human Knowledge.* Oxford: Oxford University Press, 2007.

Inefuku, Harrison W. "Globalization, Open Access, and the Democratization of Knowledge." *EducauseReview,* July 3, 2017. http://er.educause.edu/articles/2017/7/globalization-open-access-and-the-democratization-of-knowledge.

Ivanov, Vjačeslav V., Jurij M. Lotman, Aleksandr M. Piatigorskij, Vladimir N. Toporov, and Boris A. Uspenskij. "Tesi per un'analisi semiotica della cultura." In *Tesi per una semiotica delle culture,* edited and translated by J.M. Lotman, 105–47. Rome: Meltemi, 2006.

Kaplan, Robert B. "Multilingualism vs. Monolingualism: The View from the USA and Its Interaction with Language Issues around the World." *Current Issues in Language Planning* 16, nos. 1–2 (2015): 149–62. DOI: 10.1080/14664208.2014.947016.

Kern, Stephen *The Culture of Time and Space, 1880–1918: With a New Preface.* Cambridge: Harvard University Press, 2003.

Kiefer, Ferenc "ERIH's Role in the Evaluation of Research Achievements in the Humanities." In *New Publication Cultures in the Humanities: Exploring the Paradigm Shift,* edited by P. Dávidházi, 173–82. Amsterdam: Amsterdam University Press, 2014.

Kiriya, Ilya. "Les études médiatiques dans les BRICS contre les bases de données occidentales: critique de la domination académique anglophone." *Hermès. La Revue* 79, no. 3 (2017): 71–77. https://www.cairn.info/revue-hermes-la-revue–2017–3-page–71.htm.

Kirschenbaum, Matthew G. *Mechanisms: New Media and the Forensic Imagination.* Cambridge: MIT Press, 2008.

Kittler, Friedrich. "Code (or, How You Can Write Something Differently)." In *Software Studies: A Lexicon,* edited by Matthew Fuller, 40–47. Cambridge: MIT Press, 2008.

Kontra, Miklós, Robert Phillipson, Tove Skutnabb-Kangas, and Tibor Várady, eds. *Language: A Right and a Resource: Approaching Linguistic Human Rights.* Budapest: Central European University Press, 1999.

Kornai, András. "Digital Language Death." *PLOS ONE* 8, no. 10 (2013): e77056. DOI: 10.1371/journal.pone.0077056.

Koskenniemi, M. *The Gentle Civilizer of Nations: The Rise and Fall of International Law 1870–1960*. Cambridge: Cambridge University Press, 2004.

Kulesz, Octavio. *La edición digital en los países en desarrollo.* Paris: Alianza Internacional de Editores Independientes — Prince Claus Fund for Culture and Development, 2011.

Larivière, Vincent, and Nadine Desrochers. "Langues et diffusion de la recherche: le cas des sciences humaines et sociales." *Découvrir. Le magazine de l'Acfas,* November 2015. http://www.acfas.ca/publications/decouvrir/2015/11/langues-diffusion-recherche-cas-sciences-humaines-sociales.

Limes: Rivista Italiana di Geopolitica 10: "La rete a stelle e strisce" (July 2018).

Kovács, Gergely. *Economic Aspects of Language Inequality in the European Union.* College for Modern Business Studies, Tatabánya, Hungary, 2007. http://www.ekolingvo.com/Eco_languages.pdf.

Maffi, Luisa, ed. *On Biocultural Diversity: Linking Language, Knowledge, and the Environment.* Washington, DC: Smithsonian Institution Press, 2001.

Maffi, Luisa, and Ellen Woodley, eds. *Biocultural Diversity Conservation: A Global Sourcebook.* Washington, DC and London: Earthscan, 2010.

Manovich, Lev. *Software Takes Command: Extending the Language of New Media.* London: Bloomsbury Publishing, 2013.

Maraschio, Nicoletta, and Domenico De Martino, eds. *Fuori l'italiano dall'università? Inglese, internazionalizzazione, politica linguistica.* Rome and Bari: Accademia della Crusca–Laterza, 2012.

Martel, Frédéric. *Mainstream. Enquête sur cette culture qui plaît à tout le monde.* Paris: Flammarion, 2010.

Mignolo, Walter *The Darker Side of Western Modernity.* Durham: Duke University Press Books, 2011.

———. *Local Histories/Global Designs: Coloniality, Subaltern Knowledges, and Border Thinking.* Princeton: Princeton University Press, 2012.

Monella, Paolo. "Scritture dimenticate, scritture colonizzate: sistemi grafici e codifiche digitali." Paper presentatino, Ricerca scientifica, monopoli della conoscenza e Digital Humanities. Prospettive critiche dall'Europa del Sud. Rome, Italy, 24–25 October 2018. Università Roma Tre. http://www1.unipa.it/paolo.monella/scritture2018/.

———. "Forme del testo digitale". In *Filologia Digitale. Problemi e Prospettive,* edited by Raul Mordenti, 143–61. Rome: Bardi Edizioni, 2017.

Ngũgĩ wa Thiong'o. *Decolonising the Mind: The Politics of Language in African Literature.* Harare: Zimbabwe Publishing House, 1994.

Noble, Safiya Umoja *Algorithms of Oppression: How Search Engines Reinforce Racism.* New York: New York University Press, 2018.

Ortega, Élika. "Local and International Scalability in DH." *Élika Ortega,* July 2, 2014. https://elikaortegadotnet.wordpress.com/2014/07/02/scalability/.

Perri, Antonio. "Al di là della tecnologia, la scrittura. Il caso Unicode." *Annali dell'Università degli Studi Suor Orsola Benincasa* II (2009): 725–48.

Phillipson, Robert *English-only Europe? Language Policy Challenges.* London: Routledge, 2003.

———. *Linguistic Imperialism.* Oxford: Oxford University Press, 1992.

———. *Linguistic Imperialism Continued.* New York and London: Routledge, 2009.

———. "Realities and Myths of Linguistic Imperialism." *Journal of Multilingual and Multicultural Development* 18, no. 3 (1997): 238–48. DOI: 10.1080/01434639708666317.

Pino-Díaz, José, and Domenico Fiormonte. "La geopolítica de las humanidades digitales: un caso de estudio de DH2017 Montreal." Poster presentation, DH2018. Puentes-Bridges, Mexico City, June 26–29, 2018. https://dh2018.adho.org/

la-geopolitica-de-las-humanidades-digitales-un-caso-de-estudio-de-dh2017-montreal/.

——— "Aportaciones al conocimiento de la colaboración internacional en Humanidades Digitales según Scopus. Un estudio de Science Mapping Analysis." Paper presentation, III Congreso Internacional: Humanidades Digitales. La Cultura de los Datos, Universidad de Rosario, Santa Fe, November 7–9, 2018. https://rephip.unr.edu.ar/handle/2133/13468.

Risam, Roopika "Rethinking Peer Review in the Age of Digital Humanities." *Ada: A Journal of Gender, New Media, and Technology* 4 (2014). https://adanewmedia.org/2014/04/issue4-risam/.

Rodotà, Stefano. *Il mondo nella rete. Quali i diritti, quali i vincoli.* Rome and Bari: Laterza, 2014.

Romero Frías, Esteban, and Salvador Del-Barrio-García. "Una visión de las Humanidades Digitales a través de sus centros." *El profesional de la Información* 23, no. 5 (September–October 2014): 485–92. http://www.elprofesionaldelainformacion.com/contenidos/2014/sept/05.html.

Santos, Boaventura de Sousa, ed. *Another Knowledge Is Possible: Beyond Northern Epistemologies.* London: Verso, 2008.

———. *Descolonizar el saber, reinventar el poder.* Montevideo: Extensión, Universidad de la República-Ediciones Trilce, 2010.

Santos, Boaventura de Sousa, Joiio Arriscado Nunes, and Maria Paula Meneses. "Introduction: Opening up the Canon of Knowledge and Recognition of Difference." In *Another Knowledge Is Possible: Beyond Northern Epistemologies,* edited by Boaventura de Sousa Santos, xix-xv. London: Verso, 2008.

Schneider, Edgar W. "Asian Englishes — Into the Future: A Bird's Eye View." *Asian Englishes* 16, no. 3 (2014): 249–56. DOI: 10.1080/21639159.2014.949439.

Smith, Linda Tuhiwai. *Decolonizing Methodologies: Research and Indigenous Peoples.* London: Zed Books, 2013.

Steiner, George. *After Babel: Aspects of Language and Translation.* Oxford: Oxford University Press, 1998.

Terralingua. "Linguistic Diversity." https://terralingua.org/our-work/linguistic-diversity/.

UNESCO. "UNESCO Universal Declaration on Cultural Diversity." November 2, 2001. http://portal.unesco.org/en/ev.php-URL_ID=13179&URL_DO=DO_TOPIC&URL_SECTION=201.html.

Van Parijs, Philippe. *Linguistic Justice for Europe and for the World.* Oxford: Oxford University, 2011.

Veugelers, Reinhilde. "The Challenge of China's Rise as a Science and Technology Powerhouse." *bruegel,* July 4, 2017. http://bruegel.org/reader/Chinas_rise_as_a_science_and_technology_powerhouse#.

Weingart, Scott B., and Nickoal Eichmann-Kalwara. "What's under the Big Tent? A Study of ADHO Conference Abstracts." *Digital Studies/Le Champ Numérique* 7, no. 1 (2017): art. 6. DOI: 10.16995/dscn.284.

Yoshiki, Mikami, and Shigeaki Kodama. "Measuring Linguistic Diversity on the Web." In *Net.Lang: Towards the Multilingual Cyberspace,* edited by Laurent Vannini and Hervé Le Crosnier, 121–39. Caen: C&F Éditions, 2012.

13

Pitching the "Big Tent" Outside: An Argument for the Digital Environmental Humanities

Alenda Y. Chang

While some digital humanists have been struggling to make good on the "big tent" promises of the 2011 Digital Humanities conference,[1] other scholars have theorized a similar umbrella term — the environmental humanities (EH) — to encompass long-established and, in some cases, long-marginalized subfields like environmental history, environmental philosophy, and literary ecocriticism. Although those subfields and others have engaged with environmental issues since at least the 1970s, the environmental humanities designation is relatively new, having gained traction only in the past decade. Like the digital humanities (DH), which enfolds work across a wide range of subjects united by the use or study of digital tools and methods, the environmental humanities connects otherwise disparate fields via

1 For instance, Matthew Gold raises the issue of inclusivity in the DH community in his introduction to *Debates in the Digital Humanities* (Minneapolis: University of Minnesota Press, 2012), and many of the volume's contributors address it, sometimes directly, sometimes obliquely, including Tara McPherson, George H. Williams, Patrick Svensson, and Matthew Kirschenbaum.

a common interest in human environmental impact. DH efforts to fuse traditional humanistic research with more computational approaches also mirror EH attempts to insert humanistic scholarship into ongoing discussions in the social and natural sciences. Other, looser parallels could be drawn, for instance between DH's troublesome relationship to consumer technology (epitomized by Google) and EH's equally vexed association with mainstream environmentalism, or between these movements' founding exigencies — while DH often gains its sense of rhetorical urgency from the contested "newness" of new media, EH is manifestly a response to growing scientific and public awareness of planetary ecological crisis.[2]

It is probably not mere coincidence that two such broad humanistic enterprises would emerge close upon each other's heels, in a period increasingly characterized by interdisciplinary mandates and the popular valorization of science and industry. However, there is clearly more at work here than a circling of disciplinary wagons. As Hannes Bergthaller and his colleagues have argued in the case of the environmental humanities, the recent gathering of nature-minded scholars represents both an opportunity to "map common ground" and a danger of reinforcing old orthodoxies — the same juncture that the digital humanities has already passed and yet seems fated to revisit as the field consolidates.[3] Broadly speaking, then, why might the nexus of digi-

---

2 For a good, general overview of the environmental humanities, touching on its history, core concepts, and key texts and authors, see UCLA's "What Is the Environmental Humanities?" webpage, produced during the course of a Mellon Foundation-funded Sawyer Seminar on the Environmental Humanities in 2014-2015, http://environmental.humanities.ucla.edu/?page_id=52.

3 Hannes Bergthaller, Rob Emmett, Adeline Johns-Putra, Agnes Kneitz, Susanna Lidström, Shane McCorristine, Isabel Pérez Ramos, Dana Phillips, Kate Rigby, and Libby Robin, "Mapping Common Ground: Ecocriticism, Environmental History, and the Environmental Humanities," *Environmental Humanities* 5 (2014): 261–76. On the one hand, they write, "The effort to reframe our work as part of the emerging environmental humanities thus presents an opportunity to address several problems of definition, delivery, and scope" (263). "However, the environmental humanities need to beware of the trap into which so many other academic

tal and environmental humanistic scholarship be particularly important to this volume's focus on alternative historiographies and modes of DH? In my view, the environmental humanities offers at least three potential correctives or enhancements to existing DH scholarship, which we might shorthand as inclusion, materiality, and deceleration. In plain terms, an EH perspective could show digital humanists how to broaden the scope and stakes of their work while mitigating some of the oversights characteristic of technical solutions, in particular false abstraction from the physical world and the valorization of speed — whether of innovation, development, or deployment — over deliberation.

Inclusion

"Our belief that science alone could deliver us from the planetary quagmire is long dead."
— Environmental historian Sverker Sörlin, "Environmental Humanities: Why Should Biologists Interested in the Environment Take the Humanities Seriously?"[4]

First, and perhaps least controversially, the environmental humanities furnishes the historically insular digital humanities with a model of more inclusive scholarship. Not only has much

enterprises with interdisciplinary aspirations have been lured: to avoid being marginalized as eccentric specialties or subfields within their home disciplines and the university at large, they have in turn marginalized the kinds of scholarship that fail to conform to established protocols, and thus they have betrayed the heterodox impulses and category-busting ambitions that gave rise to them in the first place" (ibid.). For an account of DH's own prolonged cycles of self-questioning, see Matthew Kirschenbaum's essay in *Debates in the Digital Humanities*, entitled "What Is Digital Humanities and What's It Doing in English Departments?," in which he claims that pieces addressing the question of the field's constitution have by now become "genre pieces."

4 Sverker Sörlin, "Environmental Humanities: Why Should Biologists Interested in the Environment Take the Humanities Seriously?" *BioScience* 62, no. 9 (September 2012): 788–89.

of the pioneering environmental-humanities work been done outside the US in Australia, Europe, and Canada, but academics associated with the environmental humanities regularly reach across the aisle or outside of the academy to scientists, social scientists, environmental-justice activists, and artists, all of whom provide valuable and necessary perspectives. For example, the journal *Environmental Humanities* (2012–) grew out of the Environmental Humanities Program at the University of New South Wales in Australia, and it was jointly managed by individuals and institutions in Canada, Sweden, the United States, and Australia before it joined Duke University Press. In Europe, the European Society for Environmental History has been particularly active since its founding in 1999, and the extraordinary Rachel Carson Center for Environment and Society was established in Munich in 2009. In Canada, the Network in Canadian History and Environment (Nouvelle initiative canadienne en histoire de l'environnement), or NiCHE, was established in 2004. Beyond these institutional precedents, the recent wellsprings of EH work surrounding anthropogenic climate change and the Anthropocene have featured not only humanists, but climate scientists, anthropologists and sociologists, political scientists, economists, communications experts, and human geographers, as evidenced by classes, centers, and year-long initiatives at universities like Stanford, the University of California, Santa Barbara (UCSB), UCLA, and the University of Texas at Austin. Indeed, at UCSB, I have been fortunate to be part of a multi-year Climate Futures series that regularly brought together academic and non-academic specialists in everything from community organizing and documentary filmmaking to food policy, marine environments, and speculative fiction.

Perhaps it is the sheer scale of the ecological challenges that face us, or the long tradition of environmental activism that informs such research, but in the environmental humanities, regional, disciplinary, and occupational inclusivity are seen as prerequisites to conversation and the development of responses to global environmental change. I would venture to assert that all environmental humanists recognize that collective action is required, as well as camaraderie in the face of species annihilation — witness concepts such as object-oriented feminism (as applied by Katherine Behar and others), Stacy Alaimo's trans-corporeality, and Timothy Morton's queer ecology.[5] For me, the environmental humanities give me a reassuring sense that I am not the only one troubled by the excesses of capitalist production, that I am not the only one keeping a watchful eye on the behavior of consumers, corporations, and governments, and that I am not the only one trying, in my own small way, to make things better. The alternatives are, frankly, less attractive: gibbering fear, blind optimism, or a paralyzing misanthropy. This was not always the case. The environmental humanities did not mystically achieve such a harmonious inclusivity from the outset, but rather learned from many years of disciplinary negotiation. In the introduction to the first issue of the journal *Environmental Humanities,* editors Deborah Rose, Thom van Dooren, Matthew Chrulew, Stuart Cooke, Matthew Kearnes, and Emily O'Gorman describe the environmental humanities as a response to more limited conceptions of environmental work in fields such as political science, history, and literature, and the historic tendency to dismiss humanistic work on the environment as either unscientific or mere science communication.[6] And as Law-

5 See Katherine Behar, ed., *Object-Oriented Feminism* (Minneapolis: University of Minnesota Press, 2016); Stacy Alaimo, *Bodily Natures: Science, Environment, and the Material Self* (Indianapolis: Indiana University Press, 2010), and Timothy Morton, "Guest Column: Queer Ecology," *PMLA* 125, no. 2 (2010): 273–82.

6 Deborah Rose, Thom van Dooren, Matthew Chrulew, Stuart Cooke, Matthew Kearnes, and Emily O'Gorman, "Thinking Through the Environment, Unsettling the Humanities," *Environmental Humanities* 1 (2012): 1–5. Notably, the editors abstain from offering a conclusive definition of EH, focusing on its catalyzing impact rather than its composition: "In many ways it is not yet clear what the environmental humanities are or will become. On one level, the environmental humanities might be understood as a useful umbrella, bringing together many sub-fields that have emerged over the past few decades and facilitating new conversations between them. On another, perhaps more ambitious level, the environmental humanities also challenges these disciplinary fields of inquiry, functioning as a provocation to a more

rence Buell describes in *The Future of Environmental Criticism*, the "first wave" of literary environmental criticism (one of the cornerstones of contemporary EH) was anything but inclusive in its devotion to canonical authors in the British Romantic, American Transcendentalist, and environmental nonfiction traditions, among them William Wordsworth, Ralph Waldo Emerson, Henry David Thoreau, John Muir, Aldo Leopold, Edward Abbey, and Wendell Berry.[7] Today, literary environmental criticism opens onto much broader discursive and geographic zones, including science fiction (and the closely related genres of speculative fiction and climate fiction, or "cli-fi"), postcolonial studies, activist journalism, and diverse African, Asian, and Latin American contexts.[8] Given these shifts, it is not surprising that many scholars in the environmental humanities take pains to distance themselves from the environmentalist stereotype, namely, the white, upper-middle-class tree-hugger who cares more about plants and animals than people.[9] "Second-wave" en-

---

interdisciplinary set of interventions directed toward some of the most pressing issues of our time" (5).

7 Buell's own work is not exempted, as his *The Environmental Imagination: Thoreau, Nature Writing, and the Formation of American Culture* (Cambridge: Harvard University Press, 1996) is often cited as a seminal work in literary environmental criticism. See also Lawrence Buell, *The Future of Environmental Criticism: Environmental Crisis and Literary Imagination* (Malden: Blackwell, 2005).

8 The scholarship on science-fiction ecologies is too copious to address here, but good starting points can be found in the work of authors like Eric Otto, Lindsay Thomas, and Gerry Canavan, for instance Gerry Canavan and Kim Stanley Robinson, eds., *Green Planets: Ecology and Science Fiction*, (Middletown: Wesleyan University Press, 2014). Examples of activist environmental journalists and more globally minded environmental scholars include Michael Pollan and Naomi Klein, historians Naomi Oreskes, Erik Conway, and Ramachandra Guha, and literature scholar Rob Nixon.

9 I have always found historian Richard White's essay on the cultural barriers between work and nature appreciation to be instructive in this regard. See Richard White, "'Are You an Environmentalist, or Do You Work for a Living?': Work and Nature," in *Uncommon Ground: Rethinking the Human Place in Nature*, ed. William Cronon (New York: Norton, 1996), 171–85.

vironmental criticism, as Buell confirms, has wisely expanded its concerns and stakeholders to urban communities, environmental justice or "EJ" activism, the global south, Indigenous peoples, nonhumans, and non-literary media forms. In many ways, this expansion recapitulates some of the major theoretical outcomes of environmental scholarship from the past three decades or more, from feminist scholars and environmental historians like Carolyn Merchant, Donna Haraway, William Cronon, and many others who have worked to explode easy definitions of "nature" and the natural. Having recognized that a narrow love for wilderness and pastoral fails to account for cities and posthuman bodies as environments in their own right, EH continues to stretch its mandate beyond privileged sites and persons. I am a regular participant at the biennial Association for the Study of Literature and Environment (ASLE) conferences, in part because the parent organization and conference planners make it a point to include authors, artists, and residents from the conference location's community, as well as opportunities to learn about the region, often well off the usual conference circuit. At the 2004 ASLE-UK symposium at University College Chichester in West Sussex, I went on a sponsored trip to Kingley Vale, known for its ruins and ancient yews; at the 2011 ASLE conference in Bloomington, Indiana, I tried birding at Lake Monroe (actually an engineered reservoir); at the 2015 conference in Moscow, Idaho, I went on a tour of native cultural landmarks led by members of the Nez Perce tribe; and at the 2017 conference in Detroit, I visited Belle Isle, the country's largest city island park, designed by Frederick Law Olmsted. Of course, many of these excursions are indistinguishable from classic forms of privileged nature communion — hiking, biking, or ecotourism adventures — but I have always appreciated the ways in which these trips encourage conference goers to interact with the local community, campus, and natural habitats in ways far more meaningful than your typical academic conference. The kinds of conscientious care offered to the interconnection of people, land, technology, and popular discourse by Indigenous and minority scholars promise much for both EH and DH.[10] Imagining what DH would look like if it took a similar course is, of course, the commendable project of this volume. What if, for instance, DH conferences regularly invited speakers and topics related to "digital justice," whether that meant closing digital divides, promoting forms of digital activism, or challenging draconian intellectual property laws and policies? What if DH conference organizers planned field trips to corporate datacenters, underfunded public libraries, or the cybersecurity offices of the Department of Homeland Security? What if, ultimately, the humanities were seen as an essential response to the rise of the digital, rather than as lagging behind or somehow co-opting the vitality of the digital, as it is so commonly assumed? While the "digital" still languishes in an apolitical quagmire, the word "environmental," for better or for worse, tends to strike a strident tone. By allowing the modifier "environmental," the environmental humanities implicitly sheds the disinterested stance often demanded by academic study, and that is, as they say, a good thing.

Materiality

> *"It's necessary to move beyond a simple analysis of the relationship between an individual human, their data, and any single technology company in order to contend with the truly planetary scale of extraction."*
> — Kate Crawford and Vladan Joler, "Anatomy of an AI System"[11]

The environmental humanities also have a second contribution to make to the digital humanities, namely, by returning

10 For example, Marisa Elena Duarte, *Network Sovereignty: Building the Internet Across Indian Country* (Seattle: University of Washington Press, 2017) and Carolyn Finney, *Black Faces, White Spaces: Reimagining the Relationship of African Americans to the Great Outdoors* (Chapel Hill: University of North Carolina Press, 2014).

11 Kate Crawford and Vladan Joler, *Anatomy of an AI System: The Amazon Echo as an Anatomical Map of Human Labor, Data and Planetary Resources*, 2018, https://anatomyof.ai/.

the material world to often immaterial theories and histories of technology. Whether or not they identify themselves as such, environmentally minded humanists do the important work of revealing the imbrication of environmental and computing history. I still remember my first reading of Fred Turner's extraordinary *From Counterculture to Cyberculture* for this very reason.[12] Turner's book opened my eyes to the countercultural origins of modern computing, just as Jack London's novel *Call of the Wild,* which thrusts a pampered sheepdog from California's Santa Clara Valley into Alaskan gold-rush territory, evoked Silicon Valley's recent agricultural past. Today, Bay Area technology corporations still regularly take their employees out-of-doors for inspiration, and the language we use to describe our online experiences inevitably draws from nature metaphors.[13] Turner's work, along with vibrant studies like Tung-Hui Hu's *A Prehistory of the Cloud,* continues in the vein of influential environmental classics by Leo Marx and Raymond Williams, who skillfully posed technology and nature and city and country not as polar opposites but generative partners in the construction of national and cultural rhetorics.[14]

In most academic circles, materialism is likely to trigger associations with Marxist thought or philosophical idealism (as its opposite). Materiality, however, is more directly about matter — in DH, this could be taken to mean hardware, rather than software, or print, rather than digital texts. Thus the 82 copies of Shakespeare's 1623 First Folio housed at the Folger Library in Washington, DC are material, while the scans and transcriptions of the First Folio available online through sites like the World

12 Fred Turner, *From Counterculture to Cyberculture: Stewart Brand, the Whole Earth Network, and the Rise of Digital Utopianism* (Chicago: University of Chicago Press, 2006).

13 Sue Thomas, "When Geeks Go Camping: Finding California in Cyberspace," *Convergence* 15, no. 1 (February 2009): 13–30.

14 Leo Marx, *The Machine in the Garden: Technology and the Pastoral Ideal in America* (1964; repr. Oxford: Oxford University Press, 2000); Raymond Williams, *The Country and the City* (New York: Oxford University Press, 1973).

Digital Library (a project of the Library of Congress) are not. Alternatively, the laptop hard disk on which this essay is currently saved is material, while the binary digits that encode my word processor's information are not, although software studies has complicated any idealized notion of the free-flowing stuff of digital convergence, Kittlerian or otherwise.[15] In addition, important work in forensic media, media archaeology, or platform studies by people like Matthew Kirschenbaum, Erkki Huhtamo, Ian Bogost and Nick Montfort, Mark Sample, and others has already labored to correct the anti-materialist trend in early digital studies, in essence recapitulating the textual and bibliographic study of books as worldly objects.

But in the environmental humanities, others have begun to push beyond media archaeology and software or platform studies to an even more radical kind of substrate studies, in what represents a radical leveling of the conventional ontological hierarchy between humans, animals, and nonhuman things. Take, for example, the philosophy of elemental media in John Durham Peters's *The Marvelous Clouds* or Melody Jue's oceanic reorientation of media theory in *Wild Blue Media.*[16] Interestingly, in some cases, the same scholars who helped to establish digital materiality studies ended up expanding their purview to the rest of the world, among them Ian Bogost, a founder of the Platform Studies series from MIT and co-author of *Racing the Beam,* who later turned toward object-oriented ontology and a philosophy of things. Jussi Parikka, who wrote a book on media archaeology, also penned a trilogy of media ecology works that concluded with *A Geology of Media.*[17] Parikka's *A Geology*

15 Two popular paradigms of media convergence can be found in Friedrich Kittler's *Gramophone, Film, Typewriter* (Stanford: Stanford University Press, 1999) and Henry Jenkins's *Convergence Culture: Where Old and New Media Collide* (New York: New York University Press, 2006).

16 John Durham Peters, *The Marvelous Clouds: Toward A Philosophy of Elemental Media* (Chicago: University of Chicago Press, 2015); Melody Jue, *Wild Blue Media: Thinking through Seawater* (Durham: Duke University Press, 2020).

17 Jussi Parikka, *What Is Media Archaeology?* (Cambridge: Polity, 2012). Parikka also co-edited with Erkki Huhtamo the collection *Media*

of Media and Nicole Starosielski's *The Undersea Network* remain some of my favorite works in this vein, respectively calling attention to the plethora of rare-earth metals and thousands of miles of underwater cabling that underlie our digital devices and networks.[18] Parikka asks what media history would look like if it extended to the earth's crust or even orbiting space detritus, while Starosielski considers the political and geographical complexities of wiring the Earth. Their work belongs to a growing body of scholarship that reveals the technology industry's ecologically irresponsible model of planned obsolescence and the growing problem of e-waste for what they are — reminders that the very visible, some say ubiquitous mobile and screen-based devices of late history have their genesis, as well as their afterlives, in the material world.[19] Writing in this framework explodes traditional media history and media industry studies, expanding well beyond individual human actors and companies, audiences and markets, to the depth and span of geological time and space — becoming well and truly "global." At the same time, the environmental humanities' interest in technology's embeddedness and indebtedness to the material world does not mean excluding its social and cultural contexts. Labor, too, is a crucial part of these stories, from Chinese factory workers today forced to inhale the aluminum dust created by polishing Apple products to the Navajo women once upheld as the ideal pliable workforce by early semiconductor manufacturer Fairchild.[20]

Archaeology: Approaches, Applications and Implications (Berkeley: University of California Press, 2011).

18 Jussi Parikka, *A Geology of Media* (Minneapolis: University of Minnesota Press, 2015); Nicole Starosielski, *The Undersea Network* (Durham: Duke University Press, 2015).

19 Early work in this vein can be found in Charles R. Acland's edited collection *Residual Media* (Minneapolis: University of Minnesota Press, 2006).

20 Jussi Parikka, "Dust and Exhaustion: The Labor of Media Materialism," *CTHEORY* (2013), https://journals.uvic.ca/index.php/ctheory/article/view/14790; Sheldon Lu and Zhen Zhang, "Mediated Environment Across Oceans and Countries," *Media+Environment* 1 (2019), https://mediaenviron.org/article/10136-mediated-environment-across-oceans-

If the digital humanities took environmental materiality more seriously, it would find ways to address the staggering energy and natural-resource demands of digital research and consumption, the colonialist disposal of electronic waste, and phenomena typically excluded as externalities to properly functioning computer systems — workers' bodies, glitches, errors, heat, network latency, and even catastrophic failure, as in the case of the 2006 Hengchun earthquake that paralyzed massive portions of communication networks in Asia.[21] While some might argue that media ecology is best left to media studies or new media theory, rather than the digital humanities, in my opinion the broad ecological perspective provides a salutary drag on digital prophesying.

Deceleration, or Playing the Fool

There may be one final advantage to juxtaposing EH and DH, which may at first seem like a shortcoming: environmental humanists like to take things slowly. This is not to say that they are dull, or laggardly, or lack serious motivation. On the contrary, they (or perhaps I should say we) are all too aware of the urgency of our contemporary moment, but at the same time cognizant that "fast" companies and "high-speed" everything may have put us where we are today. From Rob Nixon's discussion of "slow violence" to Isabelle Stengers's well-known call for "slow science," the environmental humanities consistently urges us to mind the details and to stall, even play dumb in the face of "progress."[22] Nixon worries that many forms of environmen-

and-countries; Lisa Nakamura, "Indigenous Circuits: Navajo Women and the Racialization of Early Electronic Manufacture," *American Quarterly* 66, no. 4 (December 2014): 919–41.

21 Peter Krapp, *Noise Channels: Glitch and Error in Digital Culture* (Minneapolis: University of Minnesota Press, 2011).

22 Rob Nixon, *Slow Violence and the Environmentalism of the Poor* (Cambridge: Harvard University Press, 2011); Isabelle Stengers, "The Cosmopolitical Proposal," in *Making Things Public*, edited by Bruno Latour and Peter Weibel (Cambridge: MIT Press, 2005), 994–1003.

tal damage do not conform to our understandings of violence either as spectacle or isolated and tangible acts of aggression. Alongside the very visible consequences of war and catastrophe, how do we understand the perniciousness of something like the gradual seepage of industrial chemicals into a community's drinking-water supply, or the unpredictable action of radiation in human and animal bodies and landscapes? Nixon's articulation of slow violence challenges us to devise ways to make these subtle wounds perceptible.

Stengers, meanwhile, has made her "cosmopolitical proposal" many times over, in an effort to awaken the slumbering giant of ostensibly disinterested science to the world of politics.[23] Less a prescription or comprehensive philosophy than a call to radically expand the universe of political actors and actions, cosmopolitics is Stengers's large-scale retelling of the story of science and an attempt to reconcile it to contemporary demands. A chemist-turned-philosopher, Stengers finds solace in Gilles Deleuze's refashioning of Dostoyevsky's fool, the "idiot" figure who, by failing to or being slow to comprehend, delays resolution. The idiot is "the one who always slows the others down, who resists the consensual way in which the situation is presented and in which emergencies mobilize thought or action."[24] For Stengers, this is a boon rather than an obstacle, as she urges her fellow scientists to unhitch their careers from "fast" benchmarked research and overly cozy relations with industry. Using

---

23 Stengers's cosmopolitics is not to be confused with Kantian cosmopolitanism. Notably, Stengers's philosophy has been taken up far outside of science studies, philosophy, and sociology, in an extraordinary range of fields ranging from Indigenous and postcolonial studies to animal studies, education, and urban planning. Robert Bononno has translated her writing in *Cosmopolitics I* (2010) and *Cosmopolitics II* (2011), both from University of Minnesota Press.

24 Stengers, "The Cosmopolitical Proposal," 994. While the language of idiocy is undeniably ableist, even when valorized, I suspect that cosmopolitics is fundamentally sympathetic to the project of critical disability studies in its desire to move past mere tolerance to genuine diversity of opinion, and in its acknowledgment of the social construction of scientific fact.

examples ranging from the adoption of genetically modified organisms to the ethics of animal testing, she argues that what we need is "something more similar to the slow knowledge of a gardener than to the fast one of the so-called rational industrial agriculture"[25] (slow science is, not surprisingly, related to other "slow" movements, among them the Italian slow food movement).

Although Stengers is particularly concerned with the role of scientists, her call might resonate with those who question DH's frequently utopian refrain of technological progress — put simply, that going digital necessarily means better research, better teaching, and better collaboration.[26] Her embrace of idiocy cautions us to remember who and what disappears in such enticingly celebratory accounts, from people without the equipment, skills, or access to participate, to the material resources extracted from the planet to build and sustain such enterprises. The idiot thus notably represents not only humans but nonhumans, and not just those who may not have a seat at the table, but also those who may not even be interested in such a seat, but are nevertheless impacted by the decisions made there. Even in the present atmosphere of crisis, in which the digital humanities purportedly holds the power to save the humanities from

---

25 Isabelle Stengers, "'Another Science Is Possible!' A Plea for Slow Science," inaugural lecture of the Willy Calewaert Chair, December 13, 2011, Université Libre de Bruxelles.

26 For example, see Anne Burdick et al., eds., *Digital_Humanities* (Cambridge: MIT Press, 2012), much of which was originally found in the form of an online "manifesto." Despite the authors' reassurances that DH "bears no privileged relationship to modern or contemporary cultural corpora" (16) and that DH does create new problems alongside its solutions, the authors still lapse into extolling the "generative humanities" and "the utopian prospect that the massive spread of shared knowledge across networks could give rise to a state of 'ubiquitous scholarship'" (30). They are also prone to dismissing obdurate inequities: "The digitization of the world's knowledge and its movement across global networks, *no matter how incomplete or incompletely free,* have transformed what we understand by and how we approach the humanities in the 21st century" (26, my emphasis).

technical irrelevancy,[27] we would do well to remember Stengers's warnings. Perhaps we should second guess ourselves, or re-evaluate the stakes and stakeholders, before hastening to train our young people for this new knowledge economy. Or as Ruha Benjamin writes in *Race after Technology*, rather than espouse Facebook's original slogan of "Move Fast and Break Things," let us "*Move slower and empower people.*"[28]

To be clear, I count myself as something of a digital enthusiast. I play and write about video games, and I have taught a plethora of digitally themed classes. My point is not that we must condemn all things DH or digital, or that the environmental humanities somehow occupies a moral high ground in relation to the digital humanities. I could, in fact, write another, complementary essay about what the digital humanities has to offer the environmental humanities. In that essay, I would mention that while the digital universe may seem annoyingly unperturbed by considerations of environmental impact or continuing digital divides, most dispatches from the worlds of environmental science and activism pillory technology and technology users as beyond redemption. A few of those voices leaven their criticism with praise for the educational potential of digital tools, but the norm is to paint love for nature and technology as a zero-sum scenario, in which one must by definition take away from the other. Think, they say, of all those teenagers with their noses buried in glowing screens… they can't even see the trees, let alone the forest!

Needless to say, having one foot in each of these camps — the environmental and the digital — has rarely been an easy po-

27 Take, for example, part of the mission statement of the 4humanities collective, found at http://4humanities.org/mission/: "They [the digital humanities] catch the eye of administrators and funding agencies who otherwise dismiss the humanities as yesterday's news." Or consider experiments in treating coding as a foreign language, as described in the provocatively titled post "The Humanities Need an Ally: Could It Be Computer Code?" by Sanjena Sathian, OZY, April 8, 2014, http://www.ozy.com/c-notes/can-the-digital-humanities-save-english/30301).

28 Ruha Benjamin, *Race after Technology: Abolitionist Tools for the New Jim Code* (Cambridge: Polity, 2019), 17.

sition to occupy. Yet it would be grossly shortsighted to see only the perils, and not the pleasures, of things digital. While research to date indicates that digital media do not, in and of themselves, create civic tendencies, they can and do reinforce those tendencies once formed elsewhere.[29] And if digital media are what increasingly absorb us, especially our youth, our messages may need to follow suit. It is not by coincidence that organizations like Greenpeace and PETA were among the first environmental organizations to develop games as part of their mobilization efforts. Finally, environmental humanists may soon find themselves studying objects and practices that are close kin to those studied in the digital humanities. Ask any ecologist working today where the biggest trends are in their field or subfield, and they are likely to say that the discipline has moved radically toward mathematical and statistical modeling via the computer — witness newer journals like *Environmental Modelling and Software* (1997–), *Ecological Informatics* (2006–), and *Remote Sensing* (2009–). Some ecological research no longer takes place in the field, but rather uses satellite measurements and advanced statistical algorithms like machine learning to crunch large quantities of remotely gathered data, which may be as important as the patient and methodical observation of natural habitats and species. This should sound remarkably similar to using topic modeling algorithms or data visualization software to process concordances, databases, or library corpora, and just as scholars who cling to romantic notions of literary work, lodged purely in the text itself, may feel threatened by the advance of digital approaches, ecologists committed to research outdoors may experience an existential crisis in this age of "big data" and "big science."

I have no doubt taken unpardonable liberties in generalizing about both the digital and environmental humanities commu-

29 See, for example, two reports from the Pew Research Center's Internet & American Life Project: Amanda Lenhart et al., "Teens, Video Games, and Civics," September 16, 2008; and Aaron Smith et al., "The Internet and Civic Engagement," Septemnber 1, 2009.

nities, in the hopes of effecting their intersection. In my defense, my head has been heavy of late with such strange conjunctions: environmental remediation, elemental media, and procedurally generated galaxies among them.[30] My shelves and tabletops groan under a sometimes dizzying mix of volumes from these disparate worlds — books by Jentery Sayers, Cara New Daggett, and Nicole Seymour brush bindings with textbooks like *Phyto: Principles and Resources for Site Remediation and Landscape Design* and, my current favorite, *Mycelium Running: How Mushrooms Can Help Save the World.*[31] Rather than see this as a sign of disorder, or blatant grafting, let us playfully uncover the mycelial (or that more familiar term, rhizomatic) ground common to a newfangled digital environmental humanities.[32] As cumbersome as that moniker might seem, my hope is that this essay makes clear that the environmental humanities could provide a much-needed centrifugal counter to the centripetal tendencies of the digital humanities, even as the digital demands more and more attention from environmental humanists looking to reach broader audiences and promote greater environmental awareness. To return to Stengers, the goal is not to decide, once and for all, in favor of old or new, or less mediated or more mediated experiences of texts and environments. Rather, this is the time

30 Alenda Y. Chang, "Environmental Remediation," *electronic book review*, June 7, 2015, https://electronicbookreview.com/essay/environmental-remediation/. See also the new Elements book series from Duke University Press, and the galaxy-exploration game *No Man's Sky* (Hello Games).

31 Jentery Sayers, ed., *Making Things and Drawing Boundaries: Experiments in the Digital Humanities* (Minneapolis: University of Minnesota Press, 2017); Cara New Daggett, *The Birth of Energy: Fossil Fuels, Thermodynamics, and the Politics of Work* (Durham: Duke University Press, 2019); Kate Kennen and Niall Kirkwood, *Phyto: Principles and Resources for Site Remediation and Landscape Design* (New York: Routledge, 2015); and Paul Stamets, *Mycelium Running: How Mushrooms Can Help Save the World* (Berkeley: Ten Speed Press, 2005).

32 Jon Christensen at UCLA and the editors of the Rachel Carson Center's *Ant Spider Bee* blog are also invested in establishing the "digital environmental humanities." I have written two short pieces for the latter, entitled "Slow Violence: A Proposal for Ecological Game Studies" and "Growing Games."

to carefully consider our options, and to have open conversations about our future together.

Bibliography

Acland, Charles R., ed. *Residual Media*. Minneapolis: University of Minnesota Press, 2006.

Alaimo, Stacy. *Bodily Natures: Science, Environment, and the Material Self*. Bloomington: Indiana University Press, 2010.

Behar, Katherine, ed. *Object-Oriented Feminism*. Minneapolis: University of Minnesota Press, 2016.

Benjamin, Ruha. *Race after Technology: Abolitionist Tools for the New Jim Code*. Cambridge: Polity, 2019.

Bergthaller, Hannes, Rob Emmett, Adeline Johns-Putra, Agnes Kneitz, Susanna Lidström, Shane McCorristine, Isabel Pérez Ramos, Dana Phillips, Kate Rigby, and Libby Robin. "Mapping Common Ground: Ecocriticism, Environmental History, and the Environmental Humanities." *Environmental Humanities* 5 (2014): 261–76. DOI: 10.1215/22011919-3615505.

Buell, Lawrence. *The Future of Environmental Criticism: Environmental Crisis and Literary Imagination*. Malden: Blackwell, 2005.

Burdick, Anne, Johanna Drucker, Peter Lunenfeld, Todd Presner, and Jeffrey Schnapp, eds. *Digital_Humanities*. Cambridge: MIT Press, 2012.

Canavan, Gerry, and Kim Stanley Robinson. *Green Planets: Ecology and Science Fiction*. Middletown: Wesleyan University Press, 2014.

Chang, Alenda Y. "Environmental Remediation." *electronic book review*. June 7, 2015. https://electronicbookreview.com/essay/environmental-remediation/.

———. "Growing Games." *Ant Spider Bee*, July 2, 2015. http://www.antspiderbee.net/2015/07/02/growing-games/.

———. "'Slow Violence': A Proposal for Ecological Game Studies." *Ant Spider Bee*, January 27, 2013. http://www.antspiderbee.net/2013/01/27/slow-violence-a-proposal-for-ecological-game-studies/.

Crawford, Kate, and Vladan Joler. *Anatomy of an AI System: The Amazon Echo as an Anatomical Map of Human Labor, Data and Planetary Resources.* 2018. https://anatomyof.ai/.
Daggett, Cara New. *The Birth of Energy: Fossil Fuels, Thermodynamics, and the Politics of Work.* Durham: Duke University Press, 2019.
Duarte, Marisa Elena. *Network Sovereignty: Building the Internet across Indian Country.* Seattle: University of Washington Press, 2017.
Finney, Carolyn. *Black Faces, White Spaces: Reimagining the Relationship of African Americans to the Great Outdoors.* Chapel Hill: University of North Carolina Press, 2014.
Gold, Matthew K., ed. *Debates in the Digital Humanities.* Minneapolis: University of Minnesota Press, 2012. https://dhdebates.gc.cuny.edu/projects/debates-in-the-digital-humanities.
Huhtamo, Erkki, and Jussi Parikka, eds. *Media Archaeology: Approaches, Applications, and Implications.* Berkeley: University of California Press, 2011.
Jenkins, Henry. *Convergence Culture: Where Old and New Media Collide.* New York: New York University Press, 2006.
Jue, Melody. *Wild Blue Media: Thinking through Seawater.* Durham: Duke University Press, 2020.
Kennen, Kate and Niall Kirkwood. *Phyto: Principles and Resources for Site Remediation and Landscape Design.* New York: Routledge, 2015.
Kittler, Friedrich. *Gramophone, Film, Typewriter.* Stanford: Stanford University Press, 1999.
Krapp, Peter. *Noise Channels: Glitch and Error in Digital Culture.* Minneapolis: University of Minnesota Press, 2011.
Lenhart, Amanda, Joseph Kahne, Ellen Middaugh, Alexandra Macgill, Chris Evans, and Jessica Vitak. "Teens, Video Games, and Civics." *Pew Research Center's Internet & American Life Project.* September 16, 2008. https://files.eric.ed.gov/fulltext/ED525058.pdf.
Lu, Sheldon, and Zhen Zhang, "Mediated Environment Across Oceans and Countries." *Media+Environment* 1 (2019). DOI:

10.1525/001c.10136. https://mediaenviron.org/article/10136-mediated-environment-across-oceans-and-countries.

Marx, Leo. *The Machine in the Garden: Technology and the Pastoral Ideal in America.* 1964; repr. Oxford: Oxford University Press, 2000.

Morton, Timothy. "Guest Column: Queer Ecology." *PMLA* 125, no. 2 (2010): 273–82. https://www.jstor.org/stable/25704424.

Nakamura, Lisa. "Indigenous Circuits: Navajo Women and the Racialization of Early Electronic Manufacture." *American Quarterly* 66, no. 4 (December 2014): 919–41. https://www.jstor.org/stable/43823177.

Nixon, Rob. *Slow Violence and the Environmentalism of the Poor.* Cambridge: Harvard University Press, 2011.

Parikka, Jussi. *A Geology of Media.* Minneapolis: University of Minnesota Press, 2015.

———. "Dust and Exhaustion: The Labor of Media Materialism." *CTHEORY* (2013). https://journals.uvic.ca/index.php/ctheory/article/view/14790.

———. *What Is Media Archaeology?* Cambridge: Polity, 2012.

Peters, John Durham. *The Marvelous Clouds: Toward A Philosophy of Elemental Media.* Chicago: University of Chicago Press, 2015.

Rose, Deborah, Thom van Dooren, Matthew Chrulew, Stuart Cooke, Matthew Kearnes, and Emily O'Gorman. "Thinking Through the Environment, Unsettling the Humanities." *Environmental Humanities* 1 (2012): 1–5. DOI: 10.1215/22011919-3609940.

Sathian, Sanjena. "The Humanities Need an Ally: Could It Be Computer Code?" *OZY*, April 8, 2014. http://www.ozy.com/c-notes/can-the-digital-humanities-save-english/30301.

Sayers, Jentery, ed. *Making Things and Drawing Boundaries: Experiments in the Digital Humanities.* Minneapolis: University of Minnesota Press, 2017.

Seymour, Nicole. *Bad Environmentalism: Irony and Irreverence in the Ecological Age.* Minneapolis: University of Minnesota Press, 2018.

Smith, Aaron, Kay Lehman Schlozman, Sidney Verba, and Henry Brady. "The Internet and Civic Engagement." *Pew Research Center's Internet & American Life Project.* September 1, 2009. https://www.pewresearch.org/internet/2009/09/01/the-internet-and-civic-engagement/.

Sörlin, Sverker. "Environmental Humanities: Why Should Biologists Interested in the Environment Take the Humanities Seriously?" *BioScience* 62, no. 9 (September 2012): 788–89. DOI: 10.1525/bio.2012.62.9.2.

Stamets, Paul. *Mycelium Running: How Mushrooms Can Help Save the World.* Berkeley: Ten Speed Press, 2005.

Starosielski, Nicole. *The Undersea Network.* Durham: Duke University Press, 2015.

Stengers, Isabelle. "'Another Science Is Possible!' A Plea for Slow Science." Inaugural lecture of the Willy Calewaert Chair. December 13, 2011. Université Libre de Bruxelles.

———. *Cosmopolitics I.* Translated by Robert Bononno. Minneapolis: University of Minnesota Press, 2010.

———. *Cosmopolitics II.* Translated by Robert Bononno. Minneapolis: University of Minnesota Press, 2011.

———. "The Cosmopolitical Proposal." In *Making Things Public,* edited by Bruno Latour and Peter Weibel, 994–1003. Cambridge: MIT Press, 2005.

Thomas, Sue. "When Geeks Go Camping: Finding California in Cyberspace." *Convergence* 15, no. 1 (February 2009): 13–30. DOI: 10.1177/1354856508097016.

Turner, Fred. *From Counterculture to Cyberculture: Stewart Brand, the Whole Earth Network, and the Rise of Digital Utopianism.* Chicago: University of Chicago Press, 2006.

White, Richard. "'Are You an Environmentalist, or Do You Work for a Living?': Work and Nature." In *Uncommon Ground: Rethinking the Human Place in Nature,* edited by William Cronon, 171–85. New York: Norton, 1996.

Williams, Raymond. *The Country and the City.* New York: Oxford University Press, 1973.

Indigenous Futures

14

An Indigenist Internet for Indigenous Futures: DH Beyond the Academy and "Preservation"

Siobhan Senier

Origin stories are charged for Indigenous people, who have narratives of their own: traditional emergence stories explaining how they came to be on their land, as well as dynamic accounts of their survival and resurgence. Indigenous origin stories counter colonialism's own creation myths, which try to install settlers as the true "first peoples," rendering aboriginal people as vanishing remnants.

Digital humanities' own emergence narratives have likewise tended to elide the original contributions of Indigenous people. In the academy at least, digital projects involving Indigenous content have tended to be dominated by one concern: archives and their "virtual repatriation." In virtual repatriation, activist scholars help create electronic surrogates of cultural heritage materials (historic photographs, primary documents, even material objects) held in major collecting institutions, making them newly available to their communities of origin. The best such projects engage Indigenous people on equal terms: they consult with elders and tribal historians; they bring tribal members into physical archives and effectively indigenize these collections' metadata and interpretation. In North America and Australia, some of the most visible digital repatriation projects include "Through Indigenous Eyes," a partnership among Ojibwe, Cherokee, Passamaquoddy and Penobscot knowledge keepers and the American Philosophical Society; the Reciprocal Research Network, brokered by the University of British Columbia and regional tribal councils; and AUSTLANG, an Aboriginal and Torres Strait Islanders language database.[1] These projects go far beyond offering new access to old archives: they are what the Cherokee sociologist Eva Garroutte might call Indigen*ist,* insofar as they move "beyond an aspiration to 'preserve' cultures" and seek to bring "more personnel, more resources, more perspectives to the collective project of maintaining and restoring the intellectual and spiritual heritage of tribal peoples."[2]

Meanwhile, tribal communities have also been pursuing their own electronic and new media projects, more or less independent of academic DH. These include, probably most dramatically, hashtag activism like the #IdleNoMore, #MMIW (Missing

1 "APS Collections through Indigenous Eyes," *American Philosophical Society,* 2013, http://www.amphilsoc.org/library/exhibit/indigeyes; Reciprocal Research Network, November 22, 2014, https://www.rrncommunity.org/; *AUSTLANG: Australian Indigenous Languages Database,* http://austlang.aiatsis.gov.au/main.php. For more on virtual repatriation and the politics of digital archives, see Robin Boast and Jim Enote, "Virtual Repatriation: It Is Neither Virtual nor Repatriation," in *Heritage in the Context of Globalization,* eds. Peter Biehl and Christopher Prescott, Vol. 8, SpringerBriefs in Archaeology (New York: Springer New York, 2013), 103–13; Kimberly Christen, "Opening Archives: Respectful Repatriation," *American Archivist* 74 (Spring/Summer 2011): 185–210; Paul Grant-Costa, Tobias Glaza, and Michael Sletcher, "The Common Pot: Editing Native American Materials," *Scholarly Editing* 33 (2012), http://www.scholarlyediting.org/2012/essays/essay.commonpot.html; Timothy Powell and Larry Aitken, "Encoding Culture: Building a Digital Archive Based on Traditional Ojibwe Teachings," in *The American Literature Scholar in the Digital Age,* eds. Amy Earhart and Andrew Jewell (Ann Arbor: University of Michigan Press, 2010), 250–74; and Susan Rowley, "The Reciprocal Research Network: The Development Process," *Museum Anthropology Review* 7, nos. 1–2 (2013): 22–43.

2 Eva Garroutte, *Real Indians: Identity and the Survival of Native America* (Berkeley: University of California Press, 2003), 149.

and Murdered Indigenous Women), and #NoDAPL (No Dakota Access Pipeline) campaigns, which have convened large groups of Native people, on and off their reservations, for political protest.[3] They include digital art projects like *Robohontas*, in which Fox Spears (Karuk) photoshopped a metallic feminized figurine in a series of "exotic" poses; and the magnificent curatorial work of Paul Seesequasis (Cree), who floods Twitter with deliberately upbeat old photographs of Indigenous people, and elicits richly detailed information about those photographs from his Indigenous followers.[4] A survey of extra-academic Native DH might also include the many tribal websites used to convey information to Native community members and sometimes to the larger public; and curated hyperlinked sites like NativeWeb (nativeweb.org), which gathers a wide range of electronic resources related to history, language and culture. It would include the panoply of YouTube channel hosts from sketch comedy troupe The 1491s to vlogger Crystal Starr Szczepanski (Athapaskan/Yupik/Colville), who offers beauty tips as well as Chinuk Wawa language lessons; it would look at the creativity, play and resistance of NDN TikTok, where you can see Two-Spirit Passamaquoddy artist Geo Soctomah Neptune (@passamahottie) voguing while skinning a hide.[5] It would include the proliferation of Soundcloud channels by bands like the Ottawa-based DJ crew A Tribe Called Red, and news programs like Native America Calling. An Indigenous-centric genealogy of DH would survey video games like the Iñupiats' much-hailed *Never Alone* and Elizabeth LaPensée's (Anishinaabe/Métis) *Thunderbird Strike*.[6]

3 For more on these campaigns, see Karyn Recollet, "Glyphing Decolonial Love through Urban Flash Mobbing and Walking with Our Sisters," *Curriculum Inquiry* 45, no. 1 (January 1, 2015): 129–45.

4 Fox Spears, *Robohontas*, http://www.robohontas.com/. Seesequasis's Twitter handle is @PaulSeesequasis, and his photographs led to a book, *Blanket Toss Under the Midnight Sun* (Toronto: Knopf Canada, 2019).

5 Jessie Loyer, "Indigenous TikTok Is Transforming Cultural Knowledge," *Canadian Art*, April 23, 2020, https://canadianart.ca/essays/indigenous-tiktok-is-transforming-cultural-knowledge/.

6 David Gaertner has aggregated some excellent readings and resources about *Never Alone* at *Never Alone: Resources and Reflections*, https://

Turning our attention to such cultural production and situating it in its tribal contexts would complement the current digital humanities focus on archives and tribal-academic collaboration; it would highlight emphatically *contemporary* scenes of self-representation and sovereignty. Indeed, as an evolving discipline whose struggles around inclusion and diversity seem only to intensify with each passing year, DH would do well to attend to the great diversity of Indigenous digital projects, and to the ways that such projects have managed to sustain or reinvent themselves without major institutional investments or recognition. Amy Earhart is one scholar who has acknowledged that, in the short history of the discipline, early sites, which might "now seem simplistic and out of date," are nevertheless "pivotal to the formation of digital literary culture."[7] Similarly, we might say that rudimentary, early websites like NativeWeb were critical because they drew on the power of community and helped build it further, such that — even if the particular digital iteration or medium disappears — the community itself endures. I say this not to romanticize or make static the notion of Indigenous "community," which is as contested and fraught as any other. I mean only to underscore what James Clifford has called the "Indigenous longue durée" — an understanding that the violence of settler colonialism has, in the end, offered only temporary disruptions to Indigenous people's longstanding presence and their ability to adapt cultural practices.[8]

In what follows, I discuss a small selection of Indigenist Internet projects conducted outside — or better put, *alongside* — the academic and nonprofit industrial complexes. The re-

---

ilsaneveralone.wordpress.com/. For a discussion of some energy industry reactions to LaPensée's game, see Jacob Dubé, "Oil Lobbyists: Thunderbird Strike Video Game 'Promotes Ecoterrorism,'" *Vice*, October 27, 2017, https://www.vice.com/en_us/article/xwawq3/oil-lobbyists-thunderbird-strike-videogame-promotes-ecoterrorism.

7 Amy E. Earhart, *Traces of the Old, Uses of the New: The Emergence of Digital Literary Studies* (Ann Arbor: University of Michigan Press, 2015).

8 James Clifford, "Varieties of Indigenous Experience: Diasporas, Homelands, Sovereignties," in *Indigenous Experience Today*, eds. Marisol de la Cadena and Orin Stran (London: Berg Publishers, 2008), 199.

lationship between the academy and Indigenous communities is indisputably shifting, not least because more and more Indigenous scholars are entering the academy and working on digital projects, and because Indigenous communities are increasingly attuned to (often concerned with) what academics are writing about them. Still, inasmuch as the various boundaries (between academic and non-academic, Native and non-Native, "DH" and New Media) may be dissolving, there is one line that seems alive and well, and that is the split between the haves and the have-nots: large and well-funded non-Native museums and archives, on the one hand, versus small and precarious tribal or artists' enterprises on the other. In looking at just a small selection of bootstrap web-based projects, this chapter considers the possibilities and limits of so-called big tent DH. Arguably, Indigenous digital projects have been effective precisely because they have tended to operate outside of academic DH, with its particular reward systems demanding particular kinds of communication, particular kinds of technological "innovation." Given that institutionalized DH has tended to emphasize themes of "access," "preservation," and "big data," DH practitioners might honestly ask ourselves about the colonial outlines of our field. Historically, those impulses have been part and parcel of an effort to relegate Indigenous people to the past, to "mine" them for useful information and resources. The projects I describe below are far less invested in such impulses than in community-building, self-representation, and Indigenous futures.

I. Multimedia Literature: As/Us Journal

DH scholars working on virtual repatriation are wisely concerned about the politics of archives and about protecting Indigenous intellectual property; the best of them seek, in Elizabeth Povinelli's characterization, to make their content "concealed and exposed, expanded and contracted according to the dialogical conditions of a social network."[9] Still, many of the more grassroots Indigenous projects express much greater optimism about digital media's representational possibilities, and the ability to share Native voice. Perhaps this is because such projects are not in fact much concerned with ethnographic fetishes, but rather with Indigenous *futures*. Métis activist Molly Swain puts it plainly: "People don't expect Indigenous people to be interested in the future. That's partially because nobody expects Indigenous people to have a future, which is what colonialism is."[10]

Indigenous artists and activists see some hope, therefore, that new media might offer new possibilities for Indigenous resurgence. When Mohawk artist Skawennati helped launch the online gallery/chatroom *Cyberpowwow* — an "aboriginally determined territory in cyberspace" — she expressed a sentiment still quite common among Indigenous people using the web:

> When we finally realized that photography was a medium that we too could use to represent our ideas, our culture, and our selves, the medium, and our relationship to it, had already been defined. The same can be said about film and, for that matter, print. We were the subjects, and not the photographers, filmmakers or authors [...]. [But] [t]he World Wide Web, the latest story-telling medium to arrive on the scene, is as enticing to us Indians as it is to everyone with (and even some without) a modem. The number of web pages by and about First Nations, Aboriginals, Native Americans, Indigenous peoples, and Indians is staggering, and very satisfying. There are pages for band councils and tribal councils, Native languages and Native organizations. For the first time, Native people are in on the ground floor of a new technology, and

9 Elizabeth A. Povinelli, "The Woman on the Other Side of the Wall: Archiving the Otherwise in Postcolonial Digital Archives," *differences: A Journal of Feminist Cultural Studies* 22, no. 1 (January 1, 2011): 161.

10 Nadya Domingo, "The Trope Slayers," *This Magazine*, March 20, 2015, http://this.org/magazine/2015/03/20/the-trope-slayers/.

are helping to define the way it will be used to describe our cultures.[11]

The optimism is not only that an uncharted, virtual territory might be a space where Indigenous people can speak and be heard; it's that virtual space can reconnect Indigenous people to their lands and each other. *Cyberpowwow* had virtual galleries and a chat room with avatars; but it also organized live gatherings, which put "the powwow in Cyberpowwow," by letting people "get together in the REAL world to talk, laugh, surf and meet live human beings."

In recent years, Indigenous writers have followed *Cyberpowwow*'s lead in harnessing the affordances of multimedia to build community while also promoting the spoken and written word. In some cases, like many literary magazines, existing print publications have moved online. This was the case with *RED INK: International Journal of Indigenous Literature, Art & Humanities,* published out of the University of Arizona since 1982.[12]

11 Skawennati Fragnito, "CPW: FAQ," *Cyberpowwow,* April 6, 1997, http://www.cyberpowwow.net/nation2nation/triciawork1.html. For more on the history of Cyberpowwow and its new iteration, AbTeC (Aboriginal Territories in Cyberspace), see Skawennati Fragnito and Jason Lewis, "Aboriginal Territories in Cyberspace," *Cultural Survival,* Summer 2005, http://www.culturalsurvival.org/publications/cultural-survival-quarterly/canada/aboriginal-territories-cyberspace and David Gaertner, "Indigenous in Cyberspace: CyberPowWow, God's Lake Narrows and the Challenges of Creating Indigenous Territory in Cyberspace," *American Indian Culture and Research Journal* 39, no. 4 (2015): 55–78.

12 Historically, Indigenous-published and Indigenous-edited literary magazines have been relatively few and far between; many fold after a period of time — even *Red Ink* seems to go in and out of production. Some of the longest-running publications, like *Yellow Medicine Review* and *Raven Chronicles,* have not transitioned to an online format. Despite the apparent ease and affordability of electronic publishing, the move to the Internet has not appreciably increased the number of Indigenous magazines, though it has perhaps offered Indigenous writers other, multicultural and mainstream venues to publish their work. See Meghan Bacino, "RED INK Journal: Preserving, Promoting an Indigenous Voice," *Accents on English: Newsletter of the Department of English at Arizona State University* 19, no. 1 (Fall 2015–Winter 2016), https://english.asu.edu/news-

Other, born-digital publications have emerged as well, taking advantage of free online publishing technologies. *Four Winds Literary Magazine,* which has published some prestigious writers including Anita Endrezze (Yaqui), Tiffany Midge (Standing Rock Sioux) and Suzanne Rancourt (Abenaki), has two issues to date, formatted in pdf and posted to WordPress.[13]

As/Us: A Literary Space for Women of the World likewise began online. Poet Tanaya Winder (Southern Ute/Duckwater Shoshone/Pyramid Lake Paiute) and fiction writer Casandra Lopez (Cahuilla//Tongva/Luiseño), who met while doing their MFAs at the University of New Mexico, envisioned a journal that could respond to the lack of diversity in mainstream publishing by embracing established and emergent writers, creative and scholarly works, and a wide variety of genres from fiction and poetry to visual art and spoken word. Launched online in February 2013, *As/Us* followed just two months later with a print version. Winder and Lopez have been profoundly interested in physical gatherings, hosting author regular author, artist, and activist events. They also distributed print issues of the journal to Native schools and communities through the "Reach the Rez" campaign: "By promoting art and literature, the campaign aligns with progressive empowerment within the *future* [emphasis added] of our nations."

As/Us has six issues to date and a seventh under construction, with a roster of heavy hitters from Indigenous literary circles. The first issue included an interview with none other than Joy Harjo (Muscogee), now the US Poet Laureate; work by up-and-coming Native writers like poet Marianne Broyles (Cherokee) and novelist Erika Wurth (Apache/Chickasaw/Cherokee); and the work of emergent artists with strong community ties. There was, for instance, a powerful video recording by poet/filmmaker/activist Lyla June Johnston (Diné):

---

events/newsletter/accents-english-fall-2015-winter-2016/red-ink-journal-preserving-promoting-indigenous-voice.

13 Jordan Clapper and Misty Shipman Ellingburg, eds., *Four Winds Literary Magazine,* https://fourwindslitmag.wordpress.com/.

Hozho is the prayer that carried us
through genocide and disease,
It is the prayer that will carry us through global warming
and through this global fear that has set our hearts on fire.[14]

The special "V-Day Issue" sprang from a collaboration with Lauren Chief Elk (Assiniboine/Blackfeet), a cofounder of another grassroots digital project, Save Wiyabi, which maps the epidemic of murdered and Indigenous women across the United States and Canada.[15] *As/Us* has also published poetry and interviews with Leanne Simpson (Michi Saagiig Nishnaabeg), a highly regarded and successfully published scholar who is well known for having left the academy to pursue work in decolonization.

Indeed, *As/Us* provides a critical look at what DH looks like on the margins of university resources. It regularly publishes pieces by artists who may have academic training and connections, but not much academic privilege. Winder and Lopez themselves have remained committed to writing and scholarship without the benefit of highly remunerated academic positions: Lopez is a full-time faculty member at North Seattle College, while Winder has cobbled together administrative and teaching work in Colorado, California and New Mexico. They have managed *As/Us* with next to nothing in the way of material support — no expensive apparatus, no major grants. They run the journal on WordPress to contain costs, and enlist entirely volunteer labor. At the same time, their position has arguably enabled them to accomplish and publish things they might not have been able to, for example, if they were under the gun to publish individual monographs for tenure. *As/Us* is resolutely communit*ist*, as Jace Weaver (Cherokee) might say, with an ac-

14 Lyla June Johnston, "Dawn," *As Us: A Literary Space for Women of the World* 1, http://asusjournal.org/issue-1/lyla-june-johnston-spoken-word/.

15 Lauren Chief Elk, "The Missing Women You Don't Hear about: How the Media Fails Indigenous Communities," *Salon*, February 14, 2014, http://www.salon.com/2014/02/14/the_missing_women_you_dont_hear_about_how_the_media_fails_Indigenous_communities/.

tivist commitment to Indigenous community-building rather than scholarly self-promotion.[16]

It is also resolutely *future*-oriented. In 2015, *As/Us* hosted a Native youth poetry contest. They published winners — selected by an array of prestigious Indigenous writers including Marcie Rendon (Anishinaabe) and Gyasi Ross (Blackfeet) — in their Fall 2015 issue. They also brought these young writers to read at the Survival of the First Voices Festival (SFVF), which encourages Native youth to pursue higher education "and follow their passions," and where they could rub shoulders with popular young Native artists like the hip-hop musician Frank Waln (a frequent collaborator with Winder) and actor Justin Rain. The writing contest included prompts that reflect the goals of community and self-representation: e.g., "Describing how you can be a leader in your community," or "Describing the person you see in the mirror (how you see yourself in 5–10 years)." While deprived of some of the more sophisticated interfaces and platforms of more widely hailed electronic literature and performance projects, *As/Us* makes visible the dynamic relays between online and face-to-face interactions, between older and younger generations of people and technology.

II. Podcasting: Indian & Cowboy

Indigenous radio, and Indigenous radio archived on the web, has been around for some time, but Indigenous podcasting has positively exploded in the past five years.[17] Indigenous podcasting is now a widespread and global phenomenon, including shows like the Australian Broadcasting Corporation's *Awaye!*

---

16 Jace Weaver, *That the People Might Live: Native American Literatures and Native American Community* (New York: Oxford University Press, 1997), 43.

17 Many people date the beginnings of podcasting to the early 2000s, when the term began to appear in the popular press. Internet radio began a little earlier, in the 1990s; like other podcasts, some Indigenous shows began as Internet radio and continue in that format even as they make their episodes available in downloadable podcast format.

(Listen Up!) on Aboriginal Arts and Culture and the Canadian Broadcasting Corporation's (CBC) *Unreserved.* Journalist Johnnie Jae (Otoe-Missouria/Choctaw) has been podcasting for years on her multimedia platform, *A Tribe Called Geek,* which builds community among self-proclaimed Indigenerds.[18] Another long-running online Indigenous radio show is *Native Trailblazers,* in which journalists Vincent Schilling (Akwesasne Mohawk) and Delores Schilling talk to Indigenous leaders, entertainers, artists and activists. The CBC has produced podcasts devoted expressly to violence against Indigenous women, including *Missing & Murdered* and *Island Crime.*[19] In recent years, some highly regarded arrivals to podcasting include *All My Relations* by Adrienne Keene (Cherokee) and Matika Wilbur (Swinomish/Tulalip), and *This Land,* by Cherokee journalist Rebecca Nagle.[20]

One of the first and most influential Native podcasts in North America was *Red Man Laughing* (RML), by comedian Ryan McMahon (Anishinaabe/Métis).[21] It includes routines from his national tours and appearances from some of his comedic personae, like the self-proclaimed sage Clarence Two Toes and the raunchy Powwow Pickup Pimp. McMahon also has a signature bit, the "rant," which is a freestyle monologue on whatever is bothering him — bad hotel rooms, his FitBit, the media frenzy over Amy Winehouse's death, how "kids fuck up your

18 Johnnie Jae, *A Tribe Called Geek,* http://atribecalledgeek.com/. For more on Johnnie Jae, see her roundtable with Rebecca Roanhorse, Elizabeth LaPensée, and Darcie Little Badger, "Decolonizing Science Fiction and Imagining Futures: An Indigenous Futurisms Roundtable," *Strange Horizons,* January 30, 2017, http://strangehorizons.com/non-fiction/articles/decolonizing-science-fiction-and-imagining-futures-an-indigenous-futurisms-roundtable/.

19 Elon Green, "Using True Crime to Teach Indigenous History: Reporter Connie Walker on 'Finding Cleo,'" *Columbia Journalism Review,* July 5, 2018, https://www.cjr.org/q_and_a/finding-cleo.php.

20 See Adrienne Keene and Matika Wilbur, *All My Relations,* https://www.allmyrelationspodcast.com/ and Rebecca Nagle, *This Land,* https://crooked.com/podcast-series/this-land/.

21 Ryan McMahon, *Red Man Laughing,* http://www.redmanlaughing.com/.

life" when you're a parent. Additionally, he interviews special guests — high-profile Native Studies scholars (Leanne Simpson, Taiaiake Alfred), authors (Richard Van Camp, Lee Maracle), and chiefs from the Assembly of First Nations. *RML* also breaks new music, and has sophisticated music beds created by hip-hop artists like A Tribe Called Red and Stomp of RezOfficial.

While McMahon has always revealed a strong political sensibility, *RML* has become increasingly focused on Indigenous sovereignty issues, especially since the rise of Idle No More. Since December 2012, individual episodes have often been given over entirely to interviews with activists or to live recordings at major gatherings, and an entire season focused on the politics of "reconciliation" in Canada. McMahon describes this as an organic evolution. At the beginning of Season 2, he explains that subscriptions and downloads spiked with the addition of guests who talked about pressing issues affecting aboriginal people. Therefore, he says, he'll talk "head-on" about decolonization: "Basically that's what this show is about. That idea — the idea of creating a podcast that sort of addresses, through the side door, in a light way, decolonization and that process and what it's all about [...] that's what this show sort of melded into, that's what it kind of turned into on its own." For McMahon, the podcast is about more than comedy. He has often spoken about how theater and comedy saved his own life, but for him, this is more than personal: "it is about the survival of our communities, the revival of our peoples" (S2.E1).

Radio and podcasting are powerful ways to build community, and *RML* takes seriously the building of Indigenous community. Like many podcasters, McMahon begins most episodes by talking about how to find the show, how to download it, how (and why) to use the app, how to get in touch by email. But this is more than self-promotion; he is using podcasting technology to teach other Indigenous people about electronic communications and self-representation. In early episodes especially, he creates joking dialogues to answer questions like "what's a podcast?" "what's an iTune?" "what's the cloud?" (a place, he explains, to watch cat videos). He also invites musicians to submit their audio files for consideration on the show, telling them how to do it, in a laughing way: "I'm not gonna go to your MySpace and rip them to mp3 myself, do some work SON [...]. It's 2011, that's what people do is SoundCloud, get off MySpace" (S1.E1). In May 2014, McMahon offered a whole episode on "how to podcast."

In addition to *talking* about technology and its importance in Indigenous resurgence, McMahon has also used his resources to support other content producers more materially. His startup, "Indian & Cowboy" (spoofing the Internet as a new "frontier") aspires to be nothing less than "the world's ONLY Indigenous podcast network."[22] It supports the brilliant *Métis in Space*, cohosted by Montreal-based activists Molly Swain and Chelsea Vowel — "unapologetically Indigenous, unabashedly female, unblinkingly nerdy, and unwaveringly in love with Dune."[23] Swain and Vowel challenge multiple stereotypes at the same time: they drink wine while watching and wittily commenting on some of their favorite (or most loathed) science fiction films. Indian & Cowboy also supports a more putatively "traditional"-themed podcast, *Stories from the Land*, which is similarly futural in its vision. It issues a challenge to listeners, inspired by a Facebook video posted by a listener: "take your cellphone camera out to the land and show/tell the world about the place they are from [...] take us out to the land/place you're from and share the story/history of that place in your own words." This is radical broadcasting, embedded in Indigenous community and Indigenous resurgence.

To all appearances, McMahon himself is now highly successful. But *RML* began as a scrappy, bootstrapping project, what he likes to call "my ugly baby," "a guy sitting in his living room with his cat." He started it in 2008, but didn't regularize the show until August 2011, when he made it available on iTunes as well as his own website. As he put it in that first new episode, "This is sup-

22 Ryan McMahon, *Indian & Cowboy*, http://www.indianandcowboy.com/

23 "Métis in Space," *Indian & Cowboy*, https://www.indianandcowboy.com/metis-in-space/.

posed to have been a reoccurring, once a month, twice a week, three times a day, type of podcast project, but ah, you know, that didn't happen. And there's a lot of reasons why that didn't, and mostly because people weren't listening, people weren't downloading it, and people weren't paying attention to it, so I said, 'fuck it' and I stopped doing it because it's a lotta goddamn work, and uh, but I love it, so uh, I'm coming back to it and I don't care who listens anymore, I don't give a shit. I don't care, I'm gonna continue, I'm gonna do it." And he tells his listeners *how* he's doing it, not only in its technical aspects, but also in its philosophical dimensions. He speaks frankly of the difficulties of podcasting, and his own mixed feelings about monetizing content — what he calls "the great Indian paradox," navigating between traditional ideals, the exigencies of capitalism and the demands of technology. He ponders that "it's not very Indian of me to be charging for it," but he is also searching for a sustainable model (S1.E3). Thus, by the end of his first season he had an app, he got the show on podcast networks like Stitcher.com, Earwolf.com and satellite radio, and he leveraged other social media, particularly Twitter and YouTube, to promote the show. By the summer of 2014 *RML* picked up a major sponsor, audible.com, which sponsors other major podcasts like Marc Maron's *WTF*? Along the way, McMahon has always talked self-consciously and critically about the implications of commercial success. In one of his best episodes (a November 2013 panel discussion with filmmaker Sterlin Harjo) he discusses how he was brought up on the theater community model of grant writing: "if you got money you had a project, but if you didn't have money you didn't have a project." In McMahon's view, "what the internet has offered us now is a chance to build a following or a fan base or a like-minded collective of artists where we can take a project that we make ourselves for no money and bring it to an audience." And by "we," he means Indigenous people, people whose stories have been summarily dismissed and unheard.

III. Language Revitalization: westernabenaki.com

Language documentation and revitalization represent a significant proportion of currently available Indigenous digital projects. Language loss and revitalization have always been important to Native people themselves, but they have received larger national attention since the passage of legislation like the Native American Languages Act (1990). Digital tools — websites, social media, and apps — are playing an ever-bigger role in these efforts. Linguist Mairead Moriarty argues that while, in and of themselves, digital media "cannot secure the future of such languages, their role in language maintenance and revitalization cannot be ignored"[24] In her assessment, the Internet allows communities to circumvent some of the factors that have historically contributed to language erosion (e.g., shrinkage of the speaking community by out-migration or death), even though, she admits, access and training continue to be major problems in poorer and rural communities.[25] Mobile phones and gaming, two quite powerful tools in language revitalization efforts, depend on broadband access, for the former, and a high level of technical expertise to develop, for the latter.

Digital humanities conferences and journals seem to address language-revitalization projects relatively infrequently, perhaps because they are considered more often under the domain of science and social science, with the National Science Foundation acting as a major funder. Moreover, many digital language projects simply operate with next to no institutional support. Westernabenaki.com is one such example. It depends entirely on the labor and resources of one man — Jesse Bruchac (son of the well-known writer Joseph Bruchac), who has become known as one of the preeminent, if not the preeminent, scholar and teacher of Abenaki, though he has yet to pursue a formal

24 Mairead Moriarty, "New Roles for Endangered Languages," in *The Cambridge Handbook of Endangered Languages*, ed. Peter K. Austin, Cambridge Handbooks in Language and Linguistics (Cambridge: Cambridge University Press, 2011), 447.

25 Ibid., 454.

academic degree in linguistics. Abenaki is an Algonquian language considered "critically endangered," with very few remaining speakers; the Abenaki community is also highly diasporic, with three small reserves in Quebec and no federally recognized groups in the US, though Abenaki families and communities live throughout northern New England, most visibly at Missisquoi in Vermont. Bruchac, who lives in upstate New York, studied the language on his own initiative in the 1990s with Cecile Wawanolette (1908–2006), an elder who was teaching at the Odanak reserve in Quebec as well as in the Abenaki community at Missisquoi, Vermont.

His website, westernabenaki.com, offers language lessons, an online radio show, and videos of people speaking Abenaki. The site is what the ethnographer Renya Ramirez (Winnebago) might call a "Native hub" — a space for tribal people in diaspora to gather, exchange knowledge, and take that knowledge home again.[26] It is loaded with links to other Abenaki communities, book sales, and event information. Like *As/Us Journal* and other sites, it puts a premium on physical gatherings; Bruchac tells us, "Aln8banaki waj8nemak kwinatta wd'alamitoal lintow8ganal. The Abenaki have many greeting songs. Kw8gweni gez8wado wji maahl8mek. Because of the importance of gathering together" (Episode 3). He holds face-to-face language camps, many of which are archived in video so that — hub-like — the site encourages people to gather, to bring their knowledge back to their families, and so on. Like *As/Us* and Indian & Cowboy, too, this site is invested in the future. Videos include Bruchac speaking with his children; and in one episode, he and his daughter (then four years old) dubbed the famous "Battle of the Wits" scene from *The Princess Bride* in Abenaki.[27]

The radio show now includes seventeen episodes, each just about ten minutes or less, entirely in Abenaki. You can hear a

26 Renya Ramirez, *Native Hubs: Culture, Community, and Belonging in Silicon Valley and Beyond* (Durham: Duke University Press, 2007).

27 "Princess Bride: The Battle of Witts (Aln8baiwi)," *YouTube*, January 15, 2010, https://www.youtube.com/watch?v=WCkcYV7OVoo.

powwow announcement, a traditional oral narrative, and interviews with other speakers, including Cecile Wawanolette her son, Joseph Elie Joubert. Although the number of speakers — and this radio effort — may seem small, the goal is nothing less than an Abenaki soundscape. Charles Hirschkind, who has studied the use of Islamic cassette sermons in the Middle East, makes an observation that could apply well here:

> The contribution of this aural media to shaping the contemporary moral and political landscape [...] lies not just in its capacity to disseminate ideas or instill religious ideologies but in its effect on the human sensorium, on the affects, sensibilities, and perceptual habits of its vast audience. The soundscape produced through the circulation of this medium animates and sustains the substrate of sensory knowledges and embodied aptitudes undergirding a broad revival movement[28]

In an episode of the *Sounding Out!* Podcast, where Indigenous activists talk about the current state of their traditional languages, it becomes clear that even in communities where there may not be large numbers of speakers, and there may still be a profound feeling of frustration and loss, the affective experience of hearing Native-language words — even on old ethnographic recordings, or when young people use "slang Shoshone" — has tremendous power. Leading this discussion, Ojibwe video artist and scholar Marcella Ernest remarks, "the spoken language is a cherished intellectual treasure. Each sound captures how we see the world"[29] Thus, Jesse Bruchac delights in speaking before audiences, Native and non-Native, and teaching as many individual words as he can. On the radio show, similarly, he

28 Charles Hirschkind, *The Ethical Soundscape: Cassette Sermons and Islamic Counterpublics* (New York: Columbia University Press, 2009), 2.

29 Marcella Ernest, "Linguicide, Indigenous Community and the Search for Lost Sounds," *Sounding Out!*, March 26, 2015, http://soundstudiesblog.com/2015/03/26/sounding-out-podcast-40-linguicide-Indigenous-community-and-the-search-for-lost-sounds/.

assures listeners that "chaga nda kd'aln8ba8dwaw, chaga nda k'wawtamowen, akwi saagidah8ziw! if you don't speak Indian, if you can't understand, don't worry! K'kizi askwa ibitta tbestam ta wig8damen. You can still just listen and enjoy it."

Like *As/Us Journal*, westernabenaki.com retains an appreciation for the ways that print and digital dissemination of texts are mutually interpenetrating and sustaining. He is using another web-based technology, lulu.com, to publish bilingual books in Abenaki and English, with the hope that printing such books on demand might be a more sustainable publishing model. *As/Us* uses a similar idea, making print copies available through amazon.com. Alan Liu describes these kinds of relays as "thick affordances between media regimes": despite scholars' desire for straightforward narratives of technological and communicative progress, he argues, different media — orality, writing, broadcasting, Internet, and so on — have historically always overlapped, contradicted, worked with and against each other in multiple simultaneous directions.[30]

Conclusion

Finally, the Indigenist Internet includes Native people's own origin stories of all this activity, including the frequently-heard assertion that "wampum was code": wampum, with its binary system of purple and white shell beads, its ability to "hyperlink" to oral traditions and political protocols, and its ability to morph into new designs to meet the needs of the future. Elizabeth LaPensée is among proponents of this idea, seeing new multimedia environments as continuous with much older Indigenous communication methods:

30 Alan Liu, "Imagining the New Media Encounter," in *Companion to Digital Literary Studies*, eds. Ray Siemens and Susan Schreibman, Blackwell Companions to Literature and Culture (Oxford: Blackwell Publishing Professional, 2007), 11, http://www.digitalhumanities.org/companionDLS/.

> [T]he Internet and three-dimensional representations have always existed for Indigenous people. We have always perceived the connectivity between all and life in many dimensions [...]. As we root ourselves to grow into this future, every game we make, every design we sketch, every conversation we have contributes to what has been unfolding since time immemorial — games that shift perspectives and reinforce ours.[31]

Indigenous autoethnographic views of new media challenge neocolonial narratives of progress. They represent what Liu calls "good narratives of new media encounter [that] are in the endless stories than whole imaginative environments [...] [that] imagine affordances and configurations of potentiality."[32] For many of the Indigenous digital artists and activists working outside of academic DH (and indeed outside of or marginalized in academia) those "affordances of potentiality" are much more than postmodern imaginings or intellectual games: they are survival. In their projects, we find much less emphasis on digital archives than on Indigenous *futurism,* an idea given wider airing by Grace Dillon (Anishinaabe)'s esteemed collection *Walking the Clouds: An Anthology of Indigenous Science Fiction.* The idea of Indigenous futurism has had resonance for Indigenous scholars far beyond the realm of literary sci-fi: Lou Cornum (Navajo), for instance, calls it "a disavowal of western progress," a movement "centered on bringing traditions to distant, future locations rather than abandoning them as relics."[33]

31 See *Red Man Laughing,* February 17, 2015 and Elizabeth LaPensée, "Indigenously-Determined Games of the Future," *Kimiwan Zine* 8 "Indigenous Futurisms" (2014). See also Angela Haas, "Wampum as Hypertext: An American Indian Intellectual Tradition of Multimedia Theory and Practice," *Studies in American Indian Literatures* 19, no. 4 (Winter 2007): 77–100 and Steven Loft and Kerry Swanson, eds., *Coded Territories: Tracing Indigenous Pathways in New Media Art* (Calgary: University of Calgary Press, 2014).

32 Liu, "Imagining the New Media Encounter," 16.

33 Lou Cornum, "The Space NDN's Star Map," *The New Inquiry,* January 26, 2015, http://thenewinquiry.com/essays/the-space-ndns-star-map/.

During the 1990s — the headiest days of literary canon-busting and canon expansion — it was common to hear Native scholars and writers saying "we don't need the canon; we have our own."[34] In our own moment, it is possible that DH needs Indigenous genealogies more than Indigenous communities need DH. The ethnographic digital archives mentioned in the introduction to this chapter are a first step in this direction, with their emphases on Native co-curation and their respect for current Indigenous sovereignty protocols. But an alternative genealogy asks us to go still further; it asks, as did Adeline Koh, who first envisioned this essay collection, to "cast our formulation of the digital humanities beyond the field of humanities computing to incorporate into its intellectual genealogy such fields as new media studies, DIY (do-it-yourself) digital recovery projects from the 1990s, digital projects on postcolonial studies," and more.[35] Witnessing Indigenous people's dynamic uses of electronic tools and platforms, it's clear that they have already intuited the need to keep community and social justice first, ahead of tool- or c.v.-building. In looking so resolutely to the future, they have in fact preserved not just "data sets," but them*selves.*

34 Most famously articulated, perhaps, in Craig Womack, *Red on Red: Native American Literary Separatism* (Minneapolis: University of Minnesota Press, 1999).

35 Adeline Koh, "Niceness, Building, and Opening the Genealogy of the Digital Humanities: Beyond the Social Contract of Humanities Computing," *differences: A Journal of Feminist Cultural Studies* 25, no. 1 (January 1, 2014): 102.

Bibliography

"APS Collections through Indigenous Eyes." *American Philosophical Society,* 2013. http://www.amphilsoc.org/library/exhibit/indigeyes.

AUSTLANG: Australian Indigenous Languages Database. http://austlang.aiatsis.gov.au/main.php.

Bacino, Meghan. "RED INK Journal: Preserving, Promoting an Indigenous Voice." *Accents on English: Newsletter of the Department of English at Arizona State University* 19, no. 1 (Fall 2015–Winter 2016). https://english.asu.edu/news-events/newsletter/accents-english-fall-2015-winter-2016/red-ink-journal-preserving-promoting-indigenous-voice.

Boast, Robin, and Jim Enote. "Virtual Repatriation: It Is Neither Virtual nor Repatriation." In *Heritage in the Context of Globalization,* edited by Peter Biehl and Christopher Prescott, Vol. 8, 103–13. SpringerBriefs in Archaeology. New York: Springer New York, 2013.

Chief Elk, Lauren. "The Missing Women You Don't Hear about: How the Media Fails Indigenous Communities." *Salon,* February 14, 2014. http://www.salon.com/2014/02/14/the_missing_women_you_dont_hear_about_how_the_media_fails_Indigenous_communities/.

Christen, Kimberly. "Opening Archives: Respectful Repatriation." *American Archivist* 74 (Spring/Summer 2011): 185–210. DOI: 10.17723/aarc.74.1.4233nv6nv6428521.

Clapper, Jordan, and Misty Shipman Ellingburg, eds. *Four Winds Literary Magazine.* https://fourwindslitmag.wordpress.com/.

Clifford, James. "Varieties of Indigenous Experience: Diasporas, Homelands, Sovereignties." In *Indigenous Experience Today,* edited by Marisol de la Cadena and Orin Stran, 197–224. London: Berg Publishers, 2008.

Cornum, Lou. "The Space NDN's Star Map." *The New Inquiry,* January 26, 2015. http://thenewinquiry.com/essays/the-space-ndns-star-map/.

Domingo, Nadya. "The Trope Slayers." *This Magazine,* March 20, 2015. http://this.org/magazine/2015/03/20/the-trope-slayers/.

Dubé, Jacob. "Oil Lobbyists: Thunderbird Strike Video Game 'Promotes Ecoterrorism.'" *Vice,* October 27, 2017. https://www.vice.com/en_us/article/xwawq3/oil-lobbyists-thunderbird-strike-videogame-promotes-ecoterrorism.

Earhart, Amy E. *Traces of the Old, Uses of the New: The Emergence of Digital Literary Studies.* Ann Arbor: University of Michigan Press, 2015.

Ernest, Marcella. "Linguicide, Indigenous Community and the Search for Lost Sounds." *Sounding Out!,* March 26, 2015. http://soundstudiesblog.com/2015/03/26/sounding-out-podcast-40-linguicide-Indigenous-community-and-the-search-for-lost-sounds/.

Fox Spears. *Robohontas.* http://www.robohontas.com/.

Fragnito, Skawennati. "CPW: FAQ." *Cyberpowwow,* April 6, 1997. http://www.cyberpowwow.net/nation2nation/triciawork1.html.

Fragnito, Skawennati, and Jason Lewis. "Aboriginal Territories in Cyberspace." *Cultural Survival,* Summer 2005. http://www.culturalsurvival.org/publications/cultural-survival-quarterly/canada/aboriginal-territories-cyberspace.

Gaertner, David. "Indigenous in Cyberspace: CyberPowWow, God's Lake Narrows and the Challenges of Creating Indigenous Territory in Cyberspace." *American Indian Culture and Research Journal* 39, no. 4 (2015): 55–78.

Gaertner, David. *Never Alone: Resources and Reflections.* https://ilsaneveralone.wordpress.com/.

Garroutte, Eva. *Real Indians: Identity and the Survival of Native America.* Berkeley: University of California Press, 2003.

Grant-Costa, Paul, Tobias Glaza, and Michael Sletcher. "The Common Pot: Editing Native American Materials." *Scholarly Editing* 33 (2012). http://www.scholarlyediting.org/2012/essays/essay.commonpot.html.

Green, Elon. "Using True Crime to Teach Indigenous History: Reporter Connie Walker on 'Finding Cleo.'" *Columbia*

Journalism Review, July 5, 2018. https://www.cjr.org/q_and_a/finding-cleo.php.

Haas, Angela. "Wampum as Hypertext: An American Indian Intellectual Tradition of Multimedia Theory and Practice." *Studies in American Indian Literatures* 19, no. 4 (Winter 2007): 77–100. DOI: 10.1353/ail.2008.0005.

Hirschkind, Charles. *The Ethical Soundscape: Cassette Sermons and Islamic Counterpublics.* New York: Columbia University Press, 2009.

Jae, Johnnie. *A Tribe Called Geek.* http://atribecalledgeek.com/.

Johnston, Lyla June. "Dawn." *As Us: A Literary Space for Women of the World* 1. http://asusjournal.org/issue-1/lyla-june-johnston-spoken-word/.

Keene, Adrienne, and Matika Wilbur. *All My Relations.* https://www.allmyrelationspodcast.com/.

Koh, Adeline. "Niceness, Building, and Opening the Genealogy of the Digital Humanities: Beyond the Social Contract of Humanities Computing." *differences: A Journal of Feminist Cultural Studies* 25, no. 1 (January 1, 2014): 93–106. DOI: 10.1215/10407391-2420015.

LaPensée, Elizabeth. "Indigenously-Determined Games of the Future." *Kimiwan Zine* 8, "Indigenous Futurisms" (2014).

Liu, Alan. "Imagining the New Media Encounter." In *Companion to Digital Literary Studies,* edited by Ray Siemens and Susan Schreibman. Blackwell Companions to Literature and Culture. Oxford: Blackwell Publishing Professional, 2007. http://www.digitalhumanities.org/companionDLS/.

Loft, Steven, and Kerry Swanson, eds. *Coded Territories: Tracing Indigenous Pathways in New Media Art.* Calgary: University of Calgary Press, 2014.

Loyer, Jessie. "Indigenous TikTok Is Transforming Cultural Knowledge." *Canadian Art,* April 23, 2020. https://canadianart.ca/essays/indigenous-tiktok-is-transforming-cultural-knowledge/.

McMahon, Ryan. *Red Man Laughing.* http://www.redmanlaughing.com/.

McMahon, Ryan. *Indian & Cowboy.* http://www.indianandcowboy.com/.

Moriarty, Mairead. "New Roles for Endangered Languages." In *The Cambridge Handbook of Endangered Languages,* edited by Peter K. Austin. Cambridge Handbooks in Language and Linguistics, 446–58. Cambridge: Cambridge University Press, 2011.

Nagle, Rebecca. *This Land.* https://crooked.com/podcast-series/this-land/.

Povinelli, E. A. "The Woman on the Other Side of the Wall: Archiving the Otherwise in Postcolonial Digital Archives." *differences: A Journal of Feminist Cultural Studies* 22, no. 1 (January 1, 2011): 146–71. DOI: 10.1215/10407391-1218274.

Powell, Timothy, and Larry Aitken. "Encoding Culture: Building a Digital Archive Based on Traditional Ojibwe Teachings." In *The American Literature Scholar in the Digital Age,* edited by Amy Earhart and Andrew Jewell, 250–74. Ann Arbor: University of Michigan Press, 2010.

"Princess Bride: The Battle of Witts (Aln8baiwi)." *YouTube,* January 15, 2010. https://www.youtube.com/watch?v=WCkcYV7OVoo&list=UUDUFBq8Cu1SPuaIfgThwqOw/.

Ramirez, Renya. *Native Hubs: Culture, Community, and Belonging in Silicon Valley and Beyond.* Durham: Duke University Press, 2007.

Reciprocal Research Network. https://www.rrncommunity.org/.

Recollet, Karyn. "Glyphing Decolonial Love through Urban Flash Mobbing and Walking with Our Sisters." *Curriculum Inquiry* 45, no. 1 (January 1, 2015): 129–45. DOI: 10.1080/03626784.2014.995060.

Roanhorse, Rebecca, Elizabeth LaPensée, and Darcie Little Badger. "Decolonizing Science Fiction and Imagining Futures: An Indigenous Futurisms Roundtable." *Strange Horizons,* January 30, 2017. http://strangehorizons.com/non-fiction/articles/decolonizing-science-fiction-and-imagining-futures-an-indigenous-futurisms-roundtable/.

Rowley, Susan. "The Reciprocal Research Network: The Development Process." *Museum Anthropology Review* 7, no. 1–2 (2013): 22–43.

Seesequasis, Paul. *Blanket Toss Under the Midnight Sun: Portraits of Everyday Life in Eight Indigenous Communities.* Toronto: Knopf Canada, 2019.

Weaver, Jace. *That the People Might Live: Native American Literatures and Native American Community.* New York: Oxford University Press, 1997.

Womack, Craig. *Red on Red: Native American Literary Separatism.* Minneapolis: University of Minnesota Press, 1999.

15

Ancestors in the Machine: Indigenous Futurity and Indigenizing Games

Jordan Clapper

I learned to play video games before I learned to read. While some may remember their first book, I remember my first game: *Sonic the Hedgehog 2* on the Sega Genesis.[1] In the early 1990s, video games saw a surge in popularity as consoles became more affordable. While in no way cheap, home-based consoles became less a show of exorbitant wealth (as personal computers of earlier generations were far too expensive for the average person to own) and more a commonplace presence. This allowed many families the ability to experience interactive media. Games became part of what Steven Loft describes as my "media landscape." The "media landscape" concept describes the practice of Indigenous people in a specific media: "the 'media landscape' becomes just that: a landscape, replete with life and spirit, inclusive of beings, thought, prophecy, and the underlying connectedness of all things — a space that mirrors, memorializes, and

1 Sega, *Sonic the Hedgehog 2*, Sega Genesis, 1992.

points to the structure of Indigenous thought,"[2] and one that did not necessarily steamroll my own indigeneity as a game player.

Native Americans have been limited in their representational scope in video games. Their appearance tends to cast them in stereotypical tropes. There are representations like that in *Custer's Revenge,* where one embarks on the lofty quest to rape a busty Native woman with a stupid pixelated white penis.[3] We also have the KGB-employed, longing-to-return-to-nature Vulcan Raven from the *Metal Gear Solid* series, and of course he walks across the Bering Strait to get to Russia, as if we couldn't reinforce that tired stereotype by simply playing it in reverse.[4] For a while, the only Indigenous folks in games I could experience were those in fighting games: T. Hawk from *Street Fighter,*[5] Nightwolf from *Mortal Kombat,*[6] Wolf Hawkfield from *Virtua Fighter,*[7] and many other fighting game franchises. Most of these early American Indian fighting characters can shoot lightning, summon spirits, and wear ambiguously-themed war paint, "A little bit of modernity, a little bit of tradition rolled in there. You know, get some drums goin'"[8] (in speaking about the television show *Z Nation*). From the early days of games to the modern age, (Indigenous) players can both play and further colonize coded-Indigenous characters and reenact white settler colonialism in active and obvious ways, whether it be the rape and bodily colonization of a pixelated Indigenous woman in *Custer's Revenge,* using stereotypes to power interpersonal battles in fighting games, or the suggestion that the wronged Indian could

2 Steven Loft, "Introduction: Decolonizing the 'Web,'" in *Coded Territories: Tracing Indigenous Pathways in New Media Art,* eds. Steven Loft and Kerry Swanson (Calgary: University of Calgary Press, 2014), xvi.

3 Mystique, *Custer's Revenge,* Atari 2600, 1982.

4 Konami, *Metal Gear Solid*, PlayStation, 1998.

5 Capcom, *Super Street Fighter II,* Arcade, 1993.

6 Midway Games, *Mortal Kombat* 3, Arcade, 1995.

7 Sega AM2, *Virtua Fighter,* Arcade, 1993.

8 Molly Swain and Chelsea Vowel, "Métis in Space (S.3 EP#8) — Z Nation 'We Were Nowhere Near the Grand Canyon,'" *Indian & Cowboy,* https://www.indianandcowboy.com/episodes/2016/9/22/mtis-in-space-s3-ep-8-z-nation-we-were-nowhere-near-the-grand-canyon.

only seek refuge in the typified US-hating Soviet Union. Said players can also further their experience with colonization by ignoring said stereotypes and proclaiming, "It's only a game," a common criticism in response to calls for more socially-conscious games. In the wake of misogynistic criticism that poured from the GamerGate controversy, user Patrick Rael writes in a forum post on BoardGameGeek.com, "The 'it's only a game defense' won't work to counter this concern because games are not simply games. They are not a unique aspect of culture that bears no relation to the rest of culture, and do no cultural work. If they trivialize everything they touch (a questionable assertion in itself), that trivialization is itself a kind of cultural work."[9] This sort of mentality, which sees freedom of representation as a necessary evil to creative and artistic freedom, has led to situations like GamerGate, where game developer Zoe Quinn and journalist Anita Sarkeesian (among several other women in the games industry) received coordinated online harassment because they criticized the representation of women in games.[10]

Though Indigenous representation in any media is fraught with problematic examples, Indigenous representation in video games digs into the most violent and harmful stereotypes when programmed within the baked-in structures of settler colonialism at the heart of any media advancement since the invention of the printing press. Video games have become one of the most influential media in a very short time. From the likely many unnamed figures in the industry who have worked as developers to the intensely problematic depictions of Native characters in the games themselves, Indigenous folks have been around to experience the entirety of video game history. In my media of choice, when I can even find a Native like myself, this is what I see. The public's consumption of indigeneity includes recogniz-

9 Patrick Rael. "Why Do We Argue about Games with Socially Difficult Themes?" *BoardGameGeek*, April 25, 2017, https://boardgamegeek.com/blogpost/64810/why-do-we-argue-over-games-socially-difficult-them.

10 Michael James Heron, Pauline Belford, and Ayse Goker. "Sexism in the Circuitry: Female Participation in Male-Dominated Popular Computer Culture," *SIGCAS Computers and Society* 44, no. 4 (November 2014): 18–29.

able symbols—wars and dead bodies; cultures come and gone; Wikipedia-deep, "Native-inspired" spirits and figures—that are replaced by the dominant, colonizing norm. Active involvement by Indigenous developers is relatively new ground on which we walk. This Indigenous material is what Jackson 2bears refers to as "a virtual dog's breakfast of 'Indian' paraphernalia," the kind of things he sees in the regular celebrations and parades in public schools, "the heroism of brave European frontiersmen warding off the Natives and conquering the untamed wilderness of the 'New World.'"[11] This article asks: How have Indigenous people used games for themselves? How can their presence *indigenize* gaming practices to texture the field?

Within these stereotyped signposts of indigeneity, how does one look authentically Indigenous? Indigenous game players and scholars must deal with this expected outward signification. In the digital sphere, in video games, how does this happen? Like myself, those that grow up off-rez in the Native American context have both less access to culturally relevant upbringings and the checkmark that non-natives use to de-indigenize an individual. The American regulation of Indigenous identity, primarily relating it to access to allotted land (reservations) and heritage (blood quantum) on paper, means far more limited access to "legitimated" Indigenous identity, which is usually monitored by birth certificates and/or land titles. Similarly, as the United States education system is similarly predicated on documents and land use, the academy has the power to exclude and marginalize voices it does not deem to be authentic or useful. Access to (intellectual) property cannot be said to have been fully divested from whiteness, certainly not yet. In Cheryl Harris's "Whiteness as Property," the valuation of whiteness has been linked intimately with property:

> If property is understood as a delegation of sovereign power — the product of the power of the state — then a fair read-

11 Jackson 2bears, "My Post-Indian Technological Autobiography," in *Coded Territories,* eds. Loft and Swanson, 13.

> ing of history reveals the racial oppression of Indians inherent in the American regime of property [...] the rules of first possession and labor as a basis for property rights were qualified by race. This fact infused whiteness with significance and value because it was solely through being white that property could be acquired and secured under law. Only whites possessed whiteness, a highly valued and exclusive form of property.[12]

The distinctness of indigeneity, when viewed as a racial term, is unique in that it was one of the first formulations in the project of western expansion that was seen as a hinderance, rather than an opportunity. Patrick Wolfe suggests, "Black people were racialized as slaves; slavery constituted their blackness. Correspondingly, Indigenous North Americans were not killed, driven away, romanticized, assimilated, fenced in, bred [w]hite, and otherwise eliminated as the original owners of the land but as *Indians*."[13] As such, Indigenous populations are, at the outset of their white settler colonialist definers, always on the back foot when it comes to their imposed racial status. The path to legitimate indigeneity flows through the dispossession of land and identity, only to be fed it back again when one ticks the new boxes.

My mother was adopted before the *Indian Adoption Act* went into effect. Once her documents were tampered with, this effectively erased our documented heritage, erasing the type of indigeneity that the US tends to privilege. For those that grew up off-rez; for those that don't have immediate, distinct access to cultural images and language; for those that stand at the boundary of ethical representation; for those that cannot show what others would like them to show, how does indigeneity stand a chance in the digital, moveable sphere? As 2bears points out,

12 Cheryl I. Harris, "Whiteness as Property," *Harvard Law Review* 106, no. 8 (June 1993): 1723–24.

13 Patrick Wolfe, "Settler Colonialism and the Elimination of the Native," *Journal of Genocide Research* 8, no. 4 (2006): 388.

"According to Derrida, what this means in no uncertain terms is that one must commit oneself in a performative fashion to the conjuration and invocation of the spectres of which one (or a culture) is possessed or haunted,"[14] which suggests there are places that Indigenous individuals can express themselves using the cultures that possess them, that one does not have to win out over the other. To suggest that the west has control over forms of expression is to afford it the very authenticity and originary status that it so desperately craves to maintain its hold of power. In other words, according Mark Rifkin, this fetishization "arises only as an effect of the process of seizing Native lands and consigning Indigenous peoples to the circumscribed space of the reservation,"[15] to act only as the colonizers have deemed authentically Indigenous. If my indigeneity may not be expressed on paper, it may leave traces within my scholarship, my return to my tribe's reservation, my and my son's Ponca names, and in the weaving I perform on the computer screen. As any Indigenous storyteller, I bring my indigeneity to bear in the words I perform, in the code I write.

Projects of *indigenization* within games involve the reclamation of seemingly western game tropes and reapplying them within Indigenous frames to look toward a perceived future for ourselves. *Indigenization,* thus, is a process of both looking forward *and* looking back, of contemplating and grappling with the history of colonization and with our own individual cultural histories, of looking to where we go from here, of asserting that we have a place in the here and now and into our sovereign futures. Western games, those within the white settler colonial tradition, do not often have to make these claims of themselves, as westernism presupposes temporality—'We have always been here, we are here, we will always be here'—albeit with a heavy amount of irony and blindness to ignore the fact that western-

14 2bears, "My Post-Indian Technological Autobiography," 25.

15 Mark Rifkin, *The Erotics of Sovereignty: Queer Native Writing in the Era of Self-Determination* (Minneapolis: University of Minnesota Press, 2012), 231.

ism/whiteness has always been temporal and a project in development/defense. Indigeneity, as conceived of within western tropes, often has to contend with temporality laid upon it—'You were here, you aren't here'—by these invading forces, so futurity doesn't always seem to mesh easily within western academic and gaming frames. In her introduction to *Walking the Clouds: An Anthology of Indigenous Science Fiction*, Grace L. Dillon speaks of Indigenous futurisms as always "narratives of *biskaabiiyang*, an Anishinaabemowin word connoting the process of 'returning to ourselves,' which involves discovering how personally one is affected by colonization, discarding the emotional and psychological baggage carried from its impact, and recovering ancestral traditions in order to adapt to our post-Native Apocalypse world."[16] Games, within this framework, can aid in healing and reclaiming indigeneity "post-"/para-/con-colonization.

Indigenization is also a strategy of queering the landscape of narrative and interactive storytelling. While examples of queer-Indigenous games are nearly absent from the converging communities that will be discussed here, practices of queering literature and media are nevertheless present in reforming the methods of digital storytelling and experience. Engaging with seemingly westernized methods could be falsely equated to, as Qwo-Li Driskill and their editing partners in *Queer Indigenous Studies* highlight, the

> perpetuat[ing] notions of tragic victimry that so often haunt writing about Indigenous peoples. Instead, it is said to point out the material and political conditions that Native GLBQT2 people experience under colonization, including colonization's accompanying system of heteropatriarchy, gender regimes, capitalism, ableism, ageism, and religious oppression. Indigenous queer critiques offer a mode of analysis that more

16 Grace L. Dillon, "Imagining Indigenous Futurisms," in *Walking the Clouds: An Anthology of Indigenous Science Fiction, Sun Tracks*, ed. Grace L. Dillon (Tuscon: University of Arizona Press, 2012), 10.

> complexly facilitates an understanding of these entwined systems so that they can be interrupted.[17]

Queering and *indigenizing* are modes of critique and strategic messing-with that have their own histories and particularities. These strange bedfellows, nevertheless, upset concomitant western norms by promoting marginalized individuals' access to tools that would otherwise be seen as betraying the boxes the west has put them into.

Indigenization as a strategy is about using what we have within the bounds of our own cultural ecosystems. *Biskaabiiyang*, as Dillon mentions, is a discovery process, which doesn't involve some journey to a distant, irrecoverable past, but rather a process of decolonization, working from Linda Tuhiwai Smith's work, "*changing* rather than *imitating* Eurowestern concepts."[18] Carving out space for Indigenous creators within the video game genre means indigenizing the tools and methods used to create interactive experiences and narratives. Using tropes within video games does not necessarily constitute a becoming-with the west (i.e., westernize). These strategies, as Valerie Alia has pointed out in her examination of Indigenous pirate radio, do not condemn the Indigenous creator to such western subjectivity. Rather, "For the New Media Nation, 'progress' is not a linear movement from piracy to legitimacy, statelessness to state, outlaw tactics to citizenship, but a fluid and perpetually challenging form of resistance and collective power."[19]

We will explore this process of indigenization through the work of Elizabeth LaPensée, an Indigenous game maker that

---

17 Qwo-Li Driskill et al., "The Revolution Is for Everyone: Imagining an Emancipatory Future through Queer Indigenous Critical Theories," in *Queer Indigenous Studies: Critical Interventions in Theory, Politics, and Literature*, eds. Qwo-Li Driskill et al. (Tuscon: The University of Arizona Press, 2011), 218, 211.

18 Dillon, "Imagining Indigenous Futurisms," 10.

19 Valerie Alia, "Outlaws and Citizens: Indigenous People and the 'New Media Nation,'" *International Journal of Media and Cultural Politics* 5, nos. 1–2 (2009): 51–52.

incorporates the land and the outside world into her game formation. Then, we will see a small sampling of the collectives that are reforming gaming concepts for Indigenous stories and purposes, from Indigenous youth to Indigenous-sponsored game companies. The processes and practices covered here are a springboard into larger conversations of how we can decolonize gaming spaces to allow for Indigenous creators to exist in ways that morph to their cultural needs, as well as call to consider the question: What do we consider an Indigenous game?

The questions I approach here are about futurity, both within a game-development aspect and an academic one. Like any medium, games are not ready-made for the Indigenous purpose, and there isn't consensus that this is a medium we should be moving into. Jodi Byrd, for instance, is intensely skeptical about whether or not the "flat ontology" of games like *BioShock Infinite* can accommodate an Indigenous worldview when the very coding is, itself, an extension of western ideology:

> Within all these wildly recursive frontier analogies, we are still left, however, with the persistent and haunting question: Where does the Indian go? Within object-oriented programming languages, rather than being removed, the Indian might be said to remain as a primitive class, as something both endemic to the code and so basic as necessary to operationalize and routinize the code's recognition of complex object containers. But in itself, the Indian has little to no agency. It can be made to perform like an object under the right conditions, but it primarily serves as a baseline language through which all other objects achieve viability through reference in the system. OOOs are built, in part, upon the porting of coding languages into philosophical traditions, and the theory's insistence on a flatness that refuses the correlationist gesture runs the risk of validating the logics of our political moment. As the Indian vanishes into the code, civility and savagery, democracy and anarchy, settlement and wilderness, sovereign and beast become flip sides of the same coin. Heads or tails, the toss itself requires the coin to maintain the il-

> lusion that both sides are equally matched. In the *BioShock Infinite* universe the outcome of this toss is always the same, but what remains unanswered is whether having it come up tails would actually affect the system. We keep tossing the coin with the expectation that this time, just this once, the outcome will be different.[20]

Byrd's argument assumes the perfect western-correlative code base of the Unreal Engine 3 (the engine that powers the game), and it also assumes an unrealistic flattening of real players. No game is perfectly formed or suited to a specific purpose. I, the Indigenous player, can do things unintended by the developers but still within the scope of agential play and boundaries in the game. Byrd, in part, takes issue with the ahistorical representation of the massacre of Indigenous families at Wounded Knee, when the purpose of its carnivalesque presence in a "museum" is explicitly to ahistoricize this event to prop up white valor in a clearly genocidal act. Just outside of this false museum, a glitch—being an unintentional mishap in the representation or gaming mechanics on a technical level, "a refusal of the idea that digital games and gaming communities are the sole provenance of adolescent, straight, white, cisgender, masculine, able, male, and 'hardcore' bodies and desires and the articulation of and investment in alternative modes of play and ways of being"[21] on a theoretical level—in the programming allows one to exploit the game's economic resources. One can enter and exit one of the doors to the museum and reset the vending machines throughout the area outside of the museum, which can then be mined for money over and over again. Do I assert indigeneity through such an act by subverting the game's carefully crafted bioeconomic-correlative system, or does such an act only assert the whiteness of the character I play, a violent man able to break

20 Jodi A. Byrd, "Beast of America: Sovereignty and the Wildness of Objects," *The South Atlantic Quarterly* 117, no. 3 (July 2018): 613–14.

21 Edmond Y. Chang, "Queergaming," in *Queer Game Studies*, eds. Bonnie Ruberg and Adrienne Shaw (Minneapolis: University of Minnesota Press, 2017), 15.

diegesis and become a money-machine? Equally, what if I were to spend my time and create a mod (modification) for the game to make the player-character Indigenous? What if I were to mod it to correct the anachronicities of the Wounded Knee display? Do the purported code bases of any game engine or system presuppose my exclusion from a genre, just as the historic marginalization of many types of bodies and cultures from growing or established mediascapes? In short, no. Just as the developers may have a bit of white saviorism encoded in the game, they cannot provide measures by which I will bring my own Indigenous epistemology and ontology to my play, nor can we view all projects that hope to incorporate Indigenous developers as doomed to repeat the sins of codes past.

That said, to *indigenize,* Indigenous codes written through Indigenous bodies and minds must be present. In September of 2020, Twitter user "bascule" tested the platform's image-centering algorithm by posting two elongated images, each depicting white Republican Senator Mitch McConnell and Black former President Barack Obama. Almost predictably, Twitter's algorithm centered Senator McConnell. An image-meme formed, and numerous users attempted different configurations of the image setup, and almost all of them found McConnell to be the preview-worthy face.[22] While not the first or the last coding practice to be tested, this situation brings to light what happens when algorithms and codes are fed using majority-facing data and technologies. Equally, it should call us to question who does the coding. According to Data USA, 78.1% of computer programmers are male, and 67.7% are white.[23] Without bodied Indigenous presence, a project of *indigenizing* games, whether from a development or a playing standpoint, cannot be successful.

What is the internal futurity that needs to be built for Indigenous games to thrive? What metaphoric land needs to be

22 Tony Arcieri, *Twitter,* September 19, 2020, https://twitter.com/bascule/status/1307440596668182528?s=20.

23 Data USA, "Computer Programmers," https://datausa.io/profile/soc/computer-programmers#demographics.

reclaimed for scholars of Indigenous new media to approach the question of video games with the greatest possible range of voices? What are the exclusionary threats in play when focusing too heavily on what the academy has deemed accessibly Indigenous? And where is the audience of urban Indigenous players and scholars? The academy certainly privileges "authentic" Indigenous experience, which often is correlated to on-rez life and explicit, lifelong cultural proximity, which, because of white settler colonial genocide, many Indigenous folks do not have access to at all times. As of 2007, "nearly seven out of every 10 American Indians and Alaska Natives—2.8 million—live in or near cities, and that number is growing."[24] With this, a growing population of urban Indigenous players experience these video games, and their presence as an audience must be considered. For developers, on- or off-rez, the presence of indigeneity is vital, important, and inseparable from the games themselves. *Indigenization* is the passing on of tribal values, baking indigeneity and Indigenous experience into the very code and gameplay. Building towards Indigenous futurity in video games means overcoming the veritable numbers game of coding practices and to expand the academy's view of who is playing games and who can make games. A body removed from land cannot be seen as irrevocably lost, just as an Indigenous body/mind displaced cannot be said to have lost their Indigenous perspective. The digital realm is a landscape; "So far as indigenous people are concerned, where they are *is* who they are, and not only by their own reckoning."[25]

We *are* here, and we need lenses and language to articulate our various positions.

---

24 Urban Indian Health Commission, "Invisible Tribes: Urban Indians and Their Health in a Changing World" (Robert Wood Johnson Foundation, 2007), 1.

25 Wolfe, "Settler Colonialism and the Elimination of the Native," 388.

Indigenous Games and Indigenizing

The academy loves singular creators. A single author, despite what Barthes may think, is easier to conceive of and easier to categorize. What makes a novel a Black novel (in the American context)? Well, it has to be by a Black author, yes? Is *Beloved*[26] a work of Black literature? Of course, but reasons why and specific qualifications for entrance into racially-oriented canons should always be debated, but we might softly assume that *Beloved* fits within the canon of Black American literature because of its authorship. Okay, so how about Indigenous novels? Is *Ceremony* Indigenous? Yes, because Leslie Marmon Silko, the author, is Indigenous. Therefore, *Ceremony* is a work of Indigenous literature. Is *The Education of Little Tree*[27] a work of Indigenous literature? No, because Forrest Carter is the pseudonym for Asa Earl Carter, a prominent Ku Klux Klan leader,[28] and yet we should read it to see what appropriation taken to an extreme looks like. All this said, we don't need to constantly pressure artists to create to a specific racial vision, nor do we need to see books tackle only racialized notions of subjects, though we cannot forget how intimately entwined these matters may be.

Video games are much more complicated. While many artistic industries, from literature to films, are full of purportedly singular visions—of course, this ignores the fact that films require many, many people to accomplish—the "singular vision" in games is not so easily accomplished. One of the most famous examples is that of Toby Fox, developer of *Undertale,* a meta-RPG (roleplaying game) about the world of monsters segregated off from the world of humans. All of the writing, music, coding, management, and the majority of the art came from Toby

26 Toni Morrison, *Beloved* (New York: Vintage Books, 1987).

27 Asa Earl Carter, *The Education of Little Tree* (New York: Delacorte Press, 1976).

28 Dave Randall, "The Tall Tale of Little Tree and the Cherokee Who Was Really a Klansman," *The Independent,* September 1, 2002, https://www.independent.co.uk/news/media/the-tall-tale-of-little-tree-and-the-cherokee-who-was-really-a-klansman-175400.html.

Fox himself, with supplemental art created by artist Temmie-chan, but the vast majority of the work is his.[29] Only a handful of games can be said to be made from a single person. Ostensibly, anyone reading this, with access to language and a writing implement of some kind, can begin writing a novel. It doesn't have to be good, but it can be done. But a game? It requires a vast array of skills: computer coding, graphic artistry, writing, editing, programming, management, and many other things. Singular visions that come to mind are Todd Howard,[30] David Cage,[31] Peter Molyneux,[32] and Hideo Kojima,[33] and while many of these people, often men, possess variable skills, their overarching names tend to overshadow the vast wealth of talent at their disposal that make their successful games possible in the first place. In looking to these people, we cannot necessarily privilege the writers or directors, as we often do in literature and films, as gameplay is usually the focal criteria of the success or failure of a game, relatively speaking. But are there "singular creators" within the Indigenous gaming space? Simply put, yes. My discussion of the white western Romantic single-author/genius trope should in no way detract from this creator's work.

Elizabeth LaPensée is assuredly the poster child of the Indigenous gaming scene. While several Indigenous games, projects, studios, and contributors exist, it is her name that one will likely encounter when discussing Indigenous games. Even when the projects are collaborative, her name is the privileged one. LaPensée, who is Anishinaabe and Métis as well as settler-Irish (which more academics could do in their identificatory remarks), has a hand in many Indigenous games, most of which have education or reclamation as their focus. While video games are not the only medium that she finds deserved success, games are one of her main areas of critical research. Her ability to design and exe-

29 Chris Schilling. "The Making of Undertale," *PC Gamer*, May 5, 2018, https://www.pcgamer.com/the-making-of-undertale/.
30 *Bethesda Game Studios*, https://bethesdagamestudios.com.
31 *Quantic Dream*, https://www.quanticdream.com/en.
32 *22 Cans*, http://22cans.com.
33 *Kojima Productions*, http://www.kojimaproductions.jp/en/.

cute games that indigenize the gaming process will be discussed later in this article. For now, I argue that she is an example of the singular vision trope that also has happened in Indigenous games, with the associated benefits and pitfalls that come from such a distinction. LaPensée is careful to position herself when it comes to her games, her website listing her role in her various ventures in boldface with appropriate citations of the studios or artists that she has worked with.

LaPensée is important to note as the poster child of Indigenous games as her presence directly challenges the typical image of who one tends to see in the gaming industry: male, white, and from a privileged background. As an Indigenous woman, Indigenous in her connection and gaming practices, it's important that she has been one of the main rising stars in Indigenous gaming. As Qwo-Li Driskill and friends have pointed out, "The work of belonging to, challenging, and transforming 'the community' long has been modeled by Indigenous women activists, who include Indigenous feminist theorists linking activist and academic work."[34] Our mothers and sisters and grandmothers and aunts and daughters are important in this work to *indigenize* the communities of academic work, Indigenous storytelling, and video game development.

In pointing out LaPensée, I want to highlight how she, as well as other Indigenous game developers, have *indigenized* various elements of gaming and the gaming scene by exploring various gaming tropes and texturing them to a more Indigenous gameview. However, I equally want to point out the types of Indigenous games that tend to get funded. Much of her work is centralized to what the academy seems willing to fund: reserve(-ation)-oriented games that tend to focus on land-use and historical perspectives within traditional Indigenous storytelling practices. These stories need to be told, but the academy, where one assumes she gets most of her funding, tends to see these stories as the only ones that need to be told. To be sure, the reclaiming of traditions and the survivance work necessary on

34 Driskill et al., "The Revolution Is for Everyone," 218.

reservations and in close-knitted cultural contexts should in no way be hindered—Rather, university and governmental funding for these types of projects needs to be vastly expanded—but this work should not be seen as the end all, be all of Indigenous cultural work. Funding for creative presence, games included, is necessary for the long project of healing. The presence of Indigenous developers and their gaming practices ask us to call into question things like representation, ethical play, and survivance in the digital media we create, as well as what stories get to be told. *Indigenization* reads games back onto themselves and onto those that play/study them. Indigeneity, contrasted with other racial categories in the west, is programmed precarious to facilitate western expansion. For instance, my son, who is both Ponca and Black, will easily be racialized as Black, despite his lighter skin, while his indigeneity is rationalized out—Ponca name, Ponca upbringing, but no card, not a worthy amount of blood. Again, as Wolfe points out:

> In the wake of slavery, this taxonomy became fully racialized in the "one-drop rule," whereby any amount of African ancestry, no matter how remote, and regardless of phenotypical appearance, makes a person Black. For Indians, in stark contrast, non-Indian ancestry compromised their indigeneity, producing "half-breeds," a regime that persists in the form of blood quantum regulations.[35]

Indigeneity is a powerful political tool to speak back to the west. Just as writers like Leslie Marmon Silko used the western novel to read back onto westernism itself,[36] Indigenous game makers read game-making practices and tropes onto the gaming scene writ large, making stakes to indigeneity and sovereignty of practices as well as putting a mirror up to the west itself.

35 Wolfe, "Settler Colonialism and the Elimination of the Native," 388.
36 Leslie Marmon Silko, *Ceremony* (New York: Penguin Books, 1977).

Indigenous Digital Bodies and Play

The gaming scene is intimately entrenched in concepts of authenticity and straightforward genre purity. As we have seen from issues surrounding Gamergate, there are intense pressures upon who can play and comment on video games. With its reliance on technology and economics, the vast majority of major developers are white. According to a 2019 report produced by the International Game Developers Association, 81% of respondents identified as white/Caucasian/European, though the statistic dropped to 69% when adjusted for those who only selected white and no other category.[37] Indigenous games have to work both with and against the tide of westernized notions of play. As Espen Aarseth attempts to decouple games from the cultural foundations they are built upon, he shores up the dangers of trying to ambiguate the impacts that these bases have on the games that come from them:

> The "royal" theme of the traditional pieces [of chess] is all but irrelevant to our understanding of chess. Likewise, the dimensions of Lara Croft's body, already analyzed to death by film theorists, are irrelevant to me as a player, because a different-looking body would not make me play differently [...]. When I play, I don't even see her body, but see through it and past it.[38]

This is a relatively privileged position in games, akin to "colorblind" discourse:

---

37 International Game Developers Association, "Developer Satisfaction Survey," November 20, 2019, 13, https://s3-us-east-2.amazonaws.com/igda-website/wp-content/uploads/2020/01/29093706/IGDA-DSS-2019_Summary-Report_Nov-20-2019.pdf.

38 Espen Aarseth, "Genre Trouble: Narrativism and the Art of Simulation," in *First Person: New Media as Story, Performance, and Game,* eds. Noah Wardrip-Fruin and Pat Harrigan (Cambridge: MIT Press, 2004), 48.

> Colorblindness maintains that intergroup tensions arise from overattention to ethnic and cultural categories [...]. Colorblindness may seem to imply an acceptance of ideas from all cultures, but the vision it yields in practice is less one of color inclusiveness than color myopia.[39]

Nothing means anything; *it's only a game.*

Similarly, whether a character is depicted as Indigenous, coded with indigeneity, or Indigenously ambiguous can certainly change the ways that we play these games and how we engage with the story. One must play Nuna in *Never Alone* with Indigeneity at her core,[40] Aloy in *Horizon Zero Dawn* as (problematically) Indigenously inspired,[41] and Frisk from *Undertale* as ambiguously Indigenous.[42] Stuart Moulthrop responds to the issue of becoming "body blind" by pointing out the traditional narrativist move to trivialize what might otherwise need the cultural context:

> Seeking to exclude narrativist contraband, Aarseth embargoes all cultural implications. We are not to understand the game of chess as an allegory of feudalism or Tomb Raider as misogynist-masochist fantasy [...]. Lara Croft's physique may consist of raw data but it cannot be treated as such for critical purposes."[43]

The digital body has the capability of influencing playstyle and apprehension of the story. In the example used, Lara Croft underwent a significant change from her persona and body type

39 Jaee Cho, Carmit T. Tadmor, and Michael W. Morris, "Are All Diversity Ideologies Creatively Equal? The Diverging Consequences of Colorblindness, Multiculturalism, and Polyculturalism," *Journal of Cross-Cultural Psychology* 49, no. 9 (2018): 1378.

40 Upper One Games, *Never Alone (Kisima Iŋŋitchuŋa),* PlayStation 4, 2014.

41 Guerrilla Games, *Horizon: Zero Dawn,* PlayStation 4, 2017.

42 Toby Fox, *Undertale,* PC, 2015.

43 Stuart Moulthrop, "Online Response to 'Genre Trouble,'" in *First Person: New Media as Story, Performance, and Game* (Cambridge: MIT Press, 2004), 47–48.

in the original PlayStation releases of the games to the rebooted series on the latest generations of consoles. This was not simply to please the masses but to change a player's interaction with the character in general, a technique Jodi Byrd points out in examining the emergence of tribalism in the west. Byrd writes, "tribalography provokes a discursive pause and signals a turn away from the self (auto) and to locate life (bios) in relation to a form that refuses states and nations as its raison d'être. In a contest of stories, tribalography teaches us that references matter as much as the author."[44] The west does not get to have its coded-ed cake (not a lie) and discount it when one tries to do what they've done with it: represent bodies. Indigenous bodies will play games, and Indigenous bodies/minds will create them.

The removal of Indigenous people from the creation of Indigenous-inspired things certainly does make the job of making a game without consideration much easier, but these people need to be present for cultural context. In *Sky Loom: Native American Myth, Story, and Song,* Julie Brittain and Marguerite Mackenzie discuss the seemingly innocuous and humorous story of Umâyichîs, "Little Shit Man," a story of the Algonquian oral tradition. They admit that they misinterpreted the story of a little man born of shit: "We were asking, 'What is this story about?' when we should have been asking, 'What is this story for?'"[45] This concern is reflected in the modern landscape of digital technologies. As Âhasiw Maskêgon-Iskwêw examines in his influential "Talk Indian to Me" series, "The real question about what relevance the Internet may have for artists is not what the Internet can do for artists or what artists can do with the Internet; the most significant examination remains in the domain of what a body of artwork does and how it does it,"[46] and we can apply

44 Jodi A. Byrd, "Tribal 2.0: Digital Natives, Political Players, and the Power of Stories," *Studies in American Indian Literatures* 26, no. 2 (2014): 56.

45 Julie Brittain and Marguerite Mackenzie, "Umâyichîs," in *Sky Loom: Native American Myth, Story, and Song* (Lincoln: University of Nebraska Press, 2014), 382.

46 Âhasiw Maskêgon-Iskwêw, "Talk Indian to Me #4: Speaking Spider Languages," *Ghostkeeper,* 1996, https://ghostkeeper.gruntarchives.org/

this to any digital medium. The story of Umâyichîs, taken out of context, seems like a neutral tale meant to evoke humor, but the story is, in fact, told to change the weather. Its purpose is incredibly sensitive and evokes a certain magic. Told outside of its context or with improper ceremonies, or if it were to change media, could bring harmful effects. In the context of video games, just like textual writing, the invasion of Native spaces means that Indigenous people leave some mark on the medium that seeks to represent them. As Lisa Brooks points out, "As European writing entered Native space, it was transformed, both in interaction with Indigenous systems of communication and in response to the needs of Indigenous communities."[47] Where the west tends to privilege the content, the telling of this story "creates the magic, not the actual content of the story," which Brittain and Mackenzie go on to say that the two aren't inherently unrelated, but that the context provided by Indigenous peoples links the story to the theme of "weather amelioration."[48] As such, it would be unethical to tell or retell an Indigenous story, much less program an Indigenous game, without Indigenous peoples at the core of their creation and telling. As Brooks explains, "Without ready access to Native writers, communities were forced to seek interpretive assistance from men who were not bound by the network of relations,"[49] and without ready access to Indigenous storytellers, programmers, and designers, our images and games are left to the mercy of the ravenous west. We need Indigenous minds to view and play games; we need Indigenous minds to create new games; and we need Indigenous minds to analyze all games.

---

publication-mix-magazine-talk-indian-to-me-4.html.

47 Lisa Brooks, "Awikhigawôgan: Mapping the Genres of Indigenous Writing in the Network of Relations," in *The Common Pot: The Recovery of Native Space in the Northeast* (Minneapolis: University of Minnesota Press, 2008), 220.

48 Brittain and Mackenzie, "Umâyichîs," 382.

49 Brooks, "Awikhigawôgan," 223.

Indigenizing through Social Impact

While not a video game, I first focus on *Survivance* because of its *indigenizing* of play with the goal of creating tangible, land-based change in the individual player. *Survivance* is a game that uses the internet as a medium to begin its play but which terminates with the individual taking their play out into the world and into the landscape of their own minds. The player is meant to go on a number of journeys, where they sit and listen to the voices, songs, and stories of Indigenous elders. That this begins one's journey *indigenizes* a common mechanic in games: the narrative/text box or found object. These mechanics in games are often associated together, where the player may find an object or document, which often relates something of the world or a character to the player through narration. Take, for instance, *Dark Souls,* a Japanese-made western-style RPG that has deep lore that is related primarily through item descriptions that the player must seek out. This extradiegetic narration is related to the player, not the player character, as these items do not have words or documents attached to their diegetic objects but is relayed only through the text in the player-accessed menus and windows.[50] LaPensée plays with this gamic trope by creating a space for elders, and then players, to tell their stories.

On the Caretaker path of *Survivance,* I chose the Sacred Hoop quest, which asks players to reflected on their unhealthy relationships with others. The rules of the game, outlined on the "How to Play" section of the website, leaves the interactions up to the player. The instructions differ from typical video/board game instructions in that they put choice as the primary motivator for the player. Under "Questing," LaPensée simply asks the player to choose a quest, perform a quest, reflect, and rest. "Choose a quest" asks questions of the player rather than lays out boundaries. "Where are you at in life right now? What is helpful to you? Pick a quest from any phase of the journey at

50 FromSoftware, *Dark Souls,* PC, 2011.

any time."[51] Boundaries are some of the defining features of any game, but LaPensée challenges this from the get-go, letting a player interact at their own pace, an extension from cyberspace into Indigenous spaces in a way that reflects the work Loretta Todd sees in interactive virtual spaces:

> As science changes, perhaps the universe will be imagined in ways that reflect our interconnectedness. As cyberspace develops, perhaps it will examine augmented versus immersive technology. Perhaps it will explore narrative forms in which you do not leave your body or soul. Just as the storyteller doesn't control the psychological connections of the listener, just as the shaman doesn't invade your mind, perhaps we can create new narratives where you must call upon your own powers and your own words.[52]

This open-ended approach to play and play-creation is reflected in the instructions for the Sacred Hoop quest. The first "instruction" of this quest is a question, rather than a command or a boundary: "Where have your feelings had negative impact on your relationships?" This hits home, as I've had difficulties in maintaining my personal relationships with the world as it is. The quest goes on to say, "Work towards resolving relationships that need healing."[53] As a player, I already feel inspired, as the game doesn't ask me to sink into the act of playing, which itself can be an escapist act rather than orienting the player to social acts, but rather suggests I fix some of the things in my life that aren't working. The page goes on to highlight the focus of *Survivance,* which is to create something artistic out of one's experiences. I feel the need to point out that, while I do not have the present means to enact my act of survivance in my chosen art

51 Elizabeth LaPensée, *Survivance,* 2011, survivance.org.

52 Loretta Todd, "Aboriginal Narratives in Cyberspace," in *Immersed in Technology: Art and Virtual Environments,* eds. Mary Anne Moser and Douglas MacLeod (Cambridge: MIT Press, 1996), 193.

53 LaPensée, *Survivance.*

form (writing and game making), I will hold these with me until I can do something about them.

Survivance plays against the notion of authoritative voice present in many games, either through instructions or narration, by letting an elder's voice shine through. The Sacred Hoop quest page also contains a quote from Woodrow Morrison Jr., a Haida elder and storyteller, along with a video interview with him. Gameplay is put alongside storytelling, one of the most Indigenous ways of knowledge transferal, as the story itself is what is being transferred, not just the kernel of truth or the lesson, as western stories are often guilty of in their focus. As Morrison Jr. puts it:

> When they [his children] want advice, I don't give it to them. I never offer it to them. What I do is I tell them a story, and within the story is information they can make, they can use to make a decision, but it doesn't tell them which way to go. And to me, it's the same thing when we're praying. If I'm asking for something, I'm telling God, or whatever that spirit is, I'm smart enough to know what I need, rather than what I'm going to be given.[54]

Morrison Jr. goes on to highlight the faults in our present programs for things like alcoholism, child abuse, and western education, where the focus is on the mastering a form of knowledge rather than the engagement through stories. These narratives would otherwise ask us to figure things out for ourselves rather than vest ultimate truth in the hands of a few people privileged enough to receive training or education in these various "facts," LaPensée similarly privileges a player engaging in their own personal journey. Where have my feelings negatively impacted my important relationships? I need to think about that; I need to talk to my partners and see what ways I've brought them grief. I need to talk to myself to see what grief I am engaging in in my

54 Wisdom of the Elders, "Woodrow Morrison, Jr., Haida - 2 of 2," *Vimeo*, July 29, 2013, https://vimeo.com/71304938.

own relationship with myself. My journey through the sacred hoop is my own, and its pretenses and outcomes are moldable to my own quest as the player. The acts of narrativizing and boundaries are, here, thoroughly indigenized and personalized to me, the Indigenous player.

The "Acts of Survivance" section also leaves things up to the player. The goal of these journeys is to create something artistic through one's quest in any medium they choose with the hopes of then sharing it with the world. While modern game consoles have all incorporated some act of sharing gameplay, with the "Share" button on the PlayStation 4 and a similar button on the Nintendo Switch, these acts of "sharing" focus more on the selection of game moments that exemplify the player's achievements or skills rather than the creation of something wholly new and unique to the player. *Survivance* encourages, under the "Sharing" section, one to upload and promote their artwork. While it is unfortunate that the website either has not been updated or seemingly has less interaction in recent years—the last photo uploaded to "The Caretaker" section under "Acts of Survivance" was posted on September 10, 2016—it is heartening to see the contributions of players highlighted. From the beadwork on boots to the sharing of an entire card game (*Niiwin,* by Julia Keren-Detar and Itay Keren, which I will be playing at some point this summer),[55] Indigenous-made creations, made through play, are the focus rather than the one's success in a specific, programmed gaming endeavor. This resists the strict rules that games tend to be associated with.

LaPensée follows in the example of other digital Indigenous creators, as the work promotes going out into the world with the teachings and experiences one develops. The strategy employed here is reminiscent of works like Skawennati's CyberPowWow, a digital collaborative project that sought to combat "the ways in which cyberspace could alienate users from the land and the

55 LaPensée, *Survivance.*

body, and she worked diligently to overcome it."[56] As such, digital creators and activists like Skawennati and LaPensée work to connect the digital and the physical to make "explicit the ways in which the material and digital could be bridged, blurring the rigid material/digital binary that [Loretta] Todd identifies by connecting users to place,"[57] though this "place" can be broadened to include the digital/mental spheres enacted when playing through digital games like *Survivance* or through LaPensée's other video game work. It is with this strategy of *indigenizing* gaming practices that I want to turn to another digital endeavor of LaPensée.

Circular Indigenizing: Social Issues Experienced in Games

LaPensée extends social engagement to representing and grappling with social issues present within current Indigenous populations. *Thunderbird Strike* further *indigenizes* common gameplay mechanics to bring attention to the problem of abusing the Alberta tar sands for capitalistic growth. The game takes the form of a side-scrolling shooter and little overt narrative elements. In the game, the player takes the form of Thunderbird flying over the tar sands. The player passes mining equipment, refineries, and animals as it crackles with electricity. As far as gameplay, the player is able to move about the screen and fire lightning bolts at the ground. When the player fires lightning, it can damage and destroy the mining equipment and refineries, but it can also bring life back to animals buried in the sands, the animals springing to life and running away, what appears to be small pockets of life and light in their bodies as they escape. Just like other forms of energy, the lightning the player controls is not infinite, as the Thunderbird must fly into the clouds to replenish itself.[58] The social issues are readily apparent, with

56 David Gaertner, "Indigenous in Cyberspace: CyberPowWow, God's Lake Narrows, and the Contours of Online Indigenous Territory," *American Indian Culture and Research Journal* 39, no. 4 (2015): 59.

57 Ibid.

58 *Thunderbird Strike*, PC, 2017.

capitalism heavily represented as a destructive force and being combatted by a spirit of nature, who uses destruction as a means to reestablish life in balance. But it is two particular gameplay elements that are emblematic of the *indigenization* of typical gameplay practices.

The most readily apparent *indigenized* gameplay mechanic in *Thunderbird Strike* is the direction of the side-scrolling. Some of the earliest and most prevalent features in video games is the direction of movement in two-dimensional games, especially side-scrollers. Some of the largest icons in video games, *Super Mario Bros.*[59] and *Sonic the Hedgehog*,[60] have made their names with this directional movement. I don't see anything political about moving in that particular direction, but to violate that common mechanic occurs when a game designer is calling attention to standards, the contextualization varying depending on the game. As it pertains to *Thunderbird*, moving left flies in the face of mainstream gaming conventions. Using such a convention suggests that the game is designed with players knowledgeable of typical gaming practices, taking into account that this game's audience is both Indigenous and non-Indigenous players. LaPensée's games often seem to take this into account with their designs.

Another aspect of LaPensée's game that seems to take Indigenous direction is the seeming lack of unnecessary death. Western games are often built on the assumption that there is a limited number of stock to a character's life, represented numerically as "lives" within the context of many games, and equally, the goal of many shooting games is to remove life from another individual, whether it be player or character. The Thunderbird strikes down the numerous symbols of capitalism, such as trucks, that harvest the tar sands. Visible, living figures are only present in the animals that the Thunderbird gives life to. The only destruction present in the game is the destruction of manmade machines. The gamemakers put thought into what

59 Nintendo, *Super Mario Bros*, Nintendo Entertainment System, 1985.

60 Sega, *Sonic the Hedgehog*, Sega Genesis, 1991.

these mechanics represent and how they can be used to further a more Indigenous form of play. Like *Survivance, Thunderbird Strike* promotes education, creativity, and the pursuit of life. Its website contains educational materials, as well as other artistic representations of players' interpretation of the game's messages. The game *indigenizes* these elements of play to get across its environmental message, but these sorts of activist games are not the only ones that use *indigenization* as a gameplay strategy.

Youth at the Helm of Futurity

Much of LaPensée's work focuses on Indigenous activism. The games have clear messages and aims to challenge the norms established by the colonizers. These games often promote a certain level of self-education, where the player is encouraged to delve into the presented materials without necessarily constraining the gameplay to a particular presentation style. However, a vast swath of the field of Indigenous games is focused on education, the futurity of Indigenous cultures, stories, languages, and survival as their focus.

Skawenatti and Jason Edward Lewis established The Skins Workshop as an educational collaborative. The various workshops are formed to educate Indigenous youth in the many game development skills. From writing to directing to programming and everything in between, Indigenous youth are paired with skilled workers in the games industry and academia to plan and develop games to tell stories from within their cultures. I focus here on these workshops because of their melding of creativity with Indigenous stories to make games that serve multiple audiences. Indigenous youth empowerment is paramount in programs like this, as it allows them to obtain the tools to counter the Indigenous "antiselves," in the vein of Gerald Vizenor,[61] that are present in the current media of video games. Games like USA

61 Gerald Vizenor, "Postindian Warriors," in *Manifest Manners: Postindian Warriors of Survivance* (Hanover: University Press of New England, 1994), 1–44.

(*United Sugpiaq Alutiiq*), an educational game to teach Sugcestun languages, are designed with maintaining internally consistent Indigenous languages and practices, as are other projects in this vein.[62] These games serve particular functions and are not meant for consumption outside their intended contexts. But these sorts of games certainly receive the lion's share of academic focus and support. Vizenor addresses the prevalence of Indigenous imagery that is crafted by western subjects *for* western subjects: "Simulations are the absence of the tribes; that absence was wiser in the scenes of silence, richer in costumes, and more courageous on a ride beside simulated animals. Western movies are the muse of simulations, and the absence of humor and real tribal cultures."[63] The danger of this simulated indigeneity is present in the current landscape of games, and the presence of the Skins project helps to resist the overtly western depiction of Indigenous subjects and simulated stories. For Skins, their stated goals are for students to

> engage in 1) knowledge, in which they observe and recall factual information, 2) comprehension, in which they understand the meaning of knowledge, 3) application, in which they apply knowledge in new situations, 4) analysis, in which they identify and extract patterns in knowledge, 5) synthesis, in which they use old ideas to create new ones, and 6) evaluation, in which they reflect on the ideas.[64]

Synthesis is at the core of their approach to game design.

---

62 Leslie D. Hall and James Mountain Chief Sanderville, "United Sugpiaq Alutiiq (USA) Video Game: Preserving Traditional Knowledge, Culture, and Language," *Educational Technology* 49, no. 6 (2009): 20–24.

63 Vizenor, *Manifest Manners*, 6.

64 Beth Aileen Lameman, Jason E. Lewis, and Skawennati Fragnito, "Skins 1.0: A Curriculum for Designing Games with First Nations Youth," in *Proceedings of the International Academic Conference on the Future of Game Design and Technology* (New York: Association for Computing Machinery, 2010), 106.

He Ao Hou, a point-and-click adventure game developed through the Skins 5.0 workshop held at Hālau ʻĪnana in Honolulu in the summer of 2017, adapts kānaka maoli stories into a synthesis of gameplay. According to the game's website, *He Ao Hou* "focuses in particular on the uses of the native kukui nut, itself a symbol of knowledge" and is "set in the far future, when kānaka maoli have attained the next level of navigation: space travel."[65] The opening sequence of the game uses kānaka maoli art to situate the player within an Indigenous story. The story is introduced to the player as a conversation between two youth and their grandfather. As the grandfather grows sick, your sister goes missing, seemingly from grief. The player must travel in their grandfather's space canoe to search for her. By visiting three planets, the player learns about the kukui nut and how it relates to kānaka maoli culture.[66] Traditional western point-and-click adventure games strike a balance between searching for random items, text-based dialogue with NPCs (non-player characters), and traveling between related locations to achieve certain criteria for progression. *He Ao Hou* uses many techniques typical of this style of games, but it embeds indigeneity in certain places to better tells its story.

For my gameplay experience, I visited Wai, the water planet, first. The first humans that I encounter are a pair of people that tell me about the kukui nut, that it is chewed up and spit into the water to purify the ocean. This is enough of a prompt for me to search about the island for the kukui, then traveling to two locations to assist in purifying the waters. For my efforts, a shark arrives and tells me that they saw someone with tattoos like mine (the player character) traveling to Pele, the lava planet. Once on Pele, I have to solve a small puzzle before being taught to Hula by Hi'iaka. The game informs me that I have to push the arrow buttons to hula, but it doesn't fully explain what these buttons are. While frustrating on its surface, the lack of clarity indigenizes the process of learning. One would not simply watch

65 Skins, "Skins 5.0," http://skins.abtec.org/skins5.0/.
66 Skins 5.0, *He Ao Hou: A New World,* PC, 2017.

a hula dancer and immediately register the importance of the act or what knowledge is embedded in these bodily movements. I tried and failed for several minutes before I figured out the sequence of dance steps. Again, my effort to learn these touchstones awards me with more knowledge about the location of my sister, who seemingly has gone to Ahpua'a, the plant planet. There, I meet Kamapua'a, a demi-god that transforms into an eight-eyed boar. The game breaks convention a little, as it is up to me to throw kukui nuts at his various eyes to wake him up. Once he does, I travel back to my ship to find out several things that otherwise went unnoticed to me.

This game does not provide explicit instructions as to how to properly play the game, which affords it with the qualities of discovery. The knowledge, both cultural and narrative, are relayed to the player through their willingness to explore the various environments that they encounter. For my experience, I did not check a console next to the main control panel of the canoe until after Pele. In order, I read the heartening encouragement of my grandfather, before reading a newspaper excerpt that he had passed away. This put an extra weight onto my actions on Ahupua'a, the finding of my sister more somber. However, upon completing this last planet, I find a message that my sister has transformed into a planet herself, furthering the flow of life and allowing new land to sprout. This sequence and my ability to seek it out for myself indigenizes the ways that games can grapple with death, even in a narrative context. Death is a common trope in any medium, and games use it to more or less expected effect in their various contexts. Here, the game assumes that I have some knowledge of typical western views of death; how can I not with the west being everywhere? But it plays with that notion by showing that death is not something to be feared but something which may bring new life. The ceremonies of chewing the nut to purify the waters, hula dancing to encourage life to return to the volcanic land, hurling it as a projectile to help wake a sleeping demi-god, and seeing both my sister and my grandfather pass from this life into another, the life growing and multiplying, one cannot help but question the portrayal of life in other games, how "lives" are the colloquial term for the mechanic in games to attempt to master a skill and be punished for it by failure.

He Ao Hou does not betray its indigeneity by synthesizing several stories and knowledge bases. Against what Byrd may argue, the use of technology and western-developed engines does not exclude the Indigenous youth at the game's helm. Rather, it attempts some level of balance between westernized notions of play and Indigenous values within both the content and the storyplay itself. The game also helps further the possibilities of indigenized gameplay and storycrafting through Skins's and the Initiative for Indigenous Futures's (IIF) collective goals of educating and empowering Indigenous youth to engage with their cultures in new and interactive ways.

Toward Within and Without: Indigenous Futurity through Sponsored Development

The last game I want to talk about is likely the one someone interested in games would have heard about. Developed by Upper One Games, *Never Alone (Kisima Inŋitchuŋa)* is a platformer that follows the journey of Nuna, an Iñupiaq girl, and an arctic fox as they traverse the frozen landscape in search of the source of a devastating arctic wind, as well as other treacherous creatures and obstacles.[67] This game is notable for its direct connection with Indigenous folks, both through funding and the cultural insights from elders and community members. *Never Alone indigenizes* a number of gameplay mechanics, in particular the "collectible," small items and milestones that one gets through strategic and crafty gameplay. The game has more traditional western gameplay collectibles, like the PlayStation trophies obtained throughout play, but the most notable element of the collectible mechanic are the "cultural insights," short videos told by Iñupiaq tribe members that span traditional tales and

67 Upper One Games, *Never Alone (Kisima Inŋitchuŋa)*, PlayStation 4, 2014.

other aspects of their everyday lives.[68] Rather than describing the world of the game itself, it gives the player insight into the lives of the Iñupiaq themselves and, thus, how the story impacts their lived existences. It also lends credence to the reality that the characters in these stories aren't simply characters but ancestors, teaching tools, and important interpretive modes.

These insights put some of the gameplay into context. Like *Thunderbird Strike,* this game gives the lives of those on the screen weight. Things like falling in the water or the death of one's fox friend have small consequences where one must replay the scenario, but the lives are not calculated by numbers, nor is the player given the opportunity to take the life of another unnecessarily. Throughout the game, the player is pursued by a polar bear. The player is eventually trapped, and the boss fight that follows involves playing as the arctic fox to trick the polar bear into opening up a passage for us to escape. It would seem all too easy to give the player the agency to kill the bear, which would be the easier option if one's only goal was to simply live. However, the cultural insight "A Girl & Her Nanuq" has Fannie (Kuutuuq) Akpik relate a tale where her brother accidentally killed a mother polar bear when it attacked him. He saved himself but at the cost of the bear. He realizes the weight of his actions, as Fannie explains, "We've always known traditionally that we avoid killing a mother. It's always been sacred to us to protect them. He had to present himself to the council, and so he was given the job to mother the baby, and we kept it."[69] The seemingly tangential relationship between this story about a man mothering a bear and the player's inability to harm the bear gives the player a sense of the weight of life in the Iñupiaq view: human life is not more important than the lives of others, even animals, even coded entities imbued with cultural insight.

This *indigenized* view of death in the context of gameplay is further explored with the arctic fox character. We are given the opportunity to either switch between these characters to solve

68 Ibid.
69 Ibid.

platforming puzzles, as they each have their own skills and bodies that can perform certain actions, or to play cooperatively with another player (I played single-player, as a second controller on the PlayStation 4 is quite expensive). As we play, the fox is killed, but he becomes his spirit form and continues to aid us on our journey. Rather than trivializing the death, this element of the game gives the player more context as to the importance of animals in relation to humans. Up to this point in the game, the fox is needed for various spirits to assist us. In a platformer, *Never Alone* manages to indigenize the concept of the platform itself. Fox's life and death shows us the importance of interacting with spirits and what they are capable of. Fox is our interpreter, our translator, as Nuna cannot summon the spirit platforms herself. Humans alone may not be able to summon or negotiate with spirits, but Fox, through his own spiritual connections, is able to help us and establish the connection between humans and other creatures, life and death, our path now and our path after our passing.

Is *Doom* an Indigenous Game? Strategies and the Path Forward

This was the initial question I had as I surveyed the present landscape of Indigenous gamemakers and creators. (Alfonso) John Romero is a video game designer and director, having had a hand in some of the biggest franchises of the 1990s and 2000s, such as *Doom*,[70] *Quake*,[71] and *Wolfenstein*.[72] He was one of the founders of id Software LLC, which remains a prominent name in the games industry. Romero is Yaqui, Cherokee, and Mexican, which was something not widely known for the early part of his career, or at the very least, it was not spoken about much. I only found out about it when someone pointed out his long hair, a common trope when talking about him online. "I'm

70 id Software, *Doom*, MS-DOS, 1993.
71 id Software, *Quake*, MS-DOS, 1996.
72 id Software, *Wolfenstein 3D*, MS-DOS, 1992.

both [Mexican and Native American]. Yaqui are native to southwestern Arizona; one grandparent was Yaqui, another Mexican, another Cherokee (other side),"[73] he said in a Twitter thread in 2016.

This tweet led to the initial question I had when thinking about the state of the field: what constitutes an Indigenous game? The best I could come up with was: maybe. So why even mention it here? To me, this question represents avenues for research and development in Indigenous games. While I've argued that indigenizing certain elements of gameplay have led to things like the challenging of western notions of death, franchises like *Doom* are built upon and have expanded on the glorification of death. In the most recent installments of the franchise, *Doom* (2016) and *Doom Eternal* even have a mechanic called "glory kills," where the player receives life and ammo bonuses for executing particularly gory kills. I'm not here to question the morality of these elements, but it does put a strange twist on the concept of *indigenization* and what counts as the clever reworking of gameplay elements in order to challenge their usage in application to Indigenous games. Death and violence are no strangers in the realm of Indigenous artwork. As LaPensée says in a paper examining her game, "Another important aspect of Indigenous game development involves creating the game and then gifting it to the community fully or partially, depending on how they determine to proceed."[74] Capitalism is certainly a problem in the progress of western expansion, as it undoubtedly has privileged some and paved over others. I don't want to argue that one should not make a living off of their work, but as LaPensée has highlighted, if Indigenous game development involves reciprocity, what about instances like Romero's where he works for someone else? Is his work somehow less Indigenous?

73 John Romero, *Twitter*, February 21, 2016, https://twitter.com/romero/status/701530383863644161.

74 Elizabeth LaPensée, "Survivance Among Social Impact Games," *Loading...* 8, no. 13 (2014): 49.

These mostly unanswerable questions serve to highlight an aspect of Indigenous arts and study that tend to get traction within academia: those that are recognizably Indigenous. James Luna's influential performance piece "Take a Picture with a Real Life Indian" is an example of what the general public and academia in particular favor when it comes to Indigenous studies. This in no way detracts from the importance of reclaiming tradition and maintaining one's tribal presence and expression, whether it be in traditional dance or in video games, but Luna's piece truly highlights what has been privileged by the western white gaze. In the scope of his three installations of this piece, spanning decades, not one person wanted a picture with an Indian wearing a polo shirt and khakis. Does this mean that Indigenous people should ascribe to assimilation? Of course not. Assimilation is pure violence, and we have seen the products. But does Luna indigenize the clothes that he wears? To some degree, I would argue so. What his performances bring to light is that the larger community of outsiders to Indigenous cultures have come to recognize a narrow mode of expression, where "traditional" Indigenous art and garb is the way that the academy recognizes legitimacy, authenticity, and indigeneity. Elizabeth S. Hawley examines this peculiarity:

> *Take a Picture* is particularly pointed in its interrogation of the pose and the photograph, and how both Native and non-Native peoples are implicated in and affected by the resulting stereotypes: Native peoples are expected to adhere to the stereotypic construction of Indian identity, but in performing this role, they reify the stereotype. At the same time, non-Native peoples perpetuate the problematic cycle by only characterizing as "Indian" those Native peoples that adhere to the stereotype that non-Native peoples have constructed and come to expect.[75]

75 Elizabeth S. Hawley, "James Luna and the Paradoxically Present Vanishing Indian," *Contemporaneity: Historical Presence in Visual Culture* 5, no. 1 (2016): 7.

Even at academic conferences, I receive comments on my Indigenous appearance, specifically my long, black hair. I keep it long because I want to, but that doesn't make it any less of a calling card that puts even fellow academics at rest when I identify as Ponca; forget the fact that only a single uncle of mine has long hair.

"Is *Doom* an Indigenous game?" is a vital question, because it should provoke a conversation. *Indigenization* involves recognizing the ways that Indigenous players, developers, and academics create space and walk the digital land. Do we still have a space where Indigenous individuals can create and code games that aren't visually or symbolically coded? To be more specific, can Indigenous game-makers create games that aren't simply to express an explicitly cultural story to the tribal masses or to the general gaming population in general? Is Stephen Graham Jones's *After the People Lights Have Gone Off*[76] any less of a work of Indigenous storycrafting because of its less obvious Indigenous symbolism when compared to his work *Ledfeather*?[77] Is there space for ghosts in the narrative machine, where we can explore indigeneity in other ways? Can we pass down our gameplay as well as our stories? Does academia define the "our"? Should we mediate digital indigeneity through an access to land and documention stacked by white colonialist notions of who we get to define "we" as? Digital sovereignty and *indigenization* reclaim space to do what is necessary for our indigeneity, as well as opening that space to those that need to walk that land.

Obviously, I'm trying to carve out a space for myself and my process. I've written many stories. Not all of my characters have a stated tribe; many don't have a physical form; I'm learning my own tribal stories as much as I'm trying to weave my own. But indigeneity is there. I'm inseparable from my body, my mind, our land, our ways. I could never wall off my indigeneity from what I produce. If so, many Indigenous people do not

76 Stephen Graham Jones, *After the People Lights Have Gone Off* (Chicago: Dark House Press, 2014).

77 Stephen Graham Jones, *Ledfeather* (Tuscaloosa: FC2, 2008).

live on reservations, where are all of these stories; where is the variety? The shift to online representational modes has brought definite challenges, but it also brings opportunities, as Gabriel S. Estrada examines in his work researching and incorporating online Indigenous spaces. Similar to the written word, online spaces and coding "can evolve to serve American Indian narratives, identities and literatures even when they were not originally designed to do so" with Indigenous input.[78] Projects such as the Skins Workshops, translating 'olelo Hawai'I into *C#*, and teaching programs like *USA* show promise for futurity, but even as the developers of *USA* have looked to preserve culture, the danger is that education may be seen as enough. As they state, "Native-American and Alaska-Native cultures have endured in spite of Federal policies of forced assimilation. We believe Indigenous people do not need new images, stories, and ideologies, but need to return to their old images, stories, and ideologies."[79] This is a dangerous decree. Access and embodiment of Indigenous cultures and histories are absolutely essential for Indigenous futurities and sovereignty, but to say that Indigenous folks have equal access to their images, stories, and traditional ideologies is ignoring the devastation and tribe-splitting tactics of the white settler colonialist past-present. What of the over half of all Indigenous peoples that live in urban environments? What of those who were forced from their homes? Indigenous people are not resistant to change, as stories evolve and change all the time. Indigenous futurity rests on access to new ceremonies to aid in healing, to aid in being able to reclaim and establish their identities, which are always enduringly present.

As we move forward in our studies and our development, we need to leave space for creative explorations of Indigenous expressions that may not fall under the acceptable banner that the academy has laid out for us. And that space is certainly developing. I'm excited for an upcoming Indigenous game, *Hill Agency:*

78 Gabriel S. Estrada, "Native Avatars, Online Hubs, and Urban Indian Literature," *Studies in American Indian Literatures* 23, no. 2 (2011): 67.

79 Hall and Sanderville, "USA," 23.

BARK & byte (listed on their website with the subtitle *PURITY/ decay*), described on the Kickstarter page, which was successfully funded, as "An Indigenous Cybernoir Detective Game. Explore an Indigenous future sovereign nation and the secrets of the Akâmaskiy."[80] The game even seems to have LaPensée's seal of approval thus far, so while LaPensée nevertheless has institutional support and name recognition, it is good to see that used in support of other creative Indigenous gameplay endeavors. *Indigenizing* in a gamic context should be seen as a way to use the tools that are at our disposal. Pushing those boundaries of typical play are as much of a creative endeavor as sticking to what works and putting it in an Indigenous context. "Indigeneity" is not so easily defined when it comes to art, but "sovereignty" means that those that are Indigenous must be able to express that indigeneity in ways that relate to their lived experiences. As Jolene Rickard puts it succinctly, "Sovereignty is the border that shifts Indigenous experience from a victimized stance to a strategic one. The recognition of this puts brains in our heads, and muscle on our bones."[81] "Strategic" is a hugely operative word, as it calls for Indigenous folks to be clever with their situations, to use what they have to get their art and message across.

As I've laid out here (or, rather, how these Indigenous artists have laid out for me), part of *indigenizing* the present media of video games means challenging the mechanics and technology that we have come to take for granted. 2bears's *remix theory* is, again, applicable as it positions the *remix*, Indigenous works of combinatory sampling and reworking,

> as a new media performance conjuration—with the backwards and forwards scratch!...scratch!...scratch!...that becomes about the conjuration and exorcism of spectral narra-

80 Achimo Games, "Hill Agency: BARK & Byte Kickstarter," *Kickstarter*, 2020, https://www.kickstarter.com/projects/1678114327/hill-agency-bark-and-byte.

81 Jolene Rickard, "Sovereignty: A Line in the Sand," in *Strong Hearts: Native American Visions and Voices*, eds. Nancy Ackerman and Peggy Roalf (New York: Aperture Foundation, 1995), 51.

> tives and the animate shadows that haunt our mediascape; a recombinant act that involves the slicing, cutting, and deconstruction of virulent colonial mythologies.[82]

Indigenizing, like queering, upsets the veritable apple cart, takes what the west has assumed to be its own and, like Gerald Vizenor's "postindian warriors," allows Indigenous developers to become "new indications of a narrative recreation, the simulations that overcome the manifest manners of dominance."[83]

To remix the tools we've been handed is an act of decoloniality, and decolonization is an act, not a metaphor, as Tuck and Yang have observed: "Decolonization as metaphor allows people to equivocate these contradictory decolonial desires because it turns decolonization into an empty signifier to be filled by any track towards liberation."[84] In short, the academy and the gaming scene needs to give Indigenous folks the space to do their work. "Progress" is not simply having white subjects focus on marginalized works by marginalized creators. If these media landscapes are indeed "landscapes,"[85] then the project of decolonization in the field of Indigenous games requires ceding those spaces back to the Indigenous developer; "Decolonizing the Americas means all land is repatriated and all settlers become landless. It is incommensurable with the redistribution of Native land/life as common-wealth,"[86] which means that we need the space to define what we want to do with our own images and games. What does this look like in the academic sense? Increased (or in many cases merely "present") support of Indigenous creators and funding their needs. The funding is paramount, as the greatest difficulty of developing games is the capital and technological needs before one can even attempt it. This means funding for training, networking, support, food,

82 2bears, "My Post-Indian Technological Autobiography," 26.
83 Vizenor, "Postindian Warriors," 6.
84 Eve Tuck and K. Wayne Yang, "Decolonization Is Not a Metaphor," *Decolonization: Indigeneity, Education & Society* 1, no. 1 (2012): 7.
85 Loft, "Decolonizing the 'Web.'"
86 Tuck and Yang, "Decolonization," 27.

lodging, school fees, artistic supplies, programs, travel: anything the creator may need. This funding is, itself, toward an act of decolonizing university funds. But for it to be a project of decolonization, any university helping to fund these individuals cannot and should not retain the rights to the game that is created. This means giving these Indigenous gamemakers sovereignty over their work and the stories they want to tell; it is *not* for the university to own. The presence and continued support of those whose lived indigeneity attaches their cultures to the land and its people, we can only challenge ourselves to welcome them into our purview.

Bibliography

22 Cans. http://22cans.com.

2bears, Jackson. "My Post-Indian Technological Autobiography." In *Coded Territories: Tracing Indigenous Pathways in New Media Art*, edited by Steven Loft and Kerry Swanson, 1–29. Calgary: University of Calgary Press, 2014.

Aarseth, Espen. "Genre Trouble: Narrativism and the Art of Simulation." In *First Person: New Media as Story, Performance, and Game*, edited by Noah Wardrip-Fruin and Pat Harrigan, 45–55. Cambridge: MIT Press, 2004.

Achimo Games. "Hill Agency: BARK & Byte Kickstarter." *Kickstarter*, 2020. https://www.kickstarter.com/projects/1678114327/hill-agency-bark-and-byte.

Alia, Valerie. "Outlaws and Citizens: Indigenous People and the 'New Media Nation.'" *International Journal of Media and Cultural Politics* 5, no. 1 & 2 (2009): 39–54. DOI: 10.1386/macp.5.1-2.39_1.

Arcieri, Tony. *Twitter*, September 19, 2020. https://twitter.com/bascule/status/1307440596668182528?s=20.

Bethesda Game Studios. https://bethesdagamestudios.com.

Brittain, Julie, and Marguerite Mackenzie. "Umâyichîs." In *Sky Loom: Native American Myth, Story, and Song*, 379–98. Lincoln: University of Nebraska Press, 2014.

Brooks, Lisa. "Awikhigawôgan: Mapping the Genres of Indigenous Writing in the Network of Relations." In *The Common Pot: The Recovery of Native Space in the Northeast*, 219–45. Minneapolis: University of Minnesota Press, 2008.

Byrd, Jodi A. "Beast of America: Sovereignty and the Wildness of Objects." *The South Atlantic Quarterly* 117, no. 3 (July 2018): 599–615. DOI: 10.1215/00382876-6942183.

———. "Tribal 2.0: Digital Natives, Political Players, and the Power of Stories." *Studies in American Indian Literatures* 26, no. 2 (2014): 55–64. doi: 10.5250/studamerindilite.26.2.0055.

Capcom. *Super Street Fighter II*. Arcade, 1993.

Carter, Asa Earl. *The Education of Little Tree*. New York: Delacorte Press, 1976.

Chang, Edmond Y. "Queergaming." In *Queer Game Studies*, edited by Bonnie Ruberg and Adrienne Shaw, 15–23. Minneapolis: University of Minnesota Press, 2017.

Cho, Jaee, Carmit T. Tadmor, and Michael W. Morris. "Are All Diversity Ideologies Creatively Equal? The Diverging Consequences of Colorblindness, Multiculturalism, and Polyculturalism." *Journal of Cross-Cultural Psychology* 49, no. 9 (2018): 1376–1401. DOI: 10.1177/0022022118793528.

Data USA. "Computer Programmers." https://datausa.io/profile/soc/computer-programmers#demographics.

Dillon, Grace L. "Imagining Indigenous Futurisms." In *Walking the Clouds: An Anthology of Indigenous Science Fiction*, edited by Grace L. Dillon. Sun Tracks, 1–12. Tuscon: University of Arizona Press, 2012.

Driskill, Qwo-Li, Chris Finley, Brian Joseph Gilley, and Scott Lauria Morgensen. "The Revolution Is for Everyone: Imagining an Emancipatory Future through Queer Indigenous Critical Theories." In *Queer Indigenous Studies: Critical Interventions in Theory, Politics, and Literature*, edited by Qwo-Li Driskill, Chris Finley, Brian Joseph Gilley, and Scott Lauria Morgensen, 211–21. Tuscon: The University of Arizona Press, 2011.

Estrada, Gabriel S. "Native Avatars, Online Hubs, and Urban Indian Literature." *Studies in American Indian Literatures* 23, no. 2 (2011): 48–70. https://www.muse.jhu.edu/article/445200.

FromSoftware. *Dark Souls*. PC, 2011.

Gaertner, David. "Indigenous in Cyberspace: CyberPowWow, God's Lake Narrows, and the Contours of Online Indigenous Territory." *American Indian Culture and Research Journal* 39, no. 4 (2015): 55–78. DOI: 10.17953/aicrj.39.4.gaertner.

Guerrilla Games. *Horizon: Zero Dawn*. PlayStation 4, 2017.

Hall, Leslie D., and James Mountain Chief Sanderville. "United Sugpiaq Alutiiq (USA) Video Game: Preserving Traditional Knowledge, Culture, and Language." *Educational Technology* 49, no. 6 (2009): 20–24.

Harris, Cheryl I. "Whiteness as Property." *Harvard Law Review* 106, no. 8 (June 1993): 1707–91. DOI: 10.2307/1341787.
Hawley, Elizabeth S. "James Luna and the Paradoxically Present Vanishing Indian." *Contemporaneity: Historical Presence in Visual Culture* 5, no. 1 (2016): 5–26. DOI: 10.5195/contemp.2016.170.
Heron, Michael James, Pauline Belford, and Ayse Goker. "Sexism in the Circuitry: Female Participation in Male-Dominated Popular Computer Culture." *SIGCAS Computers and Society* 44, no. 4 (November 2014): 18–29. DOI: 10.1145/2695577.2695582.
id Software. *Doom*. MS-DOS, 1993.
———. *Doom (2016)*. PC, 2016.
———. *Doom Eternal*. PC, 2020.
———. *Quake*. MS-DOS, 1996.
———. *Wolfenstein 3D*. MS-DOS, 1992.
International Game Developers Association. "Developer Satisfaction Survey," November 20, 2019. https://s3-us-east-2.amazonaws.com/igda-website/wp-content/uploads/2020/01/29093706/IGDA-DSS-2019_Summary-Report_Nov-20-2019.pdf.
Irrational Games. *BioShock Infinite*. Xbox 360, 2013.
Jones, Stephen Graham. *After the People Lights Have Gone Off*. Chicago: Dark House Press, 2014.
———. *Ledfeather*. Tuscaloosa: FC2, 2008.
Kojima Productions. http://www.kojimaproductions.jp/en/.
Konami. *Metal Gear Solid*. PlayStation, 1998.
Lameman, Beth Aileen, Jason E. Lewis, and Skawennati Fragnito. "Skins 1.0: A Curriculum for Designing Games with First Nations Youth." In *Proceedings of the International Academic Conference on the Future of Game Design and Technology*, 105–12. New York: Association for Computing Machinery, 2010.
LaPensée, Elizabeth. *Survivance*. 2011. survivance.org.
———. "Survivance among Social Impact Games." *Loading...* 8, no. 13 (2014): 43–60.
———. http://www.elizabethlapensee.com.

Loft, Steven. "Introduction: Decolonizing the 'Web.'" In *Coded Territories: Tracing Indigenous Pathways in New Media Art*, edited by Steven Loft and Kerry Swanson, xv–xvii. Calgary: University of Calgary Press, 2014.

Maskêgon-Iskwêw, Âhasiw. "Talk Indian to Me #4: Speaking Spider Languages." *Ghostkeeper*, 1996. https://ghostkeeper.gruntarchives.org/publication-mix-magazine-talk-indian-to-me-4.html.

Midway Games. *Mortal Kombat 3*. Arcade, 1995.

Morrison, Toni. *Beloved*. New York: Vintage Books, 1987.

Moulthrop, Stuart. "Online Response to 'Genre Trouble.'" In *First Person: New Media as Story, Performance, and Game*, edited by Noah Wardrip-Fruin and Pat Harrigan 47–48. Cambridge: MIT Press, 2004.

Mystique. *Custer's Revenge*. Atari 2600, 1982.

Nintendo. *Super Mario Bros*. Nintendo Entertainment System, 1985.

Quantic Dream. https://www.quanticdream.com/en.

Rael, Patrick. "Why Do We Argue about Games with Socially Difficult Themes?" *BoardGameGeek*, April 25, 2017. https://boardgamegeek.com/blogpost/64810/why-do-we-argue-over-games-socially-difficult-them.

Randall, Dave. "The Tall Tale of Little Tree and the Cherokee Who Was Really a Klansman." *The Independent*, September 1, 2002. https://www.independent.co.uk/news/media/the-tall-tale-of-little-tree-and-the-cherokee-who-was-really-a-klansman-175400.html.

Retro Gamer Team. "John Romero." *Retro Gamer*, January 17, 2014. https://www.retrogamer.net/profiles/developer/john-romero/.

Rickard, Jolene. "Sovereignty: A Line in the Sand." In *Strong Hearts: Native American Visions and Voices*, edited by Nancy Ackerman and Peggy Roalf, 51–61. New York: Aperture Foundation, 1995.

Rifkin, Mark. *The Erotics of Sovereignty: Queer Native Writing in the Era of Self-Determination*. Minneapolis: University of Minnesota Press, 2012.

Romero, John. *Twitter,* February 21, 2016. https://twitter.com/romero/status/701530383863644161.
Schilling, Chris. "The Making of Undertale." *PC Gamer,* May 5, 2018. https://www.pcgamer.com/the-making-of-undertale/.
Sega. *Sonic the Hedgehog.* Sega Genesis, 1991.
———. *Sonic the Hedgehog* 2. Sega Genesis, 1992.
Sega AM2. *Virtua Fighter.* Arcade, 1993.
Silko, Leslie Marmon. *Ceremony*. New York: Penguin Books, 1977.
Skins 5.0. *He Ao Hou: A New World.* PC, 2017.
Skins. "Skins 5.0." http://skins.abtec.org/skins5.0/.
Swain, Molly, and Chelsea Vowel. "Métis in Space (S.3 EP#8) – Z Nation 'We Were Nowhere Near the Grand Canyon.'" *Indian & Cowboy.* https://www.indianandcowboy.com/episodes/2016/9/22/mtis-in-space-s3-ep-8-z-nation-we-were-nowhere-near-the-grand-canyon.
Thunderbird Strike. PC, 2017.
Toby Fox. *Undertale.* PC, 2015.
Todd, Loretta. "Aboriginal Narratives in Cyberspace." In *Immersed in Technology: Art and Virtual Environments,* edited by Mary Anne Moser and Douglas MacLeod, 179–94. Cambridge: MIT Press, 1996.
Tuck, Eve, and K. Wayne Yang. "Decolonization Is Not a Metaphor." *Decolonization: Indigeneity, Education & Society* 1, no. 1 (2012): 1–40.
Upper One Games. *Never Alone (Kisima Iŋŋitchuŋa).* PlayStation 4, 2014.
Urban Indian Health Commission. "Invisible Tribes: Urban Indians and Their Health in a Changing World." *Robert Wood Johnson Foundation,* 2007. https://www2.census.gov/cac/nac/meetings/2015-10-13/invisible-tribes.pdf.
Vizenor, Gerald. "Postindian Warriors." In *Manifest Manners: Postindian Warriors of Survivance,* 1–44. Hanover: University Press of New England, 1994.
Wisdom of the Elders. "Woodrow Morrison, Jr., Haida - 2 of 2." *Vimeo,* July 29, 2013. https://vimeo.com/71304938. DOI: 10.1080/14623520601056240.

Wolfe, Patrick. "Settler Colonialism and the Elimination of the Native." *Journal of Genocide Research* 8, no. 4 (2006): 387–409.

Break (Up, Down, Out, In) DH and Black Futurities

16

Breaking and (Re)Making

Ravynn K. Stringfield

The interesting thing about the digital humanities is that it is exceptionally fragile. As Christy Hyman notes in "Black Scholars and Disciplinary Gatekeeping," digital humanists often spend their time gatekeeping and policing what "counts" as digital humanities rather than use the digital to dream up new futures. Black DH, or digital humanities that is concerned with and uses the methodologies, praxes and epistemologies of Black intellectual thought, uses the preoccupation of these gatekeepers to slip into the cracks of the code and break it apart.

As Andre Brock notes in *Distributed Blackness,* much of the digital humanities canon has done its best to separate Black people from the digital, as if these two things together are counterintuitive, when in fact, Brock argues, they are inherently intertwined.[1] Black digital humanists such as Brock, Jessica Marie Johnson, Catherine Knight Steele and others use their work as opportunities to showcase how Black people use the digital as extensions of Black cultural traditions. When Steele writes about the digital barber shop, she draws on the long tradition of African diasporic oral tradition that evolves and manifests on-

1 André L. Brock, *Distributed Blackness: African American Cybercultures* (New York: New York University Press, 2020).

line. When Johnson writes of "alter egos and infinite literacies," she evokes the practice of developing personas, which while we attribute primarily to the digital age of avatars and profile pictures, can be attributed to the multiple personas which populate hip hop culture. Black people regularly find a multitude of ways to reinvent ourselves, and the digital is simply the newest tool in expressing our infinite selves. Brock aptly writes that when we, Black people, go online and perform Blackness, it is for the simple fact that we enjoy being Black.

And that, in and of itself, breaks digital humanities.

Like many other forms of humanities, *digital* humanities is no different in its desire to strip Black people of our humanity, despite its very name. In the same way that Black digital humanities recodes various practices of Black culture in the digital, digital humanities as a field is also able to, and does, replicate various modes of harm. Gatekeeping is one of these practices that transcends fields, but master/slave binaries continue to exist in metadata languages and dismissing Black digital humanities theoretical work is prevalent, just to name a few.

Black DH and the scholars and artists and activists who engage in Black digital humanities practices continue to create and theorize while the gatekeepers fuss over boundaries. Boundaries that we jump over with interdisciplinary projects, like those of Marisa Parham's remixing digital essays; with communal effort, like that of the Digital Alchemists, who support each other in their (digital) intellectual pursuits; with a mass of digital content created and curated by Black graduate students with the express intention of leading more and more students of color into and through the Academy.[2]

---

2 See Marisa Parham, ".Break .Dance," *sx archipelagos*, July 10, 2019, http://smallaxe.net/sxarchipelagos/issue03/parham/parham.html; Yomaira C. Figueroa and Jessica Marie Johnson, eds., *Taller Electric Marronage*, https://www.electricmarronage.com/; Kim Gallon, *Black Press Research Collective*, http://blackpressresearchcollective.org/; Allanté Whitmore, *BLK + IN GRAD SCHOOL*, https://www.blkingradschool.com/; and Tiffany Lee and Autumn Adia Griffin, *Blackademia*, http://www.readblackademia.com/; and on and on.

Some digital humanists are coders; some are breakers and (re)makers. Others use the digital humanities to design new futures for us. The ethical concern I have about the digital humanities is that too often projects exist simply because *they can,* with no regard for the potential harm it may do. Black digital humanists' projects often center humanity and approach digital tools with an ethos of care.

My hope for the future(s) is that digital humanities will look to the practices and ethos of Black digital humanists for ways to extend their own ethos of care in their projects. My hope is that the norm will no longer be to exact boundaries, but to observe what has been done to break those parameters and *why* it was necessary to break them. My hope is that Black digital humanities' innovation and further breaking is not contingent upon white digital humanists ignoring, dismissing or even stealing the labor of digital humanists of color. My hope is that our future(s) as a field is not contingent upon further erasure.

This is a vision that is informed by the Black radical tradition, which in turn informs Black digital humanists, who are often Afrofuturists. But futures, as Afrofuturists know, are not created without a firm understanding and appreciation of histories. Black cultural (and in this case, digital) innovation is, and has often been, a product of extreme duress.

That does not mean it needs to be.

Bibliography

Brock, André L. *Distributed Blackness: African American Cybercultures.* New York: New York University Press, 2020.

Figueroa, Yomaira C., and Jessica Marie Johnson, eds. *Taller Electric Marronage.* https://www.electricmarronage.com/.

Gallon, Kim. *Black Press Research Collective.* http://blackpressresearchcollective.org/.

Lee, Tiffany, and Autumn Adia Griffin. *Blackademia.* http://www.readblackademia.com/.

Parham, Marisa. ".Break .Dance." *sx archipelagos,* July 10, 2019. http://smallaxe.net/sxarchipelagos/issue03/parham/parham.html.

Whitmore, Allanté. *BLK + IN GRAD SCHOOL.* https://www.blkingradschool.com/.

17

Black Scholars and Disciplinary Gatekeeping

Christy Hyman

Afrofuturism is here defined as responsible storytelling, a challenge to remember a past that instructs the present and can build a future.
—De Witt Douglas Kilgore[1]

(I think of this as a kind of provocation as I imagine Black Futurities alongside the material realities of Black Scholarship within the Digital Humanities.)

Scholars enrolled in graduate programs go through a process where faculty supervisors decide if thesis/dissertation topics are rigorous enough for effective completion.[2] If a topic is compel-

1 Douglas Kilgore, "Afrofuturism," in *The Oxford Handbook of Science Fiction,* ed. Rob Latham (Oxford: Oxford University Press, 2014), 563.

2 P. Gabrielle Foreman, *Twitter,* January 4, 2020, https://twitter.com/profgabrielle/status/1213268486258135041?s=20: "Barbara Christian Was Told by Her English Dept Colleagues She Couldn't Write a 1st Book on Black Women Writers. Don't These Folks Get Tired of Having Us Prove Them so Dramatically Wrong over and Again. @viet_t_nguyen. #MLA2020 https://T.co/IEK1e3uAFX." In this tweet Foreman points out how scholars who have gone on to do groundbreaking work were initially discouraged by their programs to pursue their research agendas because

ling but lacks the available sources to respond to the historical questions posed then the student is advised to seek a topic that has a trail of sources from which the student can draw on for historical interpretation. The central tenet of the historical profession requires a critical engagement with records from the past. However, Black scholars engaged in recovery projects whose central questions relate to silenced legacies are forced to abandon those projects that reveal a dearth of archival sources.[3] In this way digital recovery can act as a prescriptive allowing the scholar to build projects that are based on different methods of verifying information that may not be recognized as rigorous by the discipline.

Accessing the traces of Black life in archival sources, noticing the silences is a key method in historical recovery work.

Humanist scholars "are the long-recognized monitors of cultural memory" and "exposing the richness" of the Black past is the "office" of the Black scholar engaged in recovery work."[4] The results from these technologies of recovery represent artifacts of digital cultural memory, creating avenues for the survival of cultural narratives for future generations to access.[5]

---

they were rooted in hidden and obscured histories of people historically marginalized.

3 Martha C. Howell and Walter Prevenier, *From Reliable Sources: An Introduction to Historical Methods* (Ithaca: Cornell University Press, 2001). Howell and Prevenier assert that the "central paradox of the historical profession is that historians are prisoners of sources that are not always reliable but skilled readings of those sources can yield meaningful stories about the past and the human relationship to the past." However, it still remains that sources documenting the Black lives in history are often very problematic—Jessica Marie Johnson reminds us of the violence of the past and that "the brutality of black codes [...] created a devastating archive." See Jessica Marie Johnson, "Markup Bodies: Black [life] Studies and Slavery [death] Studies at the Digital Crossroads," *Social Text* 36, no. 4 (2018): 58.

4 See Jerome McGann, *A New Republic of Letters: Memory and Scholarship in the Age of Digital Reproduction* (Cambridge: Harvard University Press, 2014), 1, 21.

5 Gallon rightfully asserts that Black digital humanities projects represent technologies of recovery. See Kim Gallon, "Making a Case for the Black Digital Humanities," in *Debates in the Digital Humanities*, eds. Matt Gold

So the hope is recover the stories of Black folks past and present whose experiences have been rendered invisible—but when the discipline confers legitimacy only on those stories with a trail of print sources that puts the Black scholar in a position where they must make a fateful choice:

Abandon the compelling story that honors Black historical agents dishonored by a colonialist, hegemonic archive?

Or...

Engage in a project of subversion, disrupting the methodological traditions that the discipline holds so dear.

And when the scholar goes rogue and chooses to recover these stories that appear often as traces, an unyielding commitment to the story is essential. Every step of the way the importance of telling the story takes precedence over everything. This sort of disruption destabilizes all those things naturalized by the discipline that recognizes only certain historical actors, events, forms of knowledge as rigorous scholarly research agendas. These stories that Black scholars are telling are those that Christina Sharpe has recognized as having been "swept up and animated by the afterlives of slavery," these are the stories that must be told as they have survived despite an "insistent violence and negation."[6] This is the inheritance of Black scholars with a view to future-oriented diasporic histories that animate a culture of survival.

---

and Lauren Klein (Minneapolis: University of Minnesota Press, 2016), 42–49, https://dhdebates.gc.cuny.edu/read/untitled/section/fa10e2e1-0c3d-4519-a958-d823aac989eb. A fine example of this important digital recovery work is the Colored Conventions Project which brings to digital life the buried history of collective Black mobilization in the nineteenth century for undergraduate and graduate students, researchers across disciplines, high school teachers, and community members interested in the history of church, educational and entrepreneurial engagement. See *Colored Conventions Project*, https://coloredconventions.org/.

6 See Christina Elizabeth Sharpe, *In the Wake: On Blackness and Being* (Durham: Duke University Press, 2017), 12–15.

Bibliography

Colored Conventions Project. *https://coloredconventions.org/.*

Foreman, P. Gabrielle. *Twitter,* January 4, 2020, https://twitter.com/profgabrielle/status/1213268486258135041?s=20.

Gallon, Kim. "Making a Case for the Black Digital Humanities." In *Debates in the Digital Humanities,* edited by Matt Gold and Lauren Klein, 42–49. Minneapolis: University of Minnesota Press, 2016. https://dhdebates.gc.cuny.edu/read/untitled/section/fa10e2e1-0c3d-4519-a958-d823aac989eb.

Howell, Martha C., and Walter Prevenier. *From Reliable Sources: An Introduction to Historical Methods.* Ithaca: Cornell University Press, 2001.

Johnson, Jessica Marie. "Markup Bodies: Black [life] Studies and Slavery [death] Studies at the Digital Crossroads." *Social Text* 36, no. 4 (2018): 57–79. DOI: 10.1215/01642472-7145658.

Kilgore, Douglas. "Afrofuturism." In *The Oxford Handbook of Science Fiction,* edited by Rob Latham, 561–72. Oxford: Oxford University Press, 2014.

McGann, Jerome. *A New Republic of Letters: Memory and Scholarship in the Age of Digital Reproduction.* Cambridge: Harvard University Press, 2014.

Sharpe, Christina Elizabeth. *In the Wake: On Blackness and Being.* Durham: Duke University Press, 2017.

18

Dr. Nyanzi's Protests: Silences, Futures, and the Present

Nalubega Ross

In the wake of the Kentucky grand jury's refusal to indict the killers of Breonna Taylor, Dr. Tressie McMillan-Cottom wrote a piece contemplating Breonna Taylor's vision board; her dreams for her future. To quote Dr. McMillan-Cottom, "Some of us are literally mapping above ground railroads [...] something that can feel more like freedom than where we have been predicted to die."[1] To imagine a Black digital future is a delicate dance; one that requires that we attend to the past and pay attention in the present. As Dr. McMillan-Cottom says, many Black people are mapping an aboveground railroad to freedom. Black people have been predicted to die whether they live in the United States or are outside the United States. And as we contend with the digital humanities' past and imagine a Black future, I present the poetry and imprisonment of Dr. Stella Nyanzi, to illustrate what mapping an above ground railroad looks like for those outside the United States and offer a new way of thinking about a digital Black future.

1 Tressie McMillan-Cottom, "Post-it Dreams," *Medium*, September 24, 2020, https://medium.com/@tressiemcphd/post-it-dreams-9d12095a7342.

In her poem, "Political Prisoner," Dr. Nyanzi presents her prison numbers from the two years she was imprisoned, 2017 and 2018.[2] Dr. Nyanzi was imprisoned for cyber harassment by the president of Uganda in 2017 and once again in 2018 for the same charge.[3] The charge for cyber harassment was a poem she wrote, referring to the said president as *matako* (pair of buttocks).[4] The poem that led to her arrest was digitally written, on Facebook. However, "Political Prisoner" was written while she was on remand at Luzira Maximum Security Prison. In this particular poem Dr. Nyanzi reaffirms that she will continue her poetry to fight against a dictatorship.

In reexamining the digital past of the humanities, and the power that runs through the digital past and how that affects the digital present and the digital future, we must consider who continues to be silenced in the ever present digital. Though Dr. Nyanzi's resistance began online, her use of poetry as a form of resistance continued despite her imprisonment. But without access to the digital she had to smuggle her handwritten poems out of prison. Despite the government's attempt to silence her, Dr. Nyanzi continues to map a route to freedom even while her body is behind bars and she doesn't have access to the "digital."

I wonder, will the letters that were smuggled out of prison ever be found in any archive? Will future scholars be able to visit an archive somewhere and interact with the poems Dr. Nyanzi

---

2 Stella Nyanzi, *No Roses from My Mouth* (Uganda: Ubuntu Reading Group, 2020), 16

3 "PEN SA Condemns Re-Arrest in Uganda of Dr Stella Nyanzi," *PEN South Africa*, November 14, 2018, http://pensouthafrica.co.za/pen-sa-condemns-re-arrest-in-uganda-of-dr-stella-nyanzi/.

4 "Museveni matako nyo! Ebyo byeyayogedde e Masindi yabadde ayogera lutako. I mean, seriously, when buttocks shake and jiggle, while the legs are walking, do you hear other body parts complaining? When buttocks produce shit, while the brain is thinking, is anyone shocked? When buttocks fart, are we surprised? That is what buttocks do. They shake, jiggle, shit and fart. Museveni is just another pair of buttocks. Rather than being shocked by what the matako said in Masindi, Ugandans should be shocked that we allowed these buttocks to continue leading our country. Matako butako." Stella Nyanzi, *Facebook*, January 27, 2017, https://www.facebook.com/stella.nyanzi/posts/10154878225000053.

wrote and learn of the stories of the multiple men and women who worked to smuggle these letters out of Luzira prison to be published? Or given the precariousness of Dr. Nyanzi's activism is it best to keep her conspirators a secret; creating a necessary silence in the archive with the understanding that memories of the oppressors are long and brutal? Or is this knowledge, as Tuck and Yang argue,[5] one that the academy and digital humanists do not deserve?

In thinking about Dr. Nyanzi, her resistance, and her interaction with the digital, both with her handwritten poetry and her use of hashtags to get her message across,[6] Dr. Nyanzi offers us an alternative genealogy of digital humanities. One where though some things are born digital, real life means that in many instances, they have to leave the digital realm to return another time. As we consider power and reimagine the future of digital humanities, it is important to consider that there are places where even minimal computing is not available, and we must prepare a room within the digital humanities for movements that though born digital move fluidly in and outside the digital. In thinking about this fluid movement both in and out of the digital, attention must be paid to what is considered "digital" and how those of us predicted to die use multiple modalities, from poetry (as was the case of Dr. Nyanzi) to post-it notes (as was the case of Breonna Taylor).

As Hyman points out, digital humanities often spends its time policing what "counts" and I would add, "who" counts. As we look towards a new future for the digital humanities, continuing to dismiss Black scholars, especially the work of Black scholars that identify as women, at a time when the world is trying to reimagine a new and equitable world, means that digital humanities will continue to reproduce over and over again the same inequities that we see today. And in this reproduction, the

5 Eve Tuck and K. Wayne Yang, "Unbecoming Claims: Pedagogies of Refusal in Qualitative Research," *Qualitative Inquiry* 20, no. 6 (2014): 813.

6 Wairimu Muriithi, "Review: No Roses from My Mouth," *GenderIT*, March 14, 2020, https://genderit.org/articles/review-no-roses-my-mouth.

necessary recovery work that Hyman notes will be stalled or at worst completely erased.

I use Dr. Nyanzi's story because she refuses to be silenced. And Black digital humanists too have not been silenced. But the use of Dr. Nyanzi's story is not just to tell her story, it serves two things: (1) As we reconsider the old genealogies of the past and imagine new futures, we cannot forget the present. And the present, as it currently is, is in dire need of reshaping. And to reshape the present we must diligently attend to the different modalities those most oppressed among us are using to tell our stories. Because those different modalities offer a counter narrative, and a new way to imagine a Black digital future. (2) Dr. Nyanzi's story is a reminder of how much of the digital humanities is built on instruments of surveillance. Her story illustrates quite clearly how digital tools are consistently used by countries worldwide to silence the voice of dissidents. As we imagine a new digital future, let us not forget those who are routinely silenced and whose physical bodies are harmed because of their work in the digital. Audre Lorde reminds us, "The master's tools will never dismantle the master's house." We have looked at the house that Father Busa created. And Black scholars, Black makers, Black Dreamers, Black digital humanists, have given us a very clear and easy-to-follow blueprint for a new house, we simply have to look at their tools. It is time we made that house a reality.

Bibliography

McMillan-Cottom, Tressie. "Post-it Dreams." *Medium*, September 24, 2020. https://medium.com/@tressiemcphd/post-it-dreams-9d12095a7342.

Muriithi, Wairimu. "Review: No Roses from My Mouth." *GenderIT*, March 14, 2020, https://genderit.org/articles/review-no-roses-my-mouth.

Nyanzi, Stella. *Facebook*, January 27, 2017. https://www.facebook.com/stella.nyanzi/posts/10154878225000053.

———. *No Roses from My Mouth*. Uganda: Ubuntu Reading Group, 2020.

"PEN SA Condemns Re-Arrest in Uganda of Dr Stella Nyanzi." *PEN South Africa*, November 14, 2018. http://pensouthafrica.co.za/pen-sa-condemns-re-arrest-in-uganda-of-dr-stella-nyanzi/.

Tuck, Eve, and K. Wayne Yang. "Unbecoming Claims: Pedagogies of Refusal in Qualitative Research." *Qualitative Inquiry* 20, no. 6 (2014): 811–18. DOI: 10.1177/1077800414530265.

19

Against Lenticular Modeling: Missives on Locating Blackness from the WhatEvery1Says Project

Jamal Russell

In his 2014 book *Habeas Viscus,* Alexander Weheliye describes Blackness as designating "a changing system of unequal power structures that apportion and delimit which humans can lay claim to full human status and which humans cannot."[1] Kim Gallon employs this definition as a point of reference from which she argues that:

> [A]ny connection between humanity and the digital therefore requires an investigation into how computational processes might reinforce the notion of humanity developed out of racializing systems, even as they foster efforts to assemble or otherwise build alternative human modalities.[2]

1 Alexander Weheliye, *Habeas Viscus: Racializing Assemblages, Biopolitics, and Black Feminist Theories of the Human* (Durham: Duke University Press, 2014), 3.

2 Kim Gallon, "Making a Case for the Black Digital Humanities," in *Debates in the Digital Humanities,* eds. Matthew K. Gold and Lauren F. Klein (Minneapolis: University of Minnesota Press, 2019), 44.

What is implied by both Weheliye and Gallon is that Blackness is not a discrete thing, but an ever changing social relation imposed upon the bodies of Black people that can be manipulated toward a number of ends depending on context and objective. From this point, I argue that a future for Blackness in the disciplinary sphere of digital humanities must account for the various valences of this social relation, as opposed to indulging in what Tara McPherson terms a *lenticular* logic. McPherson uses the term lenticular, referring to the lenses that allow one to see different images printed on objects such as post cards as one rotates or moves around them, to describe a cultural logic that "makes simultaneously viewing the various images contained on one card nearly impossible."[3] The effects of such a logic within DH become particularly important when considering the goals of modeling as a DH method; modeling, in the words of Willard McCarty, is "an explicit, delimited conception of the world" that "instantiates an attempt to capture the dynamic, experimental aspects of a phenomenon rather than to freeze it into an ahistorical abstraction."[4]

Based on my experience with various modeling methods, particularly topic modeling, during my five-year tenure as a member of 4Humanities's WhatEvery1Says (WE1S) project, I find that due to a lack of consideration for the contexts and uses of language through which the racial dynamics Weheliye and Gallon describe above, many models instantiate the very ahistorical abstractions McCarty warns against as they pertain to Blackness. I call such models lenticular models, arguing that they present data visualizations to their viewers that are predicated on the disarticulation of social and technical categories. Furthermore, these models represent their data without regard to the contexts within which their constitutive corpora were themselves collected, or the contexts within which the model

3 Tara McPherson, "Why Are the Digital Humanities So White? or Thinking the Histories of Race and Computation," in *Debates in the Digital Humanities*, eds. Gold and Klein, 144.

4 Willard McCarty, *Humanities Computing* (Basingstoke: Palgrave MacMillan, 2005), 22–23.

was created. This piece draws on my experiences with the WE1S project to examine how lenticular models are the product of a lack of consideration for how DH modeling methods can render specific valences of Blackness invisible within topic models. This piece also places these experiences and concepts alongside work done by DH theorists and scholars such as Johanna Drucker, Katherine Bode, and WE1S project director Alan Liu regarding the representational power of corpus collection and modeling to begin sketching out what a non-lenticular DH modeling practice would entail. Such a model, I argue, would have to make the act of relating the social to the technical a foundational aspect of the modeling workflow, encompassing not just the generation of the modeling interface, but acts such as corpus collection, stopword list creation, and tokenization as well.

McPherson argues that the lenticular not only describes the post-1960s United States' racial climate, particularly as it pertains to the rise of an identity politics that increasingly focused on the concerns of particular identity groups at the expense of collective identification and action (intentionally or otherwise), but also the impulses toward modularity, encapsulation, and simplicity McPherson derives from the development history of the UNIX programming language and sees as embedded in our computational culture. In McPherson's words, "a lenticular logic is a logic of the fragment or the chunk, a way of seeing the world as discrete modules or nodes, a mode that suppresses relation and context."[5] I find that there is a fundamental connection between McPherson's insights and Johanna Drucker's longstanding interest in representational and non-representational modeling in DH contexts. For Drucker, the former is defined by a unidirectional relationship between data and display, wherein the data precede the display and the display both "stands for the data" and is "generally taken to be a presentation, a statement (of fact, or argument, or process), rather than a representation (surrogate) produced by a complex process," namely the interconnected cultural, technical, and historical conditions of its pro-

5 McPherson, "Why Are the Digital Humanities So White?" 144.

duction as data and/or display.[6] The latter constitutes Drucker's corrective to this condition in that non-representational models would "use graphical means to produce interpretive work using visual argument structures such as contradiction, ambiguity, parallax, and point of view that are fundamentally hermeneutic in character."[7] In this context, the means of presentation are not occluding operations, but rather become the foundations of an interpretive poetics, the operations of which must be modeled as a means of integrating traditionally humanistic approaches with the computational methods of DH. In Drucker's case, this is exemplified by the 3DH (Three-Dimensional/Digital Humanities) project hosted at the University of Hamburg in 2016, where she developed many of the ideas underpinning her nonrepresentational modeling concept (which themselves were outgrowths of long-standing concerns of her scholarly research and her artistic practice as a book artist). To put it another way, Drucker's proposal is her answer to the dilemma presented by McPherson: a non-representational, and thus non-lenticular, modeling approach that allows one to "capture the dynamic, experimental aspects of a phenomenon" through the model's conception, design, and use.[8]

Topic modeling, as a means of presenting a delimited conception of the corpus modeled, has many of the traits of a representational model, in Drucker's parlance, and thus those of a

6 Johanna Drucker, "Non-representational Approaches to Modeling Interpretation in a Graphical Environment," *Digital Scholarship in the Humanities* 33, no. 2 (2018): 249.

7 Ibid.

8 Although outside of the scope of this essay, one could articulate a number of resonances between Drucker's non-representational modeling practice, and the non-representational theory that has developed in Human Geography via the work of researchers such as Nigel Thrift and Tim Ingold. In particular, both Drucker and the researchers noted share an interest in contesting, or at least examining, representation's centrality to analyses of cultural practice. See, for example, Nigel Thrift, *Non-Representational Theory: Space, Politics, Affect* (London: Routledge, 2007); and Tim Ingold, *Being Alive: Essays on Movement, Knowledge, and Description* (London: Routledge, 2011).

lenticular model as well. Per Ted Underwood, topic modeling is a means of "extrapolating backward from a collection of documents to infer the discourses ('topics') that could have generated them."[9] This is achieved by using topic modeling packages such as MALLET, along with interfaces used to visualize one's results in specific fashions, to convert text into bags of words that are "vectorized for use in a variety of black-box procedures developed by systems engineers and computer scientists."[10] The procedure in question for topic modeling is computer scientist David Blei's Latent Dirichlet Allocation (LDA) method, which intuits as a first principle that documents exhibit multiple topics that can be categorized by sorting said documents according to the proportion of words they contain that are representative of a given topic.

The issue with topic modeling as a humanistic method, and certainly as a means of examining Blackness in DH contexts, can be broken down into two components. One component is that, when one uses topic modeling packages to generate a model of a given corpus, there are a number of decisions made throughout the process that will determine how the model is shaped, but are not themselves modeled. Technically, this not only entails determining how many topics the model will produce, but also encompasses anything that falls under the umbrella of "pre-processing": the tokenization process that breaks down documents into bags of words and eliminates all punctuation and upper-case letters from the corpus, curating a stopword list (or simply using one of the many pre-produced stopword lists floating around online) and using it to remove words such as articles and prepositions that do not on their face resolve into the types of topics LDA would intuit in an article, lemmatizing words so that first-person nouns and present-tense verbs stand in for all

9 Ted Underwood, "Topic Modeling Made Just Simple Enough," *The Stone and the Shell*, April 7, 2012, https://tedunderwood.com/2012/04/07/topic-modeling-made-just-simple-enough/.

10 R.C. Alvarado, "Digital Humanities and the Great Project: Why We Should Operationalize Everything — and Study Those Who Are Doing So Now," in *Debates in the Digital Humanities*, eds. Gold and Klein, 77.

versions of a given token, and stemming words by reducing them to their root forms. This process is not represented in a topic model apart from the final results of the modeling process itself, and it is this issue that animates Drucker's discussions of DH modeling practices. The other component appends to this problem, namely that these decisions entail a previous decision regarding what the most basic unit of analysis will be. Most often, this is a singular entity of semantic consequence such as the word, and anything that is not a semantically consequential word potentially representative of a topic must be treated as noise and stopped out, never to be intentionally included in the model. This is a good practice if one wants to model discrete objects or data points, to remain in the realm of the lenticular, but makes the modeling of social relations nigh-impossible.

The goal of a non-lenticular model as it pertains to depictions of Blackness, then, should be akin to how Fred Moten understands the workings of glossy blacks in his 2018 book *The Universal Machine*. The final essay of this volume, "Chromatic Saturation," is rooted in a dialogue between Ad Reinhardt and Cecil Taylor conducted as part of a larger forum on the topic of "Black" for a 1967 issue of *Arts/Canada* magazine. Reinhardt, known for the accented matte black canvases he produced between 1954 and 1967, mentioned during the interview that he was not fond of glossy blacks because they were "unstable," "surreal," and because it "reflects all the social activity that's going on in a room."[11] Moten adds "necessarily social" to the quote and contrasts Reinhardt's view with that of Taylor, who understood Blackness to be "aesthetic sociality, of and from the eternal, internal, and subterranean alien/nation of black things in their unregulatable chromaticism."[12] Blackness always already implies the multiplicity, mutability, and opacity of relation, simultaneously absorbing into itself and excluding from itself to extremes

11 Ad Reinhardt, "Black as Symbol and Concept," in *Art-as-Art: The Selected Writings of Ad Reinhardt*, ed. Barbara Rose (New York: The Viking Press, 1975), 87. See also Fred Moten, *The Universal Machine* (Durham: Duke University Press, 2018), 162.

12 Ibid.

at both ends, qualities that can be emphasized and deemphasized depending on how the Blackness is contextualized. To not model relation is to attend to none of these fundamental qualities of Blackness, and consequently, is to not model Blackness itself.[13]

My observations on this subject are the product of my five-year tenure as a member of 4Humanities's WhatEvery1Says project (WE1S). The project, beginning as a pilot project developed and spearheaded by Alan Liu at the University of California, Santa Barbara in 2013 and eventually expanding into a Mellon Foundation-funded initiative for the final three years of its lifespan between 2017 and 2020, aimed to "use digital humanities methods to study public discourse on the humanities in journalistic media and other sources at large data scales."[14] This was primarily pursued through the use of the MALLET topic modeling toolkit, with our results visualized primarily using Andrew Goldstone's DfR-Browser topic modeling interface. For the final two years of the project, I was a member, and eventually leader, of a project subgroup devoted to analyzing and articulating the connections between public-facing humanities narratives and the interests of a wide range of social groups, most notably Black Americans.

The team initially was not able to find substantive results within the models of our main corpus, which necessitated the decision to build our own corpus of minority- and LGBTQ-serving publications to be modeled and examined. When we finally built the corpus (derived largely from ProQuest's Ethnic NewsWatch and GenderWatch databases, as they were the only

13 Attending to relation also entails attending to the negation of relation and its poetics, as well. To this end, a supplement to this discussion can be found in Édouard Glissant's call for a "right to opacity" and his explication of opacity as the foundation of a relation with the Other. See Édouard Glissant, *Poetics of Relation*, trans. Betsy Wing (Ann Arbor: University of Michigan Press, 1997).

14 WhatEvery1Says Project, "The WhatEvery1Says (WE1S) Project: A Prospectus," October 10, 2017, https://we1s.ucsb.edu/about/we1s-prospectus/.

platform that allowed us to easily generate the plain text files we needed for our topic modeling workflow from their collections), we found similar results to what we found in the main corpus: no direct links between the two subjects of our study. We did not encounter *nothing*, far from it in fact, as there were many latent connections between public facing humanities narratives and the concerns of these "groups of interest" (a term I find problematic, but the necessity of referring to disparate groups defined by a wide range of ethnic, racial, classed, gendered, and sexual indicators will always involve an unavoidable measure of erasure) via a given publication's inclusion of humanistic commentary on various political and economic issues. Publications, particularly newspapers of record such as *The New York Times* and *The Washington Post* did not hesitate to call on the knowledge of humanists, and increasingly over time humanists of color, when expert opinions on ethnic or racial issues of note such as the Black Lives Matter movement were needed. What it also told the team, however, is that one of the key questions we needed to ask and answer for ourselves was not only *what* the connections between public-facing humanities narratives and the concerns of these groups of interest were, or *where* they might be located in our models, but also *why* was it so difficult for us to find anything to begin with, particularly as it concerned Blackness?

It should be telling that the group's findings reflected what we were *not* able to find as much as what we did find in our models. Many times, they had to address not merely what the model conveyed to us about our corpora, but how our topic modeling workflow produced models to begin with. We increasingly found that not only did our topic models's disarticulation of words from one another create major issues for our capacity to even discuss Blackness's presence or absence in our corpora, but even modeling words such as "Black," "African," or even "American" strictly as unigrams afforded those words the ability to appear in topics not only about race and the humanities, but topics about color, fashion, and global politics, among other subjects. This is in no way a terrible outcome (for many digital humanists, such serendipitous groupings are the intended outcome), but it becomes an issue when it occurs at the expense of a model's ability to convey the social relations constitutive of Blackness and relate them public discourses on the humanities. The problem is not merely that race appeared alongside these other subjects as Blacks signified within the model, but that the social relations that would link them together within a semi-coherent conception of the corpus's conception of Blackness did not exist. In other words, constructing and exhibiting these relations in language is ultimately not the work of unigrams by themselves, but bigrams, trigrams, hyphens, conjugation, conjunctions, and prepositions, among other para-word aspects of language that are often treated as noise by a standard topic modeling workflow.[15]

In a certain sense, our work both strived for and ran up against the limits of modeling methods such as topic modeling for thinking through not only the question of how cultural criticism can meet DH in the middle, but also discovering through iterative inquiry how data domains, Liu's term for the "ontological, epistemological, formal, and social-political-economic provenances- put more generally, contexts- in which datasets arise no matter how richly or poorly faceted,"[16] overlap and intersect with one another. A model's ability to depict such connections between and within data domains will be the purview not of lenticular practices such as topic modeling currently conceived, but of practices that are self-conscious about the means of their production and allow their users to design, for lack of a better word, their interpretations of that self-consciousness and

---

15 To this end, Jennifer DeVere Brody's examination of the myriad ways in which punctuation marks articulate, perform, and think through the affects of cultural gestures is particularly relevant to questions of how Blackness, and social relation more generally, is presented in DH text modeling practices such as topic modeling. See Jennifer DeVere Brody, *Punctuation: Art, Politics, and Play* (Durham: Duke University Press, 2008).

16 Alan Liu, "N+1: A Plea for Cross-Domain Data in the Digital Humanities," in *Debates in the Digital Humanities*, eds. Gold and Klein, 562.

the contexts within which the model and its constitutive corpora operate.

Beyond Drucker's 3DH project,, there are a number of DH approaches to modeling and presenting collections that could lead to useful non-lenticular approaches for DH research. Miriam Posner, working from the premise that "technically speaking, we frankly have not figured out how to deal with categories... that are not binary or one-dimensional or stable," writes about a number of projects that attempt to solve the dilemma she poses in "What's Next: The Radical Unrealized Potential of Digital Humanities."[17] Of particular interest is a model built by David Kim for a project about photographer Edward S. Curtis. When building a spreadsheet about Curtis's photographs of Native Americans that would later provide the data structure for the project's models, Kim acknowledged that the photographs only provided a "highly mediated and carefully constructed" view of their subjects, and thus he "turned the data visualizations back around, focusing scrutiny on Curtis himself and the Western ideology that he represented,"[18] not dissimilar to work done on the exploitative relationship between scientific knowledge and indigenous populations by Linda Tuhiwai Smith. In addition, constructing something akin to what Katherine Bode terms a "scholarly edition of a literary system" could also be of value as a non-lenticular approach to DH modeling, in that its objective is to create a "model of literary works that were published, circulated, and read — and thereby accrued meaning — in a specific historical context, constructed with reference to the history of transmission by which documentary evidence of those works is constituted."[19] In short, without the ability to model the relations instantiated by the connectors and/or the connected of language, models will remain lenticular, and Blackness will remain largely outside of DH paradigms. The decoupling of meth-

17 Miriam Posner, "What's Next: The Radical, Unrealized Potential of Digital Humanities," in *Debates in the Digital Humanities*, eds. Gold and Klein, 34.

18 Ibid., 37.

19 Katherine Bode, *A World of Fiction: Digital Collections and the Future of Literary History* (Ann Arbor: University of Michigan Press, 2018), 4.

od from theory, Tanya E. Clement observes in critiques of DH, becomes an important impulse to reverse. It is exactly in DH's modeling methods that insights about Blackness coming out of humanistic fields of inquiry that can then be a fully-realized element of DH as a discipline.

Bibliography

Alvarado, R.C. "Digital Humanities and the Great Project: Why We Should Operationalize Everything — and Study Those Who Are Doing So Now." In *Debates in the Digital Humanities,* edited by Matthew K. Gold and Lauren F. Klein, 75–82. Minneapolis: University of Minnesota Press, 2019.

Bode, Katherine. *A World of Fiction: Digital Collections and the Future of Literary History.* Ann Arbor: University of Michigan Press, 2018.

Brody, Jennifer DeVere. *Punctuation: Art, Politics, and Play.* Durham: Duke University Press, 2008.

Drucker, Johanna. "Non-representational Approaches to Modeling Interpretation in a Graphical Environment." *Digital Scholarship in the Humanities* 33, no. 2 (2018): 248–63. DOI: 10.1093/llc/fqx034.

Gallon, Kim. "Making a Case for the Black Digital Humanities." In *Debates in the Digital Humanities,* edited by Matthew K. Gold and Lauren F. Klein, 42–49. Minneapolis: University of Minnesota Press, 2019.

Glissant, Édouard. *Poetics of Relation.* Translated by Betsy Reed. Ann Arbor: University of Michigan Press, 1997.

Gold, Matthew K., and Lauren F. Klein, eds. *Debates in the Digital Humanities.* Minneapolis: University of Minnesota Press, 2016.

Ingold, Tim. *Being Alive: Essays on Movement, Knowledge, and Description.* London: Routledge, 2011.

Liu, Alan. "N+1: A Plea for Cross-Domain Data in the Digital Humanities." In *Debates in the Digital Humanities,* edited by Matthew K. Gold and Lauren F. Klein, 559–68. Minneapolis: University of Minnesota Press, 2019.

McCarty, Willard. *Humanities Computing.* Basingstoke: Palgrave MacMillan, 2005.

McPherson, Tara. "Why are the Digital Humanities So White? or Thinking the Histories of Race and Computation." In *Debates in the Digital Humanities,* edited by Matthew K.

Gold and Lauren F. Klein, 139–60. Minneapolis: University of Minnesota Press, 2019.

Moten, Fred. *The Universal Machine.* Durham: Duke University Press, 2018.

Posner, Miriam. "What's Next: The Radical, Unrealized Potential of Digital Humanities." In *Debates in the Digital Humanities,* edited by Matthew K. Gold and Lauren F. Klein, 32–41. Minneapolis: University of Minnesota Press, 2019.

Reinhardt, Ad. "Black as Symbol and Concept." In *Art-as-Art: The Selected Writings of Ad Reinhardt,* edited by Barbara Rose, 86–88. New York: The Viking Press, 1975.

Thrift, Nigel. *Non-Representational Theory: Space, Politics, Affect.* London: Routledge, 2007.

Underwood, Ted. "Topic Modeling Made Just Simple Enough." *The Stone and the Shell,* April 7, 2012. https://tedunderwood.com/2012/04/07/topic-modeling-made-just-simple-enough/.

Weheliye, Alexander. *Habeas Viscus: Racializing Assemblages, Biopolitics, and Black Feminist Theories of the Human.* Durham: Duke University Press, 2014.

WhatEvery1Says Project. "The WhatEvery1Says (WE1S) Project: A Prospectus," October 10, 2017. https://we1s.ucsb.edu/about/we1s-prospectus/.

I would like to thank the principle investigators for the WhatEvery1Says project (Alan Liu, Jeremy Douglass, Lindsay Thomas, and Scott Kleinman), as well as my teammates on the project's Social Groups and the Humanities team (Sami Alsalloom, Susan Burtner, Melissa Filbeck, sam goli, Giorgina Paiella, and Tyler Shoemaker) for their intellectual and technical contributions to the work from which the findings of this piece were produced. It would not exist without the collaborative work I did alongside these individuals.

Contributors

Bridget Blodgett is an associate professor in the Division of Science, Information Arts, and Technology at the University of Baltimore. Her research analyzes Internet culture and the social impacts thereof on offline life. Her current research takes a critical eye to online game communities regarding gender, inclusiveness, and identity. *Toxic Geek Masculinity in Media* (with Anastasia Salter) was released in 2017 by Palgrave MacMillan and is the summation of this work to date.

Alenda Y. Chang is an Associate Professor of Film and Media Studies at the University of California, Santa Barbara. Her research and teaching interests include environmental media, histories and theories of the digital, game studies, science and technology studies, and sound studies. Chang's articles have appeared in numerous journals, among them *Qui Parle, Interdisciplinary Studies in Literature and Environment, electronic book review, Feminist Media Histories,* and *Resilience*. Her first book, *Playing Nature: Ecology in Video Games,* develops environmentally informed frameworks for understanding and designing digital games (University of Minnesota Press, 2019). At UC Santa Barbara, Chang directs the Creative Computing Initiative and co-directs Wireframe, a studio promoting collaborative theoretical and creative media practice with investments in global social and environmental justice. She is also a founding co-editor of the UC Press open-access journal, *Media+Environment.*

Edmond Y. Chang is an Assistant Professor of English at Ohio University. His areas of research include technoculture, race/gender/sexuality, feminist media studies, video games, popular culture, and 20th-/21st-century American literature. He teaches undergraduate and graduate courses on American literature, speculative literature of color, queer theory, games, and writing. Recent publications include "Drawing the Oankali: Imagining Race, Gender, and the Posthuman in Octavia Butler's Dawn" in *Approaches to Teaching the Works of Octavia E. Butler,* "Playing as Making" in *Disrupting the Digital Humanities,* and "Queergaming" in *Queer Game Studies.* He is completing his first book on algorithmic queerness and digital games tentatively entitled *Queerness Cannot Be Designed.*

Jordan Clapper is a doctoral candidate in the English program at Brandeis University. They are an unenrolled Ponca of Oklahoma, and they study indigenous and queer literature and video games. They are a member of the 2020–21 cohort of the Palah Light Lab, a creative and critical community for queer and feminist new media. They are working on several video and board games that address positions at the margins as places of power and narrative possibility.

Domenico Fiormonte is lecturer in the Sociology of Communication and Culture in the Department of Political Sciences at University Roma Tre. In 1996 he created one of the first online resources on literary textual variation (www.digitalvariants.org). He has edited and co-edited a number of collections of digital humanities texts, and has published books and articles on digital philology, digital writing, text encoding, and cultural criticism of DH. Since 2008 Domenico has been working on educational projects in the South of India and has recently edited an Italian collection of interdisciplinary essays on consciousness (*La coscienza. Un dialogo interdisciplinare e interculturale*, Rome, 2018). His latest book is *Per una critica del testo digitale. Filologia, letteratura e rete* (Rome, 2018). With Sukanta Chaodouri and Paola Ricaurte he is currently editing for the University of Minnesota Press the first Digital Humanities collection devoted to developing countries and the Global South.

David Golumbia is an Associate Professor of English at Virginia Commonwealth University. He is the author of *The Cultural Logic of Computation* (Harvard University Press, 2009), *The Politics of Bitcoin: Software as Right-Wing Extremism* (University of Minnesota Press, 2016), and many articles on digital culture, language, and literary studies.

Christy Hyman is a digital humanist, environmental advocate, and PhD student in the program of Geography at the University of Nebraska Lincoln. Her dissertation research focuses on African-American efforts toward cultural and political assertion in the Great Dismal Swamp region during the antebellum era as well as the attendant social and environmental costs of human/landscape resource exploitation. Hyman uses Geographic Information Systems to observe to what extent digital cartography can inform us of the human experience while acknowledging phenomena deriving from oppressive systems in society threatening sustainable futures. Hyman has been invited to share her work at a range of humanities centers including the Dave Rumsey Map Center at Stanford University, the Institute for Digital Research in the Humanities at the University of Kansas, and the Maryland Institute for Technology in the Humanities Digital Dialogues series to name a few.

Arun Jacob is a Ph.D. student at the Faculty of Information, University of Toronto, working in the Media, Technology, and Culture concentration. His research interests include examining the media history of educational technologies.

Alexandra Juhasz is Distinguished Professor of Film at Brooklyn College, CUNY. She makes and studies committed media practices that contribute to political change and individual and community growth. Author and/or editor since 1995 of scholarly books on activist media in light of AIDS (*AIDS TV*, Duke University Press, 1995 and *AIDS and the Distribution of Crises*, Duke University Press, 2020), Black lesbian and queer representation (*Sisters in the Life*, Duke University Press, 2018), feminism (*Women of Vision*, University of Minnesota Press, 2001), and digital culture (*Learning from YouTube*, MIT Press, 2011), Dr. Juhasz also makes videotapes on feminist issues from AIDS to teen pregnancy as well as producing the feature fakes *The Watermelon Woman* (Cheryl Dunye, 1997) and *The Owls* (Dunye, 2010). She writes reviews, interviews, and opinion pieces about these subjects for non-academic venues like *MS*, *Bomb*, *Hyperallergic*, and the *Brooklyn Rail*. Her current work is on and about fake news and radical digital media literacy (fakenews-poetry.org).

Dorothy Kim teaches medieval literature at Brandeis University. Her research focuses on race, gender, digital humanities, medieval women's literary cultures, medievalism, Jewish/Christian difference, book history, digital media, and the alt-right. Her book, *Jewish/Christian Entanglements: Ancrene Wisse and Its Material Worlds*, is set to be published with the University of Pennsylvania Press. She has a forthcoming book, *The Alt-Medieval: Digital Whiteness and Medieval Studies* from the University of Minnesota Press in 2021. She has received fellowships from the SSHRC, Ford Foundation, Fulbright, Mellon, and AAUW. She is the co-project director in the NEH-funded Scholarly Editions and Translations project *An Archive of Early Middle English*. She is a project co-director for the Global Middle Ages Project (http://globalmiddleages.org) and is scheduled to co-write a book with Lynn Ramey (Vanderbilt University) on *Medieval Global Digital Humanities* for Cambridge UP for 2021. She has co-edited two collections in the Digital Humanities. The first collection, co-edited with Jesse Stommel (University of Mary Washington), on *Disrupting the Digital Humanities* (punctum books, 2018), discusses the marginal methodologies and critical diversities in the Digital Humanities. This current volume is her second edited DH collection. She has an edited volume in the Cultural History of Race series (the Cultural History of Race 1350–1550) with Kim Coles (University of Maryland) forthcoming in October 2021 at Bloomsbury. She is the associate editor for the *Journal of Early Middle English* and the co-editor for the medieval to early modern section of *Literature Compass.*

Carly A. Kocurek is Associate Professor of Digital Humanities and Media Studies at the Illinois Institute of Technology. She researches the cultural history of video games with an emphasis on gender identity and also makes games. Her books include *Coin-Operated Americans: Rebooting Boyhood at the Video Game Arcade* (University of Minnesota Press, 2015) and *Brenda Laurel: Pioneering Games for Girls* (Bloomsbury, 2017). Currently, she is researching the history and impact of the games for girls' movement as part of a project funded by the National Science Foundation. Her articles have appeared in outlets such as *The American Journal of Play, Feminist Media Histories, Game Studies, Velvet Light Trap,* and others.

Viola Lasmana works at the intersections of transpacific studies and digital media, with an emphasis on literature, film, and media arts. She is currently completing a book, *Shadow Imaginations: Transpacific Approaches to Post-1965 Indonesian Archives,* on the reconstitution of Indonesia's decimated cultural archive. Her work has appeared in *Film Quarterly, The Cine-Files, Visual Anthropology, make/shift: feminisms in motion, Computers and Composition,* and *Interdisciplinary Humanities.* During 2020–21, she was ACLS Emerging Voices Fellow at Columbia University's Center for the Study of Ethnicity and Race.

Born and raised in Uganda, **Janet Nalubega Ross,** who goes by her middle name Nalubega, is interested in how people learn about sex, birth, and childcare. Her current dissertation work focuses on how refugees resettled in the United States learn, paying attention to how race, age, sexuality, cultural values, political landscapes, geographical location, and the ever-changing social media landscape shape learning processes. Nalubega holds a degree in Community Health Education and Promotion from the University of Utah (2011), and a Master's degree in Bioinformatics from the University of Missouri-Kansas City (2014). When not working on her dissertation, Nalubega can be found tending an ever-growing collection of plants.

Jamal Russell is a PhD candidate in English at the University of California, Santa Barbara. His research interests span media theory, electronic literature, 20th- and 21st-century experimental poetics, and the digital humanities. He is currently writing a dissertation that examines Black media forms as a means of articulating both the history of interface and the poetics of the interface's formation through their modes of interaction.

Anastasia Salter is an Associate Professor of English at the University of Central Florida, and the coauthor of *Twining: Critical and Creative Approaches to Hypertext Narrative* (Amherst College Press, with Stuart Moulthrop, forthcoming 2021); *A Portrait of the Auteur as Fanboy* (University of Mississippi Press, with Mel Stanfill, 2020); and *Adventure Games: Playing the Outsider* (Bloomsbury, with Aaron Reed and John Murray, 2020).

Cathy J. Schlund-Vials is Professor of English and Asian American Studies at the University of Texas at Austin; she is also the president-elect of the American Studies Association. Prior to these recent appointments, Schlund-Vials served as the Associate Dean for Humanities, Undergraduate Affairs, and Diversity, Equity, & Inclusion at the University of Connecticut, Storrs. In addition to numerous articles, book chapters, and edited collections, she is author of two monographs: *Modeling Citizenship: Jewish and Asian American Writing* (Temple University Press, 2011) and *War, Genocide, and Justice: Cambodian American Memory Work* (University of Minnesota Press, 2012). She is presently completing a book-length project focused on the institutionalized rise and fall of ethnic, gender, and sexuality studies in higher education.

Siobhan Senier is a Professor of English and Chair of the Department of Women's and Gender Studies at the University of New Hampshire. She is the editor of *Dawnland Voices: An Anthology of Writing from Indigenous New England* (Univerity of Nebraska Press, 2014) and dawnlandvoices.org. Her other publications include *Voices of American Indian Assimilation and Resistance* (University of Oklahoma Press, 2001), *Sovereignty and Sustainability: Indigenous Literary Stewardship in New England* (University of Nebraska Press, 2020), and essays in journals including *American Literature, American Indian Quarterly, Studies in American Indian Literatures, MELUS, Disability Studies Quarterly,* and *Resilience.*

Ravynn K. Stringfield is a PhD candidate in American Studies at William & Mary. Her dissertation project, which was recently awarded a 2021–22 Halleran Dissertation Completion Fellowship, centers Black women and girls in new media fantasy narratives. Stringfield currently serves on the American Studies Association Digital Humanities Caucus and is an Equality Lab Fellow at William & Mary under the direction of Dr. Elizabeth Losh. Committed to public facing scholarship, Stringfield's intellectual practice also includes creative nonfiction and fiction writing, which has appeared in a number of publications including *ZORA, Shondaland, Catapult, Voyage Young Adult Journal,* and *midnight & indigo.*

CPSIA information can be obtained
at www.ICGtesting.com
Printed in the USA
FSHW010523140122
87659FS